Networks of Rebellion

A volume in the series

CORNELL STUDIES IN SECURITY AFFAIRS

edited by Robert J. Art, Robert Jervis, and Stephen M. Walt

A list of titles in this series is available at www.cornellpress.cornell.edu.

Networks of Rebellion

EXPLAINING INSURGENT
COHESION AND COLLAPSE

PAUL STANILAND

Cornell University Press

ITHACA AND LONDON

For my parents

Copyright © 2014 by Cornell University

All rights reserved. Except for brief quotations in a review, this book, or parts thereof, must not be reproduced in any form without permission in writing from the publisher. For information, address Cornell University Press, Sage House, 512 East State Street, Ithaca, New York 14850.

First published 2014 by Cornell University Press
First printing, Cornell Paperbacks, 2014

Printed in the United States of America

Library of Congress Cataloging-in-Publication Data

Staniland, Paul, 1982– author.
   Networks of rebellion : explaining insurgent cohesion and collapse / Paul Staniland.
      pages cm. — (Cornell studies in security affairs)
   Includes bibliographical references and index.
   ISBN 978-0-8014-5266-6 (cloth : alk. paper)
   ISBN 978-0-8014-7929-8 (pbk. : alk. paper)
  1. Insurgency—Cross-cultural studies. 2. Social networks—Cross-cultural studies. 3. Insurgency—South Asia—Case studies. 4. Insurgency—Southeast Asia—Case studies. I. Title.
   JC328.5.S83   2014
   303.6'4—dc23   2013042305

Cornell University Press strives to use environmentally responsible suppliers and materials to the fullest extent possible in the publishing of its books. Such materials include vegetable-based, low-VOC inks and acid-free papers that are recycled, totally chlorine-free, or partly composed of nonwood fibers. For further information, visit our website at www.cornellpress.cornell.edu.

Cloth printing   10 9 8 7 6 5 4 3 2 1
Paperback printing   10 9 8 7 6 5 4 3 2 1

Contents

List of Tables	vii
Acknowledgments	ix
1. Organizing Insurgency	1

Part I. Theorizing Rebellion

2. Insurgent Origins	17
3. Insurgent Change	35

Part II. Comparative Evidence from South Asia

4. Azad and Jihad: Trajectories of Insurgency in Kashmir	59
5. Organizing Rebellion in Afghanistan	100
6. Explaining Tamil Militancy in Sri Lanka	141

Part III. Extensions and Implications

7. "Peasants and Commissars": Communist Tides in Southeast Asia	181
8. Insurgency, War, and Politics	217
Notes	233
Index	285

List of Tables

1.1.	Types of insurgent organizations	6
1.2.	Prewar social bases and wartime organization	9
2.1.	Political categories of prewar social bases	19
3.1.	Pathways of insurgent change	38
4.1.	Patterns of organization in Kashmir	62
5.1.	Patterns of organization in Afghanistan	103
6.1.	Patterns of organization in Sri Lanka	143
7.1.	Patterns of organization in Southeast Asia, 1928–1960	182

Acknowledgments

I owe a profound debt to the many people who shared their knowledge with me during my field research. The core question driving this book—why some insurgent groups are unified and disciplined while others struggle with splits and feuds—emerged during a summer I spent in Northern Ireland, and it took on fuller form during my research in India and Sri Lanka. I knew remarkably little when I began researching this topic, and to the extent that this book succeeds in offering new insights, it is solely because of those who helped me. My interviewees remain anonymous because of this book's sensitive subject matter, but I hope they find something of value in the pages that follow. I am grateful for the good friends and thoughtful colleagues who helped me navigate, enjoy, and learn from new places. I also often benefited from the kindness of strangers. I owe particular thanks to the institutions that hosted me in the field: Queen's University Belfast and Linen Hall Library in Northern Ireland, the Centre for Policy Research and the India International Centre in New Delhi, and the Centre for Policy Alternatives and the International Centre for Ethnic Studies in Colombo.

This book has its roots in my time in the Department of Political Science and the Security Studies Program at MIT. Roger Petersen provided a unique mixture of intellectual creativity and personal support. Barry Posen's high standards kept me focused on the things that matter. Stephen Van Evera's insistence on valuing research that grapples with important questions is an inspiration. I cannot thank Steven Wilkinson enough for bringing to bear his sharp questions and encyclopedic knowledge. I am indebted to Fotini Christia, Taylor Fravel, and David Andrew Singer for their advice over the years and to the staff of the department

Acknowledgments

and the Security Studies Program for helping me survive numerous logistical adventures.

I benefited from time at Harvard University's Belfer Center for Science and International Affairs, where Sean Lynn-Jones, Susan Lynch, Steven Miller, and Robert Rotberg created a first-rate research environment. The first draft of this book was finished at Yale University's Program on Order, Conflict, and Violence. Stathis Kalyvas and Elisabeth Wood were incredible as both supporters and critics.

The University of Chicago improved this book in all respects. Dan Slater is an irrepressible source of enthusiasm and insights. My co-directors in the Program on International Security Policy, John Mearsheimer and Robert Pape, have provided excellent advice on a dizzying variety of issues. I am in awe of and grateful for Betsy Sinclair's boundless energy and good humor. I appreciate the feedback of Charles Lipson, John Padgett, Jong Hee Park, Tianna Paschel, and Alberto Simper. Kathy Anderson, Kim Schafer, and Brittan Strangways kept my head above water. I thank Chicago's graduate students for the opportunity to learn with them, especially Ahsan Butt, Eric Hundman, Morgan Kaplan, Jonathan Obert, Lindsey O'Rourke, and Sarah Parkinson. Jim Nye and Laura Ring are the best research librarians imaginable.

The Department of Political Science, led by Bernard Harcourt, generously funded a workshop on the manuscript for this book. Will Reno, Jack Snyder, Jeremy Weinstein, and Elisabeth Wood devoted an extraordinary amount of their time and energy to improving it. I cannot thank them enough and I hope they see the difference they made. I also appreciate the involvement of many colleagues and graduate students at this workshop.

I benefited enormously from the feedback of participants at presentations at Yale University, MIT, Dartmouth College, the University of Minnesota, Columbia University, the University of Chicago, Northwestern University, Harvard University, the Centre for Policy Alternatives, the "New Faces" conference of the Triangle Institute for Security Studies, and the Brown-Harvard-MIT South Asian Politics seminar. I am grateful to the many people who have helped me with and commented on this research over the years. They include Ana Arjona, Kristin Bakke, Shane Barter, Emma Belcher, Stephen Biddle, Hanna Breetz, Jonathan Caverley, Christopher Clary, Dara Kay Cohen, Teresa Cravo, Kathleen Cunningham, Sarah Zukerman Daly, Alexander Downes, Keith Edwards, Alexander Evans, Kristin Fabbe, Vanda Felbab-Brown, Sumit Ganguly, Scott Gates, Frank Gavin, Kelly Greenhill, Christopher Haid, Phil Haun, Timothy Hoyt, Llewelyn Hughes, Patrick Johnston, Stephanie Kaplan, Chaim Kaufmann, Matthew Kocher, Sameer Lalwani, Adria Lawrence, Janet

Acknowledgments

Lewis, Evan Liaras, Jason Lyall, Romain Malejacq, Tara Maller, Zachariah Mampilly, Reo Matsuzaki, Anit Mukherjee, Shivaji Mukherjee, Harris Mylonas, Ragnild Nordas, Will Norris, Wendy Pearlman, Srinath Raghavan, Jesse Dillon Savage, Alexandra Scacco, Gustavo Setrini, Lee Seymour, Jacob Shapiro, Josh Shifrinson, Erica Simmons, David Siroky, Nick Smith, Hendrik Spruyt, Monica Duffy Toft, Ben Valentino, Ashutosh Varshney, David Weinberg, and Phil Williams. I apologize to those I have inadvertently overlooked.

A number of research assistants have played a key role in developing this book; I thank Peter Austin, Maham Ayaz, Danielle Fumagalli, Meher Kairon, Sahiba Sindhu, Brian Shevenaugh, and especially Morgan Kaplan, Saalika Mela, and Jonathan Weatherwax.

I have learned a tremendous amount from Laia Balcells, Francisco Flores-Macias, Keren Fraiman, Brendan Green, Dominika Koter, Peter Krause, Jon Lindsay, Austin Long, Negeen Pegahi, Andrew Radin, Joshua Rovner, Abbey Steele, Maya Tudor, and Adam Ziegfeld. Vipin Narang and Caitlin Talmadge read the entirety of this book and have served as reliable sounding boards on truly every conceivable topic.

I received generous financial support from the Harry Frank Guggenheim Foundation, the Smith Richardson Foundation, the Center for International Studies at MIT, the MacMillan Center at Yale University, the Kennedy School of Government and the Minda de Gunzberg Center for European Studies at Harvard University, the United States Institute of Peace, and the Committee on Southern Asian Studies and Social Sciences Division at the University of Chicago.

At Cornell University Press, Roger Haydon has been an excellent guide to writing a book. I appreciate his early enthusiasm for the manuscript and his thoughtful advice as the book developed. Robert Art gave the book much-needed clarity and focus. I thank an external reviewer for carefully commenting on the manuscript. I am grateful to Kate Babbitt for her exceptional copyediting and to Susan Specter for her assistance in the production process.

Earlier versions of some of the material in this book were previously published in "Organizing Insurgency: Networks, Resources, and Rebellion in South Asia," *International Security* 37, no. 1 (Summer 2012): 142–177, © 2012 by the President and Fellows of Harvard College and the Massachusetts Institute of Technology; and "Between a Rock and a Hard Place: Insurgent Fratricide, Ethnic Defection, and the Rise of Pro-State Paramilitaries," *Journal of Conflict Resolution* 56, no. 1 (2012): 16–40, doi: 10.1177/0022002711429681, © 2012 by SAGE Publications, Inc., all rights reserved. I thank the publishers of these journals for their permission.

Acknowledgments

My family has been the most important source of support. My sister Laura's perseverance and initiative are an inspiration. My wife, Rebecca Incledon, has been extraordinarily supportive, persuaded me to have more fun, and, very simply, made everything better. This book is dedicated to my parents, Alberta Sbragia and Martin Staniland. They are models of both scholarship and parenting that I hope to emulate for the rest of my life.

[1]

Organizing Insurgency

Several times in the spring of 2008 I made my way through a set of checkpoints into a Sri Lankan military base in the heart of Colombo. After a motorcycle ride with a security guard, I entered a block of rundown apartments ensconced in barriers, barbed wire, and heavily armed security personnel. Each time I had come to interview a member of one of the Tamil political parties that had opposed the Liberation Tigers of Tamil Eelam (LTTE) and that now sheltered behind the simultaneously protective and repressive arms of the Sri Lankan state. Ironically, several of these political parties had their origins as anti-state insurgent groups in the 1970s and 1980s. One by one, organizations such as the People's Liberation Organisation of Tamil Eelam (PLOT) and the Eelam People's Revolutionary Liberation Front (EPRLF) had been ruthlessly targeted by the LTTE. The LTTE struck these groups when they were internally divided, torn by splits and feuds that made them vulnerable to fratricidal assault. They were then forced into an alliance of convenience with the government.

Though the LTTE was eventually wiped out in 2009, the Tigers' tight discipline and ability to calibrate and target violence turned them into the ultimate arbiters of Tamil politics and a key influence on Sri Lanka's politics and economy for nearly a quarter of a century. Groups such as the PLOT and EPRLF, by contrast, were plagued by problems of factionalism that doomed them to a marginal role in Colombo. Organization and power were fused together in Sri Lanka's long war. These dynamics are not unique to Sri Lanka: whether in Sudan, Pakistan, or Colombia, the ability of rebels to build strong organizations has been crucial to their military effectiveness and political influence.

This book uses a new typology of insurgent groups, a social-institutional theory of insurgent organization, and comparative evidence from South and Southeast Asia to explain how insurgent groups are constructed and why they change over time. The prewar networks in which insurgent leaders are embedded determine the nature of the organizations they can build when a war begins. Preexisting social bases vary in the kinds of social resources they can provide to organizers. Four types of insurgent groups—integrated, vanguard, parochial, and fragmented—emerge from different combinations of prewar networks. This is why insurgent groups that are otherwise similar, with the same ideology, ethnicity, state enemy, and resource flows, often have dramatically different forms of organization.

These initial organizational structures are not locked in place, though they do constrain the likelihood and nature of change. The violence and dislocation of war opens the possibility for major changes in how insurgent groups are organized. Shifting horizontal and vertical ties lead to organizational change, as social embeddedness determines whether insurgent institutions can be built and maintained in the face of counterinsurgency. Starting points create different pathways of likely change: vanguards are more vulnerable to leadership decapitation than parochial groups, for instance, but they are also better able to create coordinated strategies. Insurgents try to build and protect these social ties in order to expand their organizational power, while counterinsurgents try to disrupt them and induce collapse. This struggle is the core battle of guerrilla warfare. The evolution of insurgent groups blends historical legacies from prewar politics with counterinsurgent strategy, insurgent innovation, and international intervention during war. Explaining insurgent organization makes it possible to understand when rebels can generate military and political power and when insurgent challenges instead shatter into factionalism and collapse.

Why Insurgent Cohesion Matters

Insurgent cohesion shapes how wars are fought, how wars end, and the politics that emerge after war.[1] The organization of an insurgent group is crucial to its effectiveness in battling counterinsurgents. As Huntington argues, "Numbers, weapons, and strategy all count in war, but major deficiencies in any one of those may still be counterbalanced by superior cohesion and discipline."[2] Organizational control is central to military struggle.[3] Insurgent discipline also plays a key role in explaining violence against civilians during war. Undisciplined armed groups are often predatory toward civilians as foot soldiers pursue their own agendas without central control.[4] In Iraq, for instance, loose command and control within Moktada al-Sadr's militia contributed to opportunistic local ethnic cleansing of Sunnis in the aftermath of the American invasion. Disciplined groups, by contrast, may victimize civilians in a more systematic way according to the strategic orders of their leaders. For example, the LTTE engaged in carefully coordinated campaigns of ethnic cleansing made possible by high levels of organizational control, and its cadres stopped this behavior when LTTE leaders told them to. Different patterns of violence are linked to different patterns of organization.

Insurgent cohesion also affects the prospects for peace by influencing negotiations, demobilization, and postwar stabilization. Radical factions create splits that cause "spoiler" problems and undermine deals.[5] An organization whose leaders cannot control its fighters is not a credible bargaining partner. Disciplined organizations may be able to avoid unexpected spirals of uncontrolled violence, but fractious groups and movements find themselves torn by patterns of outbidding and competitive violence between prospective leaders that make negotiations fall apart. Keeping a group together during a controversial peace process is difficult and requires powerful mechanisms for maintaining control and unity.[6]

Insurgent organization further affects state building and regimes after conflicts.[7] Integrated insurgents can impose their favored regime once they have seized power, but fragmented groups are prone to destabilizing battles over the spoils of victory.[8] Vu, for instance, shows that the structure of insurgent movements determined the nature of state building and economic development in postcolonial Asia. Different political outcomes flow from different kinds of armed groups.[9] While insurgents care about achieving a variety of goals—taxing peasants, killing soldiers, pursuing ideological visions—all require some minimum level of control and unity. Armed groups spend enormous amounts of time and energy trying to build or protect cohesion because organization is central to the politics of civil war, state formation, and peace building.

The Limits of Existing Explanations

Most research on civil war takes the structure of insurgent groups as a given rather than trying to explain it.[10] Research that does offer explanations of insurgent organization can be broken into four broad approaches; these focus on state structure and policies, material resources, ideology, and mass support.[11] This is a rich and important literature, but it suffers from important limitations.

State-centric theories argue that insurgent groups are reflections of states and the political contexts they create.[12] For instance, Goodwin argues that insurgents will be cohesive when they face weak but exclusionary states, and Skocpol suggests that sustained peasant rebellion will be possible only when the state is suffering a crisis. While these political contexts are undoubtedly important, this approach underestimates the agency and autonomy of insurgents. They can find ways of defying states, overcoming structural constraints, and creating new opportunities. The dramatic differences that frequently emerge across insurgent groups fighting the same state at the same time make it clear that we need to pay more careful attention to the capabilities, social bases, and strategies of these groups.

A more recent wave of research argues that the material resources of insurgents affect how they are organized and how this organization determines behavior. A key claim in this work is that groups built through or reliant upon state sponsors, diamonds, oil, and other natural resources are prone to thuggishness, indiscipline, and fragmentation.[13] There are certainly cases that support this argument, but some of the most skilled, resilient, and cohesive insurgent groups in recent history have been fueled by diasporas, state sponsors, drugs, and smuggling, from the Afghan Taliban to the Provisional Irish Republican Army.[14] Other groups with the exact same resource endowments have fallen apart. Material resources alone do not determine the success or failure of insurgent groups.[15] Instead, other factors determine whether resource influxes will bolster or undermine cohesion.[16]

A third explanation highlights the mass support that armed groups receive: those with popular support can attract more recruits and greater allegiance along class or ethnic lines than groups advancing an unpopular ideology.[17] The problem with this approach is that we regularly see disciplined groups pushing aside more popular rivals and dominating insurgencies and revolutions. Organization and control can trump mass sympathy, as popular support does not seamlessly create institutions for waging war. The challenges of collective action do not make mass support irrelevant, but they do make organization a crucial precondition for taking advantage of popular sympathy.[18]

Finally, ideology has been advanced as an explanation for organizational structure. During the Cold War, the Leninist "combat party" and the Maoist model of insurgency were both hugely influential in how insurgents thought about organizing themselves.[19] Yet it is not easy to convert these blueprints into reality, as many rebels hoping to follow in the footsteps of Lenin and Mao found to their chagrin. Ideas are obviously of great importance, but they need to be turned into durable organizations in very challenging and dangerous circumstances. Insurgent leaders are not unconstrained agents who are able to create whatever organizations they please.[20] Thus, we need to identify the circumstances under which ideas can be implemented.

Organizing Insurgency

There are three more general problems with existing research. First, these works do not offer careful conceptualizations of how insurgent groups differ from one another, which makes it difficult to study groups comparatively or over time. Second, key existing theories are only loosely related to prewar political life: in this literature, insurgent groups seem to come out of nowhere once wars begin. We need to take history seriously to understand how armed groups emerge. Third, there is little explanation of change over time within war. Some influential variables that are used to explain outcomes, for example the resources available in a particular war zone or a state's regime type, are frequently static. Insurgent groups often change over time with important consequences, but we lack a convincing account of change. This book tackles each of these three challenges.

Analyzing Insurgent Groups

The first step in explaining patterns of rebel organization is identifying how insurgent groups differ from one another. An insurgent organization is a group of individuals claiming to be a collective organization that uses a name to designate itself, is made up of formal structures of command and control, and intends to seize political power using violence.[21] This distinguishes organizations from movements: Hamas is an organization while the Palestinian national movement is not, and the Taliban is an organization while "the Afghan insurgency," which combines several organizations, is not.

Insurgent groups have central processes of decision making and institution building and local processes of recruitment and tactical combat. Insurgent organizations differ in the strength of these control processes and the patterns of internal politics they create. Four types of insurgent groups can be identified according to how they combine central and local control: integrated, vanguard, parochial, and fragmented (table 1.1). Because groups can move between these organizational types over time, this typology is useful both for comparing groups with one another and for identifying changes within a group.

An organization with robust central control coordinates its strategy and retains the loyalty and unity of its key leaders as it implements strategy. It establishes and maintains institutions for monitoring cadres, creating ideological "party lines" that socialize new members, engaging in diplomacy, and distributing resources. By contrast, organizations with fragile processes of central control experience leadership splits and feuds. Their bureaucracies for socialization and discipline are nonexistent or function poorly, no single voice is capable of negotiating or speaking for the group, and policies are not consistent across factions.

Table 1.1. Types of insurgent organizations

Type of organization	Central processes of control	Local processes of control	Nature of dissent
Integrated	Robust	Robust	Minimal
Vanguard	Robust	Fragile	Central vs. local
Parochial	Fragile	Robust	Between factional commanders
Fragmented	Fragile	Fragile	Pervasive

Strong local control processes involve reliable, consistent obedience from foot soldiers and low-ranking commanders. Institutions exist on the ground to recruit and socialize fighters who become loyal to the leadership. Obedience occurs even in risky and dangerous environments where central leaders cannot easily monitor or punish local units. This distinguishes disciplined groups from those that coerce obedience purely through fear. An organization with fragile local control is characterized by disloyal or shirking local foot soldiers and revolts from below. In these situations the group lacks an institutionalized presence in local communities.

Integrated Groups

Integrated organizations are characterized by leadership unity and discipline at the center and high levels of local compliance on the ground. Formal mechanisms exist to incorporate and socialize new members, leaders and foot soldiers are connected through institutions that operate in a similar fashion across space and time, and unity of purpose is high. There are few major leadership splits and feuds and local defiance are rare. Institutional procedures and organizational policies are consistent throughout the organization. Integrated groups are the most effective militarily and are resilient in the face of pressure from counterinsurgents.

These groups are not necessarily widely popular or ultimately victorious, but their organizational cohesion makes them major political and military players in civil wars. The shift from vanguard or parochial organization to an integrated structure is a hugely important transformation. Prominent examples of integrated groups include the Viet Cong, Hezbollah, the Provisional Irish Republican Army, the Rwandan Patriotic Front, and Tito's communist partisans in World War II Yugoslavia. As this list indicates, integrated organizations can exist across very different contexts, war aims, and ideologies.

Vanguard Groups

Vanguard organizations have robust central control but fragile local control. There is a tight leadership that creates central institutions but faces recurrent difficulties in local expansion and discipline. Clear political guidelines, the production and reproduction of ideological visions, and careful attention to strategy are characteristic of these organizations. Yet the weak institutions on the ground cannot establish or sustain consistent local processes of recruitment, intelligence, and monitoring.[22] Organizations that rely on urban commissars to mobilize distant peasants or on exiled leaders abroad often have a vanguard structure, at least initially. The major challenge is to implement the leadership's goals and strategies in local communities.

Examples of vanguard organizations include Al Qaeda in Iraq since 2004, the Naxalites in West Bengal in the late 1960s and 1970s, the Ejército de Liberación Nacional de Bolivia in Bolivia in the 1960s, and the Bolsheviks in Russia in 1917. In these groups, initially coherent high commands faced endemic difficulties in mobilizing and controlling local units. Some of these vanguard groups changed toward integration, others remained the same, and yet others fragmented. The key question for vanguard groups is whether they can establish the local institutions that make them integrated; this is a crucial change that can enable an urban movement to mobilize the countryside or allow an elite leadership to reliably draw on peasants. Chapter 3 devotes special attention to explaining shifts from a vanguard to an integrated structure.

Parochial Groups

Parochial organizations are characterized by weak central discipline but robust local control.[23] Control processes on the ground work well but are not linked by coherent central institutions. This combination creates heterogeneity across factions: different leaders follow different strategies and implement different policies. Parochial organizations resemble a coalition of distinct suborganizations; even if they are loosely held together by a central leader, he or she lacks consistent control over major commanders. Despite these problems of unity and control, the presence of robust (if diverse) local factions provides fighting power. The challenges facing both the group's leaders and its counterinsurgent foes are the opposite of those of vanguard groups: vanguards are locally weak but centrally strong, while parochial groups have a strong local presence but weakly organized command cores.

Many organizations have a parochial structure for much or all of their existence. Recent examples include the Pakistani Taliban, the anti-Qaddafi military opposition in Libya in 2011–2012, Moktada Al-Sadr's Jaysh al-Mahdi in Iraq, and the Alliance of Democratic Forces for the Liberation of Congo during the late 1990s. Though driven by varying goals and operating in wildly different contexts, these organizations were characterized by strong local units and a weak central command. Distinct blocs and factional commands undermined strategic coordination and control. At the same time, because localized factions within the organization had substantial power, some of these groups were formidable on their own home turf.

Fragmented Groups

Finally, fragmented organizations cannot routinely achieve organizational control at either the central or local levels. Few expectations and norms are shared, and these organizations have weak coercive capacity for enforcing organizational decisions and little unity of purpose among leaders. They exist as loose collections of small factions and individuals but are unlikely to summon unity and institutionalized discipline for any substantial period of time. Any advantage from this structure centers on the difficulty counterinsurgent forces initially have in determining who is in charge of these organizations and how to pull them apart. This advantage, however, is fleeting.

We do not see many long-lasting fragmented groups precisely because they are relatively easy to destroy. Nevertheless, examples of this structure include the Red Brigades in Italy in the 1970s, the anarchist movement in the late nineteenth and early twentieth centuries, and the Irish National Liberation Army in Northern Ireland. These organizations were unable to reproduce either central discipline or local control and were prone to fissiparous feuding, waves of defection, and out-of-control units. This structure is often the end point for groups that begin with a different structure: as chapter 3 discusses, vanguard, parochial, and even integrated groups can become fragmented, often as a prelude to total collapse.

It is important to note that a particular organizational structure does not necessarily lead to a specific political or military overall outcome.[24] Integrated armed groups may simply be overwhelmed by massive state power despite their cohesion, while parochial or vanguard organizations may be able to take advantage of an incompetent state or the intervention of a third party to achieve their war aims. Cohesion matters in war and should have important effects on both military and political dynamics, but it certainly does not determine all outcomes. For instance, the Tamil Tigers were clearly an integrated organization, even though they were ultimately annihilated because of a staggering imbalance of power.

THE SOCIAL ROOTS OF INSURGENCY

This book offers a social-institutional explanation for both the initial organization of insurgent groups and change over time within them. Insurgent groups are built by mobilizing prewar politicized social networks. These preexisting social bases provide information, trust, and shared political meanings that organizers can use to create new armed groups. The initial organization of an insurgent group reflects the networks and institutions in which its leaders were embedded prior to violent mobilization. Political parties, kinship groups, veterans' and students' networks, and religious associations, among others, that act as politicized opposition to state power are potential sources of future insurgency. They are generally not built for war but can be deployed for violence, converting previous peaceful activities into new tasks of fighting and organizing. These social bases have a variety of possible structures, however, which lead to different initial insurgent structures. The prewar horizontal ties between organizers and vertical ties between organizers and local communities within a social base determine the strength of central and local organizational control when rebel leaders mobilize that base for rebellion.

This link between prewar politics and initial wartime organization can be found, for instance, in Syria in 2011–2012: as the rebellion against Assad took on greater fury, new armed groups began as "small personal networks or groups of army defectors"[25] who had transitioned into rebellion. In this case, the localized nature of these networks tended to create parochial organizational structures. Table 1.2 shows how horizontal and vertical prewar networks combine to create new initial wartime organizations. The social-institutional theory I am offering answers the crucial question of where armed organizations come from and why they vary so dramatically. Ethnic or ideological solidarity, mass popular support, or material resources alone are not enough to organize rebellion; instead, it is necessary for a group to mobilize prior linkages of trust and commitment for the purposes of violence. Chapter 2 explains which prewar networks are most likely to become relevant to rebellion, how these

Table 1.2. Prewar social bases and wartime organization

	Strong vertical ties	**Weak vertical ties**
Strong horizontal ties	*Integrated organization* Robust central processes Robust local processes	*Vanguard organization* Robust central processes Fragile local processes
Weak horizontal ties	*Parochial organization* Fragile central processes Robust local processes	*Fragmented organization* Fragile central processes Fragile local processes

ties are turned into institutions, and what types of initial organizations emerge as a result.

The dynamics of war impose crushing pressures and create new openings that can move groups from their initial organizational structure into a different one. Chapter 3 explains how organizational evolution occurs: changing social linkages determine where institutions can be built and maintained. Nevertheless, initial organizational starting points determine the most likely pathways of insurgent change over time. Rather than having to choose between structure and agency, this book combines structural constraints rooted in prewar politics with specific mechanisms of strategy and evolution during conflict.

Integrated groups tend to be fragmented only by comprehensive state counterinsurgency or disastrously mismanaged expansion. Their initial organizational advantages make them a difficult foe for states. Vanguard groups become integrated by exploiting local conflicts and gaining trust on the ground that helps them build vertical ties to communities and create new institutions of local control. They are vulnerable to leadership decapitation and revolts from below that can cause a change to a fragmented structure. Parochial groups integrate by forging new relationships of trust and monitoring among commanders of factions. This process is most likely when it is encouraged by unified foreign sponsors and when a group faces indiscriminate violence by counterinsurgents. Parochial groups become fragmented when elite feuding spirals into warfare between factions and when local infiltration by state forces shatters the vertical ties that sustain local control. Groups that begin as fragmented find it very difficult to change and are likely to be quickly marginalized.

SCOPE CONDITIONS

This theory should apply to insurgent organizations that originate as irregular guerrilla forces, are faced with consistent pressures on their survival, and seek to politically govern territory.[26] I include armed groups that seek both secession and central power, although these different goals can lead to different strategies. My argument should be most useful for understanding wars in which insurgents fight capable, resolved central states or powerful armed competitors because this is where the difficulty of organization building is most pronounced and collective action is most challenging.

This book's claims are less likely to apply to armed groups emerging from state collapse in a situation where parts of the state itself become nonstate armed groups (these usually become "warlords"), armed groups that are born in highly collusive relationships with the counterinsurgent state forces (such as pro-state paramilitaries), organizations that do not seek to govern or control territory for political purposes (purely criminal actors)[27], or groups that emerge and operate outside of a contested war zone, such as a purely exile movement. My analysis ends when insurgent groups sign a peace deal that demobilizes them as fighting forces; when they abandon violence in favor of party politics, crime, or collusive arrangements with the state; or when they are wiped out. I do not seek to define the "optimal" structure for all organizations. Integrated insurgent groups may be marginal electoral forces, they may be incompetent launchers of military coups, they may be bad at running a state, or they may be unable to marshal mass protests. Conversely, electorally popular parties, innovative religious groups, or powerful labor union organizers may be poor insurgents.

These scope conditions limit the number of groups to which my theory applies. Roughly half of post-1945 civil wars have been waged as irregular guerrilla conflicts, but many others have involved conventional warfare or nebulous militia conflicts in which armed groups remain linked to state power.[28] I privilege a strong explanation of a small number of cases rather than a vague, lowest-common-denominator explanation of a large number of cases. The book's scope nevertheless remains applicable to many contemporary and historical conflicts.

The Empirical Approach: Comparative Rebellions in Southern Asia

Assessing whether the social-institutional theory explains patterns of insurgent organization requires a mix of careful comparisons and detailed information about the origins and evolution of insurgent groups. We need to identify the prewar social bases upon which armed groups were built, the initial organizational structure of these groups, and whether and how these organizations changed over time. This approach is data intensive because it reaches back before a war and then follows insurgent behavior through the course of secretive and chaotic conflicts. Controlled comparisons in which many factors are similar across groups are needed to plausibly identify the effects of different variables. Picking wildly dissimilar cases does not make for credible conclusions, and thin or highly aggregated empirical evidence cannot provide the detail necessary for tracing the actual processes through which insurgent groups are constructed and change.

Case Selection and Comparative Method

I deal with these challenges by using within-conflict comparisons of groups in three wars in South Asia and a set of cross-conflict comparisons in Southeast Asia. These contexts allow me to examine the prewar political terrain that gave birth to new armed groups in order to see whether preexisting social bases provided the underpinning for new wartime organizations and to then compare the trajectories of militancy over time as insurgents dealt with similar kinds of challenges.

The first cluster of empirical work is built around South Asia and constitutes part 2 of this book. This part focuses on civil wars in Kashmir, Afghanistan, and Sri Lanka. Within each conflict, I examine multiple armed groups characterized by varying levels and patterns of organizational cohesion. This allows me to explore group origins and change while holding key structural variables constant across space and, in some cases, over time. Each chapter combines detailed process tracing of how mobilization occurred and what happened to armed groups over the course of the war with tight comparisons that eliminate a number of alternative explanations.

Within each of these wars, the ethnic makeup of the armed groups was often similar. In addition, each of the groups pursued the same war aims and/or operated in the same international and economic environment. This comparative framework is crucial for disentangling the social-institutional elements of my theory from counterinsurgency, resource flows, and other possibly confounding variables. It allows a tight focus on how organization building occurs in an environment that puts similar pressures on groups.[29] This research design follows the model that Leites and Wolf recommend in their influential work to compare rebel groups within a shared context[30] and follows a growing trend of carefully studying the dynamics of mobilization and violence in war.[31]

The data is based on field research and detailed historical information about prewar politics and wartime insurgency. This research is underpinned by approximately ten months of fieldwork in India and Sri Lanka. In addition to the wide variety of secondary sources I use here, I conducted interviews with current and former militants, security force and government officials, politicians, journalists, academics and analysts, and normal citizens to gain insight into how armed groups were built and how they operated in the demanding environment of insurgent warfare. The comparative cases I examine from Afghanistan draw upon the rich existing literature on political violence in Afghanistan since the early 1970s.[32]

I study indigenous armed groups in Kashmir between 1988 and 2003 in chapter 4, arguing that the prewar networks of insurgents created organizational structures that explain major differences in how armed groups used Pakistani aid and in whether these armed groups could handle the stresses of Indian counterinsurgency. Chapter 5 examines several key insurgent groups that tried to seize control of Afghanistan during the period 1973 to 2013. I show that the social roots of organizations explain why some groups were able to carve out enduring power while others splintered or collapsed. The chapter examines organizational change in several groups.

Chapter 6 compares five Tamil militant groups in Sri Lanka's long war, focusing on the Tamil Tigers. The comparisons from Sri Lanka provide mixed support for my argument. Varying caste and student networks appear to have primed armed groups for different organizational structures, but other factors were very important, particularly individual leadership, ideology, and recalcitrant state policy.

Part 3 moves beyond these South Asian conflicts to explore patterns of communist rebellion in Southeast Asia from 1928 to 1960. I compare communist movements in the Philippines, French Indochina, and Malaya, seeking to explain why the Huks in the Philippines emerged as a parochial group and then fragmented, why the Malayan Communist Party started its armed struggle as a moderately integrated group but then became a vanguard organization, and why the Viet Minh was able to shift from a vanguard to an integrated structure in the mid-1940s. A mixture of cross-conflict variation and variation over time, despite shared ideological goals and similar dislocations during World War II, forms the core puzzle of chapter 7. The chapter shows powerful continuities between prewar communist mobilization and initial wartime organization. Change occurred through shifts in state counterinsurgency policy that interacted with the specific organizational strengths and vulnerabilities of insurgent groups. I also point to the problems the changing organization of the Viet Minh pose for my argument and the implications of this for future research.

This research addresses four key empirical issues. First, my identification of the prewar social bases that were politically salient for a potential armed conflict significantly narrowed the array of social and political networks, associations, and organizations that needed to be accounted for. Second, I systematically categorized and compared the structure of these salient social bases by assessing prewar horizontal ties among organizers and vertical linkages between organizers and local communities within each social base. Historical and field research provided insights into why and how organizers found themselves embedded in different social structures, what those social structures looked like, and how they operated before war actually broke out.

Third, I studied the organizational structures of the groups when they began their wars. I examined whether initial wartime organization tracked prewar politics in the ways I predicted and whether the causes of continuity resembled the mechanisms of my theory. I used process-tracing to identify how groups were built—who did what with whom and to what end.[33] Finally, I examined organizational change over time. Some groups continued on the same trajectory as their original structure, but others changed dramatically. Explaining change required an understanding of which factors changed and why (ranging from counterinsurgency strategy to international politics) and which remained the same.

A critique of this method is that case study researchers can always find cherry-picked support for their arguments. However, in this book I explicitly identify instances when my argument failed to explain important aspects of cases, particularly in French Indochina and Sri Lanka. A virtue of qualitative historical research is its careful attention to detail and sequence that makes possible an assessment of causal mechanisms and alternative explanations.[34] This bore fruit when I was doing the empirical work: I uncovered unexpected processes, identified cases that did not work for my argument, and used tight comparisons to make compelling claims about the underlying causes of insurgent origins and change.[35]

Part I

Theorizing Rebellion

[2]

Insurgent Origins

Where do insurgent groups come from? This chapter argues that preexisting networks provide the underpinnings for new insurgent groups. Prewar political parties, students' and veterans' groups, and religious organizations, among others, are repurposed for rebellion. Nonviolent prewar bases can create integrated and effective insurgent groups. The trust, information, and shared political beliefs embedded in these networks help organizers construct new institutions and convert old organizations to new purposes in the chaos of an escalating war. But these social bases also place constraints on insurgent leaders. Integrated, vanguard, parochial, and fragmented groups emerge from different combinations of horizontal ties between organizers and vertical ties between organizers and local communities.

This chapter first identifies which types of social bases are likely to have the political orientation necessary for potential rebellion. It then explains how the structure of these social bases shapes the organization of new insurgent groups. Ideology, resource endowments, and state policy do not straightforwardly create insurgent groups. Instead, the ability of leaders to overcome a set of shared organizational challenges hinges on the social resources that are available to them. These social roots of insurgency in turn determine how other factors, whether they be drug money or Maoist doctrine, influence armed organization. Understanding insurgent origins establishes the basis for explaining change over time: as Kathleen Thelen has observed, "knowing how institutions were constructed provides insights into how they might come apart."[1]

SOCIAL BASES AND POLITICS

Social bases are structures of collective action and social interaction in a society.[2] They differ depending on context, from peasant associations to Islamist networks to political parties. Social bases can be identified independent of warfare or future revolt: the French Communist Party, the Brazilian branch of the Catholic Church, and the Egyptian Muslim Brotherhood are all social bases, even though none are war-fighting organizations. The vast majority of prewar social bases have nothing to do with ambushing government soldiers, smuggling guns through distant mountains, or making strategic decisions about how to overthrow a government. This means that my argument is not tautological; if it is wrong, we will see major disjunctures between prewar political life and wartime insurgency.

However, the extraordinary profusion of social ties in every society creates a different problem: How do we know what to focus on when trying to explain insurgent origins? If all social bases are equally likely to create insurgencies, then the task of measuring and assessing them ahead of time is nearly impossible.[3] To deal with this problem, I categorize social bases along two dimensions. The first is whether a social base is politicized in potential opposition to state power. Apolitical and pro-state social bases can be distinguished from politicized opposition social bases that organizers could conceivably take to war against the state. This approach takes political and ideological commitments seriously without claiming that they have deterministic effects on how groups behave or organize. The second dimension is whether the organizers of a social base are actively preparing for a violent conflict. Organizations whose members include revolutionary plotters who are waiting to launch a rebellion can be distinguished from other social bases that have not built themselves for waging war, such as opposition parties or religious associations.

Social bases can be understood in four political categories (table 2.1) that enable us to perform a social "net assessment" of a society for the purpose of identifying likely roots of rebellion.[4] Symbols, discourses, and strategies of mobilization can bring a social base into alignment with the political status quo and the regime that runs a state, orient it in opposition, or make it politically irrelevant. This is admittedly a blunt analytical device, but it helps to narrow down the universe of social bases in a society that could be sources of rebel organization. I then look for evidence of pre-insurgency planning for violence. Indicators include military training, the acquisition of weapons, or the building of institutions dedicated to rebellion.

Unpoliticized and Pro-state Social Bases

A substantial portion of any given society is not politically primed for revolt. Many social structures do not line up with major political cleavages

Table 2.1. Political categories of prewar social bases

Politicized opposition?	Planning for violence?	
	Yes	No
Yes	Revolutionary plotters; underground movements	Politicized but nonviolent social and political structures
No	Pro-state militias and party thugs; criminals	Numerous and varied, but largely irrelevant for purposes of my theory

for or against the state; they include groups such as bowling leagues or alumni groups. Few are ever truly apolitical, but it is rare that these kinds of social bases launch insurgencies. Politicized pro-state networks are the least promising terrain for insurgency. Nonviolent ruling parties, business associations linked to a regime, and pro-government intellectual networks, for instance, are unlikely to lead a rebellion.[5] Pro-state social bases that are created for the purpose of violence include regime-backed thugs, paramilitaries, and the armed wings of ruling parties.[6] If civil war breaks out, these groups will usually serve as counterinsurgents and state-backed militias.[7]

Politicized Opposition

The social bases most likely to underpin rebellion are independent from state patronage and have political beliefs that are compatible with opposing the government. The types of social bases that are most likely to be the prewar core of a future insurgency include opposition political parties, underground revolutionary groups, anticolonial nationalist movements, autonomous religious organizations, peasant associations, and networks of dissident student activists. Such groups have the "ideational resources" to challenge the state, even if most or all of their activities before war are decidedly nonviolent.[8]

There are two types of politicized opposition: revolutionary plotters and nonviolent opposition. Revolutionary plotters who prepare for violence before a war, such as underground movements and networks of militant anti-regime activists, can be the basis for rebellion. We might expect there to be little "causal distance" between prewar networks and future conflict when insurgency is launched by revolutionary plotters. Social ties could be the outcome of carefully optimized leadership strategies in expectation of war. If revolutionary plotters seamlessly built networks appropriate for insurgency and then became the dominant insurgent forces once war broke out, my argument about the importance of historically contingent, preexisting social bases would have little independent force. Networks would be simply outcomes of ideas.

In reality, the social bases of revolutionary plotters often develop in unintended ways and end up poorly suited to future wars. The goals of insurrectionary movements attract the attention of state forces and are thus more likely to be destroyed or disrupted. Revolutionary plotters may also misjudge the future contours of a conflict and build the wrong networks even when they are not repressed by the state. Strategic planning by underground movements frequently involves biased misjudgments and bad information, elements that decrease flexibility and adaptability when the unexpected inevitably happens.[9] Many movements prepare for a rapid putsch, a mass uprising, or a revolutionary seizure of power and then are surprised when a protracted guerrilla war develops; others prepare for insurgency but are overtaken by mass street protests or a coup. In such cases, we can see significant disjunctures between prewar ties and wartime needs. Insurgents go to war with the networks they have, for better and worse.

Nonviolent politicized opposition networks are the other major source of resistance to state power. In these social bases, political beliefs are linked to cleavages in a society in a way that makes rebellion politically thinkable.[10] These networks do not originate or persist for the purpose of future insurgency, but they are imbued with preferences that can lead to them opposing the state when the conditions for civil war onset are present.

Why are these social bases so potentially useful for future insurgency? First, their nonviolent activities before war begins reduce the likelihood that they will be preemptively wiped out by state repression. They have autonomy from state power through social linkages that the government cannot easily penetrate or co-opt.[11] Second, this category of social base can be more adaptable to new circumstances than revolutionary plotters because they have not tried to build networks in anticipation of any particular course of war. This provides flexibility in a highly uncertain environment. These characteristics make nonviolent opposition a crucial, if often overlooked, starting point for insurgent organization. Scholars and journalists pay too much attention to publicity-seeking revolutionaries and too little to the day-to-day networks that produce reliable cooperation.

The Structures of Social Bases: Horizontal and Vertical Ties

Contingency and history shape the political orientations of social bases, leaving some more primed for rebellion than others. The next step is studying the structure of those social bases of politicized opposition: how are people in these groups linked together? A social base has a core of organizers who connect people. These individuals are socially and geographically mobile. Each social base is also made up of a set of local communities—villages, neighborhoods, local networks—that is geographically concentrated and has limited links to other communities.

Social bases are composed of different combinations of vertical ties between organizers and local communities and horizontal ties among organizers. Some social bases strongly link members horizontally across space but have weak vertical ties to communities; other social bases have strong vertical linkages but weak horizontal ties across organizers. Ties are embedded in formal organizations and associations and in informal relationships, and often in the overlap of the two. These connections create variation in how collective action, information, and clusters of norms and shared preferences are distributed in social bases. Social bases can be compared to one another along these dimensions.[12] The structure of a social base creates clear ex ante predictions about what kind of insurgent group will emerge if the social base is mobilized for war.

Horizontal Ties

Horizontal ties link people across space and connect different geographic and social sites. They are formed between mobile individuals drawn from beyond a single social and geographic locale. Horizontal ties can differ in the flows of information, bonds of normative obligation, and shared political preferences across a given set of organizers.[13] Strong horizontal linkages underpin collective action and interactions among geographically or socially mobile leaders who are not fixed to a particular local community.[14] These ties make possible the consolidation of shared political visions at the regional or national level. Examples of strong horizontal networks would be a group of party members who regularly meet at conventions or a group of priests who trained together. These individuals are not bound to local communities but instead operate beyond them.[15] Students, activists, business elites, clerics, politicians and political entrepreneurs, labor leaders, intellectuals, and political party cadres are most likely to be enmeshed in strong horizontal ties.

Weak horizontal ties limit communication, coordination, and cooperation across localities. They make it difficult to know the political preferences of people outside a local community. Weak ties undermine the collective social resources available in a social base. An example of weak horizontal ties are those between local village strongmen who have loose links to other leaders in their ethnic group but who rarely see, talk to, or interact with them. Similarly, a political party may be a diffuse umbrella of local notables who have little in common beyond shared ambition. Enough linkages exist across localities for the local leaders to be considered part of the same social base, but they have little connection above this threshold.

Vertical Ties

Vertical ties are created by relations of information, trust, and belief that link organizers to local communities. These ties can be used by organizers as they try to build or sustain political, economic, or social projects in these communities. They are the social anchors that organizers can call upon to align extralocal goals and imperatives with local action. Local communities are where peasants, members of working classes, and other mass categories are centered, in contrast to the horizontal networks of mobile activists, elites, religious organizations, and student networks. Vertical ties do not directly connect communities; horizontal ties are what do that.

Strong vertical ties connect organizers to local communities through bonds of trust, information, and preference. People in the community know or can easily learn about organizers through direct personal experience, flows of information in their networks, or shared membership in an organization or association. Such ties make them more likely to cooperate with, obey, or listen to an organizer who attempts to mobilize a local community. An example of a strong vertical tie would be a political party member who is a native of a village and has recruited local family and friends into the party. These links provide the party member with social resources for collective action in the village.

Weak vertical ties exist when there are few social relations between organizers and communities. An organizer may want to connect a local community with others, but if he does not know its people, cannot access overlapping networks with locals that would provide information, and has few or no normative claims on their cooperation it will be hard to actually achieve this goal. Organizers in this situation "float"[16] above a community or set of communities. They are social outsiders who lack links to potential group members based on information, norms, or common political worldviews.

An example of weak vertical ties is a network of students from a middle-class background who met in a university but have few connections to the urban working classes with whom they want to cooperate. They live in separate spaces, talk to different people, and use rhetoric and frames of reference that are different from those of the people they hope to mobilize. Even if they are on the same side of a political cleavage,

[22]

the student organizers cannot easily access information and create trust in the community because of these social gaps. Weak vertical ties often undermine urban elites who are trying to mobilize peasants to build states, get votes, or impose orthodox doctrine on local folk religions.

The Social Terrain of Politics

Vertical and horizontal ties combine to create the social terrain upon which politics is conducted. Patterns of cooperation and connection are crucial to everything from electoral patronage to state infrastructural power.[17] The goals and structures of social bases vary widely. Some are political parties trying to win elections, others are religious networks trying to access the divine, while others are underground movements seeking to mobilize the proletariat for mass revolution.[18] Social ties are not locked in place or "traditional," but they are also rarely created with an eye to future insurgency. Ideological visions, state policies, the economy, and leaders' agency can all be important in creating, sustaining, and structuring social bases, but such bases are enmeshed in patterns of actual social interaction and connection (or, just as importantly, their absence). Social bases represent a complex blend of agency, structure, and contingency that determines the ideational and social resources insurgent leaders can mobilize for war.[19]

BUILDING REBELLION

Insurgent leaders construct organizations by trying to convert their prewar social networks into a wartime organization.[20] The beginning of a war is an uncertain process that puts huge strain on nascent insurgent groups.[21] Leaders do not have the freedom to make whatever kind of organization they want. Instead, they "socially appropriate"[22] existing structures of collective action for new functions. Networks provide potent advantages over other forms of mobilization based solely on common ideology, ethnicity, or class status because they can provide reliable and rapid collective action. Tapping into prewar social ties is useful for building the "the extra-local party and army organizations that are indispensable to win[ning] national state power."[23] These linkages facilitate the secrecy, discipline, and obedience that are necessary for building rebellion.[24]

Prewar politics determine the initial organization of rebel groups. While political meanings are not locked in place, they also cannot be easily transformed, which means that many social bases are politically irrelevant to insurgency. This is why the most important building blocks of rebellion are politicized oppositions. Even when organizers do draw on a politically salient social base, mobilizing rebellion is enormously difficult. Underground movements must move from stealthy organizing to real war, political parties need to shift from getting votes to training and funding fighters, and clerical networks are challenged by the transition from engaging in religious activities to creating institutions for generating coercion. The ability of leaders to overcome these challenges depends on the social ties they can mobilize. Some leaders are enmeshed in strong horizontal but weak vertical ties, others have exactly the opposite set of social resources, and yet others have few resources at all.[25]

Structure and Agency in Organizing Insurgency

The historical roots of social bases limit the freedom of action of organizers trying to get a rebellion off the ground. This raises the question of why new insurgent leaders do not simply change their social ties as a war escalates. The uncertainty of the future is the key problem leaders face; it is hard for them to know what course to pursue, and social structures are not easily changed, especially in the face of government repression. As Barnard notes in a different context, "successful cooperation in or by formal organizations is the *abnormal*, not the normal, condition. . . . Most cooperation fails in the attempt, or dies in infancy, or is short-lived."[26]

Leaders embedded in social bases cannot fluidly reshape their social relations or political meanings.[27] It is very hard to readjust social linkages on the fly: "history gives no clean slates."[28] This creates inertia and mismatches between current social ties and future needs. Leaders of a clerical association that is pro-government are unlikely to persuade the association's members to launch an insurgency. A group of revolutionary plotters hoping to rapidly seize power in the capital city cannot quickly create vertical linkages to rural peasants, especially if security forces try to repress the nascent insurgency.[29] Though social bases may be the result of years of political and social work to build relationships, there is no guarantee that these ties will be most appropriate to the specific pressures of insurgency. This is "an environment where chance and contingency cannot be underestimated."[30] Many militants end up dead, marginalized, or in jail because of the uncertainty of war and the difficulty of reshaping their networks. The left-wing students who launched a Maoist uprising in India's West Bengal in the late 1960s were methodically wiped out within several years because they lacked deep ties to the peasantry. They tried to quickly create these ties when it became clear that the war would become a protracted guerrilla conflict, but they failed to do so.[31]

Insurgent Origins

This does not mean that there is no role for creativity and individual leadership. The most important opportunity for agency comes in decisions about alliances and coalitions. Leaders may decide to combine forces, enter into an umbrella agreement, or merge their structures. Such decisions can create disjunctures between the structure of a prewar social base and the organizational type of the insurgency that develops. Structure is not the same as determinism, and the empirical research in chapters 4–7 identifies cases where smart strategies overcame the limitations of social bases and, conversely, miscalculations squandered structural advantages. Nevertheless, once the underlying structure of a group is established, it cannot be easily changed.[32]

Explaining Insurgent Structures

Chapter 1 introduced a new typology of insurgent groups: integrated, vanguard, parochial, and fragmented. Prewar social bases create these different organizational starting points. Central organizational control can be built quickly when leaders have good reasons to trust one another, confidence in broadly shared goals, and access to rich shared flows of information.[33] These social resources come from prewar horizontal ties between organizers, making possible the creation of institutions for strategy, socialization, and coordination.[34] Where horizontal ties are weak or nonexistent, central control is more difficult: as Huntington has observed, "mutual distrust and truncated loyalties mean little organization."[35]

Vertical ties between organizers and local communities lay the basis for insurgent control at the local level. The leadership reaches into communities through preexisting networks to organize war. These linkages make it possible for leaders to communicate with local fighters, socialize new members, and deter and punish internal defiance. When leaders lack vertical ties, organization building on the ground is far more challenging. The embeddedness of leaders in communities helps determine whether organizations can quickly build an organizational backbone to govern, provide services, and control the population.[36] Table 1.2 shows how prewar social bases create new insurgent group structures. This linkage between prewar politics and wartime mobilization explains why insurgent groups that seem to be similar can take on fundamentally different organizational structures.

If my social-institutional theory is wrong, there will be consistent differences between social bases and wartime organizations. If ideologies matter more than the social base, Communists reading Mao should build different types of organizations than ethno-religious separatists, regardless of the prewar social bases of each of these types of group. If material resources are the crucial determinant of organization, leaders with access to material resources will build systematically different kinds of organizations than those without resources. If state policy is essential, leaders facing population-control counterinsurgency will construct distinct organizations than those that are dealing with indiscriminate counterinsurgency. Later in this book, I draw on empirical research that helps me assess how well these alternative explanations explain patterns of insurgency.

Even if my theory is correct, these other factors will surely be important. Yet this book should help to explain how these other influences work: counterinsurgency should be more effective against some types of groups than others, the implementation of Maoist doctrines should depend on whether leaders have the social resources to turn aspiration into reality, and the effects of resources on groups should depend on social bases and the organizations they create. Similar social building blocks will lead to similar organizations and will determine the effects of other variables.

My theory cannot explain why leaders embedded in strong social ties decide not to try to create organizations. I assume that leaders want to build integrated organizations, but this assumption is surely sometimes wrong.[37] Similarly, there will be cases where innovative or creative leaders transcend their social base or other variables overwhelm social bases as a war escalates.

Origins of Integrated Organizations

Leaders embedded in social bases with strong vertical and horizontal ties use these ties to create integrated organizations. New processes and new functions are built upon preexisting connections among leaders and on the ground in local communities. Bureaucracies are most likely to emerge when social linkages pull together both central leaders and local followers who cooperate in forging new organizational processes. Integration occurs even if the group is not highly popular, and it happens regardless of what resources a group has and across different ideologies. The Provisional IRA in Northern Ireland used family and republican networks to quickly create fighting units in Belfast in 1969, even though there had been almost no insurgent violence in Belfast for decades. McCann shows the importance of social bases: "the tiny republican movement of the time, embodied in Belfast in a few families, like the Adamses, the Hannaways, the Prices and the MacAirts, provided an organizational framework, a channel for expression and a readiness to fight that matched the sudden mood of the Catholic masses."[38]

Horizontal networks help leaders create central processes of decision-making, command and control, strategic assessment, and ideological production. Normative obligations decrease the likelihood of betrayal, shared preferences reduce the odds of major splits, and information flows allow for in-group policing that can check (though never fully eliminate) infiltration and disobedience. Leaders of a disciplined prewar political party, for instance, are likely to have these collective social resources, which will enable them to create new institutions and repurpose existing networks. The specifics of organizational structure will obviously vary, but we see broad similarities: bureaucratic specialization, standard operating procedures, a clear leadership structure, and a reasonably coherent ideology that is disseminated consistently throughout the organization.[39]

Vertical ties connect central leaders to communities and make it possible to quickly establish institutions for local control. The fundamental challenge in many rebellions is linking leaders with local communities. Vertical ties mitigate this challenge because they provide trustworthy, information-rich channels for accessing villages, neighborhoods, and other local networks. These sites can be harnessed to the broader agenda of the organization by enabling leaders to gain the cooperation of villages and neighborhoods. The gaps that so often exist between "peasants and commissars"[40] are overcome. Vertical ties make it possible for leaders to share their ideology with people at the local level, facilitating political education and the reproduction of worldviews favorable to the insurgency. When these ties are in place, leaders can more easily monitor foot soldiers and local fighters are more likely to obey leadership commands.

Local networks become the basis for new fighting units that can train and socialize new foot soldiers while being linked to the broader organizational structure. For example, a party member who has long operated in a village but remains connected to party members in other areas uses his local branch as a site for identifying and recruiting fighters. A teacher identifies promising students to recruit and pass along to commanders. Because of such local processes, "insurgents have been spared the difficult task of inducing participation through the provision of new incentives of either a solidary or material nature."[41]

Strong horizontal and vertical ties lay the groundwork for providing incentives, governance, and services that can be used to mobilize broad civilian support. These strategies are important for maintaining and expanding insurgency, but an organizational structure needs to first be in place to implement them. Integrated groups will be the most effective at consistently enacting these policies. Hamas, for instance, was able to convert its Muslim Brotherhood base into robust insurgency with surprising speed and effectiveness because of its social linkages. As Mishal and Sela note, "From the beginning Hamas was organized into a small number of hard-core activists who coordinated and activated a wide network of supporters through the mosques whose preachers were often members of the movement or had close acquaintances in the Islamic students' associations and communal services."[42]

Once integrated organizations are created, they can take on greater distance from society. However, they cannot become fully autonomous as long as they need to rely on local intelligence, support, and recruits. A continued relationship to society is a great strength for integrated groups; they can use local ties to harness manpower and information without becoming captured by local interests and feuding. Although under certain circumstances the linkages that hold integrated groups together can become weakened or destroyed, thus undermining control within the organization, integration is the most promising starting point for insurgents.

Origins of Vanguard Organizations

Vanguards emerge when strong horizontal and weak vertical prewar social ties have been mobilized by rebel leaders. Networks that strongly connect activists, elites, and mobile organizers to one another are best positioned to build new central insurgent institutions. But such networks will have trouble quickly organizing local communities if they lack strong vertical ties. This trajectory is quite common, especially when urban political movements and networks attempt to reach into rural areas to organize for war, students and elites aim to mobilize socially distant communities, or exiled leaders try to control armed movements from afar.

Insurgent leaders at the top of a new organization can quickly create central institutions by mobilizing strong horizontal ties. The linkages among nascent leaders, whether they be labor organizers, clerics, or urban intellectuals, are used to construct the central command. This mixture of social relations and shared political meanings makes it easy to forge a clear party line and build central bureaucracies that can tap into resources and make decisions in difficult circumstances. The structure of leadership will be at least partially collective: there may be a key individual leader, but even if that is the case, he or she will be surrounded by a core of commanders who have connections to one another that predate the war.

Vanguard organizations are classic Leninist "combat parties." The advantage of this organizational type is the discipline and commitment of its leaders. A group's ideology is often intertwined with the prewar social ties through which the group is built, and that ideological focus tends to carry over into the command elite. In contexts where rapid coordinated action is essential, a vanguard group can become a decisive and dominant player. The Bolsheviks in 1917 Russia rose to power by using a strong party leadership to outmaneuver their rivals.

Despite these strengths, vanguard organizations lack reliable local roots that can establish and sustain local processes of control. Leaders and prospective followers drift past one another, lacking common understandings of politics and shared social relationships. The organization is forced to send socially alien recruiters into communities to try to mobilize supporters, and it is not surprising that these recruiters have problems establishing local control. This occurs even if the policies the insurgents are advocating would in fact benefit the community or if they are trying to emulate models of mobilization that succeeded elsewhere. This is why the Bolsheviks had to launch a long, fractious process of consolidation even after their seizure of power: they lacked extensive vertical ties and needed to build them through brutal warfare.

Two distinct, though closely related, variations of a vanguard group can arise, depending on initial expansion strategy. First, some vanguard groups may never build a local presence. Their fears of the negative effects of expansion forestall efforts to aggressively reach into communities. Local control barely exists because there is little to control in the first place. This type of vanguard group, which is typically confined to urban and elite social environments, finds it difficult to draw on social support for protracted irregular warfare. The failure to build connections with local communities undermines efforts to mobilize the citizenry through selective incentives or ideological appeals, because a structure must be in place to lay the groundwork for local organizing. In this situation, leadership decapitation becomes an extremely serious vulnerability since local replacements do not exist. The inability of Che Guevara to inspire the rural masses to revolution in the jungles of Bolivia is a clear example of the limits of vanguards.

In the second variation of a vanguard structure, a group may decide to accept a slew of local fighters without clear screening and control. Internal disagreements about obedience and control occur because channels of information and trust have not been established.[43] Organizers do not know who to trust, how to find fighters, or whether their foot soldiers are obeying them, all of which makes bureaucratization difficult. The coalition between a tight core of leaders and an array of local fighters and commanders is loose. This situation often leads to local defiance and dissent that undermines local control: units ignore leaders, actively work against their orders, or even rebel against them. The Communist Party of

Thailand, for instance, initially could expand only by recruiting autonomous local networks and hill tribes from Thailand's periphery, leaving party leaders vulnerable to defiance from and abandonment by local units.

In vanguard groups, an ideological and disciplined leadership is vulnerable to heavily armed local forces. The patterns of internal unrest that emerge between leaders and local units should map onto prewar social structure. In protracted guerrilla warfare, weak local control is a serious liability in building and maintaining rebellion.

Origins of Parochial Organizations

Leaders who draw on vertical linkages to local communities without strong horizontal ties to one another construct parochial organizations. The weak links between organizers undermine central institutionalization and control. Localized power centers are built into the organization and de facto sub-organizations are clustered around particular leaders, even if the official organizational chart suggests otherwise. In this situation, leaders have little trust in the other leaders and cannot monitor each other's behavior. An absence of common and consistent policies across the different factions of an organization militates against coherent strategy and bureaucratization.

These organizational factions resemble prewar cleavages and blocs in the social base.[44] A group of clerics loosely connected through an ephemeral central leadership may want to cooperate and work together, but they will face basic challenges to collective action as they build new violent organizations. The local clerical networks will serve as the primary actors instead of a central command. These collections of localized networks may go to war together for numerous reasons: an alliance of convenience, a shared identity category, common political interests, miscalculation of the needs of future war, or a lack of other options. Whatever the case may be, the core underlying dynamic remains that social structure shapes organization.

Organizations that emerge from such a social base will take on one of two leadership structures: either a single leader engaged in tenuous "brokerage" across distinct factions or a fractious collective leadership of commanders.[45] In the first leadership situation, the broker has the power to play factions against one another. This central leader may have individual power through symbolic authority, access to external resources, or both.[46] But brokerage is fragile because war creates unexpected shocks and setbacks. These arrangements are prone to coups, breakdowns, and factional feuds. Moktada Al-Sadr's militia in Iraq was built around disparate local factions and networks. Consequently, as the International Crisis Group noted in 2006, Sadr led "a movement that is short of resources traditionally considered critical in Shiite politics, is rife with internal contradictions, and remains both unpredictable and undisciplined."[47]

In the second situation, we see a coalition of commanders of factions who act autonomously despite the existence of an ostensible collective leadership. This occurs when there is no charismatic or credible central leader who can rise above the different factions. Some degree of central coordination may exist, but without consistent policies for making and enacting decisions. Commanders will not trust one another enough to become subordinate to or obey the others.[48] In Syria in the period 2011 to 2013, the insurgency represented "a rebellion divided into little fiefdoms"[49] even though some umbrella organizations claimed to unite local units. In such a situation, each faction corresponds to a preexisting network, at least initially.

The tight strategy, bureaucratic specialization, and central unity that we see in vanguard and integrated organizations are absent in parochial groups because of the limited social resources of their leaders. Actual processes of central strategy making and implementation are not anything like processes outlined in formal organizational charts. Efforts to reform and transform the organization are unlikely to succeed as long as the underlying social linkages remain the same, because these linkages have built powerful "veto players" into the organization.[50]

The key advantage of a parochial organization is local embeddedness, drawn from prewar vertical ties that are converted into local units and factions. Vertically embedded (but horizontally isolated) organizers use their networks on the ground to quickly establish fighting forces. They become local commanders, strongmen, and power brokers with whom both counterinsurgents and other commanders in their own organization must contend. In contrast to the fragile discipline at the center of an organization, there is consistent control and obedience in each bloc, including developed norms and expectations about appropriate behavior and mechanisms for punishing disobedience.

The disorder in the broader organization obscures local factional coherence and order on the ground. This distinctive pattern of central fluidity and local stability arises from the social origins of these organizations. We can even see integrated factions nested in parochial groups. The local units of a parochial group tend to be tough fighters who know their local areas well and are able to induce cooperation from the civilian population, both through preexisting links and through the credible manipulation of coercion and bribery. In such a situation, counterinsurgents have a difficult time establishing local dominance and rooting out embedded factions. If the central difficulty in vanguard organizations is reaching into localities, the key challenge in parochial groups is managing conflict between the leaders of armed local factions.

Origins of Fragmented Organizations

Fragmented organizations emerge when organizers are unable to draw on any kind of strong social ties to build their new group. They desperately try to recruit from wherever they can, with disastrous consequences for their organizations. Many organizers try to mobilize insurgent groups but fail to get off the ground because they lack the capacity to generate collective action or build any kind of control. If an organization does emerge from this social base, it will be fragmented. Fragmented organizations are prone to rapid, often fratricidal, failure and decay. When facing a strong state they are likely to be quickly wiped out or pushed aside. They are somewhat more potent in the context of a weak state and can also survive in exile, without a serious presence in the war zone. These are the least common type of enduring insurgent group, even though many groups rise and quickly fall as fragmented organizations.

A few key leaders recruit other commanders outside their preexisting network to form the new command of a fragmented group. Prior ties that can facilitate this organization-building task do not exist. The commanders may not have known each other at all or well before the war, they lack shared information flows, and major differences in political goals and preferences are likely to emerge as the war evolves. As a consequence, we see little or no specialized bureaucracy, careful strategic assessment, or leadership unity at the central level in fragmented groups. A fluid coalition of leaders dropping in and out of the group characterizes the initial trajectory of a fragmented organization; opportunism and alliances of convenience dominate leadership politics. This structure is extremely vulnerable to state counterinsurgency and internal unrest.[51]

Recruitment of diverse individuals, the presence of local subgroups with nowhere else to go, and diffuse collections of fighters undermine local control. Vertical ties do not exist to shepherd and structure organization building in communities. A shambolic process of recruitment occurs based largely on local incentives: a fragmented group may provide a useful organizational cover for the pursuit of parochial criminality, for instance. Leaders may have to pay for fighters or even abduct them. These are the sorts of organizations that Jeremy Weinstein refers to as

Insurgent Origins

"opportunistic"; they are held together by personal gain and coercion at best and are prone to complete collapse at worst.[52] National and local cleavages of war will be distinct since no institutional mechanisms exist to bridge them. Formal procedures will have little bearing on actual organizational activities on the ground.

The Irish National Liberation Army (INLA) in Northern Ireland is a classic example of this process: it attracted a motley collection of recruits (including criminals and expelled members of other groups) and was forced to rapidly expand because of a brutal feud when it split from the Official IRA. The INLA rapidly spiraled into internecine killings and drug dealing. Even from its early days, "factions within the INLA openly struggled for supremacy,"[53] and by 1987 even its own internal documents argued that "we have also failed to purge our membership of unsuitable material, having in the past tolerated informers, touts, careerists, opportunists, sectarians and macho militarists."[54]

The one advantage of a fragmented organization is that it can sometimes engage in low-level violence for a protracted period precisely because its lack of organization makes it hard for the state to fully wipe it out. However, this is an unpromising starting point for an organization.

The Social Underpinning of Insurgency

The origins of insurgent organizations lie in prewar politics. The vertical and horizontal ties in which leaders are embedded and the political salience of these ties shape what kinds of organizations emerge. As conflicts begin and escalate, social and political structures are transformed, appropriated, and repurposed into militant organizations. Wars are not waged from a blank slate: instead, their early days are rife with attempts to draw upon prewar political life in order to quickly form organizations that can handle the strains of violence. The social terrain of war helps some leaders and undermines others as the weight of history, choice, and contingency shapes how organizers can mobilize. This explains why some organizations forge ahead while others fall by the wayside.

Other influences, such as ideological doctrines or material resources, are filtered through this underlying social-institutional structure. Integrated groups can handle huge inflows of resources without becoming predatory thugs, while fragmented or parochial groups are much more likely to suffer from feuds linked to resources. Creating a Marxist-Leninist organizational weapon should be much easier for leaders with strong horizontal ties, whereas leaders with weak horizontal links will find it difficult to create leadership cohesion. Vanguard groups will struggle more to provide local services and governance than parochial and integrated groups will. The point is not that these other variables are irrelevant but instead their effects are contingent on the ways the organization is embedded in social forces. The next chapter builds on this argument to explain when and why insurgent groups change over time during conflict.

[3]

Insurgent Change

Change is integral to conflict. Vanguard organizations try to reach into localities, parochial organizations attempt to reform their central institutions, and integrated organizations seek to expand without fragmenting. New strategic challenges arise when insurgents need to incorporate allies, to manage influxes of illicit resources, or to deal with local power struggles in areas they control. In turn, counterinsurgent states try to break and fracture insurgents. They deploy soldiers and police to blanket geographic spaces, attempt to recruit agents within the insurgency, monitor and control the civilian population, and target insurgent leaders. This battle over organization is the core focus of both insurgents and states during war.

There are almost no existing theories about the sources of insurgent change.[1] This chapter argues that the different starting points of organizations create distinct pathways of likely change that reflect the initial strengths and weaknesses of groups.[2] The expansion or destruction of horizontal and vertical ties determines shifts in organizational control during war. Insurgent strategy, counterinsurgency policy, and the behavior of external sponsors are the key factors that explain how these changes occur. For instance, vanguard groups are more vulnerable to leadership decapitation than integrated groups, parochial groups can become integrated when unified external sponsors encourage "factional fusing," and integrated groups are most likely to degrade when counterinsurgency simultaneously controls local communities and eliminates individual leaders.[3]

These pathways out of path dependence are not the only causes of change. An endless list of other factors and contingent events can explain how organizations evolve. Instead of trying to incorporate this staggering diversity, I specify a coherent set of mechanisms that should recur across time and space and help us understand change. These "endogenous processes"[4] are more complex than the straightforward argument I offered about origins in chapter 2 but are built around the same core claim about the connection between organization and social networks. This chapter systematically identifies how the competition between insurgent groups and states develops over time. Explaining change is essential to understanding how wars are waged and how they end.

The Enduring Importance of Social Linkages

Social linkages remain essential for armed groups after they are initially built. Organizational power continues to rely on links between leaders and local communities and among leaders themselves. This is true for several reasons. First, rebels need to tap into local support and manpower in order to keep fighting. Unless an insurgent group is immediately able to completely institutionalize and dominate all aspects of its constituency, which is highly unlikely, it must rely on trust, loyalty, and information on the ground. Insurgents need tips from peasants about the movement of government soldiers, local networks provide new manpower, and commanders use vertical ties to monitor their foot soldiers.[5] Without connections to society, an insurgent group will be isolated in exile abroad, will wither away on the ground, or will become fatally vulnerable to state repression. Vertical ties and local control form the core of guerrilla warfare.

Second, insurgents rely heavily on social links within their organizations. Inside armed groups, trust, political consensus, information flows, and norms among members are essential in an environment in which secrecy is needed and risk is endemic.[6] Robust control should persist where social relations have been established and intertwined with formal institutions.[7] These social ties within a group bolster the organization against counterinsurgency by providing a crucial layer of internal cooperation.

The Double-Edged Sword of Social Embeddedness

Although social connections keep armed groups fighting, they also create vulnerabilities. Organizational control responds to shifts in the networks that institutions are built upon. Counterinsurgents can undermine armed groups by targeting social ties, divisions within society can play out within organizations, and social linkages need to be sustained and reproduced to avoid ossification and self-encapsulation of insurgents.[8] As Mahoney and Thelen argue, "Where institutions represent compromises or relatively durable though still contested settlements based on specific coalitional dynamics, they are always vulnerable to shifts."[9]

Insurgent Change

We can explain how organizations change by studying what happens to these social building blocks. Counterinsurgents want to push groups toward fragmentation by breaking linkages, while insurgents seek to stay at or move toward integration by developing new ties. A struggle ensues over who can access and control society.[10] While I cannot predict ex ante when insurgents and counterinsurgents will make decisions about the policies to pursue (that would require a staggeringly complex theory), my social-institutional argument can explain the broad patterns of organizational change that result from the interaction of these strategies.

Carefully working through how insurgents and counterinsurgents try to build or destroy rebel organizations requires us to avoid assigning state policy the role of a deus ex machina, yet still take counterinsurgency seriously.[11] The quest for a single set of strategic "best practices"[12] in counterinsurgency that was so fashionable during America's Iraq and Afghanistan wars is intellectually fruitless, because different types of insurgent organizations present very different challenges. What works against a vanguard insurgent group may have little to do with success against a parochial organization. To understand insurgency, we need to know when it becomes vulnerable to counterinsurgency, and to understand the success of counterinsurgency we need to identify differences across insurgent groups.[13]

Pathways of Insurgent Change

This section identifies key pathways of change between different organizational structures. Structural origins, drawn from prewar social ties, create powerful tendencies of path dependence. These tendencies can be overcome when insurgents change the social ties that underpin processes of control or when counterinsurgents are able to break down these ties. Table 3.1 summarizes the pathways of change that the rest of this chapter explains.

The core principle guiding this argument is that we should see similar dilemmas facing similar types of insurgent organizations. Vanguard groups, for instance, change through a set of mechanisms that are different from how parochial groups change. These patterns arise because the social-institutional origins of groups create distinctive opportunities and constraints; as Kathleen Thelen notes, "Different institutions rest on different foundations, and so the processes that are likely to disrupt them will also be different, though predictable."[14] Counterinsurgent strategies will similarly vary in effectiveness depending on what kind of group they are targeting. To avoid unfalsifiable ad hoc

Table 3.1. Pathways of insurgent change

	Integrated	Vanguard	Parochial	Fragmented
Mechanisms of increased central control			Factional fusing Cooperation under fire	Forced merger
Mechanisms of increased local control		Local alliance Local imposition		Rising warlord
Mechanisms of fragmentation	Comprehensive counterinsurgency Mismanaged expansion	Leadership decapitation Fratricide from below	Interleadership fratricide Local disembedding	Numerous

explanations, any theory of change must be driven by specific, observable conditions.

Crucially, insurgents and counterinsurgents cannot reshape organizations as they please. Explanations of change require a careful assessment of how different rebel and government policies intersect with the social-institutional constraints on insurgent groups. Skocpol made this point decades ago:

> Once a political movement is in contact with the countryside, *there may be only some possible policies that will "work" to mobilize the peasantry,* given, on the one side, the constraints faced by revolutionaries and, on the other side, the specific features of local class, community, and political arrangements among the peasantry.[15]

It is necessary to identify when particular strategies and mechanisms of change are relevant because otherwise we will end up with an unrealistic voluntarism, in which insurgent leaders could easily change if only they put enough thought and effort into it or states could break any insurgent group as long as they adopted a universally effective set of counterinsurgency policies. I argue instead that options can be foreclosed even if leaders are creative and innovative. The same is true on the counterinsurgent side. Understanding why organizations fail and collapse is just as important as explaining how they adapt and innovate.[16]

CHANGE IN INTEGRATED ORGANIZATIONS

Integrated groups are initially formed when leaders use strong vertical and horizontal linkages to rapidly construct central and local control.

In this process, the social resources of prewar politics are converted into a war-fighting organization. As long as central and local institutions continue to be intertwined with trust, monitoring, and shared political preferences, the organization should be able to reproduce itself as a relatively disciplined force. This is the optimal starting point for insurgent groups.

Yet we can see instances where groups that were originally integrated change toward vanguard or parochial organizational structures. Two primary mechanisms drive changes—and even collapse—for such groups: comprehensive counterinsurgency that simultaneously targets the horizontal and vertical ties that sustain control, and mismanaged expansion by insurgent leaders triggered by military desperation or political competition. The first is a result of external pressures, while the second results from a mix of external incentives and internal agency. Both pathways can undermine the organizational control necessary for integrated rebellion.

Comprehensive Counterinsurgency and Insurgent Fragmentation

The first mechanism of change is caused by sustained counterinsurgency campaigns that effectively target leaders and at the same time impose pervasive state control at the local level. To survive as a cohesive fighting force, integrated groups must be impermeable to the counterinsurgent state yet still benefit from internal and external social links. Counterinsurgents try to snap these linkages to disrupt the organizational processes that rely on trust and information. When can they actually achieve this goal? Two state strategies must operate in tandem: leadership decapitation aimed at the organizers and commanders of the group and local disembedding aimed at the organization's connections to local units on the ground. Each alone is insufficient to force organizational fragmentation when directed against integrated groups. Instead, dramatic change requires their simultaneous application. The ability to implement this comprehensive counterinsurgency strategy at an acceptable political and military cost is beyond the reach of many counterinsurgent states. It involves extraordinary resources, fine-grained intelligence, high levels of political resolve, and capable state organization.[17]

Breaking down central control is most effective when states can use extensive *leadership decapitation* that disrupts how leaders interact with one another.[18] This strategy targets both formal processes and informal linkages of trust and commitment among the leadership. Leadership decapitation against integrated organizations is more difficult than against other types because the greater discipline of the group makes intelligence scarce. Detailed information has to be slowly and painstakingly acquired through recruiting informants, using signals intercepts, and deploying forces to make travel and communication difficult. This intelligence then needs to be carefully used by trained forces without inflicting indiscriminate violence on civilians.

Shattering the local roots of an integrated group necessitates disembedding it from society by displacing populations, implementing intense social control and surveillance, and using local counterinsurgent forces and "flipped" former militants to target insurgent fighters and sympathizers. The local disembedding strategy makes it possible to control and monitor the local population and creates incentives for informants to betray local insurgent units. If carried out properly—a time- and resource-intensive task—this strategy should make it increasingly difficult for insurgent leaders to draw on the local areas for support. Local control breaks down as access to communities is denied.[19]

Decapitation and disembedding can destroy, respectively, vanguard and parochial groups, as I discuss below. However, each strategy on its own is less likely to be as successful against integrated groups. This is because these groups have the flexibility and capacity to adapt to each type of strategy.[20] The efforts of counterinsurgents to target one or a few communities for disembedding can be overcome by insurgents moving men and resources toward or away from the targeted area, thus limiting the damage. Integrated groups can respond to leadership decapitation by reaching into local units for loyal and motivated fighters to replace the targeted leaders. Counterinsurgents must implement a challenging mix of policies to substantially degrade integrated organizations, and that is what makes these organizations different from other types of insurgent groups.

It is possible that comprehensive counterinsurgency will succeed in some ways but fail in others: policies may be implemented unevenly, insurgents may face resource constraints that limit their adaptation, militant leaders may be able to flee to foreign sanctuary, and innovative state strategies may be able to get around some insurgent countermeasures but not others. Insurgent groups can survive without fragmenting even if they are weakened in the face of comprehensive counterinsurgency. If vertical ties degrade and local control processes break down but the leadership remains protected, an initially integrated group should begin to look more like a vanguard. This occurs when the government is able to surge forces and build reliable local control on the ground but is unable to thoroughly target the high command. In India's Assam state, the ability of key United Liberation Front of Asom military leaders to escape into Bangladesh and Burma/Myanmar despite crushing Indian counterinsurgency has changed the group from an integrated structure to at least a semblance of a vanguard structure.[21] By contrast, if local ties endure but the leadership becomes isolated and divided, we should see a shift toward a parochial organization. When the leadership is unable to coordinate and communicate because of state policies that cut off travel and communication across regions and key leaders that link localities are incapacitated, powerful local enclaves may still be able to keep fighting if local disembedding does not occur.

Integrated groups are potent foes and only under fairly rare circumstances will counterinsurgency alone induce collapse. The governments that can decisively defeat integrated groups tend to be either the richest, most powerful, and most administratively capable (precisely the kinds of states least likely to face rebellion on their own soil to begin with) or extremely highly resolved and willing and able to incur heavy costs over long years of intense warfare, state building, and social transformation.

Mismanaged Expansion and the Dilemma of Incorporation

The second potential source of a shift toward fragmentation comes from within. Insurgent leaders may engage in mismanaged expansion that undermines social relationships and strains processes of socialization and control. Expansion is a particularly severe challenge for groups trying to capture central power that need to seize territory and bring in new social blocs in order to march on the capital, separatist organizations that face intense military pressure, and groups that are trying to unify a broader movement under their aegis.[22] Leaders in these contexts face a choice between relying on their original social base and moving beyond it.

Organizational change can result from internal miscalculations by insurgent leaders about their ability to incorporate and homogenize new commanders and local fighters from outside the original social base. Agency opens space for leaders to both make mistakes and cleverly innovate. Many integrated organizations do expand successfully. The most effective expansion for integrated organizations is carefully channeled through powerful socializing institutions that instill values and norms in new commanders and recruits.

Only specific forms of expansion can cause a group that begins as integrated to change its organizational structure. Two mechanisms of mismanaged expansion can lead to such a shift. The first mechanism, rapid incorporation of leaders, undermines the horizontal relationships that hold together the central leadership. The second mechanism occurs when promotion of new, socially distinct foot soldiers is blocked, creating gaps and resentments between local combat units and the central leadership. The first mechanism causes integrated organizations to become parochial and the second mechanism converts them to vanguard groups as central and local control processes break down. They result from strategic choices driven by considerations of political competition, attempted unification, and military desperation.

The first form of mismanaged expansion occurs when a group incorporates new commanders in a way that undermines horizontal ties and reduces the ability of central institutions to maintain control and cooperation. This happens when groups try to outcompete rivals by growing more quickly than them or by absorbing other factions as part of a broader political strategy of controlled unity. Rapid leadership expansion is most common in groups trying to navigate divided, fractious movements.[23] New commanders without prior ties to existing leaders are brought into the organization to bolster its size and reach. This weakens central control because these new leaders lack social linkages to the existing command.[24] In this situation, an integrated organization comes to increasingly resemble a parochial group as the bonds that previously underpinned the central command become more diffuse. Rapid leadership expansion increases the risk of debilitating factionalism, even if the formal organization of the group remains the same as before.

The second mechanism toward fragmentation driven by strategic miscalculation occurs when new fighters enter the organization but are not provided with a pathway to move into leadership roles.[25] Blocked promotion causes discontent. This scenario is most likely to arise when the organization needs more military strength. A desperate need for military power leads to aggressive local recruiting of foot soldiers who previously would not have been trusted or incorporated while the leadership core tries to maintain its dominance. A vanguard organizational structure emerges from this shift in social composition. Revolts from below and tensions between local and central leaders become more likely, triggered by shocks, unexpected setbacks, or divide-and-conquer manipulation on the part of the state. This dynamic helped destroy the Communist Party of Burma. Although it was a powerful and coherent organization for much of its history, its decision to aggressively recruit foot soldiers from Burma's ethnic minorities while retaining a leadership dominated by ethnic Burmans eventually led to devastating internal splits along ethnic lines that destroyed the group.[26]

Integrated groups are the most potent foes of states, but their structure is not locked in place. Governments are sometimes capable of deploying enormous resources to target and disrupt the central and local social resources that underpin organizational power. The demands of war and the need to compete with other militant factions can encourage counterproductively rapid expansion that undermines an integrated organization from within. Strategy and agency interact with initial structural constraints to create both powerful forces for continuity and potential pathways of change.

Change in Vanguard Organizations

Vanguard organizations face the problem of how to mobilize local communities. While strong horizontal linkages between organizers make it easier to set up central institutions—politburos and leadership councils, internal policing, bureaucracies for socializing and training group members—the weak prewar vertical ties between leaders limit their presence and control on the ground. Leaders of vanguard groups need to build vertical linkages to villages and neighborhoods if they are to increase integration, but this is a real challenge, especially in the face of counterinsurgency. Many vanguard organizations retain their original structure over the course of a war: peasants and commissars and exiles and locals fail to connect with one another as the organization operates parallel to mass society. Local units ignore orders, defect, or simply do not exist.

Yet some of the most important insurgent groups in the world managed to move from this starting point toward integration. Sometimes students, urban intellectuals, and other organizers with weak prewar ties to local communities have been able to build new organizations at the local level. These organizers become the hinges of an expanding armed movement by merging committed central leadership with locally mobilized units. The National Resistance Army in Uganda, the Viet Minh in French Indochina, and the Tigrayan People's Liberation Front in Ethiopia are cases in which armed groups penetrated, mobilized, and then organized localities even though they began as vanguard groups.[27] I devote special attention to vanguards because they have the greatest potential for important change.

My social-institutional theory identifies two mechanisms through which vanguard organizations can become integrated organizations: making alliances with local groups and imposing an organization on a local area. The strategy of making local alliances tends to be more durable and resilient because it is organically links local conflicts with the "master cleavage" of the war, whereas imposing a vanguard group takes advantage of vacuums of power to establish a local presence. I then specify two mechanisms of fragmentation—leadership decapitation and fratricide from below—that undermine horizontal ties and central processes of control. Fragmentation through decapitation is a result of state counterinsurgency that degrades central processes by targeting leaders who have been unable to mobilize localities. Fratricide from below arises from the internal tensions that emerge when vanguard groups accept new local factions and fighters on the ground without being able to control them.

When Vanguards Mobilize Communities: Local Alliances and Local Imposition

The first and most powerful mechanism through which vanguards move toward being integrated organizations is by creating local alliances. These alliances occur when insurgents take advantage of local feuds and tensions that can be aligned with the master cleavage of the war that the insurgents are waging. Organizers infiltrate the locality by allying with one side in a local conflict, using a shared enemy to establish new ties. Over time, these alliances create social ties of trust and allow formal organization to be built. Local conflicts—peasants against landlords, interethnic tension, feuds between key families, oppressive state forces versus villagers—are yoked to the broader aims of the organization.[28] In return, local actors benefit from the resources, protection, and power of the insurgents. To have a substantial effect on organization, these local conflicts need to be widespread so that insurgent leaders can mobilize a substantial number of communities.

Vanguard groups frequently attempt this strategy to escape the constraints created by their social origins. Building vertical ties is especially important for groups of urban leaders who need to mobilize rural peasants.[29] Yet the success of this strategy is highly variable. Whether or not this strategy will succeed is contingent on political structure, state policy, and insurgent adaptability. For local alliances to work, local cleavages and master cleavages must align, at least in broad terms; the insurgent leadership must be flexible about how it adopts its ideology to local conditions, and the state must be unable to defuse local conflicts.[30] The alignment of cleavages is necessary because shared political interests help forge new coalitions that can evolve into the successful expansion of an organization. Pragmatic alliances based on local politics are the surest route to the mobilization of local areas by insurgents. If these alliances can be built, insurgents' favored ideology can be "grafted" onto these ties and then disseminated at the local level.

Counterinsurgency creates space for local alliances when the state's political and organizational constraints leave it unable to move its own policies and those of local allies away from counterproductive local conflicts.[31] State policy—which can be driven by a large number of factors—is crucial for determining what opportunities are available to insurgents.[32] Within this structural context, patience and pragmatism are essential for insurgents: local alliance is a demanding strategy that is easy to propose and difficult to implement. The conditions under which the pursuit of local alliances can create major organizational shifts are restrictive and require insurgent skill, counterproductive counterinsurgent strategy, and an overlap of national and local interests that creates space for local alliances. Will Reno has argued that rebel groups in Uganda and Ethiopia achieved a change from vanguard to integrated structure by taking advantage of deep contradictions in an incumbent regime and paying attention to local dynamics that provided openings for rebel organizers.[33]

By contrast, creating local alliances as a pathway to change is far more difficult to achieve across the master cleavage of a war (for example, a clash between two Serbian farming families in north Kosovo would not have been fertile ground for the Kosovo Liberation Army), when local conflicts are not aligned with the cleavage between the state and insurgents (a leftist insurgent group may not benefit from a division between evangelical Protestant and Catholic peasants), and when states have the population under extensive control and surveillance.[34] When these conditions hold, there may be spurts of expedient cooperation between insurgents and locals but not substantial change in a group's structure.

Failure may also result from insurgent strategy.[35] Local alliances do not occur when the insurgency is ideologically rigid in its beliefs about how local social and political life should be structured and unwilling to accommodate local norms and interests: if commissars ignore these norms and interests, peasants will not trust or cooperate with them, much less help them create a robust organization.[36] Failure can also result if attempts of insurgents to embed their group in a local area undermine strong connections across the commanders who have been sent to mobilize the localities. They risk being manipulated by local factions if central processes of control break down as a result of leaders' dispersion to communities. Ironically, excessive pursuit of local alliances can create parochial organizations when efforts to strengthen vertical ties undermine central control by building up powerful local fiefdoms.

There are clear limits on using the strategy of building local alliances as a means of creating vertical linkages and transforming a vanguard group into an integrated organization. Embedding an insurgent group in a local area involves more than reading Mao just right: it must also be the case that counterinsurgents are unable to manage local conflict, the political interests of local residents and the insurgent group are aligned, and the insurgent leadership is willing to accommodate local input while still maintaining central control. These conditions explain why vanguard groups often fail to build local control despite serious efforts. When insurgent strategy does intersect with a promising political and military context, this organizational change is important because it

Chapter 3

transforms the social and geographical space the state must defend. Counterinsurgents are forced to change their strategy from containing isolated leaders to garrisoning vast areas and trying to resolve destructive local conflicts.

The second mechanism of integration for groups that begin as vanguards is imposing an insurgent presence on a local area. This process of local imposition occurs when a vanguard group establishes control without previously creating social ties in the local area. The opportunity to use this strategy is created when the counterinsurgent presence is significantly reduced by government strategy, regime politics, or military constraints. This is not common at the national level, but it may happen regionally in ways that create openings for a vanguard group to establish a presence. The group can outmaneuver local opposition because it is better at violent, coordinated collective action. This is a less organic and thus less resilient process than creating local alliances: instead of establishing relations of trust and cooperation as a way of establishing local organizational processes, an ideological blueprint from the center is put in place.

Uncontested territory creates valuable space for vanguards to create quasi-state structures that can make possible greater integration over long periods of time. If the state never tries to or is never able to retake a local area where insurgents have imposed control, that control may become a taken-for-granted fact of life that eventually creates vertical ties and reliable local institutions. But in general, local organization resulting from local imposition strategies is less robust and reliable than that resulting from creating local alliances. As a consequence, the local imposition mechanism of change is more fragile and easily disrupted by governments.[37]

From the perspective of counterinsurgents, the strategy of creating local alliance is much more dangerous and difficult to counteract since it builds on complex conflicts that states are unable or unwilling to solve. The strategy of imposing local control is, by contrast, an opportunistic, though potentially important, response to a vacuum in state power. Creating local alliances should be the dominant means vanguard groups use to change into resilient integrated groups and thus to create a fundamental shift in the nature of a guerrilla war.

Fragmenting Vanguard Organizations: Targeting Leaders and Fratricide from Below

Two mechanisms of change can seriously undermine vanguard organizations and create change toward a fragmented structure. I noted in chapter 2 that vanguards can have subtly different forms: some lack any substantial local presence, while others expand on the ground but have few strong vertical ties. Each structure creates different vulnerabilities that can lead to fragmentation.

One strategy that can undermine vanguard groups is sustained decapitation of leaders by the counterinsurgent state. Vanguards are vulnerable because they lack deep local roots that regenerate manpower and build new cadres of leaders. Leadership is crucial: these are the people who Selznick, writing of communism, calls "the steeled cadres upon whom the continuity and the basic power of the party rest."[38] In a vanguard group, the local units that should be recruiting, socializing, and controlling the next generation of fighters do not exist or do not function well. If the state is able to regularly arrest or kill key leaders, central processes will decay and perhaps collapse altogether. Simply inserting new people into formal leadership positions will be less effective if these leaders lack ties to one another; trust and cooperation will break down as attrition takes its toll. The horizontal bonds within the leadership cannot be easily reproduced when leaders are systematically removed by counterinsurgents, especially when there are few or no local units on the ground.

Leadership decapitation is the dominant means by which vanguard groups are destroyed. Many urban leftist organizations in Latin America suffered this fate when they were unable to embed themselves in local communities.[39] For this strategy to succeed, however, a state must have detailed intelligence *and* be discriminating in its use of violence.[40] This requires extensive infrastructure, a tightly coordinated security apparatus, and informants who can provide precise information about who leaders are and how to get them. The capacity of states to carry out these operations varies dramatically. If they do have these capabilities, we should see vanguards being degraded through targeted campaigns that move them into a fragmented structure or even wipe them out completely. If states lack this capacity, attempts at decapitation are likely to lead to targeting mistakes that turn civilians against the government, which can backfire and lay the basis for local alliances.[41]

Timing is essential if state efforts to fragment vanguard groups are to succeed. The state needs to quickly break apart leadership networks before local alliances can be formed. If it does not do so, newly established vertical ties and organization at the local level will minimize the damage decapitation does by reaching into local units to find new leaders who are tied to one another and to the broader organization. Depending on the type of armed group being targeted, a state's use of the same policy may have fundamentally different results.[42]

The second mechanism of fragmentation, fratricide from below, arises from the problem of weak local control. A vanguard group may decide to expand by recruiting a loose array of local strongmen and foot soldiers who are not linked to the leadership. The absence of preexisting vertical linkages makes this strategy dangerous. This is a problem even for integrated groups and can be totally devastating for vanguard groups. When vertical ties are absent, expansion creates a dangerous dependence on autonomous local forces and shifts the internal balance of power toward new fighters. Weak socialization of new members and poor incorporation of these soldiers exacerbate tensions and increase the potential for escalation of conflict between the commanders and foot soldiers. Although Al Qaeda in Iraq had a coherent and institutionalized leadership core, its reliance on cooperation with local Sunni nationalists left it extremely vulnerable to shifts in the allegiance of these factions when the Anbar Awakening occurred.[43]

In this context, coups and defections from below can trigger fratricide that may fragment the organization or leave it open to debilitating attacks from the state and rival militants. As local units rebel against or ignore a distant original leadership, horizontal ties and their associated central processes of control can also break down. Leaders can be assassinated or exiled, communication can falter, distrust can grow, and unrest from below can eventually spill over into conflict at the command level. Leadership unity thus collapses amid attrition, debates about who is to blame, and general tumult within the organization. This opens space for counterinsurgents to acquire information, play leaders off against followers, and make taking on command responsibility a dangerous affair. Fratricide is prone to rapid spirals of escalation that are difficult to control or manage short of violence. Sometimes leaders can stave off these threats through purges or organizational innovations, but this is a very tenuous structural situation.

Both of these mechanisms of fragmentation show how essential it is for vanguard insurgents to build social links to local communities, lest they be isolated and targeted. Leaders of vanguard groups are caught between the pressures of counterinsurgency from without and the dangers of a coup or split by local units from within. The survival of the group depends on whether leaders can create local institutions that can prevent internal feuding and train fighters to take the reins of command. The ability of leaders to achieve this goal depends on how their strategy relates to the broader political and military context; in some contexts, vanguards will be able to build new vertical ties and become integrated organizations but in others they will become marginalized or torn apart from within. Groups that begin as vanguards have the greatest potential for radical change, either by rapidly collapsing after leadership decapitation and internal revolts or by painstakingly building up a local organization that powerfully challenges the state.

Change in Parochial Organizations

Parochial organizations arise from social bases in which distinct local social blocs are loosely aggregated into a formal organization but strong horizontal ties between leaders do not exist. These prewar social roots create weak central control and a distinctive pattern of factional conflict among leaders. The result is either a coalition of commanders of mobilized local networks or an individual who acts as a central commander but has no consistent authority over factional elites. This is a difficult structure to change because local leaders have powerful incentives to favor the status quo in order to maintain control over their own blocs and to avoid being controlled by people they do not trust.[44] Reliable central institutions do not emerge, and war is waged by a shambolic, if locally potent, coalition.

Continuity is the most likely outcome for an organization that has been created by mobilizing this kind of prewar social base. Parochial groups are less able to move toward integration than are vanguard groups, which are better positioned to take advantage of changes in state power and have a greater capacity to coordinate strategic responses to new challenges. Conversely, it is more difficult for states to quickly wipe out parochial groups because of their embeddedness on the ground. Killing or arresting a few top commanders will not effectively decapitate this sort of organization because these individuals have no control over other parts of the group.

Nevertheless, it is possible for a group that begins as parochial to change its organizational structure. I identify two mechanisms of integration—factional fusing and cooperation under fire—and two mechanisms of fragmentation—local disembedding and interleadership fratricide. The latter two are substantially more likely than the former. Without tight central control, even popular struggles can falter into factional disarray or become fragmented by state strategies.[45] The distinctive characteristics of parochial groups determine their most likely mechanisms of change.

Overcoming Parochialism: Factional Fusing and Cooperation under Fire

There are two important pathways to integration from a parochial starting point. The first is factional fusing. When factional fusing occurs, leaders interact with each other, gain trust, and become more experienced in shared collective action. These strengthened horizontal ties facilitate the reform or creation of new formal organizational processes of decision-making, discipline, and socialization. Factional fusing is difficult to achieve in a war zone because the state has powerful incentives to isolate, marginalize, and target leadership ties. War can put an extraordinary strain on the coalitions that underpin parochial organizations, especially if counterinsurgents use selective violence in a way that encourages defection and manipulates distrust.[46]

An important arena where factional fusing can take place is the international system. External sanctuaries can provide a relatively safe place for factional elites to interact, discuss strategy, and establish new intraleadership linkages that sustain more formal organizational processes.[47] This factional fusing is particularly likely to occur if a state sponsor or powerful figures in a diaspora push for unity and provide the venue and resources to bring commanders together to build new relationships. Consolidating these linkages can then open space for formal institutions to operate more smoothly and move toward integration. Sanctuary from pressure by counterinsurgents is an important enabling condition for this mechanism, and careful brokering by states or diaspora leaders provides a direct mechanism for building unity among commanders who previously were linked only by weak horizontal ties and fragile central control.[48]

The involvement of international actors is not an unalloyed good. Such actors can also choose to undermine cohesion by exploiting divisions between factions. Parochial organizations are the most prone to divide-and-control strategies by external state sponsors who play factions off against one another. A divided international system in which external sponsors compete with each other for influence can also prevent unification: rival patrons may back different factions even within the same organization.[49] But unified international pressure is a potentially powerful means of change. For example, Will Reno argues that anticolonial rebels in Africa were forced to unify in order to get international backing: "Internal unity—the domination of a single narrative to explain why the rebels fought—remained a critical ingredient for attracting foreign diplomatic and material support, because most foreign states and governments, at least up to the 1970s, would only support one rebel group in each conflict."[50]

The second mechanism of increased central control in parochial groups is cooperation under fire. This occurs when counterinsurgents push factional commanders together through indiscriminate and ineffective violence. Mass violence becomes a spur for greater cooperation among factions and the creation of new bonds of trust and monitoring because there is no way to shirk organizational tasks: noncooperation will push a faction into the crosshairs of the state regardless of what it does. Relentlessly indiscriminate violence over long periods of time builds up a greater level of trust and more routinized norms about cooperation and coordination that bolster leadership unity and institutionalization. The crucible of war, under these specific circumstances, may shift an organization from a parochial to a more integrated structure. This mechanism relies on static state policy, in a variation of Goodwin's theory that rebels will cooperate with each other against the ruling regime when they are left with "no other way out."[51] Such policies can be caused by regime type, counterinsurgency doctrine, organizational dysfunction, or state perception of a particular form of threat that drives mass indiscriminate violence.[52]

Counterinsurgency can thus have two very different effects on parochial organizations: as I explain below, selective local disembedding fragments these groups, while indiscriminate violence forges new cooperation among leaders (unless they are all killed in the process). Cooperation under fire is a more tenuous mechanism than factional fusing because changes in state strategy may reopen wedges between rebel leaders. Unless state violence remains counterproductive for a long time, underlying social-institutional fissures will remain latent and recur when counterinsurgency policy changes. As with local imposition for vanguard groups, this mechanism can create movement toward integration, but such movement is short lived if states have the political and organizational means to self-correct. Factional fusing in the international realm is more difficult for counterinsurgents to deal with.[53]

Fragmentation in Parochial Groups: Local Counterinsurgency and Leadership Feuds

When do parochial groups fragment? The first important mechanism is driven by counterinsurgency. States can push parochial organizations toward fragmentation when they successfully create locally rooted security forces, sponsor "flipped" former militants and recruit informers, and establish pervasive social control on the ground. This sustained strategy of disembedding leads to fragmentation when the state exerts comprehensive local control and acquires detailed intelligence, making insurgent commanders unable to access networks in local communities.[54] As these vertical ties break down, insurgent institutions wither because the information and high-risk cooperation they rely on disappear. Organization charts may still claim that local units are operating in a particular area, but disembedding removes these units from actual fighting.

The absence of central control undermines the careful response of parochial insurgents to this state strategy. It is easier for a motivated and capable government to systematically isolate and wipe out local units in a parochial group than in an integrated group. Commanders in a parochial group cannot readily move to and mobilize other locales because their links to these other areas are weak. This divide-and-conquer policy should slowly but surely deliver results. We would expect the parochial group to move toward a fragmented group and eventually to total collapse if all of the major factions are wiped out or abandon the fight. The degree of local state control is the crucial determinant of when this mechanism is likely to drive major change. This is a resource- and time-intensive counterinsurgent strategy that does not induce a quick organizational collapse, unlike the effects of a strategy that targets the leaders of vanguards. In India's Punjab, for instance, the government's deployment of massive army and police resources at the local level played a crucial role in penetrating and destroying the local networks upon which Sikh militants relied; the lack of unified central leadership in turn made it difficult for the insurgents to respond.[55]

The second mechanism of fragmentation in initially parochial groups is interleadership fratricide. In parochial groups, leadership interactions are weakly institutionalized and are characterized by low levels of information and trust. Without robust central control, relationships in a coalition are unstable, even when a skilled leader acts as a broker among factions. Shocks to intra-organizational bargains are common, whether from changes in economic gains, government peace parleys and counterinsurgency offensives, state infiltration, differences in losses or gains on the battlefield among factions, or local power struggles.[56] Feuds and conflicts within parochial groups may lead only to recurrent squabbles and loose coordination, but virulent battles can essentially wipe out the organization altogether if escalation gets out of control.

This potential for internal destruction has its roots in the prewar political and social landscape. Expectations of future instability in the absence of strong central control and the presence of shocks and military pressure create powerful incentives for factions to strike first against rivals and defect from leadership arrangements. The strategic situation created by the parochial structure is enormously complex for leaders of factions, increasing the likelihood of miscalculation and the fragility of cooperation.[57] This is different from the fratricide-from-below route to fragmentation for groups that begin as vanguards. In parochial organizations, senior commanders and their factions go to war with one another; in vanguard groups, local units clash with a coherent group of central leaders.

The outcomes of intraleadership warfare are difficult to predict ahead of time. Rapid and successful internal fratricide—where one faction decisively defeats the other—can restore a tenuous unity to a group, but this will not be enduring or resilient unless the victory reshapes the social composition of the leadership. When direct targeting of rival factional leadership occurs that does not wipe out its targets, it will trigger fragmentation within the organization as the targeted leaders effectively fight back and/or defect to the side of the state.[58] States that previously had trouble exploiting internal divisions will now face a far easier task. Counterinsurgency effectiveness should increase during and after messy rounds of infighting.

Parochial groups have distinctive strengths and vulnerabilities that determine which dynamics lead to change. Such groups have fewer options for internal initiative and reform than vanguard groups. This makes them vulnerable to local counterinsurgency strategies that push leaders out of their communities and to intense internal feuds and fratricide that destroy factional cooperation from within. However, pathways of change that are driven by unified international support and indiscriminate state violence can create new horizontal linkages and consequently stronger central control processes during the heat of conflict.

Fragmented Organizations

Fragmented organizations face severe problems of command and control from the beginning. Because their social base lacks strong linkages either horizontally or vertically, this is a poor starting place for organization building. It is extremely difficult for the leaders of these groups to build strong new ties because of the effects of counterinsurgency and organizational dysfunction. States and better-organized rival militant groups should be able to easily dispense with these types of organizations over the course of long wars. We commonly see numerous fragmented groups emerging during the early period of a conflict and then being weeded out.

How might a fragmented organization develop new social ties that would enable it to move into another organizational trajectory? Answering this question requires imaginative thinking since the structural preconditions are so unpromising. One route to greater horizontal ties is backing by a state sponsor that takes on the job of arranging and supporting cooperation. Central control can emerge under the wing of a sponsor who manages the new group in a safe sanctuary. International politics may thus counteract social weaknesses domestically. This forced merger arrangement will not build vertical ties to localities on the ground, but it can allow a fragmented group to become a vanguard group by facilitating the creation and deepening of horizontal ties and consequent central institutions among leaders. The success of this mechanism hinges on a deeply involved external actor that wants greater cohesion and is willing invest serious time and effort.[59] Exile and/or proxy armies often arise through this mechanism.

The other possible means of change for a fragmented group is the emergence of a powerful rising warlord in wartime.[60] Some leaders are simply good at fighting or are able to tap into local resources or are skilled at taking advantage of a contingent event. They can emerge from below and build up a local network. This is most likely when other insurgent groups are not operating in the same social and geographic area and counterinsurgents are not very capable. Space then opens up for a new warlord to enter the scene. This leader may be able to attract the loyalty of the other fragments of the group and consolidate at least loose control of a parochial group. This control will be fragile and contingent since the rising leader remains bound to disparate local networks instead of having ties to other organizers that can forge robust central processes of control. Brief periods of organizational coherence in the Irish National Liberation Army occurred when a powerful local figure temporarily stabilized the organization due to his prowess with violence and his ability to acquire funds through crime. These arrangements collapsed when the leader was removed from the scene or could not manage new spirals of conflict.

Neither of these mechanisms is very likely. Fragmented groups are likely to be consistently marginalized and annihilated in intense wars since their social underpinnings are not up to the task of sustaining insurgency. This reinforces the importance of prewar politics and structural starting points, even in a realm as fluid and uncertain as guerrilla war.

Civil War and Insurgent Change

Organizational change is entwined with social change. Prewar social bases lay the foundations for wartime organizations. Insurgent leaders try to maintain or change their ties in order to build organizations, while counterinsurgents attempt to shatter processes of insurgent control. The social-institutional argument I offer specifies how this process plays out by identifying key pathways of change from each organizational starting point. These routes are shaped by the strategies counterinsurgents use, the decisions insurgents make, and the involvement of international actors. The core focus of all of these mechanisms is the relationship between social links and organizational control. Many other factors surely matter, but my theory provides a coherent, consistent approach to explaining organizational variation over time.

This is a more complex theory than research that embraces rigid path dependence or ignores change, but it helps us understand the most important dynamics in civil conflict.[61] When insurgent change occurs, the nature of the war can shift dramatically. Insurgent groups that are able to build new linkages will prove to be daunting foes, as will be those that can maintain discipline even in the face of long odds and a severe imbalance of military power. Organizations that shatter under the weight of counterinsurgency or are torn apart by internecine battles are unable to prolong wars, create local control and governance, or negotiate deals that satisfy their political goals. Explaining why and how insurgent groups change is central to explaining the duration of conflicts, the outcome of wars, the effectiveness of counterinsurgents, the dynamics of negotiations, and the shape of postwar orders. The following chapters shift to detailed comparative research that assesses how well my social-institutional theory explains trajectories of militancy across groups and over time in a set of protracted civil wars.

Part II

*Comparative Evidence
from South Asia*

[4]

Azad and Jihad

Trajectories of Insurgency in Kashmir

The trajectories of indigenous armed groups in Indian-administered Jammu and Kashmir demonstrate how preexisting social bases influence insurgent organization building. The prewar politics of Jammu and Kashmir fragmented opposition politics as state strategies of co-optation and repression and strategic decisions by political leaders prevented the formation of a unified political front. Instead, over the course of several decades a variety of opposition parties, networks, and organizations developed with different goals and structures. When mass protest and simmering unrest exploded into insurgency in 1987–1988, these social bases determined the initial organization of armed groups, as nascent insurgent leaders were forced to rely on preexisting ties in the face of massive Indian counterinsurgency.

These starting points created distinctive strengths and weaknesses in insurgent groups that structured how these groups changed over time. The emergence of the Jammu and Kashmir Liberation Front (JKLF) as a vanguard organization can be traced to its leadership core of diaspora activists and young urban students. The Hizbul Mujahideen became an integrated group because it mobilized the existing horizontal and vertical ties of the Jamaat-e-Islami party. The Muslim Janbaz Force and Al-Jehad, both parochial groups, reflected the fractured, feuding, and personalized factions of the People's League they were constructed upon, while the JKLF splinter group Ikhwan-ul Muslimeen became a parochial organization in large part because it was a coalition of local rural networks that were only weakly linked to one another. An exception to this pattern of groups whose trajectory follows their origins is the Al-Umar Mujahideen, a fragmented group: though it had links to a religious organization, it became fragmented and rapidly criminalized.

War put brutal pressures on these initial structures. The collapse of most of the Kashmiri armed groups occurred when internal feuds exploded into fratricide and the Indian state exploited these organizational divisions. Manipulation by Pakistan was also a significant factor, but Pakistan's ability to influence groups was conditional on how well insurgents were able to organize local areas and how autonomous insurgent groups were from society. Indian counterinsurgency became increasingly effective because of feuding and fragmentation within and across insurgent groups in Kashmir, a process that created new allies for the Indian forces and facilitated campaigns of decapitation and disembedding.

The JKLF suffered from leadership decapitation and revolts from below, while the Muslim Janbaz Force and the Ikhwan-ul Muslimeen were torn apart by internal clashes between leaders that made local disembedding possible. The Hizbul Mujahideen moved from an integrated to a vanguard group because comprehensive Indian counterinsurgency shattered local Jamaat networks with the help of flipped former militants. Its leaders were targeted but were able to take shelter in Pakistan and thus prevent the total collapse of the organization. Although Al-Umar Mujahideen's trajectory does not work for my theory, it shows how leaders can squander possible structural advantages.

There is no single explanation for what happened to insurgent groups in Kashmir, but the political-social terrain that leaders were embedded in systematically shaped what types of groups they could build. Social bases created the organizational terrain on which insurgent, Indian, and Pakistani policies played out. The decimation of the Kashmiri insurgency did not occur simply because of changes in the doctrine of Indian counterinsurgents, changes in state sponsorship, growth in the legitimacy of the Indian government in Kashmir or its capacity to provide services to its population, or the inadequacies of particular ideologies. Patterns of insurgent organization played an important role in any analysis of these events; they explain when and how these other factors mattered.

This chapter introduces basic information about the conflict, including its historical roots and the prewar political organizations and social networks that constituted opposition to the Indian state. It then explores how new and reborn insurgent groups were built in the late 1980s, the strengths and weaknesses of these groups, and the mechanisms that led to both continuity and change as counterinsurgency and international pressures buffeted the militancy of indigenous Kashmiris. I focus on the JKLF and the Hizbul Mujahideen because the comparison is theoretically informative, but I use the other cases to explore the broader applicability of my theory and to address other possible explanations. The chapter concludes by discussing the implications of these findings for understanding insurgency and for contemporary politics in Kashmir.

Methodology

I use comparisons among indigenous Kashmir groups to examine variation in organizational control. Dozens of armed groups existed in the early days of the war, and for most of them we have almost no information. Rather than trying to examine this hazy universe of Kashmiri armed groups, I focus on specific comparisons. I also discuss social bases that did not enter into militancy in order to show how politics shaped the propensity to rebel. This approach reduces the number of cases, but its combination of careful comparisons within a shared political setting, attention to sequencing, and empirical detail makes my inferences more credible than those I might draw from a study of a larger but more heterogeneous and less detailed set of cases. This comparison includes the major indigenous armed groups in the conflict, so it also helps to explain the broader course of the war. I exclude a set of Pakistani armed groups that rose to prominence in the late 1990s because they originated in a friendly Pakistan. The organizational challenges these groups faced were different from those of indigenous groups, and thus those groups are outside the scope conditions of my theory.[1]

This chapter analyzes the contest between the pro-independence JKLF and the pro-Pakistan Hizbul Mujahideen to mobilize insurgent Kashmiris. It also offers less detailed comparisons of the Muslim Janbaz Force, Al-Jehad, Ikhwan-ul Muslimeen, and Al-Umar Mujahideen. The JKLF was initially a vanguard group but then fragmented; the Hizbul Mujahideen arose as an integrated group and moved into a vanguard structure; the Muslim Janbaz Force, Al-Jehad, and Ikhwan changed from parochial to fragmented groups; and the Al-Umar emerged as a fragmented group and then collapsed.

This is a byzantine topic, rife with acronyms, shifting names, aliases, lies, and simple factual errors in much of the literature. In addition, "There is a dearth of written scholarly work on armed militants in Kashmir."[2] To get around these empirical problems I have used multiple sources to support my claims. Good analytical, historical, and journalistic books and articles have emerged in recent years that provide an acceptably fine-grained level of detail about these organizations.[3] I also did confidential interviews in New Delhi and Srinagar with journalists, academics, analysts, and retired security force officials. The interviews provided new insights and were essential in helping me sort through which parts of the written record were plausible. While there are obvious limitations in these sources, they have helped me create a comparative study of the militant organizations that have fought in Kashmir.

Table 4.1. Patterns of organization in Kashmir

Organization	Initial organizational type	Organizational change
Jammu and Kashmir Liberation Front	Vanguard	Fragmented by mid-1990s
Hizbul Mujahideen	Integrated	Shifted toward integrated/vanguard hybrid form by 2003
Muslim Janbaz Force	Parochial	Fragmented and collapsed by mid-1990s
Jihad Force/Al-Jehad	Parochial	Fragmented and collapsed by mid-1990s
Al-Umar Mujahideen	Fragmented	Collapsed by 1992
Ikhwan-ul Muslimeen	Parochial	Fragmented and collapsed by 1998

OVERVIEW OF ARMED CONFLICT IN KASHMIR

The Indian state of Jammu and Kashmir is divided into three areas: Ladakh, which is dominated by Buddhists and Shia Muslims and borders China; the Kashmir Valley, where Muslims are the majority; and Jammu, where Hindus constitute a slight majority. The Kashmir Valley has roughly 5 million inhabitants, Jammu approximately 4.5 million, and Ladakh less than 300,000. In the Kashmir Valley and the Muslim areas of Jammu, Muslim Kashmiris are divided: some favor independence for the entire former princely state, others support accession of the state to Pakistan, and others want to retain the link with India (with greater autonomy). A Line of Control divides Indian-controlled Jammu and Kashmir from the Pakistan-administered state of Azad Jammu and Kashmir (also known as Azad Kashmir), part of the former princely state of Jammu and Kashmir. This line is a heavily patrolled military boundary.

These political divisions are rooted in the history of colonialism in South Asia. British colonial rule in India involved both direct administration of territory and indirect rule in hundreds of princely states. The princely state of Jammu and Kashmir was cobbled together in the mid-nineteenth century during the Anglo-Sikh wars. The Hindu family that ruled in Jammu and Kashmir governed a predominantly Muslim population.[4] Before 1947, two kinds of mobilization characterized opposition to the maharaja's rule: one dominated by Kashmiri nationalists and the other by religious Muslims. These overlapped, particularly until the late 1930s, but they can also be distinguished from each other. The nationalists argued that Kashmiri identity was distinct from other identities on the subcontinent, including that of other Muslims. Islam was an important component of this Kashmiri identity, but the behavior of the

[62]

dominant Kashmiri nationalist, Sheikh Mohammed Abdullah, also stressed the Kashmiri language and territory instead of focusing solely on religious affiliation. In the 1930s and 1940s, Sheikh Abdullah led the rise of the National Conference (NC) in opposition to Maharajah Hari Singh.[5] However, mobilization around Islam was also prominent in Kashmir, led by the Muslim Conference and by a new, albeit relatively small wave of Islamists under the aegis of the Jamaat-e-Islami.[6] Variations of these ideological strands persisted for decades, shaping the social and organizational resources available to political actors.

The maharajah of Jammu and Kashmir attempted to hedge his bets by not committing to either India or Pakistan. In the summer of 1947, a revolt by Muslim ex-servicemen in Poonch spread and Pashtun tribesmen from the northwest frontier joined them. A surge of tribesmen toward Srinagar, which was backed by Pakistani government officials, forced the maharajah to choose a state, and he chose India. Indian troops arrived in Srinagar in 1947 and a war broke out between the Indian and Pakistani armies.[7] When the dust settled in 1949, Jammu and Kashmir was divided and India had maintained its hold on the Kashmir Valley. A crucial ceasefire line (which later became the Line of Control) demarcated the reach of the armies.

The maharajah was removed from power and Sheikh Abdullah took control of the state's administrative machinery. Abdullah embarked on a campaign of consolidation and entrenchment. However, Abdullah and Prime Minister Nehru had fallen out by 1953 because of Nehru's suspicions that Abdullah was either attempting to move toward independence or was seeking accession to Pakistan. From 1953 until 1975, Jammu and Kashmir was largely ruled by Delhi's chosen officials in Srinagar. Abdullah was jailed for most of this time and both the NC and the state branch of the Congress became reliant on Delhi for patronage and power. Recurrent mass protests and instability marked Kashmir in the 1950s and 1960s. Though Abdullah returned in 1975 as leader of the NC and the state, his death in 1982 returned Jammu and Kashmir to a state of unrest.

The 1987 state election in Kashmir was marked by substantial irregularities. Amid large-scale accusations of vote-rigging, the dominant National Conference swept to power once more in the state. Young Kashmiri Muslim men, many of whom had been involved in the 1987 electoral campaign, began crossing the Line of Control into Pakistani Jammu and Kashmir to receive training and arms. This movement was matched by a growing tide of mass protest and militancy, particularly in Srinagar, the Kashmir Valley's major city.

These militants were met in 1990 with a massive Indian counterinsurgency effort that involved the Indian Army, paramilitaries of the

Chapter 4

Ministry of Home Affairs, and Jammu and Kashmir police. The conflict initially focused on the Kashmir Valley, including both urban and rural areas, but over time the conflict moved into the rural parts of the Valley and then into rural Jammu, and new counterinsurgent militias emerged that were built around former militants.[8] Since the late 1990s, Pakistani fighters have grown in importance. Alexander Evans noted in 2000 that the Kashmir insurgency was "as bad as it gets."[9] This conflict provides an arena for studying the ability (and inability) of highly motivated, well-armed militants to survive a powerful Indian security apparatus. However, since 2003 a cease-fire between India and Pakistan and shifting politics within the Valley have significantly reduced the level of insurgent violence. I end my analysis in 2003 since the war fundamentally changed when Pakistan reduced infiltration across the border and because the indigenous groups had largely been wiped out by then.

Kashmir's Social-Political Terrain, 1953–1987

The post-1953 order in Kashmir, after the removal from power of Sheikh of Abdullah, was marked by instability and cycles of protest and repression. A number of movements emerged that combined social ties with political goals. The social and political structures that emerged during the period 1953 to 1987 provided the raw underpinnings that insurgents could later draw upon to wage war. This section first differentiates between the key political groups in Jammu and Kashmir. It then focuses on several key opposition networks and shows substantial variation in their structures.[10] This assessment of prewar politics and society historicizes the trajectories of militancy that emerged after 1987: insurgency was embedded in a social and political context that both opened and restricted opportunities for militant leaders.

Pro-State Social Bases

The dominant political organization in the Kashmir Valley was the National Conference. After Abdullah's arrest, this group became largely a pawn of Delhi. When Abdullah was released as part of a deal with Indira Gandhi, the NC returned to some degree of autonomy but remained both dominated by his personality and bound by patronage ties to the Indian state. Its potential as an insurgent actor diminished over time as it adopted a generally pro-accession political stance. The Indian National Congress never became a powerful force in the Kashmir Valley. Instead, the party allied with (and/or controlled) the NC in the Muslim-majority areas of the state. For the NC to have actively rebelled against the Indian state after its penetration and co-optation, it would have had to have abandoned the tools that sustained key NC leaders and their patronage-based followers. The NC and the Congress party (more marginal in the Kashmir Valley) thus fall into the pro-state and largely nonviolent category in the typology of salience I outlined in chapter 2. They drop out of the picture as likely insurgent social bases. The political meanings embedded in formal and informal ties play an important role in understanding which prewar structures are likely to be mobilized for rebellion. In this case, such political loyalties eliminate these social bases from consideration as roots of warfare.

Politicized Opposition

Other social forces actively contested accession and its terms. The periods when Abdullah was jailed were particularly restive, as was Kashmir after his death in 1982. The 1960s saw waves of mass mobilization against the political status quo by a number of networks and organizations. They advanced different political goals and had very different social and institutional structures, but they all opposed the political status quo in Kashmir. Key players in this politicized opposition were the Plebiscite Front (a coalition established by Sheikh Abdullah's followers while he was in jail)[11], the People's League, the Awami Action Committee, the Jammu and Kashmir Liberation Front, the People's Conference, and the Jamaat-e-Islami. Numerous other groups and splinter factions also emerged and disappeared during mass protests and the state repression and co-optation that followed. These were the key bases of politicized opposition that were possible sources of insurgency.

The vast majority of participants in this movement were nonviolent and did not anticipate a protracted guerrilla struggle: they fall into the category of nonviolent politicized opposition blocs. Even the few revolutionary plotters who embraced violence or strategized in anticipation of it expected that conflict would take the form of rapid, symbolic attacks that would likely be followed by a quick Pakistani intervention or international pressure. For decades, only sporadic militancy accompanied anti-India mobilization. This was not a political milieu built for protracted warfare; the theories of victory that animated activists did not foresee the grim reality of the future.

This movement was not a unified whole. The parties and protest networks had different identities and structures. Some were full-fledged political parties, others were collections of angry young men, and others mixed political and social activism. Some opposition leaders hoped that street protests could bring change, others emphasized social transformation, and a few hoped that violence could be used as a tool of propaganda. Even within broad ideological categories there was variation in the horizontal ties that connected organizers and the vertical ties that embedded organizers in local communities. These social bases emerged prior to the onset of the insurgency and were formed by a complex mix of leadership strategies, social and class dynamics, and state policies.

Here I explore three specific social bases: the pro-independence activists linked to the JKLF; the pro-Pakistan, Islamist Jamaat-e-Islami; and the moderately pro-Pakistan People's League. My analysis shows that substantial variation existed in the types of social ties these activists were embedded in and explains why these ties developed as they did. The Jamaat-e-Islami developed vertical and horizontal ties at the cost of mass expansion and electoral success. By contrast, the pro-independence networks were weakly embedded in most of Kashmir and were only occasionally able to generate strong horizontal ties among leaders despite substantial popular support. The People's League leaders could summon large-scale contentious politics but this emphasis on mass street mobilization undermined leadership unity. The greater popularity of the pro-independence and People's League groupings also made them a more consistent target for state repression that disrupted their social linkages.

Jamaat-e-Islami

I start with the Jamaat-e-Islami (JI), a nonviolent opposition political party/religious organization that was founded in 1941 by Syed Abul Ala Mawdudi.[12] The Jamaat first arrived in Jammu and Kashmir in an informal form in the mid-1940s and soon became organized.[13] Following the Pakistani Jamaat's model, the JI pursued a strategy of deep but limited social mobilization aimed at social transformation. An important aspect of the Jamaat's underpinnings in Kashmir was the predominance of local notables in its early ranks, including middle- and lower-middle-class professionals such as schoolteachers and doctors, some landowners, and families with links to current or former Sufi religious figures.[14] As Sikand notes:

> a common thread seems to run through the biographies of most of the early activists of the JIJK, who later went on to become leaders of the movement. They all seem to have belonged to middle-class families, many with Pir backgrounds. Their standing as members of Pir families gave them a position of leadership and authority within their own local communities, in which the Pirs and their descendants were traditionally looked upon with considerable respect and reverence.[15]

Azad and Jihad

This social base, which combined different forms of traditional religious authority and local economic power, was linked to an extensive and growing system of Jamaat-run schools.[16] The structure of the Jamaat was (and is) highly institutionalized and hierarchical and includes multiple tiers of members and affiliation.[17] The Jamaat features numerous levels of organization, from the leadership at the top down to local subunits. It thus attempted to combine organizational discipline, education, and appeals to the "pious middle class."[18] A shared class and family background was a source of social homogeneity.

This strategy in Kashmir created an institution in which the "cadres, workers, and co-travelers were the great asset for the Jamat, rather were its backbone. They had emerged out of continued process of disciplined training for years together."[19] Family and village ties became intertwined with organizational processes.[20] The early leaders of Jamaat traveled around the state with their message, and partially as a result the party was spread throughout Muslim-majority areas of Jammu and Kashmir, even if not in great numbers in most places. This social base combined vertical embeddedness in local communities with horizontal social ties across communities.[21]

However, as Sumantra Bose notes, the Jamaat's "ideology of *Kashmir banega Pakistan* (Kashmir will become Pakistan) remained a minority orientation, at odds with the continuing popular appeal of independentist ideology in the pro-*azaadi* areas of [Indian Jammu and Kashmir]"[22]; indeed, as Basharat Peer has observed, to the present day "the Jamaat continues to be a minority in Kashmir."[23] The Jamaat is the only pro-Pakistani political organization in Jammu and Kashmir that had a significant presence in rural areas, but because "the large majority [of Kashmiris] remained committed to traditional religiosity," "the Jamaat has not been as popular in the valley as it had hoped to be" and has "proved incapable of reaching out to vast numbers of ordinary Kashmiris."[24] The Jamaat's base always remained small, in part because of its focus on literacy in Urdu; its austere brand of Islam, which was at odds with traditional Kashmiri practices; and its unflinching commitment to Pakistan. These outcomes resulted from Mawdudi's model of transformation: he sought to Islamicize society from the top down by first reaching literate elites and the middle class.[25] The party was not successful electorally; before 1987 Jamaat "never won more than 5 seats in an election." This metric, however, understates the party's social influence.[26] Although Devadas notes that the Jamaat's core "remained isolated to a few families, often of first-generation professionals," Bose focuses on the loyalty of its membership:

> The JI shows a uniform pattern: a committed, hard-core following that amounts to only a small fraction of the population. Thus, as a political

party the JI has consistently fared poorly in electoral contests in Pakistan, Bangladesh, and Kashmir, incapable of mustering more than a few percentage points of the popular vote. Nonetheless, all these JI branches have a *long-standing reputation for committed cadres and organizational acumen.*[27]

The Jamaat's "quietist"[28] approach slowly layered a robust organizational infrastructure atop its network of educated local notables.[29] It spread out beyond localized enclaves into various rural areas.[30] These cadres became enmeshed over time and space in a broader social context through meetings, travel, and intermarriage. It "tried to extend its influence by running schools [and] holding regular cadre meetings.... It remained close-knit, cadre-based, and grew in its self-righteousness."[31] Journalists who have dealt with the Jamaat describe it as remarkably homogeneous and consciously part of a self-enclosed community.[32] Respondents in Kashmir note that members are unlikely to leave the party once they are in it because of its socially encapsulating nature.[33] Strong vertical ties were formed through local presence, while training and intermarriage (as well as common social and class backgrounds) contributed to the consolidation of strong horizontal links among organizers.

The Jamaat was not building or sustaining itself for war. It was able to avoid substantial state repression until the 1970s because it largely avoided the spotlight, unlike many of the young radicals of the People's League, the JKLF, and the Plebiscite Front. Politics, organization, and social life were intertwined.

Pro-Independence Activists and the JKLF

A very different set of linkages and political ideas can be found among the activists in and associated with the Jammu Kashmir Liberation Front (in its earlier days known as the Jammu and Kashmir National Liberation Front).[34] These activists generally fit into the "revolutionary plotters" category of politicized opposition because some expected and prepared for violence, though even militant members did not expect the kind of war that ended up consuming Kashmir in the 1990s. The JKLF/JKNLF was essentially reborn, almost from scratch, in the Kashmir Valley in the mid- to late 1980s. The idea the group propounded of an independent Jammu and Kashmir, unbeholden to either India or Pakistan, had substantial mass support. However, the travails of the organization and its sympathizers from 1964 until the mid-1980s meant that few vertical ties were available to nascent insurgent organizers and horizontal ties were only moderately strong because of the transnational nature of the leadership.

The JKNLF was founded in 1964 by Amanullah Khan and Maqbool Butt, drawing some supporters from the Plebiscite Front.[35] It was the

Azad and Jihad

primary group that "spoke of secular, egalitarian freedom,"[36] as opposed to a variant of pro-Pakistan Islamism. Although Butt and a few followers attempted to generate high-profile militancy in Kashmir, they had little success during the 1960s and 1970s. The organization was quickly suppressed in the Kashmir Valley, and Butt was arrested twice and then, in 1984, hanged in Delhi. Butt was well respected, but the pro-independence activists' organizational prowess did not match his personal popularity. They did not successfully tap into or establish new networks. State repression played a key role in disrupting the organization's ability to mobilize new members. Most of the JKNLF ended up based either in Pakistan-administered Jammu and Kashmir or in the UK.[37] Amanullah Khan emigrated to the United Kingdom, largely detaching the movement from both the Indian- and Pakistani-administered sections of Kashmir (though offices remained in Muzaffarabad). The organization had support in the British-Kashmiri diaspora but this diasporic base was not tied to the Valley (it was primarily from the Mirpur area) and lacked the levels of wealth and education to be a major player.[38] Diaspora networks were weak grounds for either solidarity-building or material support.

The organization formally named itself the Jammu and Kashmir Liberation Front (JKLF) in 1977, arguing that it was carrying forward the mantle of the Plebiscite Front after Sheikh Abdullah made his peace with Indira Gandhi. The JKLF languished with almost no activity until 1988. Instead, the killing of an Indian diplomat in Britain and Khan's wanderings to and from conferences were what endured of the JKLF. A presence remained in Pakistani Jammu and Kashmir and the UK, but during the 1970s and most of the 1980s, "only an isolated handful of young men from [Indian Jammu and Kashmir] were attracted to the JKLF"[39] and "until the late 1980s [the JKLF] had negligible presence and support on the Indian side of the LOC."[40] In the Valley itself—the future war zone—there was limited interaction or communication through the mid-1980s.[41]

The JKLF's social linkages were limited even though its ideology had resonance with the mass public. This was a social base marked by some horizontal linkages but very weak vertical ties: though the top leaders knew each other well (as would also be the case among the renascent JKLF in Srinagar in 1988), they lacked embeddedness in local communities in Indian Kashmir itself. Few vertical ties existed because of the exclusion of the JKLF from the Valley, the legacies of Indian countermeasures in the 1960s and 1970s, an earlier embrace of high-profile attacks over quiet social mobilization, and the absence of Pakistani support for an independent Jammu and Kashmir. Political popularity was not matched by actual presence on the ground. To paraphrase one knowledgeable interviewee in Kashmir, the JKLF had a "floating constituency."[42]

The People's League

The People's League, which made its mark during the street protests of the 1960s, was a third important player. Unlike the Jamaat or the JKLF, the People's League became a collection of local factions and cliques arrayed around particular personal leaders. Strong vertical ties connected the group's leaders to particular social networks and geographic sites, but horizontal ties between these leaders were weak. The People's League was launched largely by militants from the former Students' and Youth League and Al Fatah and "brought together many of the incipient insurgents of the 1960s."[43] The charismatic young Shabir Shah, one of the People's League heroes, was joined by a variety of well-known pro-plebiscite individuals such as S. Hamid, Naeem Khan, and Sheikh Abdul Aziz, who came together in 1974 to form the league in an effort to create and sustain momentum against further integration into India.[44] These were iconic figures who had credibility as opponents of Delhi.

However, as Noorani notes, this party was "by no means a mass movement.... They spent more time outmaneuvering each other than fighting India."[45] Despite influence derived from its ability to mobilize participants in contentious politics and urban protest, the league lost leaders such as Azam Inquilabi to splits and had broken into several distinct subfactions by the mid-1980s, including groups that mobilized around Shah and Farooq Rehmani. This illustrated the ability of Sheikh Abdullah and then his son Farooq to close the space for political opposition and the disruptions of the 1975–1977 Emergency. Some young activists of the league were also co-opted into the bureaucracy and the political system. Along with these structural factors, lack of party discipline was driven by the origins of the People's League in the chaotic aftermath of the Plebiscite Front's fragmentation.[46] The league's roots in contentious street politics left a legacy that favored breadth over depth and diffuse weak ties over narrower but stronger ties. Interviewees in Srinagar emphasized how the personality conflicts and turf battles within the party created a debilitating check on collective action and party building from the very beginning.[47]

Political context and social divisions undermined the "optimal" creation of new social and organizational linkages. Even if this had not been the case, the People's League leaders had little inkling of what was to come in 1988. By the mid- to late 1980s, there was continual "sniping" between various People's League satraps.[48] The league lacked robust horizontal social ties across factional leaders. Built for rapid, mass contentious politics and torn by internal factionalization, this was not a promising underpinning for bloody, protracted insurgency even if it was helpful for other important political purposes.

Networks of Politics in Kashmir

This section has shown that there was substantial variation in both the political salience and structure of social bases in prewar Kashmir. Parties such as the NC and the Congress were unlikely hotbeds of insurgency because of their links to the Indian state. Groups such as the Jamaat, the People's League, and the JKLF were salient networks of resistance but were largely, though not entirely, nonviolent (by choice and because of constraints). The constituent social ties of these politicized opposition blocs differed substantially. The JKLF was strung out across the globe and held together by a small core group of leaders with weak links to the Kashmiri masses, despite the popularity of the group's ideology. The Jamaat built much stronger vertical ties to accompany horizontal linkages, but its ideology and strategy did not generate broad support. The People's League's roots in mass protest and contentious politics led to a loose coalition of personalized social networks. Each emerged and evolved in this way for a complex set of reasons that cannot be attributed to any single cause; agency, state policy, and contingent events created intricate mixtures of political meaning and social structure. I now turn to the consequences of these social bases as insurgency erupted.

Mobilizing for War: The JKLF and the Hizbul Mujahideen in the Valley, 1987–1990

In the period from 1987 to 1990 insurgency erupted. Many of the organizers, networks, and parties that had constituted the opposition to the NC and Delhi went to war. This section explains the initial organizational forms of the JKLF and the Hizbul Mujahideen. The groups that arose bore a clear resemblance to prior patterns of social interaction and collective action: institutions did not emerge from nothing. History gave leaders different opportunities and imposed different constraints. The continuity between prewar ties and wartime organization is particularly strong in the case of the Hizbul Mujahideen. I discuss other armed groups later in this chapter, but here I focus on a core comparison of the JKLF and the Hizbul Mujahideen.

Building Rebellion: Social Appropriation

Sheikh Abdullah's death in 1982 was followed by a problematic dynastic succession to his son Farooq Abdullah, who lacked the political acumen of his father.[49] Continued political instability characterized the mid-1980s. The tipping point came in 1987 when a state assembly election was tampered with, denying a representative share of seats to the

Muslim United Front, a loose coalition that combined the Jamaat, the People's League, the People's Conference, and a variety of smaller separatist parties. Its thwarted 1987 electoral campaign attracted significant enthusiasm, and the manipulation of the election was a potent spur to militant sympathies.

Street militancy and low-level acts of violence began in 1987 and then accelerated in 1988 as a growing stream of young Kashmiri men crossed the LOC to acquire weapons and training.[50] Bose notes that it was common for "newly minted 'commanders' to gather a band of gunmen from their locality or extended family and float a tanzeem, a guerrilla group."[51] Numerous political groups decided to try militancy. Though these insurgent organizations were new, many were in fact "closely associated with particular political parties."[52] There was no blank slate upon which to forge rebellion; leaders drew on the ties they could reliably and quickly access.[53] This was a textbook case of transforming prewar political networks into initial wartime organizations.

Pakistan was deeply involved in the uprising and provided training, arms, and sanctuary. In these early stages, however, this aid was not determinative because "the Pakistanis were operating in a cautious fashion, taking a social Darwinist approach and allowing groups to rise and fall.... The main focus was to back an outfit, any outfit, that was able to, by force of arms or otherwise, bring about the merger of Kashmir with Pakistan."[54] It hoped that one group would emerge and show its mettle. In the late 1980s, the origins emerged of what would become a diverse set of insurgent actors.[55]

The rest of this section will show that varying social bases created differing abilities to take advantage of Pakistani patronage and to construct and maintain institutions of control in the heat of war. The JKLF built itself through relatively weak vertical links (especially in rural areas) and moderate horizontal ties. It became a vanguard organization whose local control was fragile even though it had high levels of popular support and early access to Pakistani aid. The Hizbul Mujahideen emerged as an integrated organization because of its social base in the Jamaat-e-Islami party, which provided social linkages both among leaders and between leaders and local communities. While the Hizbul Mujahideen was less popular than other insurgent groups, it leveraged this infrastructure into powerful new war-fighting institutions.

The JKLF's War: Popular Mobilization and Initial Structure

Vanguard of the Insurgency

Amanullah Khan returned to Pakistani Jammu and Kashmir from the UK in 1986, wrested power from Hashim Qureshi, and proved willing to deal with Pakistan.[56] After the rigged 1987 state assembly election, young Kashmiri men began crossing the LOC into Pakistani Jammu and Kashmir in search of guns and training. At this point the Jamaat was holding back from the fight, while other separatist parties slowly became involved in insurgency. Khan's JKLF, despite its lack of size or links to the Valley itself, was the natural destination for the men crossing the LOC. It would become a vanguard armed group with, initially, a coherent central command but little local institutionalization.

The JKLF in Indian-administered Kashmir was reborn in the late 1980s Bose relates that "the first JKLF organizational unit was established in Srinagar only in early 1988, by a new generation of radicalized young men.... This core of militants made contact with the existing JKLF organization across the LOC during 1987–1988."[57] The weak social presence of the JKLF in the Valley before 1987 made organizing the group an act of creation rather than one of consolidation or the strengthening of a preexisting organization. Four men from Srinagar led the renascent JKLF's operations in the Valley: Ashfaq Majid Wani, Hamid Sheikh, Yasin Malik, and Javed Mir.[58] They were lower- and lower-middle-class urban youth who had created an Islamic Students' League in the mid-1980s and engaged in student activism of various sorts.[59] This network was not created for the purposes of waging a protracted, brutal rural insurgency; any thoughts of militancy focused on symbolic violence, social transformation, and protest. This small core of organizers became known as the "HAJY" group and later constituted the initial leadership of the JKLF in the Kashmir Valley.[60] None were strongly embedded in the networks of the Jamaat, the People's League, or the National Conference.

I focus here on the actual fighting units of the JKLF, which operated in the Valley. The JKLF was built upon strong ties at the top but weak social penetration of the countryside and areas outside the Valley. This created a vanguard structure when the time came to mobilize for war. The Pakistani Jammu and Kashmir leaders did not have much of a role in combat, since the military forces of the JKLF were drawn from the Valley when the organization reemerged there. Weak horizontal ties existed between the Pakistani Jammu and Kashmir and Indian Jammu and Kashmir–based leadership. The bulk of the fighting involved the Indian Jammu and Kashmir part of the group, so I have focused on the organization in the war zone.

Despite these initial problems, the JKLF's political project advanced the appealing goal of independence for Jammu and Kashmir. The early years of JKLF activity, especially in 1988, involved coordinated, publicly symbolic strikes carried out by a relatively small number of fighters. Central control processes at this point were handled by the four original organizers. Crackdowns by the Indian government spurred mobilization, and "within two years, the previously marginal JKLF emerged as the vanguard and spearhead of a popular uprising in the Kashmir Valley against Indian rule. It dominated the first three years of the insurgency (1990–92)."[61] Even to the present day, "most commentators agree that among Muslims in the Valley, the JKLF enjoys considerable popular support."[62] This was especially the case in the early 1990s, when contemporary observers argued that "the predominant battle cry in Kashmir is azadi (freedom) and not a merger with Pakistan"[63] and that "the JKLF, a secular militant group, is by far the most popular."[64] The support for the JKLF was clearly substantial and greater than that of its militant contemporaries.[65] In 1995, roughly 70 percent of Kashmiris claimed to favor independence rather than annexation to India or Pakistan.[66] The JKLF had captured the hearts and minds of the plurality of Kashmiris supportive of militancy; the public's response surprised even JKLF leaders.[67]

The strategic vision of the JKLF was straightforward. It hoped to generate enough popular resistance that India would withdraw from Kashmir and leave it as an independent state.[68] The goal was to hit a tipping point at which enough people were armed and on the streets to force the state to back down.[69] This strategy proved to be full of "grave miscalculations,"[70] given the actual social resources and institutional capabilities the JKLF could draw upon. The JKLF did not have access to a social infrastructure that it could deploy instead of putting its faith in this form of mass mobilization: weak vertical ties meant that the organization's local control processes could not be easily constructed to manage recruitment and expansion.

Challenges of Expansion

The JKLF's social origins became liabilities for the organization in the late 1980s as expansion further weakened local control. The HAJY group linked up with other small factions led by Hilal Beg, Abdul Ahad Waza, and others that coalesced under the banner of the JKLF.[71] The organization's size swelled dramatically.[72] While the JKLF project was clearly popular, it was forced to grow without substantial preexisting patterns of cooperation and control to rely upon. There was no party, tribe, caste, or religious network to build the organization around. As we have seen, its Valley leadership was basically a group of urban lower-middle-class teenagers and young men who knew each other from Srinagar before the war.[73] As long as the original commanders were coordinating activity, strategy was manageable, but well-developed, routinized institutional structures on the ground never emerged; this was an ad hoc war.

The urban-rural social divide undermined the creation of local institutions for training, control, and socialization. Within the valley, "most of the top JKLF militants belonged to the capital city of Srinagar and its periphery."[74] As the war became increasingly rural, the JKLF was unable to mobilize these areas and at the same time control new fighters. As Bose notes:

> The JKLF also suffered from its own limitations, in particular its overly Srinagar-centric and Valley-centric focus and organization. All four of the JKLF's top commanders in the early phase of the uprising were from Srinagar (the JKLF's other stronghold in the early 1990s was Anantnag, the main town in the southern part of the Valley) and the group failed to develop and sustain an effective organizational structure outside Srinagar, in the smaller urban centers and the rural areas.[75]

Weak vertical ties made local incorporation ineffective. The decision to grow quickly and the absence of strong preexisting networks led the JKLF to accept and train a variety of individuals and local subfactions who did not share the organization's commitments. These new members, who were not indoctrinated or socialized during their relatively brief training, were then sent back across the LOC to operate in an autonomous manner. For instance, Devadas suggests that Waza, an early faction leader, "had no time to indoctrinate every bunch of boys."[76] This approach "turned out to be a big mistake for the JKLF."[77] Social ties affected institution building in a direct and unambiguous way: where ties were missing or weak, it was hard for the leadership to create reliable processes for the organization, no matter how popular or well resourced it was.

The results were clear. In the opinion of one former militant commander, the early period of mobilization (including that of non-JKLF groups) "was simply a matter of disgruntled boys exfiltrating for arms training; there was no organisation, no leadership, no guidelines, and no explicit objectives for the movement."[78] The JKLF even agreed to train Jamaatis and People's League loyalists without forcing them to adhere to the JKLF organizational principles or ideology.[79] This provided opportunities for the JKLF's future rivals to gain training, weaponry, and access to Pakistani patronage and sanctuary. The emerging cadres of the JKLF were highly heterogeneous, both socially and ideologically.[80] To paraphrase one interviewee, the JKLF "didn't have a base, but an idea."[81] Some of these dynamics were caused by strategic decisions, but in the context of the JKLF's foundational social base, these choices had dangerous consequences. The social underpinnings of the organization created a serious risk of revolts from below and made the group vulnerable to debilitating leadership decapitation.

The Limits of Initial Pakistani Aid

Pakistan's military dictator, Zia ul-Haq Zia, was the first to provide support to the JKLF, which continued under Benazir Bhutto.[82] Joshi argues that "the Pakistanis soon realized that the Islamists had very little appeal in the valley and [that] the only viable vehicle for rebellion had to be the pro-independence JKLF."[83] Pakistani patronage did initially provide material incentives for foot soldiers and leaders to join and stay with the JKLF. For instance, Noorani quotes a pro-Pakistan insurgent leader as saying "I agreed to send some of our boys to Pakistan for training [in JKLF camps] in handling sophisticated weapons as it would have helped us in our plans."[84] While some of these were true believers in Kashmiri independence, many others knew that the JKLF was the only game in town.[85]

Unrest within the JKLF developed fairly quickly.[86] Pakistani aid and popular support did not lead to integration. The fighters who crossed the LOC often attempted to retain control of the resources they brought back. Suspicion and poor information were endemic in the JKLF and became more damning as the war escalated. Splinters began to break away in late 1989, particularly the Al-Umar Mujahideen, which was led by Mushtaq Zargar.[87] Hilal Beg's JKLF student wing, the Jammu and Kashmir Students' Liberation Front (JKSLF), acted largely on its own.[88] The lack of social embeddedness in local communities contributed to the rise of autonomous factions that were not linked to the central command through either social or organizational ties. As chapter 3 notes, rapid local expansion by vanguard groups undermines organizational control.

The JKLF was unable to build a durable organization, particularly at the local level, during this period. It could not convert mass mobilization and popular support into resilient institutions able to handle expansion and the shocks of war. Although resources from Pakistan did not turn the JKLF into a group of greedy thugs, they also did not lead to strong organization. Instead, a vanguard group emerged that initially could coordinate some central strategy and avoid immediate collapse into feuding, but could not reliably reach into and mobilize local (especially rural) communities. A key reason for this initial structure was the divided social base that nestled uncomfortably under the JKLF's banner. In the early years of the war in Kashmir, the JKLF was at the center of insurgency, but I will show later in this chapter how the social-institutional weaknesses of the organization made it vulnerable to targeting by the Indian leadership and dissension from local units.

Building Hizbul Mujahideen: Origins

The Hizbul Mujahideen became the most robust organization in the fight in Kashmir. While its rise to dominance occurred after 1990, its mobilization during 1989–1991 through the networks of the Jamaat-e-Islami laid the basis for an integrated organization that persisted until it shifted to a vanguard structure in the early to mid-2000s. The Hizbul Mujahideen achieved this unity and fighting power even though it represented the Jamaat's unpopular minority political-religious ideology. Schofield argues that remarkably, given its eventual military and organizational trajectory, the Hizbul Mujahideen "did not have widespread support within the valley."[89]

The Hizbul Mujahideen overcame this challenge by creating warfighting institutions through the Jamaat's party cadres and their kin and local sympathizers. The Hizbul Mujahideen leadership was dominated by Jamaatis. This social base provided the cooperation and control to take full advantage of the guns and money Pakistan and the Pakistani Jamaat-e-Islami pumped into the organization. Analysts agree that the Hizbul Mujahideen was, and is, the "organizationally strongest" of the indigenous Kashmiri armed groups[90], and its leader Syed Salahuddin "has continued to rule the roost."[91] It would become "the most militarily well organized of all the jehadi organizations in Pakistan and Kashmir,"[92] "a large organization having a well-equipped, disciplined, and highly trained cadre,"[93] and "the most effective" among the indigenous groups.[94] The difference between the Hizul Mujahideen and the JKLF is dramatic despite the fact that the former's ideology was less popular.[95] This divergence occurred because it was "totally differently"[96] built than the JKLF.

Leadership Consolidation: Building Central Control

An early version of Hizbul Mujahideen emerged in some form during 1989.[97] The Jamaat-e-Islami was not an original sponsor of this group. In fact, in 1988 and early 1989, some Jamaatis regarded the idea of armed struggle with skepticism and suspicion.[98] However, the Hizbul Mujahideen's founders included several JI party members and/or affiliates. One of its key leaders, Master Ahsan Dar, was a former Jamaat schoolteacher.[99] As the JKLF grew, both politically minded Jamaatis and the Pakistanis began to get nervous. The JI's decision to enter militancy in 1989–1990 was an attempt to counterbalance the JKLF.[100]

Because of its Jamaat members, pro-Pakistan ideology, and lack of sympathy with Sufi-linked Islamic practices in Kashmir, the Hizbul Mujahideen was a natural partner. The Jamaat took over the Hizbul Mujahideen from within by placing loyal personnel in key positions, rapidly expanding the already Jamaat-heavy social composition of its organizers.[101] Central processes in the Hizbul Mujahideen organization were built around horizontal ties between Jamaat cadres. Yusuf Shah, a former Muslim United Front candidate, became the key Hizbul Mujahideen commander.[102] He was a deeply committed Jamaati who had been actively involved in the party since college.[103] Shah renamed himself Syed Salahuddin and began to consolidate his dominance of the Hizbul Mujahideen, first as the group's primary patron. Master Ahsan Dar, the chief commander, pronounced the organization the "sword arm of the Jamaat" in 1990. In response, an Ahl-e Hadith Hizbul Mujahideen leader, Nasir-ul Islam, left the Hizbul Mujahideen to start his own *tanzeem* (armed group), Jamiat-ul-Mujahideen. This was not a major split, and the Jamiat had an enduringly low profile. (Nasir-ul Islam was soon killed.)[104]

The Hizbul Mujahideen's high command came to be dominated by Jamaat party members, well out of proportion to their representation in Kashmiri society.[105] As Schofield notes, "The Jamaat's support of its militant wing, the Hizb-ul Mujaheddin, had greatly contributed to the Hizb's early successes and especially its ascendancy over the militant members of the JKLF."[106] Leadership control was built around the Jamaat's *shura* council in Jammu and Kashmir. The Hizbul Mujahideen resembled the Jamaat, as "to maintain absolute control over the Hizb...[Hizb chief Syed] Salahuddin divided the organisation into administrative and military wings. The administrative wing, manned by Jamat-e-Islami leaders, controlled the military commanders in the field. District administrators, who were always senior Jamat activists, were also appointed."[107] Preexisting nonviolent social ties between Jamaat members and their networks were transformed into new insurgent institutions.[108] The organization was not built from a clean slate; instead, it reflected the terrain of collective action available to leaders. The Hizbul Mujahideen had clear processes of strategic assessment, decision-making, and internal security that provided direction and control to the group, in sharp contrast to the more popular JKLF, which was waging a more poorly organized war.

Local Expansion

With Salahuddin in control, the Hizbul Mujahideen mobilized Jamaat and Jamaat-linked party and social networks across the Kashmir Valley and into parts of Jammu, such as Doda.[109] Crucially, the Jamaat network offered access into rural areas, where the JKLF was struggling to gain a reliable hold.[110] Local institution building occurred through these vertical ties.[111] The links between the Jamaat and the Hizbul Mujahideen were clear and widespread. While most of the foot soldiers were not themselves Jamaat members, they were recruited and controlled at the local levels by members and sympathizers of the party. As Behera notes, "The organizational networks of the Hizbul Mujahideen spread down to the divisional and district levels in the Valley.... The Hizbul cadre was recruited by the Jamaat-i-Islami."[112] Social resources were converted into the underpinning of insurgency, and the Hizbul Mujahideen could find support from "a vast network of over 6,000 militants and large upper-level base of Jamat-e-Islami leaders across the Valley."[113] The Hizbul Mujahideen was the group best equipped to organizationally harness the surge of anti-India sentiment, in substantial part because the Jamaat was so deeply involved in mobilization.[114]

Interviewees in both Delhi and Srinagar provided a consistent account of how this local recruitment tended to work. Prominent Jamaatis would identify promising young men, some of whom had been taught by or were related to the local cadre. Using their moral and religious authority and their social linkages, they would persuade young men to join the Hizbul Mujahideen and then continue to monitor their behavior once they were in the group.[115] These Jamaat members and sympathizers were crucial pivots that linked local mobilization with overall organizational control and discipline. Local cadres "had regular meetings called ijtimas, where their workers would try to convince young men to join the Hizbul Mujahideen,"[116] and this proselytization and recruitment occurred in daily life as well.[117] Prominent Jamaatis lost their sons in the insurgency.[118]

The social resources of the Jamaat clearly contributed to "the decisive ascendancy of HM as the dominant guerrilla group in the armed struggle."[119] The ties and connections provided by the Jamaat forged a socially integrated armed group, as Joshi notes: "The Jamaat, never particularly popular in the valley, suddenly became a major force courtesy the gunmen of the Hizbul Mujahideen."[120] Senior Indian security force officials also confirm the importance of the Jamaat.[121]

There was one significant exception to this pattern of Jamaat-led consolidation. At some point in the early 1990s, former Afghan and Pakistani fighters began to join the Hizbul Mujahideen as a distinct regiment, Hizbul Mujahideen Al Badr.[122] According to Rana, "Al Badr leaders were given important posts in Hizbul Mujahideen, while in Pakistan the Al Badar management remained separate and held the position of a sister organization of Hizb."[123] The Al Badr was not a Jamaati organization and thus introduced a new social bloc into an otherwise relatively homogenous group.[124] This social-institutional compromise would later have consequences for Hizbul Mujahideen, but overall we see its organizational processes reflecting its access to a prewar social base with strong, overlapping horizontal and vertical social ties.

Resource Wealth: Discipline, Not Thuggishness

Despite its political weakness, the integrated Hizbul Mujahideen could keep its fighters in line and regenerate new manpower through Jamaati and related networks. Sustained Pakistani material support flowed into the organization: "The rise of militant groups like the Hizbul Mujahideen, who believe[d] that Kashmir's future lies with Pakistan, was also the result of direct intervention by the Pakistan government."[125] The Pakistani state security apparatus "assisted by steering some of these militants [often former JKLF-ers] towards the J&K Jamaat by providing them funds as well as ready access to training and weapons."[126] The Pakistani Jamaat also funneled aid to the organization.[127] The Hizbul Mujahideen used these resources to take aim at the JKLF, the Indian state, and, later, other insurgents.[128]

It is tempting to attribute the cohesion of the Hizbul Mujahideen to Pakistani support. But this was not the only armed group the Pakistani government supported. In the early years of the insurgency Pakistan also backed a variety of other pro-Pakistan organizations such as the Ikhwan-ul Muslimeen and the Muslim Janbaz Force. The crucial difference was that the Hizbul Mujahideen did not become an undisciplined proxy army or falter in battles over resources and turf, unlike other Islamist groups I discuss below. It became "a sophisticated political movement, not just a bunch of gun-toting thugs."[129] Rather than Pakistani guns and money triggering thuggish feuding within the group, they fueled political violence that was controlled through a mixture of networks and formal institutions.[130]

The processes through which the JKLF and Hizbul Mujahideen were built track theoretical expectations: preexisting linkages were used to forge institutions to handle new military and political tasks. The weaknesses and strengths of these ties were reflected in these institutions, despite the new functions of the insurgent groups. The JKLF's Valley organization became a vanguard group because it could leverage horizontal ties but not vertical ones, while the Hizbul Mujahideen used the Jamaat's linkages to rapidly construct an integrated organization.

WAR AND CHANGE IN KASHMIR: THE JKLF AND THE
HIZBUL MUJAHIDEEN FACE INDIA, 1990–2003

Having established the initial structures of the Hizbul Mujahideen and JKLF organizations at the onset of war, we can now explore how the dynamics of warfare affected these two groups. India and Pakistan became even more centrally involved in the conflict, putting intense pressure on armed groups. However, the outcomes of these policies were shaped by social linkages underpinning the insurgent groups and the implications of these links for control within the groups. When social linkages were broken, organizational activity ground to a halt. The brutal military coercion and intelligence penetration the insurgents faced put a premium on information, trust, and shared commitment, and when these decayed the organizations could no longer function. These processes explain the shifting trajectories of insurgency and clearly show when and how counterinsurgency and state sponsorship affect the organization of armed groups.

Both India and Pakistan exploited the JKLF's preexisting weaknesses. Sustained leadership decapitation by Indian counterinsurgents essentially wiped out its central control. Pakistan pulled splinter factions away from the original leadership to use as pawns in the battle for supremacy of the insurgency. This combination of pressures shattered the JKLF by slicing apart the linkages underpinning central control and exploiting the fragility of local control. It became a fragmented group that was pushed out of militancy by 1996. In contrast, the Hizbul Mujahideen was able to hold itself together far better against an extraordinary Indian onslaught. However, it began to lose local control over the course of the 1990s as the Indian state turned insurgent defectors against it while simultaneously targeting Hizbul Mujahideen commanders. By 2003, the Hizbul Mujahideen had begun to look more like a vanguard group and its leaders were isolated in Pakistan as a result of this local disembedding. This section describes divergent trajectories of change over time driven by shifts in the social linkages that insurgent leaders called upon as they tried to sustain war.

Collapse of the JKLF: Indian Counterinsurgency and Abandonment by Pakistan

The JKLF was born as a vanguard group. It began to show signs of splintering as early as 1989, as new members formed their own factions and broke away. The process of fragmentation accelerated from late 1990 onward.[131] The Pakistani security establishment had accepted the difference between the war aims of the JKLF and its own goals as a necessary compromise in the early days of the insurgency, but once a full-blown revolt erupted it saw an opportunity to push Kashmir to join Pakistan.[132] As Bose notes, "the JKLF became an obstacle to this design," and Pakistan cast it aside.[133] The JKLF's inability to prevent its members from defecting, stop them from allying with a manipulative Pakistan, and protect its leaders from decapitation led to fragmentation within the organization and military collapse.

Pakistan's abandonment of the organization exacerbated the already-pressing structural strains it was experiencing. Lacking reliable external sanctuary or deep ties in rural communities, the JKLF began to wither in the face of a mounting counteroffensive from India.[134] Its military weaknesses and its vulnerable social infrastructure combined to shatter its fighting power. Leadership decapitation was devastating because there were no local institutions that could replace leaders with loyal second-tier fighters. The JKLF "lost almost all of its top commanders and the cream of its fighting cadres," Bose notes, even though it retained its popularity with the masses.[135] India consolidated its position as troops, paramilitaries, and intelligence agencies flowed into the Valley.[136]

Leadership decapitation played a key role in pushing this vanguard group toward fragmentation. Central processes of control devolved as each of the four founding members (the HAJY group) was either killed or spent significant time in jail. After Ashfaq Majid Wani, the first military commander of the JKLF in Jammu and Kashmir, was killed in 1990, chaos within the JKLF leadership broke out; Hamid Sheikh, Javed Mir, Yasin Malik, and Saleem Nanhaji all tried at various points to control the organization.[137] Nanhaji attempted to bring Hilal Beg's JKSLF back under the JKLF banner but was only able to get the group to change its name.[138] Hamid Sheikh, one of the founders of the organization, was released from prison in 1992 and tried to "whip some energy and discipline into the effete outfit" but was soon killed.[139] There was no consistent refilling of the ranks from below and the JKLF was unable to mobilize the rural areas. As Bose notes, "Once the Indian counterinsurgency forces gradually reasserted control over Srinagar, the erstwhile JKLF bastion, the group had no 'Plan B' to fall back on."[140] Strategic assessment and central unity devolved into chaos and feuding.

Revolts from below simultaneously occurred. Disparate factions and units outside the original leadership core became the source of defections from the JKLF, often linked to the manipulations of Pakistan's Inter-Services Intelligence (ISI).[141] The JKLF's internal divisions included numerous "pliable elements" that created vulnerability to Pakistani manipulation.[142] Crucially, these defectors were available to the ISI because of the JKLF's social and institutional structure. The Al-Umar Mujahideen split directly from the JKLF in late 1989/early 1990. Under Hilal Beg, the students' wing of the JKLF, the Jammu and Kashmir Students Liberation Front broke away formally in 1991 to become the Ikhwan-ul Muslimeen.[143] Beg had approached the ISI and built his own cadre of loyalists and was thus able to easily break away from the JKLF, which lacked the ability to discipline, deter, or destroy him.[144] Former JKLF members also helped to form Al Barq, the armed wing of the People's Conference, while others joined the Hizbul Mujahideen.[145] Unlike the Hizbul Mujahideen's ruthless crackdown on its splinter groups, the JKLF continued to have brutal and inconclusive feuds with these breakaway groups.[146]

The rise of the Hizbul Mujahideen added another hurdle, as the JKLF "faced the lethal challenge of the Hizbul Mujahideen which had

Jamaat-trained, highly disciplined cadres, better equipment, and better military strategy."[147] The Hizbul Mujahideen began to systematically target the JKLF, killing and intimidating its members and spurring others to defect. Local control completely broke down and it became very difficult for the JKLF to attract, train, and control new fighters on the ground, just as its leadership was being shattered at the top. Joshi argues that the JKLF "was almost entirely decimated and had no strike power left."[148] Despite claims of its leaders to the contrary, mass popular support was not the "most powerful weapon" in the arsenal of the militant group.[149]

While the loss of Pakistani support contributed to JKLF fragmentation, a more socially embedded organization could have adapted by trying to maintain a low-level military struggle or transitioning into a coherent nonviolent opposition organization while preventing defection. Instead, the JKLF fragmented because institutions barely existed to hold the organization together. Falling back on peasant support was impossible because of the JKLF's sparse prior links to rural communities. Its weak social underpinning and the implications of that weakness for control of the organization undermined its leaders' ability to respond to these new dynamics of war. Tensions across the LOC between the Indian Jammu and Kashmir and Pakistani Jammu and Kashmir sections of the JKLF also accelerated, though this is less important for an understanding of the JKLF's military organization. These tensions are not surprising given the tenuous prior social connections of the two groups.

Military Collapse

By 1994, the JKLF was collapsing as a military organization.[150] In 1994, it suffered a final split that essentially ended its war. When Yasin Malik, a founding member of the Valley branch of the JKLF, was released from prison he announced a unilateral cease-fire.[151] Despite his claims that he could restore unity, Malik's decision to lay down arms led to another split, this time between him and his loyalists in Jammu and Kashmir (who became JKLF-Yasin) on the one hand, and Amanullah Khan's leadership in Muzaffarabad and a few of his followers in Jammu and Kashmir on the other.[152]

The origins of the split were a combination of ideological disagreement about the future of militancy and personal rivalry between Khan and Malik.[153] This split also had a social-institutional dimension, pitting the old guard against the new (though now disintegrating) leadership that had gone to war in the 1980s. Most of the JKLF in Indian Kashmir went with Yasin, but a small faction in Jammu and Kashmir around Shabir Siddiqui remained loyal to the Khan leadership. The other surviving HAJY founder, Javed Mir, joined the Yasin Malik faction.[154] The Khan faction, led by Siddiqui, continued to bear arms but was entirely wiped out by Indian police in 1996.[155] Consequently, as Sikand observes, "By 1995, the JKLF as an armed group was no longer a force to seriously reckon with, although its agenda for a free, independent Kashmir still fired the hearts of many, if not most, Kashmiris."[156] Since then, different factions of the nonviolent JKLF in Indian Jammu and Kashmir have further splintered and coalesced again.[157]

The evolution of the JKLF shows how leadership decapitation and fragile local control can lead to the collapse of an organization. As a vanguard group, the JKLF was vulnerable to leadership decapitation because of its sparse reach into localities. The massive Indian security apparatus exploited this vulnerability at the same time that the Pakistanis drew away various local units and factions that were not linked to the founding leaders of the group. My theory cannot explain why India and Pakistan adopted their policies when and how they did, but it clearly explains why these policies had these effects on the JKLF. Its initial weaknesses, born of its prewar social base, created a distinctive trajectory of organization building and fragmentation that arose from the intersection of social-institutional structure with counterinsurgency and manipulation by state sponsors. At a broader political level, the JKLF's collapse undermined the pro-independence position in the Valley and opened space for pro-Pakistan Islamist groups to increase their power.

THE EVOLUTION OF HIZBUL MUJAHIDEEN, 1990–2003

The JKLF's collapse paralleled and was in part caused by the rise of the Hizbul Mujahideen. We have seen how the Hizbul Mujahideen was intertwined with the Jamaat-e-Islami's networks and how Pakistani aid was channeled through strong insurgent institutions. The Hizbul Mujahideen launched a bid for insurgent hegemony fueled by this organizational power. Its offensive succeeded in knocking the JKLF and several other groups out of the fight as its disciplined lethality determined the outcomes of intergroup fratricide.

However, success in pushing aside these other groups also created a backlash. Surviving factions of targeted organizations allied with the Indian security forces. They were used as counterinsurgents and their detailed intelligence about Hizbul Mujahideen and Jamaat supporters led to a concerted offensive. Leadership decapitation and local disembedding became far more effective strategies as the security forces worked hand in hand with local collaborators. Local intelligence provided by former rival insurgents systematically targeted the crucial networks on the ground that had undergirded the Hizbul Mujahideen organization. Although it survived, it was pushed into Pakistan for sanctuary and increasingly began to resemble a vanguard group.

Consolidation and Dominance, 1990–1996

A crucial step in building the Hizbul Mujahideen came in early 1991 when the Hizbul Mujahideen integrated another major group, Tehrik-e-Jihad-e-Islami (TJI), led by a Jamaat sympathizer, Abdul Majid Dar.[158] Dar had worked on Geelani's staff in Sopore, a Jamaat stronghold, and, while not a full-blown JI member, he was familiar with and sympathetic to the organization.[159] TJI was originally linked to Rehmani's faction of the People's League, but the Jamaat ties won out.[160] This was an important merger.[161] Observers from north Kashmir, the TJI base area, viewed TJI as a well-armed and well-trained organization.[162] The Hizbul Mujahideen expanded in size without losing internal cohesion by deploying Jamaat ties to underpin organizational expansion. Devadas provides some detail about how this merger and Jamaat consolidation occurred. Salahuddin "trusted [Abdul] Majid [Dar], who had once worked on Geelani's staff in Sopore, and appointed him military adviser. Then Salahuddin crossed the Line of Control and in spring [1991] dispatched Jamaat-e-Islami loyalists Ashraf Dar, Maqbool Ilahi, and Wahid Sheikh from there as district commanders."[163] The Jamaat networks were used to create and consolidate Hizbul Mujahideen's command structure.[164] Interestingly, both Maqbool Ilahi and Mohammed Ashraf Dar, like many other Islamist fighters, had first been members of or were trained by the JKLF.[165]

Ultimately the Jamaat collective leadership was made supreme. Master Ahsan Dar was the Hizbul Mujahideen's chief commander in 1991, but he had grown accustomed to running his own show with high levels of independence. The Jamaat party leadership preferred a more collective and institutionalized structure. Ahsan Dar chafed under the pressure, particularly the attempts of the JI leadership to impose a *shura* council leadership on the Hizbul Mujahideen.[166] In 1991, Salahuddin loyalists expelled Ahsan Dar from the Hizbul Mujahideen.[167] Ahsan Dar took a small group of loyalists with him to form the Muslim Mujahideen. But Dar's new group quickly fell apart after he was arrested in 1993. Both the Ahsan Dar and Nasir-ul Islam splits were low-intensity, quickly cauterized affairs that marked not leadership fragmentation but instead ruthless leadership consolidation.[168] The Hizbul Mujahideen made it through the rest of the decade without a major split.

The process of local expansion continued during the early to mid-1990s, and it was not confined to the Valley. Joshi claims that in the vast rural area of Doda in northern Jammu, for instance, "by 1993, the Hizb, led by Ahsan Ahmad, [had] emerged as the largest group in the district with some 150 men on its rolls. Using the Jamaat overground network, they were able to tap into the madrasahs, trusts and charities for support."[169] Doda became a major battleground, and militants used the close-knit rural communities and isolated terrain to challenge Indian forces. This local mobilization helped the Hizbul Mujahideen survive Indian counterinsurgency even after its urban stronghold in Sopore came under the control of the Indian state.[170]

The Hizbul Mujahideen at Bay: Explaining the Shift to a Vanguard Group, 1997–2003

The Hizbul Mujahideen was the most integrated of the indigenous groups in the first phase of the insurgency. It remained the most powerful, but by 2003 it had become more of a vanguard group that lacked resilient, active local organization. Although the Hizbul Mujahideen survives to this day as a significant force, it has become markedly weaker on the ground. Why did this change happen? A new wave of counterinsurgency was made possible by the unintended consequences of the Hizbul Mujahideen's fratricide, which created defectors to the Indian state who were willing to work as counterinsurgents in exchange for protection. Though the key early players were from the Ikhwan (and hence the counterinsurgents were broadly known as "Ikhwanis"), other groups lost splinters to the Indians through fratricide. Joshi claims that "the key to the rise of these groups lay in the incessant quarrels between the various tanzeems."[171] These new counterinsurgents played a crucial role in targeting militants and their families and sympathizers. According to Evans, they "used counter-terror brutally but effectively to decimate militant ranks."[172]

As former insurgents provided intelligence to the Indian security forces, the Hizbul Mujahideen networks on the ground were systematically degraded. There was also an increase in leadership decapitation. These two processes delinked the Hizbul Mujahideen from local communities and made central coordination more difficult. Sanctuary in Pakistan was essential for the leadership core if complete fragmentation was to be prevented. This is why the Jamaat cadres were directly attacked with the aim of shattering the local networks that kept the organization fighting.[173] The Jamaat was targeted in the feuds that helped spur the rise of the Ikhwanis, and many party members and sympathizers were killed or exiled when the targeted splinters allied with India.[174] The consensus is that "numerous Jamaat activists were eliminated together with Hizb militants," battering the social base underpinning the Hizbul

Mujahideen.[175] As Sikand notes, "Participation in the armed struggle has cost the JIJK heavily, losing hundreds, if not thousands, of its leaders, cadres, and sympathizers, in battles with and illegal killings by the Indian forces."[176]

Targeting these networks caused the Jamaat to move away from open support for the Hizbul Mujahideen in 1997.[177] Gauhar argues that "the cream of the Jamat was physically eliminated or had to migrate."[178] Interviews made it clear that the organization was on the verge of being annihilated, and the JI leadership responded, though the process was a slow and messy one.[179] Vertical ties between insurgent leaders and local communities were disrupted by the counterinsurgency operations, which had the effect of undermining local control. It became harder to find fighters, train and socialize them for an increasingly high-risk war, and then get them to actually engage in violence against counterinsurgent forces. Local units sometimes simply just put down their guns or refused to engage the security forces; the state infiltrated others. The Hizbul Mujahideen did not lose all presence on the ground but its control was weakened.

There was some leadership decapitation as well. From Ashraf Dar on, numerous unit leaders were killed, including a number of very senior military commanders. The intelligence provided by flipped counterinsurgents allowed the Indian forces to target more discriminately. With its underlying networks under pressure and its command ranks being decimated, the Hizbul Mujahideen faced severe problems refilling its leadership ranks. The group fought back: by killing various pro-India militiamen the Hizbul Mujahideen "has over time wreaked a terrible vengeance on its tormenters."[180] This was not enough to undo the damage these pro-state armed groups inflicted in the mid-1990s, however, as the degradation of the organization's central control processes had lasting effects. By the end of the 1990s, the security forces and Ikhwans had "largely beaten back" the Hizbul Mujahideen.[181]

This combination of devastating local disembedding and leadership decapitation (albeit more limited than the local-level counterinsurgency onslaught) is what can degrade groups that begin as integrated organizations. The Hizbul Mujahideen was caught in the vise of Indian counterinsurgency: though it was able to persist longer and to a greater extent than its contemporaries, the Indian effort, crucially helped by former insurgents, undermined the group's social infrastructure and thus hurt its capacity to function as an organization. Counterinsurgency had this effect only when it was yoked to detailed local intelligence that arose from conflict among insurgents.

The Hizbul Mujahideen escaped becoming a fragmented group in large part because many of its leaders were able to take refuge in

Pakistan. Local units were hammered harder than the leadership and sanctuary held off the worst effects of comprehensive counterinsurgency. Still, unrest emerged even at the central level. The first significant rupture since the 1991 split between Ahsan Dar and the Muslim Mujahideen occurred in 1998. The Al Badr faction of the Hizbul Mujahideen, which was linked to Afghanistan and Pakistan, had operated as a semi-autonomous unit within the organization.[182] According to Al Badr members, the group broke away because it "disliked the Jamaat-e-Islami's interference in organizational matters."[183] Rana quotes an Al Badr leader as saying that "Jama'at-e-Islami had so much control over Hizbul Mujahideen that it could not move an inch without orders from the Jama'at."[184] Though there was tension surrounding the Al Badr break, it was ultimately of little consequence.[185] The preexisting gaps between Al Badr and the Jamaat/Hizbul Mujahideen had created space for these later shocks to pull them apart.

Cease-Fire and Marginalization

During the period 2000 to 2003, a major split finally occurred that more clearly showed weaknesses in the central control of Hizbul Mujahideen. It bubbled up from the local destruction of Hizbul Mujahideen infrastructure and shows how local dynamics can affect central organization. We were introduced to Abdul Majid Dar earlier, the Jamaat-linked leader of Tehrik-e-Jihad-e-Islami (TJI) from Sopore who had integrated his group into the Hizbul Mujahideen and become a trusted commander of Syed Salahuddin. By 2000, Majid Dar was the field commander in Indian Kashmir and was well aware of the battering the Hizbul Mujahideen had taken on the ground. With the cautious support of Salahuddin, he began to enter into discussions with Indian security officials about the possibility of a Hizbul Mujahideen cease-fire. This is particularly interesting because he was "known until then to be a hardliner."[186] This is one of many cases for which trying to array insurgents along a "hawk-dove" spectrum is of little use. At that point, the Hizbul Mujahideen was regarded as "the leading militant group in the armed struggle against the Indian troops,"[187] but it was facing severe local pressures for reasons described above. After negotiations with Indian intelligence agencies, Majid Dar announced a unilateral cease-fire in August 2000.[188]

This move toward a possible peace deal met with two serious challenges. First, a unit commander from Pakistan-administered Kashmir named Sarfraz Masood disagreed with the move. He was expelled from the Hizbul Mujahideen and broke away with part of his Pir Panjal Regiment, clashing violently with the Pakistani Jamaat-e-Islami in the process, to form a minor splinter group named Hizbul Mujahideen-e-Islami.[189] Far more importantly, the Pakistani intelligence services, hard-liners, other jihadi groups, and even the Pakistani Jamaat-e-Islami demanded that the Hizbul Mujahideen pull back from its peace offensive.[190] This pressure led it to end its cease-fire after two weeks. From the Indian side of the LOC, Abdul Majid Dar and his loyalists looked on with concern at the rapid shift in policy in the Muzaffarabad-based Hizbul Mujahideen.[191] Majid Dar was replaced as the Kashmir Valley military commander.[192] As the rift grew, in May 2002 Majid Dar was formally expelled from the organization; he took a number of supporters from Jammu and Kashmir with him.[193] Dar was killed by alleged Hizbul Mujahideen gunmen in March 2003, eliminating this challenge to Hizbul Mujahideen cohesion. He never formed a new organization or targeted the existing leadership, so this rupture, while significant, did not cause a total collapse or wave of fratricide. The stresses on local fighters contributed to splits among central commanders.

This rupture combined with the ongoing counterinsurgency campaign weakened the local presence and control of the Hizbul Mujahideen in Jammu and Kashmir, which is now primarily the domain of Pakistani groups such as Lashkar-e-Taiba. By 2003, the Hizbul Mujahideen was relatively inactive on the ground in Jammu and Kashmir, as key leaders lived in Pakistani Jammu and Kashmir. It was been pushed toward a vanguard structure but not a military collapse like that of the JKLF. In 2004 it was still "regarded as one of the most influential groups involved in the conflict over Kashmir."[194] Even as of 2009, it remains "the brand name of the Kashmir militancy because of being the largest and the most important in terms of its effectiveness in perpetrating violence across Kashmir."[195]

The Hizbul Mujahideen's shift from an integrated organization to a vanguard group can be explained by the severe local damage Indian counterinsurgency inflicted on the group when Indian forces cooperated with flipped former militants. The Hizbul Mujahideen's lifecycle looks like what my theory predicts: its prewar social base created a new organization that could handle large resource flows and survive Indian repression, but it began to change in form when the counterinsurgents directly targeted key social ties that held the organization together, especially at the local level. Formal organizational charts could not survive the destruction of the social linkages that undergirded them. The Hizbul Mujahideen shows that the intertwining of social mobilization and organizational processes is both a strength and a weakness: Jamaati linkages were essential in building the Hizbul Mujahideen, controlling its fighters, and making use of Pakistani aid, but once these social ties become vulnerable to counterinsurgency the state was able to undermine the

Chapter 4

Hizbul Mujahideen's functioning. The mechanisms of both origins and change map nicely onto the theory I offered in chapters 2 and 3.

OTHER INDIGENOUS GROUPS: WEAK PARTIES AND
THE LIMITS OF STATE SPONSORSHIP

In the late 1980s through mid-1990s, several of the other insurgent organizations in Indian Jammu and Kashmir drew primarily on pro-Pakistani sentiments and Pakistani aid. In the early days of the insurgency they were large and prominent, but they had largely collapsed as coherent forces by 1996. This section briefly explores some of these other groups to test how well my theory works to explain their experience. The evidence from these groups is far from definitive; much of the historical record has been lost because of the arrests or death of participants. I bring in these cases to shed light on more specific theoretical questions: specifically, how "Islamist" ideology, Pakistani support, and Indian counterinsurgency affected groups other than the JKLF and Hizbul Mujahideen.

I focus on the trajectories of two offshoots of the People's League, the Muslim Janbaz Force and the Jehad Force, and two organizations that emerged from the JKLF, the Ikhwan-ul Muslimeen (originally the JKSLF) and Al-Umar Mujahideen. In three of these four cases, weak preexisting ties led to fragmentation and ultimate collapse, even though the organizations had access to weaponry and used rhetoric and symbols that were often similar to those of the Hizbul Mujahideen and even the JKLF. The onslaught of the Indian forces and the fratricidal drives of the Hizbul Mujahideen strained these organizations beyond their breaking points.

Joshi notes that in this complex insurgent space, "Pakistani handlers made heroic efforts to promote unity among the various militant groups through 1991, even as they sought to sideline the JKLF and boost the abilities of the *Islampasand* groups that openly favoured merger with Pakistan."[196] This intervention by Pakistan was insufficient because the level of discipline and control within the war zone was what determined whether a group could endure as a coherent fighting force. Regardless of how well armed a group was, if it lacked internal discipline, it failed. As these groups faltered, they in turn began to lose aid from Pakistan in a vicious cycle of underperformance and abandonment.[197] The Muslim Janbaz Force, the Jehad Force, and the Ikhwan-ul Muslimeen were parochial armed groups that eventually became fragmented and then collapsed. However, the fourth case studied here, of the Al-Umar Mujahideen, does not fit my theory. Based on its prewar links, my argument predicts that it would become a parochial armed group, but it instead rapidly became a fragmented group. Leadership appears to have led to a different result than my theory suggests.

Tanzeems of the People's League: The Muslim Janbaz Force and the Jehad Force/Al Jehad

The People's League was a factionalized opposition political party that arose out from the unrest of the 1960s and 1970s. The Muslim Janbaz Force began and ended its life as an armed wing of Shabir Shah's People's League (hereafter People's League [S]), while the Jehad Force, also later known as Al Jehad, was the military wing of the Farooq Rehmani's subfaction of the People's League.[198] We know less about Al Jehad, but it appears to have followed a similar pattern as the Muslim Janbaz Force.

The Muslim Janbaz Force advanced a pro-Pakistan agenda and received support from Pakistan. By drawing on the name of the People's League in Indian-administered Kashmir, it attracted recruits to its banner. The Muslim Janbaz Force had a substantial number of armed men at its peak and strength in north Kashmir as well as a presence in Srinagar.[199] However, the People's League (S) was a poorly organized party with weak internal ties of trust and commitment. The personalized style of its leaders contrasts sharply with the style of Jamaat leaders. As a result of these prewar moorings, "the outfit affiliated to the People's League ... would witness more ego-inspired splits than any other group in Kashmir."[200]

As the war escalated, Muslim Janbaz Force leader Firdous Syed Baba (known as Baba Badr) received clearance from Shabir Shah to cross the LOC to make contact with Pakistan in August 1989. The Muslim Janbaz Force was the group Shah sympathizers went to, as Joshi notes: "Activists of the PL(S) who crossed the border and sought Pakistani help were directed to join this force."[201] At its height, the Muslim Janbaz Force may have had as many as 4,000 cadres, though this seems like an optimistic estimate.[202] The problem in terms of recruitment was the weakness of the social organization of the People's League. This faction of the party was held together by Shah's charisma and appeal. There are indications that local leaders were involved in recruiting, but there is no evidence to suggest a disciplined and structured process.[203]

The resulting Muslim Janbaz Force was disorderly. It did not indoctrinate new recruits properly, and recruitment itself was chaotic and indiscriminate. As Sinha observes, "It was an anarchic beginning that could only culminate in disaster." No preexisting structures channeled and disciplined mobilization: "the first MJF boy to train became the local district commander. . . . anybody who landed up, and looked strong and tall enough, became a militant. The MJF hierarchy did not know who was going across to Pakistan. It was an absolute mess."[204] Al Madad's early decision to splinter away from the group showed the limits of the organization.[205] The central leadership was given the power to distribute guns and money, but this was insufficient to maintain control.[206] "Squabbling"[207] amongst cadres based in Azad Jammu and Kashmir was frequent. We can reasonably code this as a parochial organizational structure.

The Jehad Force, which was linked to the Rehmani faction of the People's League, was fighting Indian counterinsurgents at the same time the Muslim Janbaz Force was. In 1991, after Muslim Janbaz Force leader Babar Badr was arrested, the Muslim Janbaz Force was merged into Jihad Force to forge the Al Jehad.[208] With Badr and Shabir Shah under arrest, perhaps the natural home for the disorganized Muslim Janbaz Force was the armed wing of the semi-fraternal People's League faction. However, this union was not comfortable; Bose writes that the "Muslim Jaanbaz Force and Jehad Force...were only uneasily amalgamated as Al Jehad."[209] As a compromise, Al Jehad announced that People's League rivals Shah and Rehmani would be co-patrons of the armed group.[210]

The new Al Jehad was also a parochial armed group. An interviewee referred to it as a "floating"[211] *tanzeem*. Even though it was "a well-armed outfit,"[212] the leadership of Al Jehad suffered steady attrition, a sign of weak organizational structure. By 1993, the "supreme commanders" of the Al Jehad were being arrested "in almost bimonthly succession."[213] "Huge funds"[214] were available to Al Jehad, but they did not equate to a robust organization. In fact, Sinha claims, "Al Jehad had never really integrated the old MJF and the Jehad Force."[215] When Badr was released from jail in 1993, he decided that the Muslim Janbaz Force needed to be revived. With the backing of some of his loyalists he gained approval and material support from the ISI, and broke away, leaving the old Jehad Force and a few followers of S. Hamid behind. What was left of Al Jehad continued to get pounded by the Indian security forces. The group renamed itself Al-Fateh in 1995 but slid into irrelevance.[216]

The Muslim Janbaz Force, still bolstered by the "cult"[217] surrounding Shabir Shah, was back in business for a while. It continued to attract support from Pakistan's ISI. However, Badr gave up the fight in 1995 and 1996, deciding that Pakistan was not the model to emulate. Along with other former senior commanders, he entered into dialogue with the Indian government. Some Muslim Janbaz Force cadres followed him, but he did not attract major defections.[218] With his defection, the Muslim Janbaz Force disappeared from the conflict for all intents and purposes.[219] The weak social ties of the People's League undermined the Muslim Janbaz Force and the Jihad Force despite high levels of Pakistani aid. As Joshi notes, "the ISI's leverage was limited"[220] when it came to building and maintaining insurgent groups. The continuity from the People's League prewar structure to the way it waged wartime militancy is striking: weak control and feuding persisted based on factional lines established prior to the conflict. These flaws provided an opportunity for Indian counterinsurgents to break apart feuding factions, further spurring defections and abandonment as the group spun apart. The popular support for and mass mobilization of the People's League could not be converted into robust insurgency.

Al-Umar Mujahideen

We now move on to the two major splits of Islamist groups from the JKLF. The first, in late 1989, was led by Mushtaq Zargar, an "illiterate, loutish chain-smoker"[221] with a background as a criminal. He had become involved in militancy through People's League activists he met in jail and was inducted into the JKLF as a member on the day he crossed the LOC into Pakistan. Zargar, with Pakistani support, then broke away from the JKLF in late 1989/early 1990, carrying with him a group of friends and loyalists from the old-city area of downtown Srinagar, the home base of the *mirwaiz* of Srinagar and his Awami Action Committee (AAC), a religious/political organization.[222] Zargar was thus "one of the founding fathers" of militancy in the state.[223] The AAC had been deeply involved in political mobilization in the past, though its reach was limited to Srinagar. The new Al-Umar Mujahideen was related to the AAC. Some argue that the *mirwaiz* started the AAC to maintain a presence in the rapidly militarizing politics of Kashmir, while others view the link between the AAC and the Al-Umar Mujahideen as informal.[224] In any case, the Al-Umar is described as being "linked" and "very close to" the AAC.[225] Al-Umar was concentrated in Srinagar, especially the areas around the *mirwaiz*'s Jama Masjid mosque.[226]

The trajectory of Al-Umar Mujahideen does not match my theoretical expectations. My argument predicts that its ties to the AAC should provide some degree of discipline and rootedness, most likely as a parochial group based in areas in and around Srinagar. Instead, Al Umar Mujahideen had a very fractious and troubled course as a fragmented organization. It was poorly organized and its leadership was highly personalized; in addition, it attracted criminals and opportunists. In 1990, a split occurred after a leader of an infiltration group held onto his weapons and demanded a senior appointment in the group.[227] When Zargar refused, he took his weapons with him and formed a new organization, the Al Umar Commandos.[228] However, Al Umar was soon joined by Al Madad, a group that had split off from the Muslim Janbaz Force, and by the summer of 1991, Al-Umar had acquired a reputation for brutality.[229]

Chapter 4

In early 1992, internal unrest occurred that led to the end of the group. Control processes at the central level did not exist. According to Joshi, a leader of a faction within the Ikhwan-ul Muslimeen broke away from the Ikhwan and joined Al Umar, which then upset a Srinagar leader of Al Umar, who in turn broke away with some of his loyalists and joined the JKLF. But a JKLF regional leader then moved over to the Al Umar. The first major defector to the Al Umar from the JKLF got into a "scuffle" with Zargar, the group's commander, and was expelled from the group.[230] This was a group characterized by a profound lack of organization, a shifting array of opportunists, defecting factions, and feuding leaders. In addition, there is no evidence that it had any kind of mobilization routine in place. The culmination of this fragmentation came with the arrest of founder Mushtaq Zargar. Devadas describes the result: "His Al Umar was broken with his arrest in the spring of 1992. Inordinately suspicious, he had not told any colleague where the weapons or money were stored."[231] Al-Umar Mujahideen became a fragmented organization with no routinized institutions.

Confined to Srinagar, factionalized, and bereft of its leader, the group dissolved into irrelevance.[232] This case shows that my theory can be clearly disconfirmed in some cases: Zargar's personality and his willingness to bring in criminals and target civilians carried more weight than the possible benefits of the religious organization he was linked to. My theory does not perform well to explain Al-Umar's trajectory. The group had essentially collapsed by the middle of 1992.

Ikhwan-ul Muslimeen

The most important of these other groups, for unexpected reasons, was the Ikhwan-ul Muslimeen, which we have already seen in its prior incarnation as Hilal Beg's Jammu and Kashmir Liberation Front (JKSLF). The Ikhwan was initially "one of the most virulent tanzeems,"[233] but its dramatic fragmentation contributed to the rise of new counterinsurgent forces in Kashmir. The Ikhwan was built on a loose coalition of local networks, particularly in rural areas, as the group tried to rapidly expand without access to strong institutions or ties connecting leaders. This social underpinning emerged from the process of splitting from the JKLF, but we can identify distinct blocs, often built around families and villages in the Kashmir Valley's countryside. These formed a parochial organization with enduring local, autonomous factions and no powerful central leadership.

Hilal Beg was a tin salesman from Srinagar who had been recruited into the JKLF in its early days after becoming involved in the political mobilization of 1987.[234] His ties to the JKLF were not strong; he was approached by people he only knew from the previous protests and agreed to join.[235] At some point in the process of building the JKSLF and then splitting, the Ikhwan became a pro-Pakistan group. Beg carried a diverse group of followers with him into the new Ikhwan. Probably self-serving but informative accounts from Ikhwan members who flipped to the Indian side reveal how varied and chaotic their path into the group was.[236] New factions and units appear to have been amalgamated as they merged instead of flowing through and being controlled by preexisting channels of collective action. Beg embraced rapid expansion in part because the possibility of mobilizing through preexisting ties did not exist for him.[237] By 1991/1992, the Ikhwan had built a sophisticated-looking organizational apparatus.[238] However, the Ikhwan frequently clashed with the Hizbul Mujahideen because the latter "wanted complete dominance over all other tanzeems,"[239] including other groups that advanced a broadly similar ideological line. The Pakistani ISI faced limits in forging cohesion, as Joshi notes: "The persistent quarrels came in the face of great efforts to promote unity. There was only so much that could be done by the handlers across the border."[240]

Beg was unable to control the fragmentation that resulted from the escalation of these local clashes with the Hizbul Mujahideen. The Ikhwan's various factions flew apart under the impact of the conflicts with both the Indian forces and the Hizbul Mujahideen. Feuds between leaders escalated in both frequency and intensity. Most dramatic was the increasingly disconnected behavior of an Ikhwan unit in north Kashmir, led by a folk singer named Mohammed Yusuf "Kukka" Parrey. Parrey had joined the JKLF as a hedge against local Jamaatis his family was allegedly involved in confrontations with.[241] He followed Beg into the JKSLF and the Ikhwan, but his loyalties were first and foremost to his local area and his family. A series of Hizbul Mujahideen attacks against Ikhwan fighters around the Bandipore area led Parrey's faction of the Ikhwan to go to war with the Hizbul Mujahideen.[242] This area was previously a Hizbul Mujahideen stronghold that the security forces had struggled to subdue.[243]

War with the Hizbul Mujahideen was not the preferred strategy of the Ikhwan leaders, and they lost control of the Parrey faction. A major Ikhwan leader briefly forced Parrey to disarm his fighters by abducting him, which shows the dubious level of control at the center of the organization.[244] Once Parrey returned to the north Kashmir area, he received the backing of the security forces and began to attack the Hizbul Mujahideen.[245] As he said, "I knew the day I stopped fighting the HM, I would be terminated along with my gang."[246] Parrey's unit renamed itself the Ikhwan-ul Muslimoon. These local feuds between this new Ikhwan splinter and Hizbul Mujahideen units spread all the way up into the command structure. Parrey's behavior triggered further disintegration in the Ikhwan, and units and factions went their own way.[247] Liaquat Ali (alias Hilal Haider)[248] and Usman Majid[249] both jumped to Parrey's pro-India splinter force, expanding this dynamic into areas of south Kashmir.[250] The Ikhwan's local units were being "adopted" by the Indian state as countermilitias and turned against other militants, especially the Hizbul Mujahideen. Suspicion developed within the remnant leadership that undermined adaptation.[251] Localism was the fatal flaw of the faltering Ikhwan-ul Muslimeen, facilitating the defection of its local units.

As a result of this spiral of side-switching, "by mid-1995 it became clear that the Ikhwan was in trouble."[252] Though some Ikhwan fighters tried to take the war to India, the group had collapsed, and the term "Ikhwanis" came to refer to the counterinsurgents of Parrey and the other factional defectors, not to the original insurgent group. Key leaders were killed in 1996, and leadership passed to Bilal Ahmed Baig.[253] The JKIF spent two years trying to bomb urban India before going into "terminal decline" by 1998.[254] The Ikhwan-ul Muslimeen was born as a parochial organization that attracted local units and networks and collapsed because the weakness of its internal bonds of commitment and trust left its leader unable to control cascading spirals of local violence and feuding that tore the group apart. Islamism—however defined—and Pakistani support could not build a resilient Ikhwan organization.

Other Kashmiri Groups in Comparative Perspective

Despite the limits of what we know about these groups, several plausible conclusions follow. First, "Islamism" did not lead to any particular outcome. Second, the effects of resource endowments and state sponsorship were largely determined by prior social ties and structure. Third, Indian counterinsurgency took advantage of, rather than directly caused, organizational fragmentation. India pushed these groups to collapse, but only after internal feuding opened wedges the state could exploit. Fourth, Al Umar is a case of a disjuncture between prewar social base and wartime organization, as Zargar appears to have not taken advantage of the AAC's social linkages. He made his own decisions about recruitment, and structure went by the wayside in favor of personal agency. My argument cannot explain this case.

These patterns of variation are not straightforwardly linked to Islam, counterinsurgency, or resources, but they do appear to be consistently (but not universally, as with the Al-Umar) tied to the appropriation of prewar networks for organization building. These underpinnings opened or closed space for India, Pakistan, and insurgent political entrepreneurs to pursue their preferred strategies, and thus they fundamentally shaped the structure and trajectory of the conflict.

Insurgent Organizations in Kashmir: Findings and Implications

Findings

My social-institutional theory does well in Kashmir. In my examination of prewar politics, I identified the most likely sources of rebellion and the networks that, by contrast, we would expect to side with the state. This allowed me to then focus on the prewar structure of several opposition social bases. Abundant evidence links this prewar social mobilization to the starting points of insurgent organizations. The processes of change then map onto the mechanisms identified in chapter 3, especially in revealing how decapitation strategies, local disembedding by counterinsurgent militias, and state sponsorship affected armed groups differentially. Social ties were essential to insurgency in Kashmir: they created and held together formal institutions in the face of an extraordinarily intense counterinsurgency effort from India. Where such ties did not exist or were broken, organizations—no matter what their formal structure was—stopped functioning. Organizational power needs to be built and reproduced, and this requires trust and cooperation. As the networks that facilitated this cooperation were targeted, groups faltered and collapsed.

A number of implications can be drawn from a careful comparative study of Kashmir's war. It shows the limits of pure popular support. Armed groups need fighters and supporters, and thus popular support is essential. But there is no clear linear relationship between popular backing and organizational outcomes. In the early 1990s, the apparently most popular group in Kashmir, the JKLF, was systematically sidelined by the Hizbul Mujahideen, while other groups that might have been able to politically appeal to portions of the population (such as the Muslim Janbaz Force of the People's League) also fragmented. The Hizbul Mujahideen pulled ahead both because of its Pakistani support and because it could fall back on a preexisting set of Jamaat local and regional networks that provided a ready-made command structure for militancy. The crucial question about mass support is whether it can be harnessed into an organization; if not, it is of only limited use in insurgent warfare.

Ideological visions played a central role in building prewar networks and in motivating fighters in war. However, ideology did not lead to any particular outcome. Preexisting ties were also affected by state repression and co-optation, contingent events, and leadership decisions. Ideas that were embedded first in social networks and then in formal institutions affected the extent to which these visions could be translated into strong organizations. No matter how powerful and resonant these ideas were, they were not easy to turn into actual institutions. Interestingly, the trajectories of most of the Pakistan-backed armed groups in Kashmir show that external material aid alone was also insufficient to forge a disciplined insurgent organization. These groups drew on fractured political parties and ad hoc collections of personal networks. But the Hizbul Mujahideen was not undermined by greedy loot-seeking linked to Pakistani aid. Resource flows did not determine the structure of the organization one way or another; resources followed lines of internal social division instead of reshaping group cohesion. Both ideational and material resources were important, but their impact was conditional on social bases and the organizational structures they created.

Kashmir also shows the power and limits of external state support. Pakistan has been deeply implicated in shaping the trajectory of the Kashmir insurgency. It has favored some groups and dismissed others, distributing guns, money, and sanctuary in a strategic way that left some organizations shattered and others riding high. But the ISI was not omniscient. The Pakistani security establishment attempted to control a variety of pro-Pakistan forces in the early to mid-1990s in order to maintain a diversified strategic portfolio, but the fragmentation of the Ikhwan and the Al-Umar occurred despite ISI attempts to hold them together. Similarly, the Hizbul Mujahideen's activities on the ground were influenced only broadly by ISI manipulation, as local dynamics of rivalry, greed, and collusion also shaped patterns of violence.[255] Social autonomy and organizational capacity creates space for sponsored armed groups to defy, manipulate, and ignore state sponsors.

Finally, the effectiveness of counterinsurgency differed by the type of organization it was targeting. My theory does not try to explain Indian policy, but it does explain the varying consequences of counterinsurgency initiatives. Where India had the information needed to target organizational processes or was facing a divided group, counterinsurgency was ruthlessly effective. But when it took on the Hizbul Mujahideen in the first half of the 1990s, the policies that had worked against other groups did not have the same effects. It was only after the defection of former insurgents—flowing out of the fragmentation of those groups—that Indian counterinsurgency could effectively undermine the Hizbul Mujahideen.

There are areas where my theory does not perform well. The case of Al-Umar Mujahideen is a failure for my argument: the social linkages of the Awami Action Committee do not appear to have helped the group build a robust organization. Here we see a disjuncture between prewar social ties and wartime insurgent organization. The Al-Umar became a fragmented organization that quickly collapsed. We need a clearer understanding of when group leaders ignore or dispense with initial social resources. There was also substantial human agency at work in the case of the JKLF. Though it would have been difficult, it is possible that its leaders could have adopted a different strategy in 1988–1989 that would have led to better control of the organization. Moreover, once the JKLF entered the war, it experienced extensive coalition-building and fluid splintering that was not structurally determined. Though my theory of change incorporates key elements of this process, contingency was rife during the clash of arms from 1991 to 1997.

What are the broader legacies of insurgent organization in Kashmir? Violence has markedly declined since the India-Pakistan cease-fire in 2003. Yet the shattered rebellion in Kashmir has left enduring scars. The Hizbul Mujahideen clings to life with an enduring but battered organization. The JKLF retains a public presence but has no militant power. The remnants of other armed groups have linked up with either mainstream electoral parties or factions of the Hurriyat Conference. Elections have occurred but with widely varying turnouts and impacts. The state's politics lie perpetually on the edge of another round of mass protest and internal division, as was evidenced during massive marches and protests during the summers of 2008, 2009, and 2010 and the winter of 2013. The fissures that emerged in the fratricidal collapse of the insurgency have created legacies of distrust and disunity, while much of the population views the Indian counterinsurgency machine that exploited these splits with contempt and fear. This combination has contributed to deep political instability in Kashmir that is likely to persist. The consequences of Kashmir's insurgency are still being felt long after most of its guns have fallen silent.

[5]

Organizing Rebellion in Afghanistan

Afghanistan has been the site of brutal conflict since 1979. This violence has included a number of distinct but intertwined wars: the resistance to the Soviet invasion, the attempt of the Najibullah regime to cling to power in Kabul, the factional wars of the mid-1990s, the rise of the Taliban, and most recently the overthrow and return of the Taliban in the aftermath of 9/11. Afghanistan's wars constitute an extraordinarily intricate history, one that eludes easy categories and simple explanations. Despite this complexity, this chapter shows that my argument can offer new insights into the origins and evolution of the war's key insurgent groups since the mid-1970s.

Politicized social ties are essential to understanding patterns of insurgent organization in Afghanistan. The social bases in which leaders were embedded shaped their ability to build organizations. The long-run trajectories of organizations were determined by whether institutional control could be created and maintained in the face of intense military competition. Armed groups were not seamless manifestations of ethnic identity or other macro-level categories; as Dorronsoro notes, "It was not 'ethnicities' that made war, but political organisations with ideological objectives and particular institutional practices."[1] Leaders brought new goals and identities to the political space but faced recurrent challenges in converting these agendas into resilient armed organizations.

These tensions between ideological visions and social realities created remarkable variation in Afghanistan's major armed groups. A few leaders forged integrated organizations. The fighting power and adaptability of these groups—the Taliban and the Shura-yi Nazar—have made them key players who are able to adjust to a complex military terrain and shifting international politics. The Hezb-e Islami of Gulbuddin Hekmatyar emerged as a vanguard organization built around a detribalized urban Islamist core. Its inability to penetrate local areas left it with a distinctive combination of tightly disciplined central leadership and unreliable influence on the ground. These were the most disciplined major fighting forces in the war and have remained active to the present day.

The more common pattern in the Afghan war, however, involved armed groups that mobilized around strong vertical but weak horizontal social linkages. Localized networks went to war as components of loose coalitions. The parochial groups that emerged were held together by a charismatic leader and were composed of distinct factional blocs. This pattern can be found in the Pashtun tribal fighting force of Yunis Khalis's faction of the Hezb-e Islami in the 1980s, Burhanuddin Rabbani's expansive Jamiat-e Islami throughout its existence, and the southern group Harakat-e Inqelab of the 1980s, which was dominated by clerics. These groups differed greatly in ideology, ethnic composition, and material resources, yet their similar social structures pushed them toward a particular trajectory. Afghanistan also provides an example of a fragmented group: the Ittehad of Sayyaf was cobbled together in the sanctuary of Pakistan from a diffuse mix of exiles, marginalized commanders, and local opportunists, all connected by Saudi money.

The changes that occurred in these organizations during the war were primarily in the direction of fragmentation, driven by revolts from below in vanguard groups and feuds among leaders in parochial groups. These trends were exacerbated by counterinsurgency and external meddling. The major change in the other direction occurred in Massoud's Shura-yi Nazar, which used a slow and careful process of building local alliances to shift from an initial vanguard form into an integrated organization. As Harpviken argues of Afghanistan's militancy, "One needs to take the social structures in which people are already embedded as a starting-point."[2] The tides of war have shifted for many reasons, but social ties and their consequences for organizations help explain why armed groups flourished or foundered amid these challenges.

This chapter provides background for the wars in Afghanistan and outlines the patterns of insurgency in these conflicts. I lay out the origins of different social networks and political organizations in the lead-up to the first attempts at rebellion in 1975 and explore the ensuing dynamics of organization building and evolution from 1979 until 1988, the period when the Afghan mujahideen challenged the Soviet Union and the Kabul regime. I then examine how these older organizations responded in the 1990s to changing political contexts and assess whether my theory can explain the rise of the Taliban. The chapter concludes with a discussion of the evidence from the post-9/11 Taliban and of the important findings from this chapter and their implications.

Chapter 5
Methodology

Dozens of formal armed organizations have waged war in Afghanistan and many more informal local networks and groups have been involved in violence. Trying to study all of these organizations is unlikely to bear much fruit because the data on most of them is so limited. Instead, I have chosen specific comparisons of a small number of groups to assess my theory's power and its relationship to other arguments. I compare insurgent groups that have actively tried to seize central power rather than "warlord" and regional armed groups that have focused on maintaining some degree of autonomy but have not sought national power. I begin by exploring the social and political roots of social bases in pre-1975 Afghanistan. The movements and networks that emerged in the period 1955–1975 played a central role once war began, but prewar development of these networks had very little to do with planning for protracted rural insurgency against the Soviet military. The strategies of these politicized networks centered on political protest, military coups and rapid uprisings, and infiltration of elite institutions, not preparations for the war that actually later arose.

My research design examines three periods of insurgency after the onset of war. First, I compare the vanguard group Hezb-e Islami, the initially vanguard and then integrated group Shura-yi Nazar, the parochial group Jamiat-e Islami, and the parochial group Harakat during the period 1975–1988. I also briefly discuss other cases to show that my argument explains them as well. Second, I continue to study the evolution of the Shura-yi Nazar, the Hezb-e Islami, and the Jamiat-e Islami during the years 1989–2001 and examine the origins and rise of the Taliban. I argue that the Taliban arose from a social base that had been reshaped by migration and war during the 1980s: though inadvertent and painful, the social transformations of the 1980s created horizontal networks that pulled leaders together while keeping them vertically embedded in local communities, thus facilitating rapid and impressive institutionalization. The third period, since 2001, studies the organizational staying power of the Taliban in the face of U.S.-led counterinsurgency in Afghanistan.

I have not done fieldwork in Afghanistan. Instead, I rely on academic literature and press accounts to construct a comparative history of the war. I take care to offer direct quotations and multiple citations from the secondary literature to show that I am not cherry picking to my theoretical tastes. The social-institutional theory does not claim to explain all aspects of the war or its constituent organizations. Instead, the goal is to assess whether it provides consistent insights that help make sense of patterns of insurgency in Afghanistan's wars.

Table 5.1. Patterns of organization in Afghanistan

Organization	Initial organizational type	Organizational change
Hezb-i Islami (Hekmatyar)	Vanguard	Period of fragmentation, 1996–2001
Jamiat-e Islami	Parochial	Loosely integrated into state, 2001
Harakat-i Inquilab Islami-i Afghanistan	Parochial	Fragmented and then disappeared from around 1988
Shura-yi Nezar	Vanguard	Integrated by mid-1980s; loosely integrated into state in 2001
Ittihad-i Islami Bara-yi Azadi-yi Afghanistan	Fragmented	Disappeared as major force in early 1990s
Hezb-i Islami (Khalis)	Parochial	Loosely incorporated into Taliban in mid-1990s
Taliban	Integrated	No change

MILITANCY AND MOBILIZATION IN AFGHANISTAN

Historical Origins

Afghanistan's history over the last three decades is extraordinarily complex. Here I briefly summarize the aspects of that history that are relevant for understanding the emergence and development of nonstate armed groups. In broad terms, ethnic divisions in Afghanistan shaped the contours of political rule. Pashtuns—who are internally differentiated along numerous dimensions—are based in eastern and southern Afghanistan and form a plurality of the population. Northern and western Afghanistan have significant concentrations of Tajiks, Uzbeks, Turkmens, Chahar Aimaqs, and Nuristanis (among others), and central Afghanistan is the home of a sizable minority of (primarily Shiite) Hazaras. These ethnic divisions have varied in salience and form over time; they are important but not fixed.

Afghanistan's political development in the nineteenth century was shaped by its geopolitical position between Russia and British India. A rentier state developed that exploited ties to external patrons to keep ruling elites (tenuously) in power.[3] During the 1950s and 1960s, modernization developed, at least in Kabul and in central state institutions. The military and education became key vehicles of upward mobility in the state. However, most of the economy remained heavily agricultural and experienced minimal industrialization. The increase in education available in Kabul, the growth of the military, and the introduction of limited parliamentary democracy in 1964 and a coup against the king in 1973 combined to create a volatile political environment. Communists and modernist Islamists did battle on university campuses, the army became a hotbed of political competition between different factions, and modernization efforts tried to push state power into rural areas.

The overthrow of the king, Muhammed Zahir Shah, by his nephew, Daud Khan, in 1973 was pivotal. This increased the power of the military, led to a crackdown on Islamists, and spurred growing communist mobilization. Small-scale Islamist revolts in 1975 fizzled out but were followed by a communist military coup against Daud in 1978 and the establishment of a new regime led by the People's Democratic Party of Afghanistan (PDPA). The PDPA launched a massive program of social transformation in Kabul and beyond. The reaction to the PDPA initiative was violently negative, with revolts breaking out throughout the country.

Armed Groups in Afghanistan

Splits and factionalism within the PDPA and growing unrest led to internal conflict in the regime that impelled the Soviet intervention of 1979. The Soviets attempted to bring order to the PDPA regime and stabilize the Afghan countryside. The challenging terrain, weak Afghan government forces, and intense opposition from numerous Afghan social blocs made this a difficult task. A set of major armed groups emerged in opposition to the Kabul regime and its Soviet backers. Seven in particular would become prominent, in part because they had access to sanctuary in Peshawar and support from the Pakistani security services. Despite their shared goal of opposing the Kabul regime, the trajectories of these organizations differed significantly. This variation shaped which organizations could take advantage of Pakistani aid and carve out areas of territorial influence.

The anti-Soviet war of 1979 until 1988 was followed by chaos after the Soviet forces withdrew. The Najibullah regime in Kabul was able to use patronage, innovative alliances, and a rebranding of the regime to keep itself alive until 1992 in the face of a divided mujahideen movement. The task of generating quasi-conventional forces from internally divided and localized social structures was insurmountable for most of the insurgent groups. The only organizations able to meet the challenge were Massoud's Shura and, to a lesser extent, the Jamiat-e Islami, within which it was loosely enclosed; Hekmatyar's Hezb-e Islami; the Hazara armed group Hezb-i Wahdat; and new territorial militias of Ismail Khan in the west and Abdul Rashid Dostum in the north. Large parts of the country came under the control of local organizations that lacked both the capacity to project their influence beyond these local areas and reliable internal command and control.

Organizing Rebellion in Afghanistan

This multisided battle to control Kabul was interrupted by the rise of the Taliban. From its base in Kandahar in the south in 1994, the Taliban swept into other areas of Afghanistan, capturing Kabul in 1996 and driving back the forces of the Northern Alliance (a loose coalition of Rabbani, Massoud, Dostum, and other ethnic minority groups). The Taliban solved the challenge of coordinated mobilization in Afghanistan's intricate social environment, forging impressive cohesion and unity, especially in comparison to its foes. By the time of the 9/11 terrorist attacks in the United States, the Taliban controlled most of the country.

The period since 9/11 has seen the return of a Taliban insurgency. Unlike its earlier conventional warfare, the "neo-Taliban" has engaged in classic guerrilla tactics. Hekmatyar's Hezb-e Islami has also reappeared in the east. The Haqqani network, an organization that was involved in the previous wars as a component of the Khalis faction of the Hezb-e Islami, has become an important player as well. This broad array of variation across groups and over time forms a fascinating comparative setting in which to understand which factors shaped the trajectories of insurgent organizations.

Political Mobilization and Social Change in Afghanistan before 1975

This section outlines the major prewar social bases that characterized Afghanistan's political life before the first Islamist uprising of 1975. Between 1928 and 1975, the Afghan state was focused on Kabul and on a few key institutions and social networks, but the state apparatus did not reach deep into the countryside. Pervasive localism contributed to weak ties across communities. From the 1950s onward, modernization attempts and the impact of international ideological currents facilitated urban-based mobilization associated with Islamist, communist, and middle-class nationalist political projects. Ideas and interaction in Kabul created new horizontal linkages that took on greater prominence on the national stage.

Assessing the political salience of prewar social bases in Afghanistan is a complex task: unlike in Kashmir, there was no enduring state-opposition cleavage that marked groups as clearly pro- or anti-state. Instead, I examine politicized actors that had an interest in shaping patterns of governance and access to state power. Social bases that focused on political mobilization can be distinguished from the innumerable networks that cut across politically relevant cleavages or were detached from political practice at the national level. Through 1972, these social bases were nonviolent, but from 1972 to 1975 some began to prepare for war. I identify four categories of politicized social bases: clerics, modern "Islamists," communists, and urban nationalist modernizers.[4] Some later

[105]

became involved in insurgency while others focused on coups and rivalries in Kabul, but none initially came together or reshaped their ties in anticipation of an impending protracted war.

Clerics

Clerics in Afghanistan, the ulama, had significant political power until the 1950s. While clerics were influential, they were focused on civil society and social norms. The type of modernity suggested by the rise of the central state had little appeal for members of Afghanistan's clerical networks. This is because the increasing, if uneven, reach of the state in the 1950s and 1960s undermined clerical influence.[5] The modernization strategy of Kabul regimes tried to minimize the autonomous role of the clerical establishment. The regimes mixed crackdowns and arrests with a policy of co-opting clerical authority figures into state structures. As a result, by the early 1970s "the *ulama* network had no clearly defined centre: the Mujaddidi family which led the revolt of the clergy in 1928 [had] lost a great deal of its influence. There was no specific place where the clerical opposition might come together, for the faculty of theology [in Kabul] was in the hands of the Islamists."[6] Clerical embeddedness was strongest in rural areas, where state power was most lightly felt.

The combination of a worldview that turned away from clerical involvement in "modern" politics and state efforts to co-opt and disrupt clerical networks created a situation in which "there were many networks of 'ulama, but [they had] no political organization."[7] In the religious school system, "schools were scattered all over the country and had little connection with one another.... In Afghanistan, no theological center of activity was equivalent to Qom in Iran or al-Azhar in Egypt, which made organizing difficult."[8] Clerical authority remained localized until the effects of the war led to the joining together of local networks in the refugee camps and madrasas of Pakistan in the 1980s and early 1990s. Clerics were not connected to each other by social ties beyond their local areas in the 1970s. Though the evidence is far from definitive, the assessment offered by experts seems to indicate strong vertical ties but weak horizontal ties among clerics: this social base was bound by shared identity but not systematic linkages at national level.

Islamists

A very different set of social structures emerged among urban Islamists.[9] Influenced by the models of the Jamaat-e-Islami in Pakistan and the Muslim Brotherhood in Egypt, Islamists stressed the need to reshape the nature of the state in accordance with perceived religious imperatives. For these new intellectual entrepreneurs, the route to influencing the state lay in part in education and social transformation but also in the formation of new party organizations that could coordinate and control mobilization while members infiltrated state institutions. However, the process of successfully building new networks and organizations to follow an organization's blueprint is difficult, as Afghanistan's Islamists learned. The major leaders to emerge from this politicized opposition bloc were primarily urban students and middle classes who were only loosely connected to rural areas or the "traditional" religious establishment. Strong horizontal ties characterized most of the networks in this broad social base, born of overlapping ethnic and university networks, but weak vertical ties to localities were the norm.

A key social milieu from which the Islamists emerged was Kabul University, where new intellectual influences from abroad were introduced in a climate of rapid change and educational expansion.[10] Ironically, this was the source of the eventual "core leadership for all sides in the war"[11]: Marxists, Maoists, and Islamists operated in close proximity at the university. Islamist party building developed among the educated classes; as Roy notes, "The Islamists are intellectuals, the product of modernist enclaves within traditional society."[12] The new Islamist movement viewed clerics as obsolete and unequipped to do political battle with the new forces that were making their presence felt in Kabul.[13]

Party building followed two tracks: "the movement functioned on an open level, the Muslim Youth, and a more secret level, centred upon the 'professors.'"[14] Until 1972, the Islamist movement had no avowed political agenda beyond spiritual reinvigoration and anti-communism.[15] The Organization of Muslim Youth emerged as a manifestation of this movement.[16] Its structure was cellular, and the group attempted to expand beyond Kabul after being driven underground following Daud's coup in 1973.[17] Many who would become the key figures of the next three decades were members of this group.[18] After 1973, we begin to see a shift from politicized opposition toward revolutionary planning in anticipation of violence. A number of distinct networks were part of this broader (though quite small) movement that drew on different classes, ethnic groups, and identity cleavages: for instance, Tajiks were more associated with Rabbani and Pashtuns with Hekmatyar.

Although the Islamists "had as their goal the establishment of a mass movement,"[19] Roy argues, "in tribal zones they had absolutely no support."[20] Harpviken and Rashid agree with this assessment: Harpviken writes that "prior to the war, there was no rural support for the Islamists,"[21] and Rashid argues that "prior to the war the Islamicists barely had a base in Afghan society."[22] The urban educational system that birthed the new Islamist class was "external to the rural community."[23] These activists faced dilemmas that were similar to those of their communist enemies: the lure of the modern and the interests the modernizers represented were seen as very urban in an overwhelmingly rural country.[24] The linkages to the countryside that were necessary for large-scale social transformation and political mobilization were absent; the social structure of the modernist Islamists was the opposite of that of the traditional, localistic clerics.

Communists and Modernizers

Two other social bases can be identified by the early 1970s: middle-class modernizers and communists. Both were politicized in opposition to particular regimes, though in very different ways. Neither transformed into an insurgent group; instead, each launched an urban coup that brought them to power. Middle-class modernizers were based in Kabul and aimed to supplant the monarchy in order to turn Afghanistan into a more stable, powerful, and administratively advanced state that would be able to direct programs of economic development and social control. Linked to Daud, this constituency seized power in a 1973 coup that embarked on an aggressive state-building project in a loose temporary alliance with the left.

Communism became important in the military and among students during the 1960s and 1970s. The dominant strand was associated with the pro-Soviet People's Democratic Party of Afghanistan (PDPA), which was formed in 1965. Communists were locked in a broader struggle with Islamists and modernizers in the urban core of Afghanistan. Yet like these rivals, the PDPA had weak links to the rural countryside. They believed that their path to power was the central state's institutions, which were the target of communist infiltration and persuasion.

The communists became increasingly powerful in the army during the 1970s, setting the stage for their coup of 1978 against the Daud regime. The deep structural flaws within the PDPA regime that took power in 1978 can be traced back to the social loyalties and linkages of the communist party prior to its coups: it was an urban-based party that was divided by leadership factions. These problems were reflected in the new regime's structure and operation. Though my theory is intended to explain insurgent groups, it also helps explain the structure of the new Afghan regime that was built around the PDPA from 1978.

Social Bases in Afghanistan

Social bases emerged from a complex intertwining of political belief, social structure, and agency.[25] They were forged as opposition groups and political parties but were not built for protracted war. Indeed, as Dorronsoro notes, "In the 1970s the political parties were not highly structured organizations, but served mainly as discussion forums."[26] While some came to embrace violence, none were interested in rural insurgency: even the most militant Islamists and communists aimed to seize the state's top institutions, not launch a twilight war on distant peripheries. Groups expected their battles to play out in infiltration and seizure of the state, competition over the loyalties of the urban classes, and a rapid series of moves and countermoves.[27]

There was no single underlying logic by which networks formed and evolved in Afghanistan. Politics and social life were intertwined, but in many ways and for many reasons. The ideological influences were varied, from Islamists learning about Leninist models of organization through battles with campus communists to the historical lessons rural clerics embraced in the countryside. Politics were embedded in social life—as Roy observes, "the idea of a social network is fundamental to the way in which politics operate in Afghanistan"[28]—and these politicized networks were hurled into war, became spearheads of coups, and were transformed into aspirant states and counterstates in wholly unanticipated ways.

Origins and Evolution of Insurgency, 1973–1988

This section studies the origins and evolution of major insurgent groups in Afghanistan from 1973 through the Soviet withdrawal of 1988. It examines four organizations in detail and more briefly considers evidence from two others. These armed groups emerged in 1974–1978 and then took on a central role when fighting the PDPA regime and the Soviets after 1978. Newer groups then emerged over the course of the rest of the war. I compare four groups: Gulbuddin Hekmatyar's Hezb-e Islami; the Shura-yi Nazar, the armed faction of Massoud; the Jamiat-e-Islami of Rabbani, and the Harakat. Hezb-e Islami was a vanguard group with relatively strong leadership control and discipline but weak local control. The Shura-yi Nazar was technically nested within Jamiat but operated autonomously as first a vanguard and then an integrated organization with strong central discipline that extended to the local level by the mid-1980s. Most of the rest of the groups in the war "functioned ... as coalitions of mobilized social segments."[29] This is certainly true of both the Jamiat-e Islami and the Harakat. Rabbani's Jamiat-e Islami took on a parochial organizational form built around distinct commanders of factions (including Massoud): autonomous armed groups operated underneath the Jamiat-e Islami umbrella. The Harakat was a parochial armed group with extremely loose central control and eventually collapsed after fragmenting. In all four cases, we see politicized opposition social blocs going to war and creating insurgent institutions whose linkages resembled the prior social ties of group members. Both the Shura-yi Nazar and the Harakat thus show change over time.

Other groups exhibit a range of types of control. Sayyaf's Ittehad mobilized through weak preexisting social ties and consequently had almost no semblance of organization. It was a fragmented organization held together by money, desperation, and opportunistic alliances. The Khalis faction of the Hezb-e-Islami emerged as a parochial armed group because of the tribal terrain it mobilized. No nationally dominant group emerged during this period: as Harpviken notes, "Neither of the existing tribal or religious forms of organization were able to generate the organizational coherence necessary for larger-scale organization."[30]

The First Uprising and Its Aftermath, 1973–1978

Political shocks in 1973 and 1978 laid the groundwork for insurgency. The escalation of political competition in Kabul took on a new form when Daud overthrew King Zahir and established a new "modernist" regime in 1973. The urban modernizing social base made its bid for the state. The communists (particularly the Marxist-Leninists, not the Maoists) became temporary allies of the new regime, while Islamists shifted into firm opposition. The pre-1972 social bases were starting to go to war. After the Daud regime came to power in 1973, its suppression of the Islamists pushed many into exile, both in Pakistan and Saudi Arabia. During the period 1973–1975, Islamist activists began to plot to overthrow the new regime.

After the failures of coup plots, some Islamists decided to pursue a rapid uprising strategy in order to attract popular support against the regime. This social base crystallized into distinct networks around particular leaders. By 1975 these newly rebellious Islamist cells "had built up small armed groups clandestinely, but did not connect up with existing community structures."[31] Weak vertical ties shaped the outcome of the rebellion: the attempted rebel uprising was quickly and effectively shattered.[32] There was little coordination or cooperation and locals did not flock to the banner of rebellion. Dorronsoro argues that there was a "total lack of support from the population, who neither knew nor understood the Islamists. This attempted coup also gives some indication of the movement's roots—it was in fact weak and geographically restricted."[33] Vanguard groups did emerge, but the organizers did not realize their plan of creating an integrated mass rebellion.

Distinctions within the movement became more prominent from 1975. Networks and affiliations turned into formal organizations as the hope of a straightforward seizure of power faded. Dorronsoro reminds us that while ideology was important in determining social bases, it could not be separated from social connections: "within the same ideological movement individuals gravitate together according to their social profile."[34] The two key leaders who emerged among the Islamists at this point were Rabbani and Hekmatyar, and they quickly began a brutal rivalry that lasted for decades. Both had come up through the political competition in Kabul University but they were linked to distinct networks. In Roy's analysis, their split "may be represented as following the line of cleavage within the social structure which underlies everything else: the social environment of the government madrasa, the brotherhoods of the west and the Persian-speaking Islamists were pro-Rabbani, while the radical students, especially the Pashtun, were pro-Hekmatyar."[35] Roy further notes that lines of recruitment involved "teachers in the Hizb, students of government madrasa in the Jamiat."[36]

After a complex process that involved splitting, building united fronts, and feuding again, Hekmatyar's Hezb-e Islami and Rabbani's Jamiat-e Islami become major contenders for power by 1978.[37] Hekmatyar's subgroup within the Islamist movement drew from the urban Islamist milieu. The disciplined believers around Hekmatyar formed a comparatively durable central leadership whose members trusted each other and shared a political worldview embedded in common experiences in the 1960s and 1970s. Rabbani, by contrast, attempted to build a coalition around the disparate networks he connected. The Jamiat-e Islami emerged as a parochial organization with Rabbani as a broker among commanders of factions.

The 1978 PDPA Coup, Soviet Intervention, and Escalation

National politics in Afghanistan received a massive jolt in 1978 when the PDPA used its military faction to seize power and embark on an attempt to bring about revolution from above. This effort was disastrous. Another major insurgent contender joined the fray after the Communist coup in 1978 (but before the Soviet intervention). The Harakat arose from networks of rural clerics and immediately leveraged these vertical ties into local strength in eastern and southern Afghanistan.

Unrest accelerated dramatically when the Soviets intervened in late 1979 to bolster one faction of the PDPA. The Harakat, the Hezb-i Islami, and the Jamiat-e Islami all based their leadership in Peshawar with Pakistani backing. On the ground, this phase of the Afghan resistance initially took place in "spontaneous, decentralized organizational forms."[38]

Chapter 5

The Islamist parties mobilized to take advantage of these revolts, but they faced social-institutional challenges: they "were too few—about three thousand, including those in Pakistan—to set off a national revolt. They were also split by faction and ethnicity and thus did not have the nationwide cadre structure necessary to organize an uprising."[39] The insurgent forces were not "optimized" ahead of time for this new war; instead, they had to make do with the social resources they had.[40]

Insurgent organizations were not perfectly aligned with social networks; leadership choices and contingent events played a role in shaping how new fighting forces emerged. Nevertheless, there is a strong link between prewar social bases and wartime organizational structure. Leaders tapped their networks to find commanders and fighters who were willing to pledge at least a tenuous allegiance to them.[41] The key challenge was building institutions at both the central and local levels.[42] This was a major problem because of the sparse number of parties, networks, or institutions that could link people across Afghanistan.[43]

In the next decade, these new armed groups were challenged by counterinsurgency and manipulation by outside powers. The Soviets became deeply involved in the Kabul regime. Over the course of the 1980s, the Soviets launched numerous rounds of offensives against the insurgents and the Afghan regime used intelligence and violence to try to break apart the insurgency. Insurgent organizations that were not favored by Pakistan's ISI were marginalized, and this certainly played an important role (though not a decisive one, as I discuss below) in determining which groups were able to establish themselves. After a final push from 1986 to 1988, the Soviets left Afghanistan in the hands of Mohammed Najibullah Ahmadzai, who was propped up with Soviet aid until 1992.

Social origins and institutional processes determined how armed groups dealt with these challenges and thus whether and how the groups changed over time. The Soviets, the Afghan regime and rival militants were able to take advantage of internal divisions in the Harakat to pull away defectors, encourage splits, and degrade the group as a functional national organization. By 1988, it had shifted into a fragmented structure. In contrast, Massoud's armed group—technically part of Jamiat-e Islami but militarily autonomous—established new vertical linkages that facilitated local organization. It shifted from a vanguard to integrated structure, though it remained concentrated in one region. The Hezb-e Islami of Gulbuddin Hekmatyar could not turn massive Pakistani support into organization at the local level but was able to keep fighting and continued on its vanguard trajectory. Similarly, Rabbani's Jamiat-e Islami continued to be a parochial organization with powerful factions based in particular areas. Social linkages endured in the case of Jamiat-e Islami and Hezb-e Islami and structured the mechanisms of change for both the Shura-y Nazar and the Harakat.

The Hezb-i Islami at War

I begin with the most "modern" organization that waged war in Afghanistan, the Hezb-i Islami of Gulbuddin Hekmatyar.[44] There is clear consensus that the Hezb-i Islami was a tightly disciplined, Islamist cadre group: "Hizb-i Islami was a political party in the modern and specifically Leninist sense...the most hierarchical, disciplined, and secretive."[45] It had coherent institutionalized central processes, command discipline, and relatively few major splits. Yet the Hezb-i Islami experienced recurring problems related to local mobilization and control that undermined the ability of the leadership core to create an integrated organization. The Hezb-i Islami became a vanguard group because of the strong horizontal but weak preexisting vertical ties it was built upon. The group's inability to change over time reflected its social distance from much of eastern and southern Afghanistan and the rigid ideology of Hekmatyar. These two factors undermined local alliance processes that could have led to a shift toward integration. Later on in the war, the Hezb-i Islami would sometimes impose itself on local communities, but it never achieved widespread integration.

How was the organization built? Hekmatyar did not have a powerful social position and was not embedded in important ethnic networks in Afghanistan. He was part of a group of primarily Pashtun urban Islamists who had roots in the Kabul political milieu. This social base was largely drawn from detribalized northern and eastern Pashtuns. This demographic base and the Hezb's hostility to clerical authority made it difficult for the group to mobilize either the ulama or the powerful Pashtun tribes in the east (much less the south).[46] The organizational model of the Muslim Brotherhood and the Pakistani Jamaat was successfully implemented among the leadership, in large part because of strong preexisting horizontal ties stretching back to the 1960s that combined social proximity and ideological commitment.[47]

As it went to war, the Hezb-i Islami drew on individuals and groups linked to urban modernization and Pashtun migration.[48] Dorronsoro notes that in Helmand, for instance, Hezb recruitment "took place within groups affected by modernization—schoolteachers, government employees and such like—while its recruitment in the rural and tribalised areas was negligible."[49] Roy agrees: "The establishment of Hekmatyar groups is a phenomenon which transcends tribal allegiance, but it occurs most frequently in Pashtun areas and amongst young intellectual groups. It is to be found most frequently in pockets where tribal structures have broken down or which have a mixture of groups originating from different tribes."[50] The Hezb was able to insert itself in the refugee camps, where many Afghans had been sundered from their social networks and were available to be organized from above.[51] Social structure preceded insurgency and constrained how Hekmatyar could build institutional power.

These horizontal ties made it possible to build strong central institutions during wartime. Roy writes that at its best, the Hezb resembled a cohesive combat party, as "the elite members were visionaries, dogmatic, and living their whole life for the party and devoted to Hekmatyar; they were thus more detached from the group solidarity of the qawm than was the case in the other groups."[52] Giustozzi emphasizes the internal discipline of the group: "Hizb-i Islami tried wherever it could to create a strong system of command and control, manned by educated activists. Often commanders too, particularly at the upper level, were educated activists with a strong ideological commitment."[53] Priority was given to continuity and loyalty.[54] This outcome is clearly in line with theoretical expectations. The dedicated Islamist cadre of the 1960s and early 1970s provided the essential trust and shared commitments that were needed to build a strong organization.

The result was robust central control. Dorronsoro describes how "Hezb-i Islami's organisation was a blend of centralization and military discipline on the model of the Pakistani Jamaat-i Islami. Its obsession with rules contrasted with flexibility observed elsewhere. Hezb-i Islami set up an alternative society as well as an alternative state."[55] Rubin supports this analysis: "More than other parties, Hizb was an integrated modern organization in which recruitment and promotion were based on individual ideology and skills rather than on social roles."[56] Hezb cadres became known for rigid conformity.[57] A rich set of internal institutions and bureaucracies enabled the organization to have "an impact far beyond the number of its fronts, which were many, or the effectiveness of its military operations, which was considerable."[58] Social structure and ideological visions combined to forge robust central control processes. In Coll's words, it was "the tightest, most militaristic organization in Peshawar and in the refugee camps."[59]

This does not mean that the top leadership of the Hezb was always in perfect harmony. Some elite leaders split from the group and others engaged in internal feuds during this period.[60] But it had had fewer devastating internal ruptures than other insurgent groups in Afghanistan.[61] One major split that bears out my theory was initiated by Yunis Khalis. He had been loosely linked to the urban Islamist milieu when he joined the Hezb. However, his strongest ties were with the eastern tribes from which he came. He quickly broke away from the Hezb and established his own Hezb-e Islami (Khalis) group, which was comprised a completely different set of networks based on tribal groups. Prior social division laid the basis for this organizational differentiation, which I discuss more below.

The crucial problem that recurred throughout the organization's existence was the fact that the "power base of the Hizb did not extend beyond the network of the Islamists."[62] The prewar Islamist networks had few ties to the countryside, especially the tribal eastern and southern Pashtun areas. This was reflected in its relationship with local institutions once the group was at war.[63] It "could not mobilize broadly because of its inability to integrate existing social ties."[64] As a result, the Hezb "showed the greatest autonomy from local social structures [and] followed the totalitarian model of integrating all powers into the party. Hizb did not consult with elders."[65]

Hekmatyar did not have access to strong or numerous local networks; there was little overlap between the leadership core and the local communities that were essential for fighting power. The loyalty of local commanders was fiercely sought after by national armed groups as these groups tried to generate combat power.[66] For Hekmatyar, weak vertical ties led to recurrent problems in attracting these local units and incorporating them into an integrated organization.[67] Harpviken writes that "the party's major problem was to expand beyond this organizational core; the lack of existing ties to wider segments of the population greatly restricted its mobilization potential."[68] In his analysis, "the problem for the Hezb was its inability to link its own hierarchy to existing social organization."[69]

The Hezb's goals of social transformation foundered on the rocks of social reality.[70] Edwards eloquently summarizes the roots of its limits:

> Alone among the parties, Hizb lacked a firm grounding in Afghan society that could ensure its survival. Thus, unlike Gailani and Mujaddidi, Hekmatyar didn't have a base of disciples, and he also didn't have a network of clerics to build on, as Nabi and Khales did.... He also lacked the kind of natural constituency Rabbani had with non-Pakhtuns and the outside financial resources that Sayyaf had at his disposal.... Basically, Hekmatyar had the party itself and the loyalty of young maktabis [schoolboys] who, like their leader, had been alienated from the society they sought to transform.[71]

Rashid condemns its lack of "reality-based theories of change."[72] As Hekmatyar faced these limitations, he sometimes responded by bringing in clients and loosely connected local groups.[73] These efforts led to serious problems of internal control, and Hekmatyar's group found itself caught between the limits of what a vanguard organization could do and the dangers of expansion.[74] Sinno notes that Hizb's "persistent attempts to centralize its structure and to strengthen internal control often led to the defection of disgruntled clients."[75] Roy argues that "the structure of the Hizb was opposed to that of traditional society" and says that this is why "it was generally rejected by the people."[76] It was impossible for the group to form local alliances, and attempts to impose itself on local areas—when Hezb-i Islami forces simply established control in areas where a power vacuum existed—did not lead to enduring connections. The idea of creating an encompassing combat party that could transcend social particularity remained elusive; if anything, it became counterproductive.

This is precisely the organizational structure we would expect for a group with the Hezb-i Islami's social origins. There are obviously other factors at play here, so this is not a unicausal claim. Hekmatyar's personality, the ideological rigidity of the group, and large-scale Pakistani support were undeniably important in driving the behavior of Hezb-i Islami. But personal drive, ideological commitment, and Pakistani aid could not bridge the central and local levels of war.

Despite a clear lack of mass popular support and the hammer blows of counterinsurgency, the Hezb remained alive and potent throughout the 1980s. The horizontal ties upon which central institutions were built made it "the most revolutionary and disciplined of the Islamist parties"[77] during this period of the war. Deep historical continuities can be found between the student mobilization of the late 1960s and unexpected insurgency of the 1980s. The Hezb's trajectory as an organization makes sense when we trace the social mobilization and organization building that forged it: its power was derived from its embeddedness in a strong set of horizontal ties among Islamist intellectuals, and its weaknesses were caused by the sparse vertical ties that this leadership core had access to in local communities.

Jamiat-e Islami: A Coalition of Rebellion

Most of Afghanistan is not Pashtun, and this fact limited the reach of primarily Pashtun armed groups. The Jamiat-e Islami pulled together many armed factions among the non-Pashtun population. Although Rabbani, a northerner from Badakhshan, was an Islamist, he was less vitriolic and less ruthless than Hekmatyar. He was well situated to mobilize a diverse set of ethnic and religious linkages for the purposes of violence. As Rabbani built the Jamiat in the 1970s, he drew on Islamist graduates from government madrasas and Dari-speakers, turned connections with Sufi brotherhoods into a source of recruits, and accepted local commanders into the new group. Consequently, the Jamiat emerged as a parochial organization that included a number of distinct ethnic, religious, and regional factions. Although this made it a key player in the war, it was not a tightly disciplined war machine. The contrast with the Hezb of Hekmatyar is striking: each faced trade-offs in organization building that reflected social origins, and these trade-offs went in opposite directions.

Jamiat-e Islami reflected both the social networks in which Rabbani was embedded and his theory of victory. The two were intertwined, but the networks were the specific means of organization building. In terms of strategy, Rabbani "realized that it would be impossible for them [him and his followers] to establish themselves in tribal zones by means of a simple party structure and that it was necessary to adapt to tribal institutions."[78] They hoped to build the "broadest possible coalition of all Muslims."[79] Structurally, Rabbani was at the intersection of more networks than Hekmatyar. He was connected through his travel, his teachings, and his social background to urban Islamists, some Sufi (specifically Naqshbandi) networks, and some ulama (many from the government religious schools). As a Tajik, Rabbani was also connected to minority ethnic blocs. The Jamiat thus "linked up with both ulama and Islamic mysticist networks"[80] in northern and western Afghanistan. However, Rabbani did not have access to a set of horizontal linkages that tied these various groupings together: he was the nodal point of several disparate networks.[81]

This social base had enduring consequences for the organization once it was mobilized for war. Social ties were turned into institutional processes, especially at the central level. Rubin argues that "these interconnections were reflected in factionalism among the party leadership, which was divided between ideological Islamists and more pragmatic activists linked especially to the party's regional and ethnic base."[82] Rabbani served as a broker between very different networks, a fragile position in Afghanistan's tumultuous landscape.[83] Rubin notes that because of this, "Rabbani allowed his commanders much more autonomy than did Hikmatyar."[84] He had some access to financial resources from Pakistan and other international sources, and this gave him a means of loose control over his fighters but did not create reliable central institutions.

As a result of these social roots, the Jamiat "became a more complex and heterogeneous organization, drawing on Islamist, Sufi, and ulama networks."[85] Assessing the Jamiat in detail is difficult because so much of the action occurred in specific local commanders' areas. Massoud in the northeast, Ismail Khan in the west, and Zabiullah in the north emerged as particularly powerful commanders. These men had strong links with the rural and local population, while external aid and educated cadres contributed to the Jamiat's ability to build upon networks and turn them into components of the organization.[86] Barfield notes that neither Khan nor Massoud "looked for guidance from Rabbani."[87] Indeed, Tomsen, an American diplomat in Afghanistan, notes that "nominally they were members of Burhanuddin Rabbani's Jamiat party. In reality they were autonomous power centers in Afghanistan."[88]

These local power centers dominated and established regional institutions that effectively fought the Soviets. Because of the realities of this social base and his own leadership goals, Rabbani made "no attempt to create a system of party commissars, nor to create a counter-intelligence service reporting on the military leaders affiliated to the party."[89] Institutional control was not consistent or centralized. Perched in Peshawar, Rabbani oversaw a parochial coalition that reflected the mix of ethnic and religious networks that he called upon as he went to war. Central control processes were personal rather than institutional, and the group lacked a tight, coherent strategic and decision-making core. The pattern of conflict within the Jamiat-e Islami was between commanders, rather than between local units and a unified set of elites: the organization "suffered from frictions between main commanders and smaller ones, who resented the centralization of the decision process, and (after 1992) between its two main field commanders, Ismail Khan in the West and Massoud in the East."[90]

The Shura-yi Nazar and Massoud

Ahmad Shah Massoud's faction of the Jamiat-e Islami presents a fascinating case of change over time. Massoud did not simply draw on preexisting networks to create a tightly disciplined and integrated organization from the start. Instead, he carefully formed alliances with local power holders that underpinned a shift from a vanguard to an integrated organizational structure. Massoud was one of the main figures in the 1975 failed uprising. As a Tajik Islamist from the Panjshir Valley, he joined Rabbani's Jamiat and generally remained loyal to Rabbani. But he built up his own organization that was autonomous from the Jamiat, even when it acted in support of Rabbani. It transformed from a vanguard organization built around a narrow cadre of Islamists into an increasingly sophisticated proto-state both during and after the anti-Soviet jihad. Massoud's organization was named the Shura-yi Nazar for a significant part of the conflict, which is the shorthand I will use for it.

This case shows how vertical links can be created and how an organization can change from a vanguard group to an integrated structure. Massoud carefully developed ties with local power holders in the Panjshir, took advantage of ethnic networks, and used the continuing presence of urban-rural ties to embed himself deeply into the social space of the Panjshir. However, Massoud could not move beyond a narrow geographic and social space; even this paragon of modern military organization could not establish reliable connections with people outside of the Panjshir, which prevented the Shura from expanding beyond a slice of northeastern Afghanistan.

Massoud was a fairly low-ranking Islamist in the 1970s who became involved in the movement in Kabul while receiving his education. After the 1975 abortive uprising, he fled to Peshawar and joined the Jamiat. He was given significant autonomy to pursue operations as he pleased after he returned to the Panjshir Valley in 1978. Over time he rose up through the organization because of his military skills. His group started out small as a vanguard with only a limited capacity to mobilize a local area. In 1978 the group consisted of Massoud and a few followers; the group had no substantial social infrastructure. Vertical linkages were relatively weak, though horizontal ties among this group were strong.

Massoud quickly and skillfully built on this initial core to create and mobilize linkages to his local ethnic space. Roy notes that "Massoud's basic outfit was composed of Panjshiris educated or working in Kabul, thus less subjected to the duties of the qawm."[91] He argues that "Massoud's two trumps were thus the control of a homogeneous solidarity space (without tribal or other subdivisions) and control of urbanized and technically competent personnel, while nevertheless retaining a link with traditional society."[92] This was clearly a case in which social structure facilitated organization building instead of undermining it. Massoud took advantage of the homogeneity of Panjshir and the fact that many of its educated individuals retained ties to the area, and he yoked those ties to his particular vision and drive.

Over time this horizontal network of urbanized Panjshiris made accommodations and deals with local power holders in order to forge local institutions of control and extraction. Rubin argues that "the main strategic task of the resistance, as Massoud saw it, was to overcome segmentation based on qawm and locality in order to build military institutions."[93] This segmentation, as we have seen, undermined groups such as the Harakat and Massoud's own parent organization, the Jamiat, while it restricted Hekmatyar's room to maneuver. By contrast, Massoud's group "was the product of years of work. From 1979 to 1983, Massoud worked only in Panjshir.... Massoud recognized the shura [local Panjshir shura], consulted it on a variety of issues, and incorporated it into his judicial committee."[94]

He eliminated some other armed actors in the Panjshir area to show his authority and created a fairly sophisticated organizational structure.[95] Massoud was able to overcome the challenge of expansion, at least in this specific area.[96] On the one hand, he created autonomous mobile forces and brought in some new fighters and commanders from outside the Panjshiri social bloc, then he trained and indoctrinated them.[97] On the other hand, the organization remained deeply embedded in Panjshiri networks, and Massoud did not interfere with local social structures.[98]

This is appears to be a case of the local alliance mechanism creating new vertical ties that were used for formal organization. Giustozzi writes that "whatever influence the commissars could muster was the result of the support of the mullahs,"[99] and Rubin adds that Massoud "adopted a grassroots strategy that integrated political and military components."[100] Massoud pragmatically cut deals and took advantage of the inability of the Soviets and the PDPA to politically manage local communities. Massoud's approach led to both significant local institutionalization—though it was certainly not perfect or uniform—and central control. Interestingly, this did not involve mass politicization à la Mao.[101] The Shura transitioned from a small vanguard core of organizers into an integrated organization by allying itself with and co-opting local social forces.[102] This was not a seamless expansion; the process of building local institutions was long and difficult.[103] My theory cannot explain Massoud's particular organizational vision and personal skill, but it can explain why the process of change involved the local bargaining and co-optation that it did.

A senior American diplomat called the Shura "the most effective Mujahidin military organization of the anti-Soviet war."[104] Massoud's forces repeatedly beat back Soviet offensives in the Panjshir by maintaining tight discipline, mobilizing civilians for support and manpower, and increasingly drawing on international aid and illicit economies. The organization dominated its political environment, from taxes to bargaining with the Soviets, and became a core component of anti-regime militancy. Soviet counterinsurgency and penetration by the KHAD (Afghanistan's intelligence agency) could not break the organization, even though other groups splintered or collapsed around it.

However, the strength of Massoud was also a source of his limitation. Expansion remained a huge challenge. Institutional control became increasingly loose beyond the Panjshir: the organizational model could not be modularly planted elsewhere. This is a crucial finding. Though social structures opened opportunities for Massoud in Panjshir, they constrained his ability to expand beyond that region because of the challenges of making alliances with other social blocs. The Shura nestled within Jamiat as one of its autonomous fighting factions, though an unusually powerful, disciplined, and militarily effective one. Hekmatyar and Massoud clearly show both the power and limits of "modern" organization-building strategies. These could be fused with preexisting networks in incredibly potent ways, yet they were not produced or maintained when leaders could not establish social connections to local communities. Organization and ideology did not float freely in Afghanistan's war.

"Traditionalist" Clerics at War: Harakat and Localized Rebellion

Hekmatyar, Rabbani, and Massoud were offshoots of the modernist Islamist movement, each linked to particular regional and religious networks that shaped how they could put their ideas into action. Other politicized social bases took different courses: Communists and the Daud-supporting middle classes launched coups, while the royalists fled into a marginal exile. The other major social base that took to insurgency emerged from the rural clerics, especially in Pashtun areas. As I showed above, this broad social class had been fragmented by modernizing state policy and by shifts in the political geography of Afghanistan. There were weak horizontal linkages among clerics. However, clerics remained embedded in local areas and played an important role in the daily lives of communities. The Harakat was built through this social base; it emerged initially as a parochial group but then became fragmented over the course of the 1980s.

The Harakat was formed in 1978 in Peshawar. Clerics and the Islamists such as Hekmatyar and Rabbani were not close; the Islamists represented the cities and the north and the ulama represented the countryside and the Pashtun tribes in the south and east. After intricate wrangling in Peshawar among various coalition leaders, the Harakat-i Inquilab-i Islami emerged, led by Maulavi Muhammad Nabi Muhammadi.[105] It was composed of the "madrasa-educated ulama"[106] who were uncomfortable with Hekmatyar's brand of modernizing radicalism and Rabbani's (primarily) ethnic minority organization. The social base of the Harakat was clerics. Maley notes that "Muhammadi's large but loosely structured party attracted many traditional religious figures"[107] even before it began to engage in serious insurgency. The Harakat played a crucial role when the war escalated after the Soviet intervention of late 1979 because of its powerful local presence in eastern and southern Afghanistan. The problems of localism among Afghanistan's clerics, however, created a parochial organizational structure. Soviet counterinsurgency and rivalry among the militants led to the fragmentation and ultimate collapse of the Harakat. This is the pathway of change we would expect for a parochial group in which powerful factional commanders break away or simply do not obey a weak central command.

In 1980, the Harakat-i Inquilab-i Islami was "the major party" of the Afghan resistance.[108] In 1978, Nabi had become the leader of the Harakat after a convoluted set of splits, coalitions, and re-splits within the exiled parties in Peshawar.[109] Nabi ended up in the leader's seat because of his good reputation, but beyond some local connections "he had no organization" at the time Harakat was forged.[110] From the beginning, therefore, a leadership problem faced Harakat. Edwards describes the shared identity that helps explain how this group became a social base of rebellion: "the clerical parties were networks of maulavis and mullas, some of whom knew each other already, but all of whom had in common their educational experiences and their commitment to a particular vision of Qur'an-centered existence."[111] This made Harakat a large and popular organization in the early days of the resistance. Roy says that in the first year after the Soviet resistance, it was the "absolute majority in the Afghan resistance movement."[112]

At the time Harakat was formed, the clerical basis of power in Afghanistan had been "decentered" by the state and by modernization that brought with it communism and Islamism. As Roy explains, "Afghanistan no longer had a focal point, either geographical or political, for the networks of the 'ulama."[113] The clerics remained locally powerful even if they did not have a strong social structure to connect them with each other.[114] Mobilization of these local networks produced the rise of ulema-commanders.[115] The Afghan resistance was immeasurably helped by local and regional mobilizations of clerics, and it was these men that the Harakat tapped into across Afghanistan.[116] Strong vertical ties created strong local units, reflecting the fact that "the clergy from the madrasa [had] created a network of personal links between teachers and pupils, comparable to the Sufi's relationships between pir and murid."[117]

This reliance on personalized and localized fronts, however, undermined institutionalization at the central leadership level. Rashid argues that "the Harakat had no coherent party structure and was just a loose alliance between commanders and tribal chiefs."[118] Roy summarizes the Harakat's structure as "the catch-all party of the resistance. Its organization consists in a series of local fronts, centred round a non-government madrasa, under the direction of mawlawi who incorporate their students into the movement as officers."[119] Giustozzi notes that the Harakat "had a following mainly among the clergy, although it did not discriminate unduly and recruited local leaders into its ranks. While the clergy gave Harakat something of an ideological line, its organizational weakness and the absence of 'modern educated' cadres from its ranks made it impossible for the leadership to have much control over what was going on in the field."[120] Weak horizontal ties among leaders created fragmentation at the top: vertically embedded commanders went their own way.

The consequences of this social structure for the organization were clear. Though it was "by all accounts the strongest front early in the war"[121] and received "a significant number of weapons from the ISI,"[122] the Harakat began losing factions by the mid-1980s. Rubin notes that "the staff was split between Muhammadi's fellow traditional ulama (who attended private madrasas) and those from the old-regime elite who attended elite secular schools,"[123] and Rubin notes that "the old-regime officials in the leadership [were] quite socially distant from the commanders."[124] These divisions within the command elite of the Harakat were the direct result of the character of the prewar social networks that constituted the group, as Harpviken explains: "Harakat's organization reflects the ulama networks, being a loose association of fronts with little administrative capacity. The unwillingness to establish formal structure became a major problem for Harakat, the ability to coordinate large-scale military action was severely restrained, and the party became an arena for conventional leadership rivalries."[125] As we would expect from a parochial organization, conflict occurred among powerful elites clashing with one another rather than from challenges to a coherent central command from local units (as we would expect in a vanguard group).

Splinter groups broke away from the Harakat in several ways. First, ethnic and regional divisions occurred as the Jamiat mobilized the non-Pashtun populations and the Islamist parties staked out terrain in the east.[126] Second, Pakistani aid to Afghan insurgent groups led to defection because other groups, such as the two Hezbs and the Jamiats, were also able to consistently offer guns and money to local commanders who had no reason to be particularly loyal to the Harakat.[127] The Pakistanis were less generous with Harakat than with other groups, but this was "an effect rather than a cause of its limited military effectiveness."[128] The Harakat was formed in the context of the deeply fragmented social landscape of the Durrani Pashtuns in the south, creating further obstacles to organizational cohesion.[129] Finally, counterinsurgency against this group was more effective because of the internal divisions and lack of trust within it. Rubin claims that it had "the worst organized and most corrupt of the party structures" and that it "seems to have been the party most easily penetrated by KHAD."[130]

By the mid- to late 1980s, the Harakat had devolved into a set of disconnected factions, many of which broke away and essentially abandoned the organization.[131] At this point in Afghanistan, clerical networks were insufficient to underpin strong central institutions because of their pervasive localism. The Harakat's origins as a parochial group and collapse into fragmentation show the organizational consequences of social structure. Yet as we will see, broader social change in Afghanistan later enabled the Taliban to deploy a reconfigured religious network that harnessed the local to the national.

Chapter 5

The Social-Institutional Argument and the Anti-Soviet War

The evidence from the period of the Soviet war in Afghanistan is generally supportive of my social-institutional theory. We see consistent linkages between prewar political networks and wartime organizations, and organizational change in the Harakat and the Shura occurred through the mechanisms we would expect to see. But other organizations also waged war in this period. I turn to two other armed actors with very different characteristics: the Hezb-e Islami of Yunis Khalis (Hezb-Khalis) and the Ittehad of Sayyed. The Hezb-Khalis splintered from Hekmatyar's Hezb almost immediately, led by the eastern tribal leader Maulavi Yunis Khalis, who mobilized tribal linkages to create a powerful but loosely organized parochial armed group. The Ittehad was a Wahhabi group supported by Saudi Arabia and Pakistan that became a fragmented fighting force despite the external aid it received. These two cases show clear support for my argument.

The Hezb-Khalis became a parochial armed group. Khalis, a cleric from Nangrahar, had some links to the Muslim Youth Organization (in part through his son) but was not heavily involved in Islamist mobilization for most of the 1970s. He had ties to Hekmatyar but was not fond of him. In the winter of 1979, Khalis broke with Hekmatyar's Hezb, and his group became known as the Hezb-Khalis.[132] This split occurred along preexisting social lines: Khalis was associated with eastern tribal and clerical networks.[133] Edwards notes that Khalis "was as much a man of the tribe as he was a party leader" and that the group was able "to work with tribal leaders and to accommodate tribal customs."[134] The links that Khalis had with tribal leaders such as Jalaluddin Haqqani enabled him to mobilize them under his organizational umbrella; as Roy notes, Khalis's "social networks were both political (Islamist) and tribal."[135]

The new organization reflected the social characteristics of the ulema and the tribes of the east. The ties between leaders were weak, as each leader primarily looked to local networks. Rubin argues that "Khalis reverted to his role as the religious leader of a mainly Ghilzai tribal coalition."[136] The Hezb-Khalis thus took on a parochial form, and "within Hezb-i Islami (Khales) a number of competing networks could be distinguished."[137] Many of these subgroups were connected to the ISI, and the networks of Jalaluddin Haqqani and Amin Wardak operated independently of Khalis.[138] There was no intense feuding or violent splits. Instead, local factions ran their own operations without interference from the center; as Dorronsoro observes, Khalis "had little concern for organizational niceties."[139] This was workable during the anti-Soviet jihad, when the focus was on maintaining guerrilla warfare rather than creating territorial forces.[140]

The key benefit the Hezb-Khalis drew from its parochial social base was an organizational presence at the local level. Yet this social base limited the Hezb-Khalis in three ways. First, centralization was weak; Khalis acted as a broker more than he did as a commander. As Edward notes, a number of the key commanders "were able to act independently and effectively."[141] Second, because of the weakness at the center, the Hezb-Khalis was unable to socialize new recruits into a shared core mission. Third, the Hezb-Khalis's networks were specific to eastern Afghanistan; the organization did not have a broad reach. The politicized networks that Khalis drew on were not created in anticipation of protracted guerrilla war, and converting them to this task carried with it both advantages and limits. Organizational function followed social form.

Sayyaf's Ittehad, by contrast, advanced an aggressive form of foreign-inflected Islam. Sayyaf, who had been part of the Islamist milieu in Kabul and had strong links with Saudi Arabia, established Ittehad after getting out of Afghan jail.[142] He was based in Peshawar and had money to offer: the organization was "mainly a vehicle by which its leader distributed the funds he collected from Arab sources."[143] However, while Sayyef had some vertical ties to his birthplace, Paghman, the other members he attracted were "a mix of disgruntled Islamists and fundamentalists... and... mercenary groups."[144] According to Rubin, "This party was linked to virtually no social networks in Afghanistan."[145] The social underpinnings created a fragmented organization with no internal control or cohesion; the structure was loose and amorphous.

Edwards argues that "Sayyaf's Ittehad and Rabbani's Jamiat were anomalous in not being strongly grounded in a prior institutional culture."[146] As a result, Sayyaf used money to gain supporters, who consisted of "marginal commanders and groups that had come into conflict with their superiors."[147] An "aggregation of isolated units" was not a recipe for cohesion and organization building, and although Sayyaf attracted followers in the 1980s, they were "fragmented and barely under the party's control."[148] This organization follows the trajectory my theory predicts: weak preexisting horizontal and vertical social ties led to a fragmented organization characterized by almost no central control. Neither ideology nor external support could overcome this structural starting point.

Building the Insurgency, 1973–1988

This chapter only scratches the surface of the extraordinary complexity of Afghanistan at war during the 1980s. It has focused on whether my social-institutional arguments provide consistent explanations for the pattern of insurgent mobilization that emerged during this period. There is a clear correspondence between the structure of politicized networks that predate the onset of war and the subsequent patterns of insurgent organization. Leaders had differential access to Afghanistan's complex social terrain, and these differences contributed to varying types of organizations. Parochial, vanguard, and fragmented groups dominated the militancy; the integrated Shura of Massoud was an exception, but even that group was restricted to a particular social terrain. The implications of these group structures for the broader resistance were profound: no single group was able to become dominant because all had key organizational limits.[149]

Major change occurred in two of the six cases I examined: the Shura shifted from a vanguard group to an integrated organization and the Harakat moved from a parochial group to a fragmented one. In both cases, the processes of change resembled what we would expect from the initial organizational forms. Massoud started with a base of urbanized Panjshiris and then cut deals and forged alliances with local power holders to build a strong local organization that remained centrally robust. The creation of local alliances made it possible to change the networks that the group could use to create and sustain formal institutions. The Harakat's social origins pushed the group toward weak central control and hyperlocalism, which all of the competing armed actors exploited and that badly undermined the organization.

Other factors cannot be dismissed. Pakistan shaped which organizations received resources, as did the Americans and the Saudis. Nationalism and religion were important motives that pushed fighters and commanders into the war in the first place. Individual leaders helped and hurt armed groups, from Massoud's skillful bargaining with local forces to Hekmatyar's contemptuous dismissal of his rivals. Understandings of identity and politics were produced and reconfigured by political and social entrepreneurs. Yet while these factors—and many others—put pressure on groups, they did not determine how they responded to challenges.[150] Patterns of organization cut across variables such as ethnicity, external support, and categories of ideological commitment.[151] These patterns demonstrate support for this book's theoretical framework.

STATE FAILURE IN AFGHANISTAN, 1989–1994

The war in Afghanistan took a new form when the Soviets finally left Afghanistan in 1988. They continued to provide resources and support to the Najibullah regime in Kabul, which managed to hold off the mujahideen groups until the loss of Russian aid in 1991–1992. The period of 1989–1994 was one of overall political fragmentation and continued violence. The mujahideen forces became either players in the battle for Kabul or localized armed actors. Former elements of the regime recoalesced into a series of militia forces, joined sides with a mujahideen force, or fled into exile. The war at the national level was complex and scattered, fought by numerous small organizations and a few larger armed groups that nevertheless did not span the nation. Rather than walking through the labyrinthine maneuverings of this period, I briefly assess the surviving insurgent groups as a precursor to addressing the rise of the Taliban from 1994 onward. I do not study the warlord groups and the Hezb-e Wahdat because they were not seeking control of either the central state or their own secessionist state; instead, they aimed to maintain loose autonomy and often grew out of the collapsed communist regime.[152]

Patterns of Continuity

There was substantial continuity in the organizational structure of the armed groups from the 1980s. Hekmatyar's Hezb could not build broad, reliable local control; Massoud's tightly disciplined forces could not expand far; the Jamiat remained a loose coalition; and the Harakat continued to be fragmented and essentially nonexistent as a coherent group. As Dorronsoro argues, "No organisation was truly represented at the national level, since party discipline was generally less strong than local solidarity."[153] In this fragmented landscape, Sinno notes, "winners differed from losers not by their ideology but by the way they structured their organizations."[154] Broadly speaking, there was some "ethnicization" of the conflict, though inter- and intraethnic alliances and clashes were endemic.[155] While external involvement continued to be important, the profusion of weaponry and shadow economies throughout Afghanistan reduced the leverage sponsors could gain from resource flows.[156]

This was a particularly complex environment for the Jamiat, which included the northeastern forces of Massoud, Ismail Khan in Herat, and alliances with Dostum and others. Maley notes that the factions within Jamiat were "based on attachments to particular individuals."[157] Rabbani was a central player in the coalitional games of government formation and collapse in Kabul, but he was not in charge of a powerful war-fighting organization of his own. Dorronsoro argues that "Masud and Ismail Khan belonged theoretically to the same party, but for the most part behaved as autonomous or even competing powers."[158] Barfield concurs: "Masud commanded his army, and the troops were loyal to him, not Rabbani."[159]

The networks Hekmatyar accessed had limited reach into local communities. He was able to create some independent standing forces, known as the Lashkar-i Isar (Army of Sacrifice). But these forces were heavily drawn from residents of refugee camps who were socially disembedded.[160] These forces were more "modern" in some ways than their competitors; they were mobile and not yoked to a particular geographic locale, making them useful in the pursuit of central power. For instance, as Rubin summarizes, "the Army of Sacrifice simply bypassed those [local] social structures as it traversed the territories of Paktia and Logar."[161]

The continual need for manpower and social support in Afghanistan's punishing military environment meant that this was not an ideal outcome. Hekmatyar still had to rely on loose alliances with local groups for presence and control in communities. This meant that he could not reliably expand his fighting power because, as Sinno observes, "the patronage component of his organization was vulnerable to the same centrifugal forces that afflicted the patronage-based parties."[162] This created problems with recruitment and socialization.[163] The Hezb remained limited by its own social geography and by its unwillingness to pragmatically ally with local social forces.[164] In this case, leadership agency pushed in the same direction as structure. The group's history of fratricide and betrayal meant that it was deeply distrusted by the other contenders for national power and was often excluded from coalitions in Kabul.[165] Pakistani aid and Hekmatyar's growing exploitation of the opium economy did not have major effects on his organization one way or another.

During this period Massoud's Shura faced off against Hekmatyar's Hezb around Kabul. (Despite its technical dissolution, I continue to refer to Massoud's organization as the Shura for the sake of continuity.)[166] The social roots of the command core remained the same throughout the 1990s, as Giustozzi explains: "At the top of his organization, until the end Massud always relied on a small network of educated and trained Panjshiris, or individuals linked to Panjshir, occasionally accommodating a few Badakhshanis among them."[167] Panjshiris dominated the military side of the Shura.[168] This was a narrow but robust social base, one that had the horizontal and vertical links that were essential for building strong institutions. Physical and administrative infrastructure was constructed in Shura-controlled areas that made both mobilization and control possible, and the organizational structure was strong enough to keep functioning while Massoud was in Kabul.[169]

The limits of Massoud's organization continued to be similar to those of the 1980s. There were problems with mobilizing non-Panjshiris.[170] Social structure created a brake on expansion, as Giustozzi observes: "Beyond Panjshir and few other areas, the structure headed by Massud remained quite loose."[171] Massoud used his organizational acumen and tactical skills to strengthen this social-institutional backing.[172] The Shura tapped into a broad array of resource flows that included smuggling, some foreign aid, and gems.[173] Like Hekmatyar's Hezb, the Shura avoided the supposedly debilitating effects of wealth, but these resources did not solve some of its core problems.

Thus during the 1989–1994 period we see substantial continuities in the major armed groups despite a radically new political context. This shifts in national power had the greatest effect on new warlord and local groups that emerged from the wreckage of the regime. The more established insurgent groups, in contrast, faced new challenges but continued to reflect prior social-institutional patterns. The crucial challenge for these organizations came with the rise of a new force on the military and political stage of Afghanistan.

1994–2001: The Rise of the Taliban

This fractured landscape of Afghanistan was transformed in 1994 by the growth of the Taliban, which swept from the south to eventually control most of the country. The Taliban was markedly more integrated than most of its competitors: it was "disciplined, motivated and ruthless in attaining [its] aims."[174] I will show that the Taliban's organizational resilience at both the central and local levels was drawn from its leaders' ability to mobilize new networks that had formed during the 1980s. Processes of migration and education created a new social base of rural clerics with stronger horizontal ties with each other who could build a central organization. These ties were born of the social circumstances created by the war in the 1980s, particularly the education of thousands of Pashtuns in schools and camps in Pakistan. This is why the Taliban, unlike the Harakat, was able to stay cohesive with clerical leaders while incorporating new local factions. As Harpviken notes, "What was remarkable was the ability to transcend the fragmentary tendencies of Pashtun society, and build a larger-scale organization with considerable coherence."[175]

The Origins of the Taliban

During the 1980s there were enormous refugee flows between Afghanistan and Pakistan as people fled the fighting. In Pakistan new networks emerged and old networks evolved in the face of massive dislocation. The outflows were driven by suffering and fear rather than a clever calculation of how to construct new networks for a possible future rebellion in the context of post-Soviet chaos. As Ruttig notes, the war "gradually undermined and transformed the traditional relationships of village, tribal, and ethnic communities."[176] Religious schools were a popular choice for the education of boys in exile.[177] Particularly prominent, though by no means unique, were the madrasas linked to the Pakistani party Jamiat Ulema-e-Islam in the Northwest Frontier Province and Balochistan.[178] These educational institutions played a key role in bringing together Afghans (primarily Pashtuns) from different areas and backgrounds. As Rubin notes, "the madrasa networks created ties among a potential new elite while other institutions were being destroyed.... The ulama became more autonomous in exile and in warlord-dominated Afghanistan."[179]

In Dorronsoro's analysis, the rise of the madrasa as a locus of socialization and mobilization had "two major consequences for their Afghan graduates: the cementing of strong solidarities, emerging from a shared experience and a common world view; and ... the appearance of transnational networks."[180] Linkages were formed that tied together individuals, disparate networks, and rural localities in a new social constituency.[181] The graduates of these schools entered the war in Afghanistan during the anti-Soviet jihad or the battle over Kabul.[182] They joined a variety of different armed groups in the Pashtun belt, but like many others, they were often disillusioned by the ineptitude and failures of the mujahideen leadership.

Southern Afghanistan in particular suffered from the organizational disarray of the mujahideen. The Harakat had a strong following in the south, but as shown above it had faltered despite early popularity. After the Harakat evaporated as an organized force, no other organization established control of the area. Hekmatyar had pockets of loyalists but little serious presence, and the northern and western militias had no access to this region.

Within this vacuum, a group of mujahideen veterans with strong ties to the madrasas of Pakistan mobilized to impose some form of stability. Led by Mullah Omar, this new proto-organization was underpinned by previous combat and educational experiences. Dorronsoro emphasizes the central importance of the shared experience of education in Pakistani madrasas in the 1980s, while Goodson notes that they also had often fought together in the Afghan-Soviet war and that they were of the same age cohort (most were in their mid-thirties or early forties).[183] Clerics, refugees, and veterans were the essential social base of the organization.[184] Harpviken analyzes the result of the similarities among the members: "Unlike the early Pashtun resistance.... the Taliban could start out with a military core, consisting of recruits from the madrasa, whose students were easily controlled."[185] One particular madrasa, that of Sami ul-Haq, trained a substantial portion of the eventual Taliban leadership.[186] Rashid quotes one of the early members discussing these relationships:

> "We all knew each other—Mullahs Omar, Ghaus, Mohammed Rabbani (no relation to President Rabbani) and myself—because we were all originally from Urozgan and had fought together," said Mullah Hassan. "I moved back and forth from Quetta and attended madrassas there, but whenever we got together we would discuss the terrible plight of our people living under these bandits. We were people of the same opinions and we got on with each very well, so it was easy to come to a decision to do something."[187]

Abou Zahab and Roy agree on the role of the madrasas in the Taliban: "The Taliban recruited mainly among the students of a network of rural and Pushtun religious schools (madrasas).... During the war the links with the Pakistani madrasas were strengthened."[188]

The initial operations of the Taliban sought to clear warlords and gangs from the Kandahar area and from important transit routes. In this they gained the support of Pakistani policymakers who had tired of Hekmatyar's inability to gain and hold territory. Various degrees of Pakistani support are suggested in the literature, and there is no doubt that Pakistan played an important role, but, as Edwards notes, "the manpower and the motivation behind the [Taliban] movement cannot be explained away entirely as a Pakistani fabrication."[189] Crucial to the Taliban's success was its ability to exploit and take advantage of Pakistani aid rather than allowing it to become a source of intraorganizational feuding or be squandered by a weak local organization.

Maley notes that many of the new Taliban had "been combatants in Mujahideen parties, most commonly the Hezb-e Islami of Khalis, and the Harakat of Mawlawi Muhammadi (who strongly supported the Taliban)."[190] Former local units of the Harakat became linked to the Taliban, and the clerics loyal to the Taliban acted as bridges across previous factional divides.[191] These forces could now be integrated into a broader structure through ties of trust and communication that had been absent earlier in the war. In Loya Paktia, for instance, "Harakat networks transferred their allegiance to the Taliban, and Taliban networks of the plain areas are still generally structured around Harakat factional lines and commanders who chose to stay with the Taliban.... Taliban networks stem from old or newly created Deobandi networks."[192] This social infrastructure enabled the organization to transcend tribal divisions: "they were linked across tribes by their common madrasa background, as well as by subethnic solidarity among Qandahari Pashtuns."[193] Barfield notes that "one of the reasons for their particular success among Pashtuns was their ability to sidestep existing tribal leaders hamstrung by local rivalries."[194]

The war in Afghanistan created new social formations that became resources for rebellion, in unexpected and unintended ways. The networks that went to war under the Taliban banner were not the result of the triumph of tradition or representations of the unchanging Afghan "tribal" past but instead the result of a wrenching process of structural change and political innovation.[195] Along with external support and access to various resources, this mosque network enabled the Taliban "to penetrate society" at both the local level and among organizers.[196] As Ruttig summarizes, "the movement emerged from religious networks that were part of the 1978–1989 resistance," and its motivation was "political, based on a religious infrastructure."[197] Rather than a spontaneous expression of ethnic solidarity, a response to political context, or a reflection of an abstract ideological vision, the Taliban was the result of a very specific social and religious network.[198]

The Taliban thus was able to tap into local communities while retaining strong links across them. Social ties also played a key role in maintaining cohesion over time, as Dorronsoro explains:

> Positions of authority were held entirely by ulema belonging to the closed circle of "historic" Taliban—those who had joined in the early days. The social homogeneity of the Taliban leadership and the unchallenged authority of *mullah* Omar may explain why there were never internecine armed clashes or moves towards defections as a result of internal tensions, even after resounding defeats such as that at Mazar-i Sharif in 1997. In this the Taliban differed from all other Afghan parties.[199]

This was true even as the organization incorporated new factions and new recruits—social heterogeneity among the top ranks was minimal, though there was more diversity among midlevel commanders.[200] Integration was not driven by Mullah Omar's charisma: according to Maley, he "had little mass charismatic appeal, and was a poor speaker, but was respected for his piety."[201] Mullah Omar was not a uniquely brilliant broker and visionary; the Taliban "governed through a collective political leadership, which was consultative and consensus-building, rather than dominated by one individual."[202] But Omar was embedded in a social base that provided distinct advantages for mobilization. Although the networks within the early Taliban were not monolithic, they cooperated with each other.[203]

Omar and his command core did not play the role of isolated brokers, as Rabbani did. The local clerics had strong ties to a variety of leadership figures and to other clerics across space.[204] This was also not a tribal organization. While it could rely on tribal ties, the Taliban also attempted to transcend particularistic tribal loyalties.[205] Dorronsoro writes that "the Taliban rebuilt a centralized authority at a local level, exploiting its alliances with local solidary networks."[206] The Taliban reached into Pashtun society in a way that Hekmatyar's Hezb had never been able to and created central control in a way that Khalis's Hezb and the Harakat had failed to do.[207] In clear contrast to the Hezb, "the success of the Taliban movement is crucially linked to its mobilization of existing organizations."[208]

The Taliban became more popular, or at least accepted, because of its ability to impose order, but this capability followed social mobilization rather than preceded it.[209] The social origins of the Taliban, therefore, laid the basis for an integrated organizational structure. As Rubin explains, "The Taliban both mobilized social capital created in madrasas to create a homogeneous leadership group linked to political networks in Pakistan and used assistance from Pakistan and Saudi governments and traders to build up a military force and buy off opponents."[210]

The Pursuit of National Power, 1995–2001

The dynamics of military offensives, counteroffensives, and campaigns that emerged from 1995 until 2001 are far too intricate to detail. Broadly speaking, the strains of war had already undermined the cohesion of most of Afghanistan's contenders for power and essentially wiped out several others. The rise of the Taliban added further stress that triggered defections and infighting. Hekmatyar's units abandoned him, Dostum's militia became internally divided, Khan's group suffered spirals of defection and feuding before collapsing, and Massoud and Rabbani were forced back into an ever-shrinking northeastern redoubt. The Taliban incorporated factions of other armed groups and absorbed blocs that were defecting from its rivals. This mix of expansion and control was enormously powerful.

In 1994 the grim game of government formation, violence, and bargaining continued in Kabul with Hekmatyar and Massoud as key adversaries. The Shiite Hezb-i Wahdat and Dostum's Jombesh were also important players around Kabul, Khan controlled the area around Herat, and a hodgepodge of Harakat, Hezb-Khalis, Hezb, and local warlords operated in the east and south.[211] The Taliban's cohesion and momentum and the Pakistani aid it received allowed it to begin a process of coercion and co-optation against these forces. The Taliban redeployed local Harakat and other networks in the south, relying on the horizontal ties between clerical leaders bound by shared educational and wartime experiences from the 1980s and early 1990s. In the east, the Taliban gained the support of key factions of Khalis's Hezb, another group with a strong clerical underpinning. It also mobilized links to Jalaluddin Haqqani in the east to co-opt this powerful factional commander after initial opposition. He became a trusted but subordinate military commander.

Unlike Rabbani's organization, however, the Taliban did not need to embrace a loose coalition of factional commanders.[212] Many commanders with clerical backgrounds and ties to Deobandi or Pakistani networks were integrated through existing connections, making expansion possible without degradation. A robust leadership with links to a variety of diverse networks managed this institutionalization process better than a single broker trying to control many unrelated factions.[213] The Taliban used local information, exploited rivalries, and provided money from sales of opium and from external support to trigger defections without having to fight, thus creating a cascade of new members.[214] Ruttig explains the usefulness of the clerical network for mobilization: once in power in an area, "the Taliban regime made [the Islamic clergy] its 'eyes and ears' in the villages."[215]

Hekmatyar was the Taliban's primary opponent in the east among the Pashtuns, and he was targeted in Taliban offensives.[216] Despite extensive Pakistani support and a clear ideology for his organization, Hekmatyar "had proven incapable of seizing and controlling defended territory: in this respect he was a bitter disappointment to his patrons."[217] The contrast with the Taliban is stark: "Hekmatyar's Hizb failed to overcome the same opponents the Taliban trounced, even though it enjoyed the exact same advantages [of Pakistani support]."[218] This organizational pattern was a result of the urban, detribalized Islamist ties that the Hezb was built upon. The legacies of this foundational social base persisted because of the Hezb's inability to build local alliances.

In the face of the Taliban, "Hekmatyar's party... proved so weakly rooted within Afghanistan's Pashtun regions that their military units dissolved in the face of the Taliban advance."[219] Hekmatyar's local commanders switched sides or gave up in remarkably short order in 1995 and 1996, further evidence of his inability to penetrate the Afghan countryside.[220] The Taliban deployed its own networks to flip Hezb factions from below. Strongholds fell, commanders defected, and the Hezb-i Islami essentially disappeared from eastern Afghanistan as a major force.[221] Thus, "even the tenacious Hekmatyar, who had patiently built his organization over some twenty years of struggle, had to see his followers abandon him without even the pretense of a fight."[222] He and a number of his loyal followers fled from Afghanistan, though they would return after 9/11. This change shows how vanguard groups can be vulnerable to revolts from below in the face of new military and organizational pressures.[223]

As Hekmatyar's organization disintegrated, the remaining key players engaged in a complex mix of alliances with and against the Taliban. Massoud's forces remained disciplined and effective and formed "the most cohesive and centralized organization facing the Taliban."[224] However, he relied on others to guard flanks and control territory beyond the Shura's home terrain. The Taliban struggled with new challenges of mobile warfare but were able to hold together in the face of defeats and adversity in early and mid-1995. Ismail Khan launched an offensive in the summer of 1995 that exposed serious cracks within his own organization, showing how rare and valuable Taliban integration was.[225] He drew on various local factions in his domain to create a mobile expeditionary force to march on Kandahar. Giustozzi describes the result: a "motley collection of disparate groups from subordinate military leaders and external allies compounded pre-existing problems linked to the absence of a professional officer corps and effective command and control."[226] Initial advances succeeded but Taliban counterattacks led to "chaos"[227] among Khan's forces, and he abandoned the field of battle. This outcome reflected deeper structural problems in his group: the military structure was only weakly integrated and relied heavily on the charisma of a few leaders at the top, and Khan's troops were "fragmented and out of control."[228] A parochial militia, Khan's organization collapsed when adversity came.

The Taliban was then able to pivot east back to Kabul, taking Jalalabad and Kabul in late 1996. Shah Ahmed Massoud, the Hezb-i Wahdat, and Rashid Abdul Dostum were forced into an alliance. However, Dostum's parochial warlord organization was under continual threat from internal feuding, which broke out most dramatically when Abdul Malik Pahlawan, Dostum's second-in-command, launched a coup against him and temporarily linked up with the Taliban in 1997.[229] The inability of Dostum's armed organization—like that of Khan's—to maintain internal cohesion shows how essential organizational control is to success in Afghanistan.

The Taliban systematically defeated its vanguard and parochial rivals. Once its forces seized control beyond the Pashtun areas, they garrisoned and controlled these regions from the center. Through September 11, 2001, the Taliban slowly but surely pushed back Rabbani and Massoud, the most organized remnants of the Northern Alliance, who clung to the northeast with the aid of foreign support and revenue from gems and other resources. The Taliban and Al-Qaeda assassinated Massoud just before 9/11, a killing that placed them tantalizingly close to completing their victory.

The Taliban was remarkably effective at conducting mobile warfare. Barfield attributes its success to its professional military arm, with other

Afghan insurgent groups lacked.[230] This made it a "highly coordinated and skilled organization."[231] The organization continued to rely heavily on Kandahari Pashtuns and clerics for leadership, which provided continuity.[232] Yet there were avenues for other commanders to join the group and become influential; in particular, the clerical networks made it possible for the group to incorporate both Durrani and Ghilzai Pashtuns.[233] This was not a perfectly unified or administratively adept organization, and there were internal tensions, resistance to conscription and taxation, and enduring armed challenges to its power.[234] Nevertheless, the Taliban was much more integrated than most of its rivals, as Mullah Omar remained in "total control of the movement."[235] Social origins built and sustained institutions that helped create an efficient system of command and control, even in the face of financial and physical constraints.[236] The Taliban's treatment of civilians was brutal and unsparing, but this victimization was not caused by loot-seeking thuggishness. Instead, it reflected a strategic and political vision that intrinsically relied on coercion and social control.

During this period the Pakistani state had trouble maintaining tight control of the Taliban. As Rashid argues, "despite [Pakistan's] efforts to help and control the Taliban, they were nobody's puppets and they resisted every attempt by Islamabad to pull their strings."[237] The Taliban charted its own course as ruler in Kabul and as governor in large swathes of Afghanistan.[238] In this governance, "they maintained some control through a polycentric system of ruling shuras, a network of informants and dedicated followers, and a monopoly over the taxation of poppy production and smuggling."[239] They also killed or drove into exile rivals in the Pashtun community as a mechanism of intimidation.

The organizational success of the Taliban can be traced to various causes, from the geopolitical maneuverings of Pakistan to foolish strategic decisions by its foes. Yet a core reason for its success was its ability to create organizational integration despite enormous challenges. Its enemies faced much deeper problems of internal control than the Taliban did, and as a consequence the Taliban was able to defeat them.

The Taliban After 9/11

The rise of the Taliban was linked to its sheltering of Osama bin Laden and Al-Qaida.[240] After the 9/11 attacks, however, the connection with Al-Qaeda led to the overthrow of the Taliban regime as the United States worked with the Northern Alliance. The Taliban were driven from the field as a conventional force because of their inability to match the "hammer and anvil"[241] combination of air and ground power that the U.S.-led coalition deployed against them. Hamid Karzai became president in Kabul and power in Afghanistan returned to a weak central regime and a variety of local power holders and warlords.[242] The Taliban leadership fled to Pakistan and revived the movement, this time as a force for guerrilla insurgency rather than the quasi-conventional combat of the 1990s.[243] Since the mid-2000s, the Taliban has waged an effective war against the Afghan government and international forces.

This book cannot consider the ultimate fate of the Taliban after 9/11, for obvious reasons. In the decade that we can study, however, it appears that the "neo-Taliban" retains underlying social-institutional similarities that help account for its ability to rebuild and maintain its war.[244] As Ruttig argues, "One of the main features of the Taliban is that it has shown more continuity than discontinuity between the pre- and post-2001 phases in its organizational structure, including the composition of its leadership, ideology, political aims, and programs. Most importantly, the movement still adheres to its undisputed and single most important leader, Mullah Muhammad Omar."[245] As my theory predicts, the Taliban continues to "rely on personal relations as an organizational tool"[246] and draws heavily on clerical networks that can coordinate collective action and control. It resisted the efforts of both the United States and Pakistan to destroy or manipulate it after 9/11 and has forged comparatively robust, albeit imperfect, institutions of command and control.[247]

Religious-institutional horizontal linkages have remained crucial for coordinating and controlling local mobilization.[248] The Taliban is embedded in social life in ways that maintain local embeddedness while surmounting the challenges of localism. There is no active defiance and there are no violent internal feuds.[249] After 9/11, Mullah Omar remained in control of a "disciplined group."[250] Crucially, "the Taliban managed to build transtribal groups (even between tribes that are normally opposed)."[251] Ruttig describes how the Taliban are linked to its social environment:

> At the core of the movement, in its Kandahari mainstream from which its leadership is recruited, the andiwali (comradeship) factor plays a decisive role in keeping the networks together. Among today's Taliban, there are three different types of andiwal networks: religious (their original madrasas and mosques), political (their original tanzim), and the tribal (their ancestry and watan).... but the common experience that unifies the Kandahari mainstream was gathered during the jihad against the Soviets.[252]

There certainly seems to be greater local autonomy and thus weaker local control than there was before 9/11. The Taliban is not a perfectly disciplined, highly centralized war machine. The systematic campaign of leadership decapitation the United States has carried out has likely had some effect in undermining the group, but as of this writing there have not been the major defections, internal feuds, or splits that were endemic in other Afghan armed groups. The Taliban has held together despite an intense, protracted campaign against it.

Alongside the Taliban, two other forces of importance have remained since 9/11. The first is the "Haqqani network" in the east, which is subordinate to Mullah Omar but acts fairly autonomously. This group is built around social ties that have been used for the purpose of war since its time as part of Khalis' Hezb.[253] The second is Hekmatyar's Hezb-i Islami. Hekmatyar returned from Iran and reactivated some organizational presence in the east in 2002. Though small and isolated, the Hezb-Gulbuddin has intriguing links to "mainstream" Afghan politics. In both cases these leaders "simply revived their old networks, shifting their opposition from the Soviets to the United States. Because they have an already-existing command structure and willing support from Pakistan, it did not take them long to breathe new life into an old conflict."[254] Social origins and legacies have shaped organizations even in the face of an entirely new political context, different counterinsurgent forces, and a shifting international environment.

Building Rebellion in Afghanistan

Politicized networks have sustained militancy in Afghanistan, from communists and Islamists in 1970s Kabul to the new social formations that wage rebellion as the Taliban. Structural origins have limited the capacity of many groups to change, but good strategy and the agency of some leaders have opened possibilities for evolution and adaptation. War created new pressures and opportunities that were responded to in different ways by different groups. Change occurred through pathways that derived from origins, while the enduring power of initial social coalitions and their institutional consequences made continuity possible. Social resources provided crucial advantages for some groups and marginalized others.

This argument explains important dynamics in Afghanistan's wars. It makes sense of the different trajectories of groups and of the effects of other variables on insurgent organizations. A number of other factors have affected the development of the insurgent groups in Afghanistan, but my argument helps us understand how these factors mattered. For instance, specific differences between the insurgent groups cannot be explained by simply pointing to Afghanistan's regime type or state weakness, which were shared across all the groups. When considered through the lens of my argument, however, we can see why Soviet, American, and Afghan counterinsurgency policies undermined some groups but not others, and why the Taliban was able to take advantage of the 1990s state failure while its rivals were not. Explaining which armed groups are able to build and maintain organizations helps us understand how they will navigate complicated war environments.

Similarly, while material resources and external state sponsorship were obviously important, my argument explains the varying effects of these endowments. The Hekmatyar's Hezb and the Taliban both received generous support from Pakistan, but the different ability of these groups to create robust local control processes can be explained by the Taliban's vertical embeddedness. The Harakat's access to sanctuary and some aid in Peshawar did not prevent the organization from collapsing. The effects of resources depended on the networks and institutions of the groups.

Ideological visions and new ideas were centrally important to the motivations and actions of armed actors but, like material resources, they affected different types of groups to varying degrees. Leaders struggled to create institutions to put their visions into action: many failed, succeeded only in part, or found themselves in wholly unanticipated circumstances. Structural constraints and the fundamental uncertainties of war caused consistent disjunctures between ideological hopes and organizational outcomes. Ideas can be very important to armed groups, but only when these ideologies are made part of daily social and institutional life, as opposed to distant, abstract doctrines.

Afghanistan's complex history presents some challenges to the social-institutional theory. First, the complex warlord politics that characterized Afghan politics during 1989–1996 and after 2001 era do not fit easily into my theoretical framework. These militias and armed groups, like those of Khan and Dostum, share some characteristics with insurgent groups, but they arose from state collapse and pursued goals of inclusion, patronage, and local autonomy that do not map onto conventional goals of insurgent groups. Continued research is needed on the world of warlord/militia organization.[255]

Second, ideologies that were diffused across nations influenced how militant leaders saw the world, including Islamist ideologies from Pakistan and the Gulf, Marxist-Leninist doctrines from the USSR, and Maoist frameworks from China, and I cannot provide insight into when and how these ideologies first became attractive or how they spread.

Finally, I do not cover how local armed leaders decided whether to join a broader armed group (and which to join) or to remain independent. Because I focused on the level of central leadership, my argument cannot explain how local leaders made decisions about how to deal with national leaders other than through social ties.[256]

The resurgence and resilience of the Taliban in the 2000s shows that war in Afghanistan cannot be delinked from social forces. The implications of this simple fact for Afghanistan's future are significant. Efforts to build the state from the center will require bargaining with and accommodating a variety of local actors; a simple Weberian model will not suffice. Complexity and heterogeneity will be essential in future governing structures. As armed groups other than the Taliban will struggle to build broad-ranging and enduring organizations, the Taliban is the pivotal insurgent actor in the country and its future hinges on its ability to continue to be an integrated organization.

[6]

Explaining Tamil Militancy in Sri Lanka

Sri Lanka's Tamil insurgency appears to have ended in the bloody overrunning of the final battle lines of the Liberation Tigers of Tamil Eelam (LTTE) in May 2009.[1] The annihilation of the LTTE, one of the world's most innovative, disciplined, and ruthless insurgent groups, brought to a close over three decades of terror, guerrilla warfare, and counterinsurgency. Though the LTTE was the most distinctive of the Tamil groups fighting the Sri Lankan state, it was not the only one: at least four other significant organizations were involved in the conflict. This chapter traces the rise and evolution of the Tamil militant organizations in Sri Lanka, comparing the LTTE to its contemporaries. As Hellman-Rajanayagam notes, "Other militant groups have been ruthless and fanatic, but it is only the LTTE which has managed to hold on against the odds, and we have to ask ourselves why this is so."[2]

Tamil militant groups other than the Tigers were unable to create integrated organizations. The Tamil Eelam Liberation Organization (TELO), the Eelam Revolutionary Organization of Students (EROS), the People's Liberation Organisation of Tamil Eelam (PLOT), and the Eelam People's Revolutionary Liberation Front (EPRLF) were far less disciplined than the LTTE. They found it more difficult to quickly create routinized control processes: the horizontal student links of the EROS and the EPRLF did not make up for their weak vertical ties to local communities and they became vanguard organizations, while the combination of diffuse caste mobilization and strategic decisions to expand rapidly turned the TELO and the PLOT into parochial groups that later collapsed amid internal unrest. Importantly, these groups and the LTTE received similar Indian aid and they faced the same political context as the LTTE, but they were unable to match its successes. Organizational starting points, attacks from the LTTE and the government, and poor decision-making combined to doom these organizations to progressively greater fragmentation that ended in collapse or defection to the side of the state.

I find less support for my theory in this conflict than in Kashmir or Afghanistan, though the broad contours of the theory do help explain important aspects of the record of militancy. Part of the problem is that detailed information is sparse because of the violence and dislocation of the part thirty years; we can be less confident about key facts in this war. Given what we know, it appears that my argument explains three important characteristics of the conflict's militant organization. First, the LTTE's founders and consequent command elite were disproportionately drawn from a caste network, particularly in the Jaffna Peninsula, that had historically been autonomous and characterized by a distinct social network. This small group of leaders quickly set up a vanguard organization that acted with unity and strategic clarity. Second, the other Tamil armed groups appear to have had different social bases that constrained their ability to build leadership unity and local presence. Third, the major internal division that existed in the Tigers—between northerners and easterners—reflected different social blocs and exploded into a split by 2004. Intraorganizational divisions were caused by politicized social networks.

Yet there are other areas of the empirical record that my theory cannot explain. We simply do not know enough about the Tigers' social base to confidently predict whether they should have been an integrated or vanguard group. Some of the other Tamil leaders made retrospectively foolish decisions that were only loosely linked to structural considerations. Most importantly, the leadership decisions of the LTTE's Velupillai Prabhakaran facilitated a rapid process of expansion that created an integrated organization on the ground without the need for the painstaking work of building local alliances. Disastrously counterproductive state policies may have facilitated the rapid creation of local institutions without a long process of alliance building. Prabhakaran created a set of symbols and institutions that innovatively socialized fighters and reconfigured Tamil identity. Social ties that existed through caste and student networks provided a leadership infrastructure, but they do not seem to have been integral to the growth and institutionalization of the LTTE. This is one of the most significant failures of my argument. Yet these findings are also quite helpful: they show how to disconfirm parts of my theory in a particular empirical case and they point to new research directions.

The chapter explores the origins of Sri Lanka's conflict, compares the five major Tamil groups during the 1970s and 1980s, and then explores the LTTE's trajectory after 1990. It concludes with findings, future questions, and implications for Sri Lanka's future.

[142]

Methodology

The five major Tamil groups were the LTTE, the PLOT, the TELO, the EPRLF, and the EROS (table 6.1). They varied significantly in their organizational structure, and this provides an opportunity to explore the origins and evolution of armed groups in a shared context. All of the groups represented some flavor of Tamil nationalism: the PLOT, the EROS, and the EPRLF offered a Marxist/leftist variant and the LTTE and the TELO advanced a more straightforwardly nationalist brand. The TELO and the PLOT were largely wiped out by the LTTE while they were engaged in internal feuds. The TELO was a parochial group, and the PLOT was fragmented even before the Tiger onslaught. The EROS was a vanguard group throughout its existence, reflecting the distance between overseas student activists and the actual war zone. The EPRLF maintained higher, though far from perfect, internal control and cooperation, becoming a mixed vanguard/integrated group by the late 1980s. However, it was physically annihilated in the wake of the withdrawal of the Indian Peace Keeping Force in 1990.

The tormentor of these groups was the LTTE, which suffered only two splits over its nearly 40-year existence: the PLOT split from it in 1980 and "the Karuna Group" (which became the Tamil Makkal Viduthalai Pulikal) split in 2004. There was also an effective purging of deputy commander Gopalaswamy Mahendrajaah (known as Mahattaya) in the early 1990s. The LTTE quickly became, and remained, "the most powerfully motivated, disciplined, and deadly of the militant groups."[3] It began as a vanguard group and then became an integrated organization by the

Table 6.1. Patterns of organization in Sri Lanka

Organization	Initial organizational type	Organizational change
Liberation Tigers of Tamil Eelam	Vanguard	Integrated by 1984, continued as integrated until annihilation in 2009
Tamil Eelam Liberation Organization	Parochial	Fragmented by 1987 and disappeared as insurgent force
Eelam Revolutionary Organisation of Students	Vanguard	Absorbed into LTTE in early 1990s
Eelam People's Revolutionary Liberation Force	Vanguard	Vanguard/integrated hybrid by 1987; vanguard in 1989; annihilated as insurgent group in 1990
People's Liberation Organisation of Tamil Eelam	Fragmented	Collapsed as insurgent force by 1987

mid-1980s. The core question that guides this chapter is why the Tigers achieved this superior organization even though they drew from the same ethnic category, fought the same state, operated in the same political economy, and pursued broadly similar goals as their militant contemporaries.

Though this comparative setting is helpful for assessing my theory, the evidence in this chapter is the weakest in the book.[4] As a retired Indian army intelligence officer with experience in Sri Lanka writes, "The LTTE is a complex organisation, totally shrouded in secrecy."[5] The bulk of evidence is from historical and press sources, including memoirs and writings by participants in militancy and by armed group propaganda. I also rely on a rich anthropological literature on Sri Lankan social structure; it is more sophisticated and detailed than much of the strictly political analysis. These sources are supplemented by two trips to Sri Lanka to interview politicians (including a number who were linked to militancy), analysts, academics, and journalists. One of these trips occurred before the end of the war and the other occurred after it. The interviews offered a variety of often-divergent perspectives that were valuable in sorting through the other available evidence.

The tight constraints under which political discourse and analysis occur in contemporary Sri Lanka made these interviews more fraught and circumscribed than elsewhere, and the scholarly literature on the Tamil groups is very thin. The often-dangerous and tense political environment contributes to what Whitaker refers to as the "almost hallucinogenic mutability and obscure complexity of Sri Lanka's military-political history."[6] Despite these significant limitations, I hope that the comparative framework will add to the study of rebellion and demonstrate how my analytical approach can shed new light on difficult questions.

Overview of the War

Sri Lanka is an island of 20 million people composed of three major ethnic groups—Sinhalese, Tamils, and Muslims.[7] Independent since 1948, Sri Lanka has experienced three serious civil wars: two uprisings by the left-nationalist Sinhalese Janatha Vimukthi Peramuna (JVP), in 1971 and 1987–1990, and by Tamil militants from the early/mid-1970s until 2009. The Tamil war is studied here. I examine the variations in the organizational structure of Tamil insurgent groups as they tried to survive Sri Lankan counterinsurgency, shifts in Indian support, and internal political contestation.

The war in Sri Lanka pitted five major Tamil insurgent groups against a Sri Lankan state that over time grew militarily powerful and politically resolved to destroy militancy. It was primarily fought in the northern and eastern areas of Sri Lanka. In the initial years, much of the fighting was in urban Jaffna and its environs, then it shifted over time to the jungles and lagoons of the Wanni region. From 1972 to 1990, this was a guerrilla conflict, though in the 1980s Tamil militants loosely controlled territory. There were five major groups at war in the 1980s. From 1987 to 1990, the Indian Peace Keeping Force (IPKF) attempted to pacify the north and east, engaging in counterinsurgency against the LTTE while supporting the EPRLF as a paramilitary.

After 1990 the conflict resumed between the LTTE and the Sri Lankan government. The four non-LTTE groups had been destroyed, were absorbed by the Tigers, or had defected to the side of the government by this point. In the 1990s, the war took on the form of mixed conventional/irregular combat. The LTTE's strategy was to carve out and hold territory as a way to eventually compel the international community to recognize an independent Tamil Eelam. After the failure of a cease-fire that had lasted from 2002 to 2006, the war ended in May 2009 after a major three-year campaign by the government's forces to destroy the Tigers and re-establish control over the entire island. The bulk of the LTTE leadership was killed, including Prabhakaran, and many of its foot soldiers were killed or captured. The remnants of the organization are now overseas or are trying to avoid capture in Sri Lanka. Over the course of the war, at least 70,000 people died, including a large number of civilians. This was one of Asia's most intense civil conflicts, in large part because of the tenacity, ruthlessness, and skill of the LTTE.

Communal Conflict in Sri Lanka

By the 1970s, a variety of student, revolutionary, and party blocs in Tamil society were opposed to the Sinhalese-dominated regime. The roots of this politicized opposition reach back deep into history.[8] By the time of partial Portuguese colonization in the sixteenth century, there were Tamil and Sinhalese kingdoms in Sri Lanka (known until 1972 as Ceylon). Though these were distinguishable identities, their salience varied significantly across time and across areas: caste and regional divisions within both blocs were enormously important, and some Tamil royal families were linked to the (Sinhalese) Kingdom of Kandy. The politics of this period featured intricate alliances, expediency, and intraethnic division.

Caste in Tamil Society

Among Tamils, an important caste structure developed, centered on the Vellala land-owning caste.[9] Vellala caste dominance was contested in three ways. First, lower groups on the Jaffna Peninsula tried to assimilate themselves into higher castes, leading to concerns among "true" Vellalas that their category was being rendered impure. Second, groups in the east, especially in Batticaloa and its environs, tried to distance themselves from Vellala dominance and often looked more to Kandy than to Jaffna.[10] An enduring distinction between northern and eastern Tamils has characterized Sri Lanka.[11] This included different social and caste structures.[12]

Third, the Karaiyar fishing caste used its distinct sea-faring occupation and higher levels of conversion to Christianity as means of maintaining autonomy distinct from Vellala control.[13] The Karaiyar and Vellala were two of the main caste groups in the north, especially around Jaffna, while the east had a distinct lower-status position. The minority Karaiyar caste carved out a distinct social space: Wilson argues that "the Karaiyars constitute an independent and powerful entity in Tamil society."[14] The Karaiyar reproduced their autonomy over time while gaining a niche in smuggling and trading activities along the northern and eastern coasts of Sri Lanka.[15] As Asaratnam notes, "The coastal villages of Vadamarachchi became their power base and remain so to the present day. They vigorously maintained their autonomy through the colonial period, and after, because their strength lay in their independent economic activity, unrelated to the lands and its rules."[16] Some Karaiyar land-owning elites existed in the east around Batticaloa, and they often had contact with northern members of the caste through trade.[17]

During British colonial rule, the Vellala became the favored caste group in Jaffna.[18] Nevertheless, as Arasaratnam points out, "The karaiyar or fishing caste had to a great extent engineered its emancipation from Vellala domination by the 1930s. Endowed with notions of peer status, a characteristic which the Tamil karaiyar caste shared with its Sinhalese counterpart the karava, the karaiyar had utilized the vehicle of the Catholic Church to free themselves from the trammels of caste obligation."[19] The fishing caste group was able to maintain its autonomy from the Vellala-dominated caste hierarchy of Jaffna. About 10 percent of Tamils in Sri Lanka are Karaiyar. Among the Vellala, who constitute 50 percent of the Tamil population, there were recurrent fears of assimilation from below as rising subcastes adopted Vellala traits as a means of upward mobility.[20] While the caste structure remained rigid, there was a persistent sense of unease and fragility within the Vellala community, which does not appear to have had the coherence of the Karaiyar.[21] Instead, processes of capital accumulation and social emulation left the Vellala category simultaneously fluid and rigid, as those holding this status attempted, often futilely, to prevent those below from achieving the same status.[22] These divisions remained salient even when Sinhalese and Tamil ethnolinguistic mobilization became the primary focus of politics in Sri Lanka.[23]

Linguistic Mobilization through 1948

The British consolidated their control of Ceylon after a series of wars with Kandy, establishing dominance throughout the island by the mid-1820s. The absence of mass political enfranchisement meant that politics was an elite game. However, growing mass and intellectual mobilization by Sinhalese Buddhists in the latter decades of the nineteenth century and early years of the twentieth opposed Ceylon's political and economic elites. Buddhist monks, the *sangha*, played an important role in this movement.[24] As Ceylon moved toward democratization, the political incentives of the elite players began to shift.[25] If majority rule were to become a major feature of the island's politics, voters would need to be found. Since Sinhalese formed the majority of the population, winning their votes became the key quest for Sinhalese politicians. Language issues took on rapidly growing salience in politics. The Tamil population attempted to blunt the rising tide of Sinhalese majoritarianism by demanding some sort of power-sharing arrangement.

Independence and Violence, 1948–1972

After independence, the Sri Lankan political elite became fractured. By 1956, it had become clear to Sinhalese political leaders that they could win votes by primarily appealing to the Sinhalese majority.[26] S. W. R. D. Bandaranaike upped the ante in this linguistic competition by declaring a "Sinhala-only" language policy. The Tamil political bloc attempted to maintain its position of predominance in the state structure: though a demographic minority, their education and skills with English had led the British to favor them for government employment.[27] A discourse of Tamil "traditional homelands" emerged in Tamil political circles.[28] Sri Lanka's unitary political system reduced the room for bargaining.[29] Intense electoral competition was accompanied by riots, civil disobedience, and rhetorics of dominance among Sinhalese and defiance among Tamils.[30] Under the Sri Lanka Freedom Party's Sirimavo Bandaranaike, especially after 1970, the language issue favored the Sinhalese even more, especially when standards for university education changed in ways that favored Sinhalese over Tamils. The Federal Party became the political voice of Tamil mobilization, but Sinhalese chauvinism created growing fractures within Tamil politics as networks of students and separatists began to emerge.

Chapter 6

SOCIAL ORIGINS OF TAMIL MILITANCY, 1970–1983

This political mobilization provided the impetus for the outbreak of Sri Lanka's ethnolinguistic war. There was low-level militant mobilization among young Tamils in the late 1960s (especially 1969)[31] but the 1970–1973 period was pivotal; that was when insurgency became more than an idle threat. The Federal Party radicalized in response to the state's language and education policies. The most prominent politicized opposition was the Tamil United Front, which was created when the Federal Party merged with other Tamil parties in 1972. The most notable feature of nonviolent Tamil agitation was the Vaddukkoddai Resolution of 1976, which transformed the Tamil United Front into the Tamil United Liberation Front and proclaimed its goal of an independent Tamil state. Through the mid-1970s, these formal parties were the dominant social bases of nonviolent opposition. In 1977, J. R. Jayawardene's United National Party decisively defeated Mrs. Bandaranaike's Sri Lanka Freedom Party; he ruled Sri Lanka for the crucial next twelve years.

Newly politicized social bases also emerged, drawing on preexisting caste and student networks that were now imbued with clear opposition to the political status quo. In 1972, Velupillai Prabhakaran, a Karaiyar from Velvethithurai, founded the Tamil New Tigers in the Jaffna Peninsula, renamed the Liberation Tigers of Tamil Eelam (LTTE) in 1976. At roughly the same time, the Tamil Eelam Liberation Organisation (TELO) was formed. In 1975, the Eelam Revolutionary Organisation of Students (EROS) was founded in London. Splinter groups later emerged in the form of the People's Liberation Organisation of Tamil Eelam (PLOT), which split from the LTTE, and the Eelam People's Revolutionary Liberation Front (EPRLF), which split from the EROS.[32]

These nascent militants were not yet key political players: Richardson explains that even as late as 1977, "proponents of militant Eelamist views were a tiny minority, fragmented into small groups with imposing titles, but limited resources."[33] Before 1983, militants were "in a hopeless minority"[34] among the Tamil population. Moreover, as Clarance notes, "in their embryonic stage, there was a certain fluidity in the composition of the various groups and on occasions some cooperation between them."[35] The historical record is very hazy, but it is possible to discern some broad outlines of insurgency during this period. The initial organization of these groups put them in different positions to manage influxes of guns, money, and recruits that occurred from 1983 onward.

Vanguard groups were the dominant form of rebellion in the 1970s: small groups of students and mobile political activists were the organizers. The links organizers had to one another and to other networks shaped how they could build new groups, as McDowell outlines: "The

Explaining Tamil Militancy in Sri Lanka

multiplicity of rebel organisations enabled Eelamist groups to tap different social bases, including caste, through different appeals rooted in immediate contexts, and through different networks of recruitment."[36] There were numerous militant organizations, but "of the thirty-seven Tamil militant groups, only five were of significance."[37]

We can tentatively identify differences in the social bases upon which these militant groups built. Caste formed an important dimension of variation, as "at least initially, each of the more significant groups had its own caste orientation."[38] The LTTE's social base was the clearest; it combined a Karaiyar caste core with student networks in the north. These linkages consisted of personal connections that reflect the relatively small size of the caste. I have been unable to assess how LTTE organizers were connected to local communities or how they operated in local areas. It seems plausible that there were strong prewar horizontal and vertical ties, but the existing evidence is centered on leaders and so we have reliable information only about horizontal ties.

The PLOT and the TELO had more diffuse upper-caste Vellala bases that lacked the clear boundaries and social relationships of the Karaiyar LTTE elite. The EROS had strong horizontal ties that were based on urban student networks in London, India, and Sri Lanka, but its vertical ties into localities within Sri Lanka were weak. These social dynamics shaped what leaders could do as they tried to build rebellion in the 1970s and early 1980s. The Tamil United Liberation Front remained nonviolent throughout this period, but the rise of Tamil militancy and escalation of government repression shattered its political power and influence. Many of its supporters joined the emerging militant structures, fled into exile, or tried to avoid politics altogether.

The LTTE and the PLOT

Building the Tigers

The conventional wisdom about the LTTE is that it was built around a combination of mass political grievance and individual leadership. There is much truth to this assessment. Richardson notes that "Prabhakaran himself deserves much credit for providing the leadership skills and building the organisation that achieved this transformation."[39] The LTTE is in many key respects an outlier in the broader universe of armed groups in terms of its eventual fighting power, its capacity for governance, and its organizational control.[40]

However, the literature on the LTTE identifies a wider array of factors that shaped the LTTE. We cannot simply explain the LTTE's cohesion as a result of pure individual leadership, as Richardson points out: "Prabhakaran's self-discipline and organizational skills set him apart from other militant leaders, but in 1977 it was by no means certain that he would emerge as the LTTE's number one. Attracting able lieutenants who were loyal and personally courageous helped him to survive both challenges from rivals and counter-terror operations mounted by Sri Lanka's security forces."[41] Nor was mass support initially essential; as noted above, through the 1970s and even the early 1980s, the LTTE was not the beneficiary of mass mobilization. The Tigers existed in the 1970s as a small, relatively disciplined core group that had no organizational presence in many localities.

The LTTE began as a vanguard organization, operating as a small group without substantial local institutionalization. This is partially in line with my theory: the LTTE could forge central control because its initial leadership was built through Karaiyar caste networks. As Roberts argues, "One can reasonably surmise that these [caste] networks were of critical importance in the survival and growth of the LTTE during the initial decades."[42] Fuglerud argues that "the differences between [militant] groups may be understood as a direct continuation of inter-caste and intra-caste conflict, that is, as conflicts of factionalism and segmentation."[43] We can see evidence of this when looking at the major split in this period (discussed more below): when the People's Liberation Organisation of Tamil Eelam (PLOT), led by Uma Maheswaran, broke away in 1980–1981, the line of division among the two organizations roughly followed caste lines: higher-caste Vellalars went with the PLOT and the Karaiyars largely (though not universally) stayed with the LTTE.[44] The politics of Tamil society could not be completely overcome in the LTTE organization.

It is important not to push this argument too far. The lack of detailed empirical data on prewar vertical ties makes it hard to know whether the social-institutional theory should predict an integrated instead of a vanguard group. My theory may make a partial misprediction of initial organizational structure based on the LTTE's original structure, but it helps to at least understand why the Tigers' leaders were able to act collectively while their contemporaries were struggling to build their organizations. Crucially, this caste base involved interactions and personal ties between its members that were linked to enduring political attitudes. This created denser networks than among either the exile student movements or the capacious Vellala caste.

The importance of this social base is clear in the key early members of the LTTE. It was most important at the level of central control. O'Duffy argues that "the nucleus of the LTTE leadership, including Prabhakaran, emerged from a subset of the Karaiyars, the higher status Kadalodiekal, who are traditionally prominent seafaring traders (and smugglers)";

these became "vital assets" for the LTTE.[45] Wilson agrees: "The leadership of the Kadalodiekal [a component of the Karaiyar caste] turned to the armed struggle. The current LTTE leader Velupillai Prabhakaran, his one-time deputy Mathaya, and Mathaya's mother's stepbrother Thurairetnam, the former Federal Party/Tamil United Liberation Front member of Parliament for Point Pedro, were all members of the Kadalodiekal elite."[46] Yogaratnam Yogi (from Kondavil in Jaffna), who was later a Jaffna commander, and Lawrence Thilakar (from Jaffna), who was later an international spokesperson, were also Karaiyar caste members.[47] According to Roberts, this caste base expanded beyond these individuals, though there is disagreement about the caste identity of some.[48] If Roberts's assessment is generally right, this Karaiyar group within the LTTE included some of the dominant military leaders of the next three decades.[49] Even where caste codings differ, a clear geographic origin around Velvethithurai is visible, as in the case of Kittu, a future Jaffna commander.[50]

Clarance agrees with this measurement of the LTTE's social base: "Many LTTE leaders came either from the *karaiyar* caste and/or from Velvethithurai and the Vaddamarachchi (most notably, Velupillai Prabhakaran and several other leading LTTE members from Velvethithurai come from the *kadalodiekal* elite)."[51] Hellman-Rajanayagam argues that "the LTTE is a group not only with mixed caste membership, but, what is much more unusual and more important, with low-caste leadership."[52] Horowitz similarly notes that "the Tigers were representative of a range of Tamil castes but were led by a member of the Karaiyu (fisher) caste distrusted by the land-owning Vellala who dominated Tamil civilian politics; he was probably distrustful of Vellala in turn."[53] Since the Karaiyar formed only 10 percent of (non-Indian) Tamils in Sri Lanka, this was clearly a disproportionate representation within the LTTE.[54] As Smith notes, this "may explain its relative cohesion and functionality over the years."[55]

Key LTTE mobilizers were also from the north[56], including uppercaste Vellalas Kittu (from Velvethithurai, and a classmate of Mahattiya) and Uma Maheswaran and the lower-caste Tamilselvan. Some had also been childhood friends (like Shankar and Prabhakaran). The Velvethithurai area (and Jaffna more broadly) "played a key role in providing a large number of volunteers when Tamil politics began getting sucked into the web of violence and counter-violence."[57] The LTTE apparently also included some students from Jaffna linked to the Tamil Students' Federation and other student associations.[58] The LTTE's caste focus overlapped with other networks of social mobilization that could be tapped into as the group went to war.[59] Horizontal linkages between prospective organizers and leaders are very clearly present. We lack data, however, about vertical linkages, which makes it hard to say whether the LTTE's vanguard form emerged solely because of social structure and, if vertical caste networks did exist on the ground, why it did not become an integrated group until nearly a decade later.

The LTTE's small core of militants engaged in sporadic but escalating violence against the Sri Lankan state from 1974–1975 on.[60] Though Prabhakaran sometimes espoused a leftist rhetoric under the influence of Anton Balasingham, there is no evidence that he had a significant commitment to Marxism.[61] He aimed to build a Leninist organizational weapon without other parts of the Leninist package. Ideology mattered, but not in a reified or static sense; it was reinterpreted, manipulated, and drawn on in ways that suited the organization's tasks.

An Exception that Proves the Rule: The PLOT Breaks Away

During the 1972–1983 period, we do see one split from the Tigers, by Uma Maheswaran, who created the People's Liberation Organization of Tamil Eelam (PLOT). At this point there was a small, "secretive and regimented"[62] core around Prabhakaran acting under his orders.[63] In 1979 and 1980, discontent emerged targeted at Prabhakaran's leadership that showed how intraethnic sociological divisions can affect organizational structure. Crucially, the split was driven by a network outside the core Karaiyar social base.

The unrest emerged over Prabhakaran's expulsion of Uma Maheswaran. Uma, a leftist upper-caste land surveyor and former Tamil United Liberation Front activist, had joined the LTTE in 1977.[64] Tension exploded when Maheswaran was accused of having sex with a woman, which at that point was against LTTE rules. Prabhakaran expelled him but Uma fought back, claiming to be the true chairman of the LTTE.[65] The split involved ideological divisions (leftist vs. nationalist), caste/social distinctions, and more mundane personal issues. Prabhakaran and his loyalists temporarily abandoned the LTTE and instead contacted Thangadurai and Kuttimani, the TELO founders from Velvethithurai. Prabhakaran operated under a "working alliance" with the TELO. Nevertheless, his group of followers obeyed his commands and not those of the TELO.[66]

The organizational split was intertwined with social linkages. Maheswaran's new People's Liberation Organization of Tamil Eelam (PLOT), unlike the LTTE, was "essentially a high-caste Vellalar-oriented organisation"[67] that espoused cross-ethnic cooperation with the Sinhalese left.[68] Maheswaran drew away the Vellalar members of the LTTE, which was in competition with the TELO for the more socially diffuse upper Vellala caste and embraced a much looser recruitment process.[69]

I tentatively code the PLOT as being built from weak horizontal and vertical links since there is little evidence of a tight preexisting social core among either the leaders or the foot soldiers. The process of splitting seems to have undermined the group's ability to consolidate its position, especially since the split created a need for rapid expansion. The conflict "led to entrenched factional fights between Uma's PLOT and LTTE which even spilled over into India."[70] Though there was some movement of PLOT militants to the LTTE (such as Balraj), as violence escalated the divisions between these two groups grew rigid. The PLOT became a potent force in some ways; indeed, as Matthews notes, "Sri Lanka's National Security Minister Lalith Athulathmudalai acknowledged [that the PLOT] was at one time the most powerful of all the 'guerrilla' organizations."[71]

This social base and Maheswaran's disastrous personal leadership style created "organizational infelicities."[72] The PLOT was a fragmented organization throughout its existence, and while we do not have much information on the 1980–1983 period, nothing in the record suggests that it was disciplined at any level in the early 1980s. The nature and quality of the social networks on which it was founded are certainly not the only reason that PLOT eventually collapsed, but its problems with social mobilization and organization can be traced to its origins.

The TELO

The Tamil Eelam Liberation Organization (TELO) was another early militant organization. The historical record about the TELO is sparse; there is even disagreement about its real date of founding, since it hails back in some ways to the small group of Tamil separatists in the late 1960s.[73] Its leaders, Thangadurai and Kuttimani, were Tamil political activists from Velvethithurai. After Thangadurai and Kuttimani were arrested in 1981, Sri Sabaratnam took over the leadership. After the arrest of the original leaders, the caste composition of TELO "was distinctly Vellala-oriented and was acknowledged by all, including Tamil expatriates, as being 'high-caste.'"[74] Like the PLOT, the TELO eventually was based on a comparatively socially diffuse network. Unlike the PLOT, some of the mini-groups left over from the mobilization done by Tamil students in the late 1960s and early 1970s were folded into the organization. The TELO appears to have been a loosely organized parochial organization by the early 1980s, especially after the arrest of its founders removed their coordinating role, but the evidence here is weak.

The EROS

Less ambiguous social origins can be found for the Eelam Revolutionary Organization of Students (EROS). It was formed in London in 1975 by expatriate Tamil students and had a student wing, the General Union of Eelam Students. The EROS was led by Eliyathamby Ratnasabapathy, Shankar Rajee, Velupillai Balakumar, and A. R. Arudpragasam. There were robust horizontal ties between organizers in the student movement, but the movement was based in exile and ended up located in several geographic locations. As Swamy notes, "Although it failed to take roots in Sri Lankan Tamil areas for a long time, it played a key role in shaping the growth of militancy."[75] While it was influential because of its ability to promote a leftist political line, "[EROS] was largely seen as a group of intellectuals based in London."[76]

The EROS faced challenges in creating local institutions because of its overseas location, and consequently lacked local embeddedness in Sri Lanka and India. There were significant disconnects between the central command and individual cadres located outside London. The EROS was not engaged in significant militancy during the 1972–1983 period, leaving the group "plodding behind in the race for militant leadership."[77] This was a vanguard organization based overseas, and it was in no position to engage in coordinated violence.[78] Wilson suggests that there was some strength in the east, around Amparai and Batticaloa, but agrees that the overall structure of the organization resembles what I term a "vanguard group."[79] These structural vulnerabilities led to discontent among group members about EROS' inability to mobilize local Sri Lankan Tamils as other militant groups rose to prominence.

The Origins of Tamil Militancy, 1972–1983

There is too little information to arrive at any firm conclusions about this period. The groups were only sporadically active and their internal organization was both opaque and extremely fluid. Nevertheless, there are aspects of this initial mobilization that support the argument I offer in this book. First, there was clearly mobilization through preexisting caste, friendship, and student networks that shaped who became a member of these organizations. There was not a single upswell of Tamil militancy driven by a unified nationalist agenda; instead, the groups had distinct social and ideological profiles: "political organizations were constructed along class and caste lines, which hindered virtually any possibility of a common front."[80]

Second, there is suggestive evidence to indicate that the LTTE's caste base represented a more defined and robust underpinning than the other groups. The historical evolution of these caste groups may have created differential capacities for violent collective action. Crucially, this evolution had nothing to do with future expectations of militancy or linguistic conflict; it instead reflected socio-economic and religious dynamics within Tamil society in response to the shocks and opportunities presented by colonial rule. The predominance of Karaiyars within the Tigers facilitated the organization's initial ability to attract and control recruits.

THE ACCELERANT: POGROMS AND INDIAN SUPPORT, 1983–1986

The conflict in Sri Lanka escalated significantly during the summer of 1983, when an LTTE ambush of an army convoy in Jaffna that killed thirteen soldiers triggered anti-Tamil riots. These "Black July" pogroms "opened a floodgate of young Tamils to various Tamil militant groups,"[81] and there was a "mass recruitment spree."[82] Vanguard groups such as the LTTE and the EROS had to cope with the problems that accompany rapid expansion, while the parochial TELO and fragmented PLOT tried to find ways of maintaining command unity. The EPRLF split from the EROS in 1980, frustrated with its exile-based leadership's inability to mobilize local communities.

The pogroms drew India into the conflict. The central government in Delhi decided to apply pressure on Sri Lanka by supporting the Tamil insurgents.[83] India's aim was to force the regime of J. R. Jayewardene to create a deal.[84] The training that India made possible "was on a mass scale, involving all the major groups (LTTE, TELO, PLOT, EROS, and EPRLF and later the ENDLF)."[85] Indian support thus played an important role in increasing the intensity of the war.[86] The level of support varied over time and among groups: the TELO and the LTTE were the clear favorites from 1983 to 1987, while the EPRLF became the main beneficiary from 1987 to 1990. As a result, Swamy notes, "Groups which had been virtually dormant or shown no special caliber for military operations were getting bloated."[87]

Muni notes that "mutual differences [among militant groups] arose from their particular ideological orientations, personality factors and sources of support. They also differed in the specific aspects of their approach towards India."[88] During this period, there was no clear leader in terms of size or manpower; although the PLOT, the TELO, and the LTTE had the most members, the TELO and the LTTE had more arms than the PLOT.[89] The LTTE and, to a much lesser extent, the EPRLF made effective use of this external support to build their organizations, while the TELO did not. The LTTE also began to receive large flows of money from

Tamils overseas. The Tigers expanded their organization by building powerful local control processes, and they quickly shifted from a vanguard group to an integrated structure during the 1980s.

The other groups that received Indian support were unable to prevent internal disputes. The TELO was particularly fractious and fell apart under the pressures of internal feuding and clashes with other groups. The EPRLF was not as cohesive as the LTTE, but it was a committed vanguard organization built around left-wing students and lower castes in the Eastern Province. This enabled it to survive the first wave of intra-Tamil LTTE fratricide in 1986–1987 and to later become an influential arm of the Indian Peace Keeping Force from 1987 to 1990. The EROS was a fairly marginal, albeit technically skilled, organization.

Swamy notes that "problems became endemic in groups which lacked firm leadership and a military agenda."[90] Organizational structure left the TELO, the EROS, the PLOT, and the EPRLF vulnerable to the LTTE. The TELO was annihilated by the Tigers as it was in the process of fragmenting, the EPRLF was wiped out when its local fighters abandoned it, and most of the EROS was merged into the Tigers. The PLOT remained fragmented and consumed itself in feuds in 1985–1986 before the LTTE took advantage of this unrest to largely wipe it out in 1986.

Expanding the Tigers after Black July

The LTTE, which had launched the ambush that triggered the 1983 pogroms, benefited from the mobilization that ensued. The organization evolved "from a group of 30 poorly armed dissidents in 1983 into one of the world's foremost paramilitary groups by 1991."[91] The benefits of this period for the LTTE had two components. First, it led to a significant increase in Indian support, which the Tigers took full advantage of. Second, it drove many more recruits into militant ranks and provided an opportunity to establish local organizational presences throughout Tamil areas.

External aid improved the LTTE's military strength.[92] Tamil Nadu played an important role in providing sanctuary and funding.[93] The central government in Delhi also provided weapons and training. The lead agency on Sri Lanka in India was the Research and Analysis Wing (RAW), India's external intelligence agency. The RAW began bringing Tamil militants to India for training after the riots in 1983.[94] This aid was taken advantage of by the LTTE: as Tiger leader Prabhakaran told an Indian journalist, "Right now I am small. I need India's help to grow."[95] As I discuss below, Prabhkaran's attitude toward Indian sponsorship was highly pragmatic and Indian backing did not create enduring Indian influence. Funding from the overseas diaspora began to supplement (and then, over time, replace) material support from India over the course of the 1980s, most dramatically once the LTTE and India clashed with each other in 1987.[96] In contrast to what happened when other groups received external aid, these resources did not undermine discipline and control in the LTTE. It therefore earned a reputation "as a formidably led and organized military force."[97]

The other major effect of the 1983–1984 surge in mobilization of militants was a broader recruiting base for the LTTE. More young Tamils were willing to fight, and they actively sought opportunities to join an organization. As Swamy notes, "Recruits rushed to Tiger ranks, attracted by its awesome military operations, its army-like discipline, and the aura of Prabhakaran."[98] But accepting a surge of new recruits could be a recipe for disaster, and it badly hurt other Tamil militant groups. The LTTE's military would be effective only if its manpower remained disciplined, and Prabhakaran made a clear decision to limit the influx. Swamy quotes him as saying "with just 50 good people I can do a good job, instead of having a bloated but useless 500."[99]

The key question is how the LTTE was able to control expansion once the strategic decision had been taken to maintain high standards and recruit selectively. At the central level, the LTTE had preexisting structures of internal control to screen recruits and socialize new members.[100] Core leaders around Prabhakaran provided the social presence that enabled the organization to homogenize and socialize new fighters. In part, this was possible because of the remarkable continuity in the social composition of the leadership of the Tigers.[101] As Hellman-Rajanayagam notes, "The Karaiyar leadership was seen as a war-time measure, not meant to be carried over into more settled times,"[102] but it endured as long as the war did.

Local control was built alongside this enduring central cohesion without the arduous process of local alliance that my theory predicts. By 1983 a consistent screening and selection process had been set up for prospective recruits.[103] Local cadres would approach suspected Tigers to indicate their interest, but before they were accepted for training they would be monitored on the local level to assess their reliability. The Tigers built powerful control institutions for recruiting, monitoring, and socializing new members even outside their core social terrain and apparently did so without cutting deals with local communities. At least based on the available evidence, the Tigers did not engage in the slow and painstaking process of building local alliances that Massoud in Afghanistan or the Viet Minh in French Indochina undertook.

Those fighters who were accepted were used both as local guerrillas and increasingly as mobile soldiers. The socialization processes in the LTTE were extremely powerful and able to substantially overcome prior social divisions (with the key exception of easterners, as discussed below). The Tigers extended their reach into Tamil society, beginning a long process of dominating and controlling it. In 1994, Hellman-Rajanayagam argued that "it is the most tightly structured, tightly disciplined and autocratically led group of the movement.... LTTE sees comparatively little scope for the population at large in the armed fight. Active fight[ing] is not something to be taken up by everybody; on the contrary, the ritual of acceptance into the movement is quite tough and elaborate."[104]

The shift from a vanguard organization to a larger, more sophisticated integrated structure thus did not occur through either creating local alliances or imposing the group on local areas, as my theory would predict.[105] Thus, my argument does not explain how the LTTE shifted from a vanguard group to an integrated organization. It seems that the Tigers' ideology, the preexisting vanguard core, and Sri Lanka's brutal but incompetent repression combined as the perfect storm that built the Tigers. A combination of leadership skill and counterproductive state policy may lead to rapid local expansion as long as a strong leadership is in place to handle it, even without the local alliance-building that my approach emphasizes.

India's High Commissioner to Colombo, J. N. Dixit, later wrote, "It would be difficult to come by a more motivated, educated, dedicated and politicized insurgent or militant group than the LTTE."[106] This opinion was widely shared; other observers noted that "compared to other Tamil groups, the LTTE cadres were clearly superior"[107] and that "of the five major groups, the LTTE, is the most powerful, disciplined and well organized."[108] The Tigers operated in the same context as their rivals, but they were far better able to navigate it.

Competitive Mobilization and Indian Support: The TELO, the EROS, and the EPRLF

The LTTE nevertheless had serious competitors within the Tamil militant movement. The TELO, the EROS, and the splinter group EPRLF (from EROS) attracted large-scale Indian support. The TELO cultivated ties with Tamil politicians in India, the EPRLF and the EROS linked themselves to Indian leftists, and all three had strong connections to the Indian security agencies. The TELO became militarily capable, but it was a parochial group that the LTTE was able to shatter while the members feuded. The EROS had little organizational presence on the ground, reflecting its social origins as an overseas student movement. The EPRLF was the most ambiguous organization among the Tamil militants. It seems to have been primarily a vanguard group that nevertheless had some local control built on lower caste ties in the east.

Only the TELO "could match the LTTE's cadres and firepower, mainly due to the head start it had enjoyed with New Delhi's initial generosity."[109] The TELO received this aid in part because its political agenda was in line with India's: it was nationalist but was not as hard line as the Tigers.[110] Consequently, "would-be militants began making their way to TELO in maximum numbers because it was the first group to have its cadres trained [by India]."[111] Indeed, "bereft of any ideology, [the TELO] benefited the most from the mad rush and enrolled hundreds."[112] Wilson refers to the TELO as a "powerful group,"[113] and it is true that its military commanders had significant power. This attracted and retained recruits.[114] Thus, Loganathan observes, "amongst the non-LTTE organizations, it was TELO, with a record of sensational attacks against the security forces, that came anywhere close to matching LTTE's prowess in the battlefield."[115] Richardson agrees, noting that the "TELO . . . gained notoriety and recruits with a series of spectacular bombings and raids."[116]

Yet at the same time the TELO was showing military power it was suffering from organizational flaws. The key faction leaders and ground-level recruits were hastily incorporated in the scramble for new members, leading to internal divisions that were exacerbated by the killing of the group's founding leaders, Thangadurai and Kuttimani, in a 1983 anti-Tamil prison riot. Leaders Bobby, Das, and Sabaratnam did not cooperate well with one another, suggesting a parochial structure with distinct factional commanders. As Richardson notes, the TELO's ground-level cadres were known for lacking discipline, and they often appear to have used power in opportunistic, self-serving, and undisciplined ways.[117] Swamy notes that "the TELO came to be accused of thuggery on a large scale."[118] Strategy and structure interacted to create a parochial, loosely controlled organization.

Rapid growth exacerbated underlying preexisting problems, opening space for conflicts over turf and resources among the commanders of TELO factions. Sri Sabaratnam did not have tight control over his commanders or his fighters. These tensions within the TELO exploded into interfactional warfare in 1986. Das, TELO's commander in Vadamarachchi, clashed with another commander, Bobby, and was killed, creating a "serious crisis within the TELO."[119] This triggered a devastating LTTE onslaught that exploited the divisions within the TELO. Parochial armed groups are particularly likely to be pushed into fragmentation by feuding among leaders, and the TELO was moving in this direction when the LTTE struck.

The Eelamist left was represented by the EROS, the EPRLF, and the PLOT. However, only the first two were close to India; for personality reasons, the PLOT's leader Uma Maheswaran was unable to maintain strong links with the Indian agencies. The EPRLF emerged when the student wing of the EROS formed its own group. This split seemed to involve discontent with the London-based leadership's lack of involvement in the actual struggle in Tamil areas of Sri Lanka.[120] The EPRLF emerged in the period 1980 to 1984.[121]

Despite the rupture caused by the EPRLF split, the EROS, led by Velupillai Balakumar and Shankar Rajee, was able to forge close ties to the RAW and the Ministry of External Affairs in India.[122] The EROS "kept an extremely low profile,"[123] though it was apparently skilled at engaging in urban bombings in Colombo.[124] As an insurgent group in the actual war zone, the EROS was not particularly prominent because of its diaspora origins and lack of links to preexisting local networks.[125] A reliance on isolated urban bombings and external backers is consistent with the actions of a vanguard organization, lacking local guerrillas to engage in more sustained activities. The EROS later essentially disappeared as the war escalated, despite Indian support and its leftist ideology.

The EPRLF is a somewhat easier case to study because it later became much larger and rose to greater prominence. Led by K. Padmanabha, Suresh Premachandran, Varatharajah Perumal, and Douglas Devananda, among others, the EPRLF advanced a left-wing agenda and adopted a classical Marxist-Leninist approach to cadre-building and mass mobilization. As Hellman-Rajanayagam argues, "The EPRLF was . . . the only group which clearly distinguished between its political and military wing[s], which is quite unique and in distinct contrast to the LTTE."[126] She suggests that the ideology of EPRLF was the most explicitly radical of all the militant groups in Sri Lanka.[127] Its main base of support was in Batticoloa, rather than in Jaffna, the LTTE's stronghold, and it had "a groundswell of strength and support in the East which other groups could never match."[128]

Unfortunately, detailed evidence about the social backgrounds of EPRLF members during this period is hard to come by; most of the comments about the EPRLF's lower-caste and eastern base are vague (though we do know that its leader, Padmanabha, was lower caste).[129] It appears to have been constructed using a social base with tight horizontal ties among its student leaders but with weaker vertical links on the ground. There appears to be regional variation; vertical linkages may have been stronger in the east than in the north. As a result of these social underpinnings, it is not surprising that the EPRLF ended up occupying an ambiguous space between a vanguard group and an integrated organization: it certainly had substantial central control but the strength and extent of the local institutions it controlled were more limited.

In July 1983, the EPRLF was the poorest among the Tamil militant groups.[130] Although the Indians continued to favor the TELO and the LTTE in the period 1983 to 1986, the EPRLF military continued to grow, and gradually it became "a formidable group."[131] The Indian agencies provided matériel and training to the EPRLF, as did the Indian Communists.[132] Instead of adopting the LTTE's ruthlessly militaristic strategy, the EPRLF chose to expand its base beyond the initial membership of intellectuals and students to include "workers, peasant, and fishers in a more broadbased movement."[133] This certainly looks like an attempt to mobilize local alliances in order to bolster the organization. Like the EROS, the EPRLF tried to adopt the Marxist-Leninist organizational blueprint, to shift from a vanguard group into an integrated organization. It had more success in doing so than the EROS, but it could not match the LTTE's organizational strength.

The PLOT: Rapid Expansion and Organizational Cannibalism

We now return to the PLOT, which broke from Prabharakan's LTTE in 1980. The PLOT explicitly drew on left-wing ideology and aimed for a cross-ethnic revolution to change the nature of Sri Lankan society. It was born as a fragmented organization, and this trajectory endured until it was destroyed. The group expanded rapidly; Swamy notes that at one point, the PLOT had the most cadres among the militant groups.[134] According to one former member who became a major Tamil journalist, at its height it had 6,000 fighters.[135] Like the TELO, it drew heavily on the upper-caste Vellala.[136] However, it ended up being consumed by "infighting and murders."[137]

The PLOT was alienated from the major sponsors of insurgency in India because of the personality of PLOT leader Uma Maheswaran.[138] The importance of human agency is clear in this case. Uma was unable (or unwilling) to build relationships with Indian power brokers who could support PLOT militancy. This one reason why it "rarely staged any significant military operations in Sri Lanka."[139] Nevertheless, even if the PLOT had received Indian aid, there is no reason to think it would have avoided the organizational problems of the TELO, the EROS, or the EPRLF, which also had India's backing.

The PLOT attributed its lack of military action to a strategic decision to build a people's army and await the right revolutionary moment. In fact, it criticized the LTTE for its guerrilla tactics.[140] The group "became inactive or militarily non-productive due to its strategy, [and] it lost ground to other militant groups."[141] This occurred despite the mass expansion of the group. Discipline was also an apparent problem. For example, its high-caste members allegedly used their guns to settle caste disputes unrelated to the broader struggle.[142] A major split in the group triggered further fragmentation. For several years, unrest had been bubbling within the organization about the lack of military action and the mysterious disappearances of many PLOT members.[143] It soon became clear that Uma and some of his loyalists had been engaged in "a Stalin-type purge,"[144] killing dozens of members and torturing many others. 1985 was the high point of this suppression of internal dissent; the angry departure of one prominent PLOT member "led to a great purge in the group, resulting in scores of cold-blooded and brutal murders."[145] The level of internal conflict was far higher in the PLOT than any other group (except in the TELO just before its collapse). These details add support for my coding of it as a fragmented organization.

Defiance of Uma's leadership was both a cause and a consequence of this violent internal unrest and contributed to the formation of the Eelam National Democratic Liberation Front (ENDLF) by Paranthan Rajan.[146] The splitters castigated the PLOT for the "high-handed and anarchic style of one-man leadership and the subsequent infighting and murders and argued for a more democratic style of leadership through a central committee."[147] The split was nasty and violent and left Uma's PLOT with "only a rump of the movement."[148] Thus, "by mid-1986 the organisation had suffered from neglect from the leadership in India and was poorly armed."[149] The PLOT was coming apart at the seams as 1986 rolled on. Worse was to come.

Escalating Tamil Militancy, 1983–1986

While the information that is available for 1983–1986 is better than for the pre-1983 period, it would be dishonest to suggest that record is sufficient to fully assess how well my theory applies to all the groups in this period. Nevertheless, it is possible to offer reasonable conclusions about the trajectories of Tamil armed groups.

First, the LTTE maintained central control while creating new local institutions and loyalties. There were no splits or open feuds and compliance was high. The social composition of the leadership did not change radically and can be traced to earlier mobilization. However, my theory cannot explain the rise of local control, which does not appear to have occurred through either local alliances or local imposition. Second, the TELO, the EROS, and the EPRLF were either vanguard or parochial armed groups. The unknown here is the EPRLF's true structure: there are tantalizing hints of particular caste and regional mobilization but not enough data for clear analysis.[150] All three of these groups suffered at least some internal unrest, however, and this distinguishes them from the Tigers. Third, the PLOT was clearly the least disciplined and least

Explaining Tamil Militancy in Sri Lanka

cohesive organization; it converted loose networks into parts of a fragmented organization. Finally, access to resources did not determine the trajectory of organizations. Different organizations were able to do different things with similar access to Indian aid.

FRATRICIDE AND INTERVENTION: LETHAL RIVALRY AND
INDIAN COUNTERINSURGENCY, 1986–1990

The array of Tamil groups narrows dramatically from 1986 onward. The major focus of the 1986–1990 period is the LTTE and the EPRLF, which became locked in a brutal war. The catalyst for this was the Tigers' decision to knock its rivals out of the field. It did so by taking advantage of feuds and fractures within the other Tamil militant groups: successful attacks by the Tigers wiped out the TELO, severely damaged the PLOT, and pushed the EPRLF back to its eastern redoubts. The Tigers then launched an insurgency against the Indian Peace Keeping Force that was sent to impose a peace deal. The EPRLF became the indigenous militia for the Indians. Once the IPKF left, the EPRLF was annihilated, in the process suffering mass desertions at the lower ranks. It did manage to retain cohesion at the command level before almost all of its commanders were killed. Its process of collapse looks like what we would expect from a vanguard group: tight control at the top but weak control of local units, and an organization that falls apart after near-total decapitation of its leadership.

The Tigers Attack

The existence of competing militant groups disturbed LTTE leader Prabhakaran, who "had apprehensions that India's involvement would elevate the other Tamil groups to the same level as the LTTE, both tactically as well as strategically."[151] He was right; India's "strategy was to maintain control by preventing any one group from becoming dominant."[152] The LTTE made ominous threats against Tamil "traitors"[153] and was increasingly unhappy with Indian efforts to broker any kind of peace that did not include an independent Eelam.[154] It was becoming clear to the Tamil militants that "India would . . . not hesitate to squeeze" them.[155] Prabhakaran's resistance to Indian influence and his fear that Indian-backed militants would surpass the LTTE led him to embark on an offensive to eliminate other militant groups.[156] The Tigers wanted to push aside Indian favorites such as the TELO and the EPRLF and shatter its longtime foe, the PLOT. They timed their attacks to closely follow fragmentation in other organizations, as Jayatilleka notes: "The LTTE

[163]

always struck at the other organizations when they were weakened and preoccupied with internal rivalries."[157] The outcomes of these clashes were determined by which group was more cohesive, the LTTE or the group it was trying to eliminate. Here we see echoes of the conflicts in Kashmir and Afghanistan in which relatively integrated groups were able to sideline more fragmented competitors, even those with popular support or external backing.

The LTTE had clashed with the TELO in previous years, since they were the two best-armed groups in Jaffna, and TELO senior commander Das was a feared presence in the LTTE's erstwhile stronghold of Vadamarachchi. After another clash, and while a factional battle was occupying the TELO, the LTTE launched a simultaneous assault on over a dozen TELO camps.[158] The secrecy and ruthlessness with which this operation was carried out are unmistakable signs of the Tigers' integration. The TELO was broken and its key leaders were killed, driven into exile, or forced out of militancy. Some TELO cadres ended up joining the LTTE, though they do not appear to have ever been allowed into the leadership's inner circle. The TELO straggled on as a political party with occasional bouts of paramilitarism, eventually becoming an LTTE-controlled political front in the 2000s.

The PLOT was next. One of its commanders, an Uma Maheswaran loyalist named Mendis, was tortured and killed by the LTTE. The PLOT was then banned from operating on Jaffna. The organization was vulnerable in the wake of the splits and feuds surrounding Uma Maheswaran and his ENDLF rivals. The PLOT tried to wage a propaganda war in response to the LTTE's onslaught, but it was not successful, according to Hellmann-Rajanayagam, who notes that the PLOT's military weakness was evident in its public statements.[159] Ultimately, she claims, the "PLOT was clearly out of its depth without money and without real support from any side," even though it stuck to its revolutionary agenda.[160] The organization disintegrated as a serious force. During the time the IPKF was present in Sri Lanka, PLOT remnants became involved as mercenaries in a coup plot in Mauritius, and after the IPKF departed the PLOT became a pro-state Tamil paramilitary working with Sri Lankan security forces around Vavuniya.

Finally, the LTTE set its sights on the EPRLF, which was the only major organization remaining other than the EROS. As noted above, the EPRLF was a more robust organization that had strong leadership and local support in the east from lower-caste groups. These ties and the organizational processes they produced served the EPRLF in good stead when the Tigers made their bid for hegemony in 1986 and 1987. However, the group suffered a split in 1986 between its military commander, Douglas Devananda, and its political leader, Pathmanabha.[161] When the LTTE attacked, the EPRLF was pushed out of Jaffna. Nevertheless, the EPRLF "retained strength in the east and some support [in] India."[162]

As co-ethnic groups were targeted, "LTTE leaders began issuing public statements arrogating to their organisation sole authority to represent the Tamil people."[163] The EROS had maintained an uneasy peace with the LTTE, and its lack of large-scale activity or presence made its survival more acceptable to the LTTE.[164] The winners and losers in this process were determined by relative organizational capacity. Importantly, as Muni notes, LTTE dominance was directly against Indian interests: "If the RAW's objective was to see that no single group should become dominant, then the emergence of the LTTE was a major failure."[165] India lost control of Tamil militancy, showing that state sponsorship is not enough to determine the trajectories of insurgent groups.

The IPKF Goes to War

As the LTTE knocked off its rivals, Sri Lanka's security forces were regrouping. The LTTE's positions in Jaffna began to fall to a major offensive, and India grew concerned. While it had no interest in an independent Eelam, the Indian government wanted to force a compromise that would address Tamil grievances in Sri Lanka. India began making increasingly vocal threats about military intervention. In 1987, Rajiv Gandhi's government forced Jayewardene to agree to the Indo-Sri Lanka Accord.[166] This agreement was intended to lead to devolution of power to Tamil areas. It also introduced an Indian Peace Keeping Force into northern and eastern Sri Lanka. After the two heads of states signed the accord, it was presented as a fait accompli to the Tamil armed groups. The LTTE at first signaled that although it could abide by the agreement, it felt that India had sold it out. The EPRLF embraced the accord and IPKF as a political solution and a hedge against the LTTE.

India's attempts to manage the Sri Lankan ethnic conflict descended into disaster.[167] As the Indians pushed the Tigers to disarm, the LTTE began attacking the IPKF in 1987.[168] Tens of thousands of Indian infantry poured into Sri Lanka. After cooperation with the Tigers ended, the IPKF launched a bloody and ill-prepared assault on Jaffna city, driving the LTTE out of its urban stronghold but taking significant losses in the process. The IPKF offensive put another layer of pressure on the Tigers.[169] The size of the IPKF force surged to approximately 100,000 by late 1988. The IPKF had an "aura of toughness and discipline,"[170] and it drove the Tigers into guerrilla warfare in the Wanni jungles.[171]

The Indians continued to support and train the remnant non-LTTE groups; most of this was done by the RAW rather than by the IPKF.[172] The EPRLF was the main beneficiary of the presence of the IPKF and many came to view it as "India's puppet government in the area."[173] The organization relied on India for firepower, money, and logistics.[174] Tamil paramilitaries were "reportedly used as 'neutral' informers to sniff out and exterminate the Tigers."[175] The EPRLF was the front-line Indian proxy and the political face of the Northeastern Provincial Council (NEPC) that was supposed to represent the devolution of power.[176] Its strength in the east, among certain caste blocs, and among its leaders enabled the EPRLF to use Indian weapons and money at least somewhat competently, if also brutally and with an eye on revenge.[177] It tried to carve out political space for itself through its operation of the NEPC and through violence on the ground.[178]

It is hard to assess the level of popular support for the LTTE during this period. Anecdotes and analyses vary dramatically. Hellman-Rajanayagam, who spent significant time in northern Sri Lanka and Tamil Nadu, assesses it this way:

> LTTE's political hold on the population has always been precarious. Few Jaffna Tamils relished the thought of Prabhakaran and his merry boys in political control. They saw, and still see, LTTE as a necessary evil. They grudgingly admitted and admired their protective function, but happily sent them about their business once the Indians came.[179]

Muni, by contrast, attributes the staying power of the LTTE against the IPKF and its Tamil paramilitary allies to a deep reservoir of public support.[180] Indian forces committed human rights abuses and often acted arbitrarily. Suspect elections in 1988 were won by the Indian-backed EPRLF, but EROS candidates did well by advocating an political line that was sympathetic to the LTTE. This suggests clear discontent with the Indian presence. In 1987, however, a contemporary observer noted that "whether the LTTE can overshadow the EPRLF in this [Eastern] province is not certain."[181] There was no clear signal about which way popular support would go, at least in the east.[182]

There was social and organizational continuity in the LTTE during this period. The Tigers' base of military operations moved from urban and semi-urban Jaffna to the dense north-central jungles of the Wanni.[183] Its recruiting efforts may have shifted toward Tamils from the Mullaitivu area in the northeast and into the east. At the level of commanders, "the contemporary militant movement then furnished a further chance for the Karaiyar to maintain their position against the Vellalar, this time on their very own turf: warfare and on their own conditions."[184] The Tigers were also able to expand their diaspora funding.[185] Contrary to theories that emphasize the effects of resource flows, these resources were the consequences of organizational structure, not the causes.

[166]

The EPRLF appears to have continued to combine high levels of central cooperation with looser control lower in the organization. There are reports of civilian victimization and thuggery by EPRLF cadres taking advantage of their power and Indian support after the group became linked to the IPKF. Yet there is no evidence of major division within the EPRLF command, whose leaders were drawn heavily from the set of student founders who had built the organization. The EPRLF thus occupies an intermediate space among the organizations in Sri Lanka: it was not prone to major leadership unrest, but it also did not have tight control over individual foot soldiers. It seems closer to a vanguard group than an integrated organization. This structure makes sense in terms of my theory, given the (admittedly sparse) evidence suggesting that a combination of students and some eastern lower castes formed the social base of the organization.

Breakdown and Three-Sided War

When Ranasinghe Premadasa took over as the Sri Lankan president in 1989, he began reaching out to the LTTE.[186] He was skeptical of India, and his strategy was to ask India to leave, to provide guns to the Tigers that would help them push out the Indians, and to cut a deal with the LTTE that would end the civil war. Premadasa began making both public and private demands that the IPKF withdraw, and he reduced the government's cooperation with the NEPC/EPRLF. Seeing the writing on the wall, the EPRLF created a Civilian Volunteer Force (CVF) based on rapid recruiting. The CVF fighters were linked to the EPRLF, though they were formally part of the NEPC, and they earned a reputation for indiscipline. This continued the EPRLF's broadly vanguard pattern of leadership cooperation alongside weak control of foot soldiers. The details are hazy but this may be a case of local imposition by a vanguard group: the EPRLF took advantage of Indian support to try to impose its will on society without thoroughgoing bargains and alliances on the ground.

A massive corruption scandal brought down the Congress regime in Delhi in the 1989 general elections, bringing V. P. Singh to power. Singh opposed the IPKF as an unnecessary foreign adventure and began to withdraw the IPKF forces in 1989 and 1990. The slow but steady withdrawal of the Indians left the EPRLF vulnerable to the LTTE. India responded to this new vulnerability by pumping even more resources into the EPRLF. The EPRLF made the strategic decision to engage in a mass recruitment drive that included abductions and conscription. The organization hoped to hold on in the east. The conversion of the CVF and the EPRLF into a "Tamil National Army" in 1989 was a disaster.[187] Loganathan blames this creation of a large, undisciplined militia on Indian intelligence agencies, but it is clear that the EPRLF was terrified of the threat from the LTTE.[188] Whatever local organization the ERPLF had built in the east was destroyed by this mass expansion, as a tide of unwilling new foot soldiers were forced into the organization. As a result, "the sophisticated weapons were wasted in the hands of child soldiers who were not committed to the EPRLF cause and would desert at the first opportunity."[189] As the IPKF withdrew, the Tamil National Army was essentially wiped out in a coordinated series of Tiger attacks. The EPRLF had failed to reach into local communities to socialize and control new recruits.[190] These recruits were massacred across the northeast and many abandoned the fight immediately.

Remarkably, the key EPRLF leadership held together and fled to Madras in south India; they evacuated together rather than joining the LTTE or the Sri Lanka Army. However, in 1990, fourteen senior commanders of the group were assassinated by an LTTE hit squad. After this near-total leadership decapitation, the EPRLF gave up the fight and transitioned into a small Tamil political party caught between the government and the LTTE.[191] The EPRLF collapse involved waves of defections of foot soldiers amid relatively high levels of cooperation among the core leadership. This is what we would expect from a vanguard organization that relied on coercion and external support rather than local alliances to build its local organization. Direct leadership decapitation is what it took to destroy central control, and this also fits what my theory predicts for a vanguard group.

Forging Domination: The LTTE and Its Foes, 1986–1990

Leadership decisions help to account for the EPRLF's decision to adopt a mass conscription strategy in 1989–1990, but they seem to have exacerbated preexisting weaknesses instead of fundamentally changing the nature of the group. The rapid expansion made the EPRLF's weaknesses on the ground more visible and more significant, while the old command core remained largely the same. Indian aid helped hold the group together, but it did not transform it and could not save it. By contrast, the Tigers emerged battered but not broken from the IPKF period. There were no splits, no feuds, and no known internal unrest at any serious level. The social core of the LTTE leadership remained fairly constant within the Tigers, providing an organizational environment that was adept at incorporating and indoctrinating new members.

The LTTE Proto-State, 1990–2002

With the EPRLF annihilated and the PLOT and the TELO taking shelter in the arms of the Sri Lankan state, only the EROS and the Tigers remained. Most of the EROS ended up being absorbed into the LTTE amid another split, and thus the group drops out of the picture.[192] Over the course of the 1990s, the Tigers constructed statelike structures and transformed themselves into a more rigidly bureaucratized rational-legal institution. During the early and mid-1990s, the LTTE moved into a new level of military effectiveness. It became "a disciplined and militarized group with a leader of remarkable military and organizational skills"[193] and used suicide bombings in a wide variety of tactical and strategic settings.[194] The LTTE faced possible internal unrest, but an alleged challenge by the group's deputy leader was crushed without any loss of organizational integrity. As of 1990 the LTTE's "leadership was intact and safe; its troops battle hardened and ready for combat; its morale high."[195] Massive aid from the diaspora continued, and the LTTE continued to grow larger and stronger.[196]

As the LTTE began to function as a "counterstate,"[197] deep elements of continuity persisted. First, variations in loyalty and control within the group can be explained in part by the nature of the social ties among members. The command core of the Tigers remained heavily centered in Jaffna and among Karaiyar, forming a robust but narrow leadership elite with Prabhakaran at the center. Although the Tigers incorporated other Tamil social blocs, particularly from the east, these new members generally did not become key commanders. The commanders remained predominantly drawn from the same broad social stratum upon which the LTTE was founded in the 1970s.[198] My theory helps explain why the alleged Mahattaya challenge of 1990 was quickly quashed while the later 2004 split of Karuna in the east succeeded (both discussed below). The horizontal linkages among commanders were strongest in the north, consolidating the northern command elite, while the social division between northerners and easterners had negative consequences for the organization.

Second, the group's vertical ties to the larger society remained very important even as the LTTE became more formal and bureaucratized. The war-fighting style of the LTTE continued to rely on monitoring and shaping the behavior of the population, whether that meant getting it to move during military retreats or preventing intelligence infiltration by the Sri Lankan government. Because of the nature of their war, the Tigers could never escape the importance of social ties. In addition to leadership continuity, this explains why the LTTE was able to overcome intense attrition and repeated military setbacks during the 1990–2002 period—and, I will argue, why it was able to continue fighting even to the very end in 2009.

Building Eelam: State Formation Amid Conflict

From 1990 onward the LTTE thus combined state-building, war, and negotiations. This section provides a sketch of the 1990s and early 2000s to show how impressive the LTTE's enduring integration was. The group's rapprochement with Premadasa's administration collapsed in 1990, and the Tigers went back to war with the state. From 1990 until 1994, Eelam War II raged in both the north and the east. Aerial bombardment, population displacement, and mass killings occurred during this period. The LTTE used both guerrilla tactics and conventional fighting forces that were able to mount coordinated attacks on Sri Lanka Army positions. In 1994–1995, President Chandrika Kumaratunga's administration engaged in a peace process with the LTTE, but this collapsed in 1995. Eelam War III, which lasted from 1995 to 2002, involved large-scale warfare. During this period, the Tigers controlled much of northern and eastern Sri Lanka. However, the government was able to wrest control of Jaffna city and parts of the Jaffna peninsula from the LTTE. In 2002, a new peace process began. From 1990 to 2006, the Tigers fought two major wars and engaged in three peace processes. They also assassinated Rajiv Gandhi in 1991 and a variety of Sri Lankan political and military leaders (including Premadasa).

To wage this war, the LTTE constructed its own network of schools, police, internal economic infrastructure, and military training and recruiting.[199] The LTTE's organization of local areas strengthened vertical linkages by creating both material and ideational sources of control that enabled it to avoid unrest from below and maintain its ability to extract local taxation.

The size of the LTTE military grew to somewhere in the area of 10,000 (although estimates vary quite widely) and became more skillful.[200] It forged "a strong internal culture of personal and professional discipline."[201] As early as the 1980s, the LTTE had begun to engage in rituals as a form of legitimation. These included "funeral processions for fallen martyrs, cyanide sacrifices, and rousing public speeches contributed towards the mythologising of Prabhakaran and the Tigers' senior commanders who advanced the invincibility of the LTTE."[202] Symbols were created and imbued with meaning that reproduced organizational integration.

Social Origins and Continuity in the Leadership: Central Command and Regional Division

Part of the Tigers' agenda was to mitigate caste divisions, especially in Jaffna.[203] As Hellmann-Rajanayagam observes, "surmounting of caste barriers [meant] for the LTTE a reform of society at large."[204] Most of the LTTE's central ranks were Karaiyar. As McDowell describes it, "The control of power was closely guarded by a core of Karaiyar men who shared a common background and became, in effect, a specialist class of feudal knights."[205] Key LTTE leaders rose from other lower-caste roots.[206] Eelam-friendly intellectuals reframed Tamil history to emphasize the military prowess of the fishing castes.[207] Writing in the 1990s, McDowell argued:

> Just how deep and significant this caste division was (and is) in the Tamil "liberation struggle" is difficult to assess. It is clear though, that members of the Karaiyar caste originating from the Peninsula's north-eastern coastal areas are the political power-players in Jaffna Tamil society. Through the Tiger organisation, this group of former sea-traders built on their reputation as being more bellicose and adventurous than Vellalar landowners, to take on the self-appointed role as protectors of "Tamilness," and forgers of a more equitable society.[208]

Even in the context of a collective ethnic identity, divisions among Tamils remained salient as caste groups battled to create (or defend) their visions of what a Tamil society should be. The LTTE continued to pay attention to the dynamics of power within Tamil society.[209] In the east, caste tensions among Tamils endured.[210] These caste divisions remained relevant even during a period when Tamils were ostensibly molded into a unitary identity category.[211]

The outcome of the only apparent major challenge to LTTE integration in the 1990s shows how close horizontal ties, including along caste lines, kept the leadership cohesive. After the IPKF left northern Sri Lanka, Mahattaya, the Karaiyar from Velvethithurai who had become Prabhakaran's deputy commander, supposedly attempted a putsch. The contours of this incident are opaque. Mahattaya had allegedly become involved in a personal rivalry with Kittu, who was from the same region and was a senior military commander in the Tigers, and with intelligence chief Pottu Amman.[212] When Kittu was captured by India in 1993 (and committed suicide), Mahattaya was accused of having links to Indian intelligence. He was put under house arrest, his bodyguards were arrested, and he was eventually executed.[213]

Almost everyone within the high command appears to have fallen into line behind Prabhakaran as Mahattaya was purged. Mahattaya was

Chapter 6

operating directly within the social milieu of the top command: if he could not engineer a cascade of defections to his side he would have no distinct base of support upon which to rely. This illustrates how the LTTE rapidly identified and blocked any potential challenge; the Mahattaya episode showed the "totalitarian grip of the leader."[214] Yet during this period the Tigers relied on "a very thick middle stratum of leaders equally committed to Eelam [as Prabhakaran]."[215] The LTTE was not a one-man organization; instead, a rich set of horizontal social ties undergirded central organizational processes. I will show below how variation in social structure shaped organization when the easterner Colonel Karuna more successfully split in 2004.

2002–2009: Peace, War, and Annihilation

By 2002, the LTTE and the Sri Lankan state had fought to a stalemate. The Tigers had shown that they could hold onto territory, and their terror strikes in and around Colombo had shattered confidence in the Sri Lankan economy. The LTTE had been unable to retake Jaffna despite concerted effort, and after 9/11, a crackdown on the LTTE's fund-raising in the diaspora "dramatically changed" the political and economic context around the Tigers.[216] A peace process took hold from 2002 to 2006. Sri Lankan prime minister Ranil Wickremasinghe believed that creating an international "safety net" and drawing the LTTE into economic and political integration would slowly force the group to abandon its war aims.[217] The Tigers, on the other hand, believed that they held "strategic parity" and bargained hard for autonomy or even independence.

The Karuna Split

The peace process was a rocky and ultimately failed initiative. Though the Tigers continued to prepare for war, the strains of peace took a toll on the group. The organization had become increasingly reliant on foot soldiers from the eastern province during the wars of the 1990s. The ethnically divided east was a site of both conventional and insurgent combat and had a history of communal violence among Sinhalese, Muslims, and Tamils. The most senior eastern commander was Vinayagamoorthy Muralitharan, known as Colonel Karuna, from the Batticaloa area. Karuna had risen to a high level within the LTTE. But he was the only prominent easterner within the command ranks. This paucity of easterners makes clear the extent to which northerners dominated the command of the LTTE.[218] In addition, the group's social ties were stronger and more

[172]

widespread in the north than in the east. This social fact had consequences for the organization.

Karuna ran his eastern command with significant autonomy from Prabhakaran. He played an important role in building the conventional forces of the Tigers during the clashes of Eelam War III.[219] Karuna had a history of brutality that included massacres of prisoners, targeting of Muslims and Sinhalese, and the annihilation of the EPRLF in 1989–1990.[220] He was given so much autonomy in order to avoid a split. This fear of division had plagued even the highly disciplined LTTE: "Historically, the authority of the LTTE central leadership had ever been weakest in the east, and consequently the primordial need to avoid a split has been one of its abiding concerns since early days."[221] As O'Duffy notes, "the LTTE's command-led domination of the Northern Province is not as easily maintained in the East."[222] This underlying structure created a division in the LTTE: the east and north were part of the same formal organization, but each had different dynamics of command and control. As I note in chapter 3, mismanaged expansion that changes the social composition of the rank and file without allowing corresponding changes in the command elite can lay the basis for internal divisions; this is what happened in the LTTE.

In 2003 and early 2004, rumors circulated within the LTTE that Karuna had been embezzling money from LTTE funds, and an investigation led by Pottu Amman was apparently begun.[223] With new resources and breathing space, the Tiger leadership was trying to centralize control. At the same time, many in the east felt that their lack of representation and disproportionately small share of Tiger resources were signals of disrespect and exclusion.[224] The combination of alleged corruption and east-north tensions was combustible. Karuna had become more comfortable with the peace process and was reportedly less interested in a return to war, even as the LTTE expected and was preparing for renewed combat.[225] At some point in late 2003 or early 2004 Karuna was called north to the LTTE's de facto capital in Kilinochchi either to answer questions about his behavior, or to be asked to send more of his troops north (there is ambiguity about the exact events triggering the split). Karuna defied his orders and raised the flag of rebellion from Batticaloa in March–April 2004. A number of senior eastern commanders abandoned Karuna and fled north to the Wanni, but Karuna was able to tap into his regional network to pull away many eastern cadres.

Karuna explicitly appealed to the intra-ethnic cleavages between north and east as justification for his defection.[226] The social foundations of insurgent organization once again make themselves clear: despite sophisticated bureaucratic structures, armed groups need to mobilize social blocs. Whitaker reports eastern Tamil journalist Sivaram's view that the propaganda of Karuna's group, the Tamil Makkal Viduthalai Pulikal:

> pointed to long-standing tensions between largely urban Jaffna and largely rural Batticaloa over such matters as the condescending hauteur with which Jaffna Tamils occasionally treated even educated Batticaloa Tamils; the scarcity of Batticaloa Tamils in the inner circles of the LTTE; the heavier burden of recruiting—especially of children—and thus larger number of casualties borne by the east; the on-going clashes with the district's Muslim population, particularly over land tenure disrupted by the war; and, finally, to the rumor that money earmarked for rebuilding war-torn communities was mostly flowing north to fund the opulent lives of northern LTTE commanders. All these grievances, Sivaram said, Karuna, as a "son of the soil," claimed to understand better than the Jaffna-oriented LTTE.[227]

There is little evidence that the Sri Lankan or Indian governments actively precipitated the Karuna split, though it is clear that the government of Sri Lanka tried to take advantage of it after the fact. Karuna defected during the peace process, when the government was internally divided and was trying not to be too aggressive toward the Tigers.[228] Instead of being the result of government intervention, the split was driven by an internal battle over the future of the LTTE, underpinned by enduring divisions that reflected the disjuncture between the social origins of the LTTE leadership and the group's more socially peripheral (but militarily important) components.[229] There is empirical support for my social-institutional theory even long after the LTTE began its war. The limits of Tiger integration were ultimately social, in this case exacerbated by the leadership's decision to limit promotion pathways for eastern fighters. When the LTTE mobilized its forces and marched south, Karuna disbanded most of his cadres and fled with a group of supporters to Colombo. The LTTE clearly "won" the split, taking back control of the east. However, Karuna and his followers created the Tamil Makkal Viduthalai Pulikal as a political party-cum-armed paramilitary under the protection of the Sri Lankan security forces. Removed from its social groundings in the east, it was forced to fall back on the Sri Lanka Army and government of Sri Lanka for protection and material support.

War and Annihilation

By 2006, the peace process had frayed badly. Internal divisions within the Sinhalese-dominated southern political sphere combined with the LTTE's lack of interest in a solution short of de facto independence to create a stalemate. A "shadow war" of assassinations and abductions had been escalating since the Karuna split. It exploded into full warfare in the summer of 2006. The first major front was the east. The Sri Lanka Army had been refitted, reformed, and expanded during the ceasefire, and was assisted by the intelligence provided by Karuna's Tamil Makkal Viduthalai Pulikal about the LTTE's eastern operations.[230] The eastern province fell to the government in 2007.

There is no need here for a blow-by-blow account of the years of war from 2006 to 2009. Even in the face of growing losses of manpower and territory, the LTTE suffered no further splits or major (publicly known) internal feuds. Massively outnumbered and increasingly outgunned, the Tigers were driven back by the Sri Lanka Army. Unlike previous offensives, the Sri Lanka Army focused on killing Tigers and protecting flanks and supply lines, not rapidly seizing large tracts of land. The Tigers moved hundreds of thousands of Tamil civilians with them so they could preserve a base from which to extract conscripts in order to deal with attrition. Late 2008 and 2009 saw a series of dramatic successes for the Sri Lankan military. The Tigers kept on fighting even in the face of increasingly low odds of success, another indicator of their integration. Yet the LTTE began relying ever more heavily on forced recruiting, a signal of its desperation.

In a brutally violent final push, the Sri Lanka Army wiped out the vast majority of the LTTE leadership by late May 2009 and took a huge number of prisoners. Given the massive attrition imposed on the organization and the interning of hundreds of thousands of Tamils in camps, the LTTE as of this writing in 2013 appears to have been annihilated as an organization with the exception of diaspora supporters. The Tigers did not collapse because of splits or feuds (although the Karuna split helped the Sri Lanka Army) but because of their inability to field sufficient forces. Even in the face of increasingly sure defeat, the LTTE remained integrated; it went down fighting. Prabhakaran and a number of other commanders were killed, numerous others were arrested, and others fled overseas.

Organizing Rebellion in Sri Lanka

Findings

Tamil militancy presents severe research challenges and it would be intellectually dishonest to offer any confident findings from this set of comparative cases. Nevertheless, some clear insights emerge that show the strengths and limits of my argument.

First, the most integrated group, the LTTE, drew on a specific preexisting social (caste) structure at the leadership level. Horizontal ties were turned into central institutions. This coding is fairly unambiguous and offers support for my theory. The fact that the command of the Tigers had such a disproportionately high representation of this Karaiyar caste base and that informed observers point to this as an important factor in LTTE organization building should make us confident that my theory provides at least some purchase on the question why the Tigers were able to maintain cohesion among its central command. The historical autonomy and robust intra-caste ties of the Karaiyar appear to have given the LTTE an edge over its competitors in terms of both collective action and organization building before and after the crucial events of 1983. This imbalance in the group endured over time, even across decades of war and political maneuvering.

Furthermore, organizational divisions within the Tigers emerged from social tensions between the north and the east, laying the basis for the Karuna split. The LTTE had substantial room to maneuver but it remained connected to society, and this affected how the organization functioned. Even the integrated Tigers were not perfectly cohesive because of enduring social divisions that made internal unrest possible.

Second, the evidence from Sri Lanka illustrates that neither ethnonationalism nor Marxism-Leninism are sufficient bases for building strong organizations. Both nationalist (TELO) and leftist (PLOT, EROS) Tamil organizations suffered severe internal unrest. Arguments about the role of ethnic solidarity falter when confronted with the evidence of the Tigers' heavy reliance on intra-ethnic violence and coercion, the caste and regional divisions within the Tamil community, and the inability of the TELO's simple nationalist ideology to gain organizational traction. Ideologies and identities are obviously important tools for mobilization but do not provide sufficient glue to hold groups together in the midst of a fluid, extremely violent war. Instead, ideologies can be the basis for organizations only when the right social networks can be used to create strong institutions. Although the LTTE became deeply infused with a particular culture and a particular set of ideological precepts, these were at least partially the result of the Tigers' ability to construct an organization that could socialize and control recruits; ideas were enacted and reproduced through organizational mechanisms.

Third, external support was important but not determinate in shaping the trajectories of organizations. The Tamil militant groups looked to the Indian state and the Tamil diaspora for resources they needed to continue fighting. The Indian government played a major role in building the military power of the armed groups through guns, money, training, and sanctuary: the increase in Indian support in 1983 transformed the Tamil insurgency from an irritant into a threat to Sri Lanka's territorial integrity. This provided the resources the TELO, the EPRLF, and the

LTTE needed to attract new fighters and keep them in the fold. As this Indian support diminished in the late 1980s and early 1990s the international Tamil diaspora provided vast sums of money to the LTTE. The experience of the Tigers demonstrates both that resources are not intrinsic spurs to indiscipline and that resource flows can be consequences rather than causes of armed group organization.[231] It is also clear that state sponsorship was not sufficient to give India leverage over the LTTE: the group "prevailed over their Tamil rivals despite all the efforts of RAW to prevent their success."[232]

Yet there are clear limitations to my argument. Even leaving aside the weakness of the evidence, the theory does not explain the creation of robust local institutions within the LTTE. Neither local alliance nor local imposition occurred. Instead, it seems that mass support created greater willingness to be loyal to the leadership even in the absence of local deal-making and compromise. The Sri Lankan government's intransigence, the simple but resonant ideological bottom line of the Tigers, and Prabhakaran's leadership decisions appear to have been crucial in driving this group from a vanguard to an integrated structure. How central leaders are able to mobilize masses without specific social linkages is very important, and my theory struggles with this issue.

Furthermore, the internal processes of the Tigers were far more elaborate and sophisticated than in even other relatively integrated groups such as the Taliban and the Hizbul Mujahideen. A remarkable degree of socialization occurred. This was important for LTTE discipline, for, as Mann says, "to monopolize norms is thus a route to power"[233]: the ability of the LTTE to create expectations of devotion and dedication even in extraordinarily difficult circumstances is unusual. These internal processes of meaning making, norm diffusion, and socialization require deeper exploration.

An implication of my argument is that we should not expect to see substantial future LTTE or Tamil militant mobilization in Sri Lanka. This is not because Tamil grievances have been addressed or the state structure has been changed but because of the profound social dislocation and control that have resulted from government policies. Local communities are tightly monitored and guarded, while regional and national Tamil mobilization is prevented or co-opted. The social-institutional basis for renewed militancy is currently absent, even as the policies of the state continue to create motivation for rebellion. The social base of Tamil insurgency has been shattered in Sri Lanka.

Part III

Extensions and Implications

[7]

"Peasants and Commissars"
Communist Tides in Southeast Asia

This chapter explores whether my argument can explain insurgent cohesion outside of South Asia. I examine three major Southeast Asian communist groups before, during, and after World War II: the Malayan Communist Party (MCP) in Malaya, Viet Minh/Indochinese Communist Party in French Indochina, and the Huks in the Philippines. The Indochinese Communist Party (ICP) was linked to three rebellions between 1930 and 1954, the MCP fought against first the Japanese and then the British, and the Huks battled the Japanese, then the Philippine state. I mix comparisons across groups and over time to examine whether my theory can account for patterns of communist organization. I focus on how "peasants and commissars"[1] interacted to create different kinds of rebellion.

Table 7.1 outlines the groups' patterns of organization. I chose these cases for three reasons. First, they are very different from the organizations studied in the previous chapters: they are anticolonial, leftist armed groups seeking control of the state rather than religious or ethno-separatist insurgents. Second, these cases allow me to carefully examine these communist parties and peasant/labor organizations as they navigated peace and war over time, including Japanese occupation, the return of colonial powers, and postwar rebellions. This historical perspective shows how contingencies and unanticipated political dynamics created consistent mismatches between insurgent leaders' expectations and reality. Third, research by Jeff Goodwin has offered explanations for this variation that can be directly compared to my social-institutional theory in these three cases.[2]

The historical record shows significant—but not total—support for my argument in three key areas. First, the ability of communist organizers to build parties, to infiltrate labor and ethnic associations, and to direct

Table 7.1. Patterns of organization in Southeast Asia, 1928–1960

Organization	Initial organizational type	Organizational change
Malayan Communist Party	Integrated/parochial	Vanguard by mid-1950s, demobilized in 1989
Indochinese Communist Party	Vanguard	Integrated by 1947
Huks	Parochial	Fragmented/collapsed by late 1950s

peasant and student movements differed significantly across the three groups and over time within them. Even prewar successes were often inadequate for the needs of future war. These political processes were generally not guided by anticipation of protracted rural insurgency, with the partial exception of the ICP from 1944 to 1946. The communist parties of Southeast Asia in the 1930s through the mid-1940s were unable to predict where they would find themselves by the late 1940s. Even when they chose war, it occurred in times and places they did not expect. As a result, we see social bases built for one purpose being repurposed for militancy, with gaps and strains induced by using structures created for labor militancy or peasant politics as the basis for new rural armed institutions.

Second, these social bases clearly shaped the first form militant organizations took as communist parties and related institutions went to war. As communist organizers hurled their parties and mass fronts into war, the insurgent groups that emerged closely tracked the strengths and weaknesses of prewar structures. The fact that the ICP's cadres were urban and that its vertical ties were weak led to a vanguard organization from 1930 to 1944, the fact that the MCP had strong ties in the Chinese community and that many members were semi-urban squatters initially forged an integrated/parochial hybrid group from 1948 to 1950, and the fact that the Huks' members were a loosely connected mixture of an urban community party and divided rural peasants' associations created a parochial armed group. Institutions were strong where there had been extensive interaction and shared linkages before the onset of insurgency; they were much harder to build where organizers had not attempted or been able to forge ties.

Third, changes over time show some support for my theory. The MCP in Malaya changed toward a vanguard structure after its initial integrated/parochial hybrid form. The Viet Minh switched from a vanguard to an integrated group in 1944–1946 after over a decade of failed opposition. The Huks remained parochial until the group eventually fragmented. Key mechanisms through which change occurred resemble those I theorize in chapter 3. The MCP was undermined by pervasive local disembedding by the British that denied it access to local communities, even as war provided new opportunities for the leadership to coalesce. The Huks collapsed because state counterinsurgency forestalled opportunities for factions to cooperate under fire and preexisting leadership disputes spiraled into open defiance and feuding.[3] The Viet Minh used local alliances carefully, although they were helped by massive shifts in political context.

However, change is also the area where my theory is the most incomplete. Ho Chi Minh's leadership, the ideological fusion of nationalism and Marxism, and transformative changes in state repression were crucial in the Viet Minh's shift from an isolated vanguard into an integrated mass war-fighting group. These other factors allowed the ICP to deploy strategies that the MCP and Huks could not. Local alliances were crucial for the ICP, but a broader portfolio of local expansion mechanisms was involved that calls for future research.

After examining how the empirical record stacks up against my theory, I compare my argument to Jeff Goodwin's explanation of the same three cases. I argue that while Goodwin is right to note the importance of political context, his theory cannot explain the continuities that marked the MCP and the Huks before, during, and immediately after World War II; the ICP's shift in 1944–1946; or the specific mechanisms through which the MCP and the Huks were affected by counterinsurgency. The chapter concludes with key findings and implications.

THE MCP, BRITISH COUNTERINSURGENCY, AND THE WAR IN MALAYA

The Malayan Communist Party and its armed wing, the Malayan National Liberation Army (MNLA), posed a potent threat to British rule in Malaya from 1948 into the mid-1950s.[4] Unlike the ICP, there would be no final success, and in contrast to the Huks, a broadly vanguard MCP survived in Thai exile until the late 1980s, though my analysis focuses on the 1940s and 1950s. The group had two periods of fighting: first, against the Japanese from 1941 to 1945, and, second, against the British and the Malaysian government from 1948 to 1989. The MCP's organizational form was integrated from 1941 to 1942 and parochial from 1942 to 1945. It was integrated/parochial from 1948 to 1950, then vanguard from the mid-1950s before eventually giving up the fight completely in 1989 after decades of almost no activity.

My theory explains this trajectory reasonably well. Communism had strong roots in the Chinese community as a spillover from the Chinese Civil War. The party built upon a rich, if fractious, Chinese associational life but was excluded from the Indian and Malay ethnic blocs. This restricted the size of the politically salient population the MCP could draw upon. As a nonviolent party in the 1930s, the MCP thus combined increasingly strong vertical ties in the Chinese community with moderate horizontal linkages among organizers. These horizontal weaknesses among the leadership reflected both past repression and contingent strategic choices. During the war against the Japanese, the MCP's armed wing had some successes but faced recurrent leadership decapitation because of infiltration.

The MCP's strategy from 1945 to 1948 centered on the mobilization of labor in urban and semi-urban areas. This created a social base that was good for contentious politics but bad for rural insurgency. After launching the war in 1948 from this social base, the MCP was an integrated/parochial group until the early 1950s. However, as the war went on, the MCP was violently disembedded from its social sources of local strength and became increasingly unable to generate reliable manpower—even as the war bound the leadership together more closely after initial purges. The British counterinsurgency that evolved explicitly targeted the local roots of the MCP, and the MCP's local organization was badly undermined, driving a shift toward a vanguard structure. The MCP's central leadership was forced into exile in Thailand, where it remained until 1989 with no presence in Malaysia.

Communist beliefs, British policy, and ethnic division played significant roles in determining how the MCP was born, how it evolved, and how it died. Yet these factors had the effects they did because they shaped the ties and resulting organization MCP organizers built. Political divisions and prewar party-building strategy constrained the initial structure of the MCP at war, and comprehensive British counterinsurgency reshaped the social topography of Malaya in ways that undermined MCP local control.

Communism in Malaya

The social origins of communism in Malaya lie in outflows of Chinese who fled to Malaya to escape unrest in China during the 1920s.[5] Anarcho-communists and then Chinese Communist Party sympathizers who came from China brought these ideologies with them.[6] They existed in Malaya within a divided Chinese community that nevertheless was marked by robust communal activities. Communist organizers originally operated within the Kuomintang and focused on schools in urban areas. As Chiang Kai-Shek fell out with the Communists in China, leftists were purged from the Kuomintang in Malaya in 1927–1928. After experiments with various types of organizations, Communists from China established the Malayan Communist Party in 1930.[7]

Crucially, at the founding meeting to form the party, representatives of the Malay left wing were not present because they had been detained by the British. The MCP thus had almost exclusively Chinese roots.[8] This created an ethnic imbalance within the party's social base that "was to bedevil the MCP in later years."[9] Leftist opposition remained primarily the province of the Chinese in Malaysia.[10]

The party had trouble building a following and suffered internal dissension in 1932 and 1935–1936.[11] A solution to internal squabbling came from the installation of Lai Teck as MCP leader. As it turns out, Lai Teck was a French agent who had been passed to the British (and would later work for the Japanese and then the British again). This successful infiltration of the party led to the leadership being successfully undermined by targeted state repression over the years. This made it difficult for the party's leadership to maintain strong horizontal ties. Though the MCP was avowedly revolutionary, it was not a party built for insurgency. The MCP was not violent, nor was it popular during most of the 1930s.

Building a Combat Party, 1937–1945

In the wake of this failure, 1937 was a crucial year.[12] A mix of labor mobilization and anti-Japanese fund-raising and organizing after the Japanese invasion of China enabled the MCP to embed itself within the Chinese community. It used all of the tactics of the communist organizational weapon, particularly by infiltrating existing institutions and networks and steering them toward the left. This was an effective way to build up vertical ties, especially within unions and schools. The MCP reshaped its networks with an eye on the urban and semi-urban populations where Chinese were concentrated (especially urban squatters) and those that held the most promise for class mobilization.[13] In Fatt's words, the "MCP was frantic in penetrating into schools, clubs, associations, and other forms of corporate life in the Chinese community."[14] The networks the MCP later relied on were created through these activities in the late 1930s. This expansion of the MCP's social base was driven by the Japanese invasion of China, the Comintern's direction, and the growth of labor power in Malaya; it was not calculated with an eye toward future rural insurgency.

The Japanese invasion and the fall of Singapore shattered British prestige and opened space for the MCP to try its hand at militancy against the Japanese. In 1942, the MCP formed the Malayan People's Anti-Japanese Army.[15] This was the MCP's first appropriation of its party and labor linkages for the purpose of violence. During the early days of the war the group was fairly integrated. However, Lai Teck, the MCP leader, became a Japanese agent and betrayed a key meeting of the leadership in 1942 that left most of them dead or arrested. The leadership decapitation caused by Lai Teck's treachery undermined central control and made it difficult to coordinate action. This event led to a more parochial structure for the group during the war. The Malayan People's Anti-Japanese Army was never a major military force but it did gain credibility and respect for standing up to the Japanese.[16] Operations appear to have been fairly localized instead of implementing a clear master strategy. This was the MCP's first taste of guerrilla warfare, but it was not its last.

Mobilization, 1945–1948

After the Japanese surrender, brutal communal violence broke out in Malaya and the MCP was involved in Chinese-Malay conflict. Facing this chaos and the return of the British army, the leadership, again with Lai Teck in charge, decided against a seizure of power.[17] The Malayan People's Anti-Japanese Army was formally disbanded and an association of veterans was established. The MCP, following Comintern guidelines, opted for building and controlling a united front of political parties, unions, and other associations.[18] A policy of nonviolence enabled the MCP to regenerate its leadership cadres without facing continual counterinsurgency. It was able to deepen both its horizontal and its vertical linkages during 1945–1948. However, the strategic decision to not pursue a seizure of power directed the MCP toward urban labor activists and squatter communities, which the party saw as the roots of an urban and semi-urban class movement that would be able to overthrow the intertwined forces of British colonialism and industrial capital.

The MCP invested heavily in infiltrating the labor movement, especially in Singapore.[19] Coates argues that by 1947, the MCP controlled 214 of the country's 277 labor unions.[20] The party also targeted the semi-urban Chinese squatter population of the peninsula, where labor agitation and violence escalated after the war. The squatter communities were ripe for mobilization because of their fluid social structures and their confrontations with employers in the postwar tumult.[21] The strategy of building vertical ties through personal and institutional connections was reasonably effective.[22] As Stubbs notes, "The key to the recruiting process was personal contact. Recruits became associated with front organizations either through 'existing friendships', such as family ties or friendships made at work or at school, or through 'created friendships', such as those resulting from one neighbor, worker, or student helping another."[23] The MCP used this control of labor to mobilize against the British and against Malaya's economic elites. Efforts to build ties to the Malay ethnic population largely failed, as the legacies of Chinese-Malay communal violence during and after World War II deepened interethnic distrust.[24] The Chinese left was therefore the primary opposition social base in postwar Malaya.

The MCP became drawn into increasing confrontation with the British authorities. Yet there was trouble at the leadership level, as Harper notes: "The MCP was divided and compromised by informers."[25] Horizontal ties within the party leadership were weaker than the party's vertical linkages with other segments of society. Lai Teck was finally uncovered as an agent in 1947 and driven from the party, succeeded by the 26-year-old Chin Peng. Chin Peng was forced to significantly reshape the party leadership in the wake of Lai Teck's treachery. His removal was crucial for consolidating horizontal ties among organizers and removing the constant threat of decapitation and repression, but the process of rebuilding party leadership was not easy.

The party faced numerous challenges at this point, as Bayly and Harper note: it "was chronically short of funds, much of its rural organization had been disbanded, and it needed time to respond to the groundswell of criticism from its grass-roots members."[26] Stubbs argues that the leadership that remained after the removal of Lai Teck was inexperienced, and it appears that it took Chin Peng about a year to restore the party core.[27] This was disastrous timing, because consolidation was still under way when the MCP began its insurgency in 1948. There was no cunning plan on the part of the MCP to create a social base for insurgency, nor was the British state able to carefully manipulate the MCP: both were struggling through partial successes and regular failures in the face of profound uncertainty about the future.

By 1948 the MCP was embedded in some crucial Chinese communities, particularly urban laborers and semi-urban squatters. Its pre-insurgent, nonviolent party base lacked roots outside the Chinese ethnic group or in rural areas apart from places where the squatter population lived. Horizontal ties were only moderately strong compared to, for instance, those of the ICP in 1944–1945 (discussed below). This social structure created distinctive weaknesses when the MCP launched its insurgency. The emergence of the MCP as a party reflects a broader pattern identified in this book: networks can be strategically created in pursuit of a particular goal or ideology, but this is difficult and expectations guiding the underlying strategy often end up at odds with future realities.

Chapter 7

War Onset and Militant Origins, 1948–1951

While the MCP's labor unrest strategy was effective in creating contention and strikes, it was undermined by divisions within the different components of the coalition the MCP was trying to fashion.[28] By 1948, repression, concessions, and communal politics all peeled away important parts of the labor front and left the MCP worried that it had peaked.[29] British repression, Malay hostility, and intra-Chinese competition put the MCP in a precarious spot, even as it looked at other communist uprisings throughout the region. As Chin Peng restored order to the young and inexperienced leadership and clashes between labor and capital increasingly turned violent, the idea of direct armed struggle became increasingly attractive.

The MCP took the decision to go underground in the spring of 1948 because it anticipated a British crackdown, which the MCP hoped would then trigger an uprising. The MCP switched from a nonviolent opposition group to a revolutionary organization preparing for rebellion. It expected that the British would strike in September 1948, leaving the group several months to reorganize on a war footing before that event. Unfortunately for the MCP, the British moved more quickly than anticipated in the summer of 1948 as labor unrest escalated. This caught the MCP by surprise.[30] Instead of implementing a carefully thought-through plan, "both sides were responding to events, rather than initiating carefully formulated strategies."[31] As my theory predicts, the MCP needed to adapt its prewar networks to new wartime challenges:

> The MCP had now to undertake the transition from a quasi-legal political organisation whose strength lay principally in the labour unions and Ex-Comrades' Associations to an entirely clandestine association in the towns; a covert but manifest force in the villages and scattered Chinese peasant areas, which were open to sporadic visitations by government security forces; and the mobilisation, training, and supply of a regular guerrilla army"[32]

Many of its cadres were still publicly exposed and its urban component was unable to escape the vise of British repression in Singapore. The urban social base of the MCP was taken off the table as an insurgent tool and the hope of combining rural insurgency with a general strike became unworkable. As a result, "from the MCP's point of view, their guerrilla campaign went off at half cock," and its early operations indicated "the Party's lack of readiness."[33] The now-insurgent party was initially characterized by fairly strong local control and more mixed central institutionalization. From 1948 to 1951, the MCP was not a fully integrated group—there was too much leadership feuding—but it was also not a

[188]

parochial organization with distinct elite factions. I view it as an integrated/parochial hybrid. It moved closer to integration by 1950, but then over the course of the 1950s shifted to a vanguard structure, in one of the more complex patterns of change found in this book.

Central control among the leadership was initially problematic: "The leadership found it impossible to co-ordinate their campaign and control the actions of the rank and file"[34] during the mobilization of summer/spring 1948. Stubbs observes that this was partly due to "the elimination of any capable leaders during Lai Tek's treacherous association with the Party."[35] He further suggests that because of leadership attrition it "took a considerable amount of time to get both the guerrilla army and the Min Yuen on to a firm operational footing."[36] In the late 1940s, serious leadership feuding and purges occurred, though they did not cause major splits.[37] Over time the leadership became more cohesive under Chin Peng.

Vertical ties were more quickly and reliably turned into wartime institutions of local mobilization and control, as Stubbs notes: "Lai Tek, the British, and the Japanese had severely depleted the ranks of the MCP leadership. But it is true that at the level of the rank and file the MCP had few problems attracting recruits."[38] Bayly and Harper observe that locally, "where families, communities, and livelihoods were secure, the tight networks of kinship and friendship in the villages and workplace took on a compelling significance, and MCP's cadres were able to enmesh themselves in this."[39] The vertical embeddedness of the party was helpful when it went to war.[40] With Singapore no longer an option for militancy, the MCP fell back on squatter communities on the peninsula, where it had been able to build vertical ties alongside existing community organizations.[41]

The Min Yuen (People's Movement) was the civilian support apparatus that provided recruits and supplies to the fighting forces.[42] This was an elaborate apparatus intended to fuel the organization with men, food, and money to keep the war alive.[43] The Leninist structure of the MCP's organization chart was less important than the actual social relationships governing the mobilization of militants on the ground. Certain areas became MCP strongholds, while others were far less helpful to the organization, despite the diffusion of communism and a shared Chinese ethnicity, as Coates observes: "Unit strengths were determined by influences outside the Central Committee's control. Each group developed in almost exact relation to the strength of its popular base and following among the local community, and the effectiveness with which individual leaders attained this by pre-existing family and local ties, by terror, or by both."[44] The historical record matches up nicely with what the social-institutional theory predicts.

The social terrain of the war in 1948–1950 left the MCP excluded from its core urban networks but with access to local Chinese squatter communities on the jungle fringes and in semi-rural areas. As a result, initially it was very difficult for the British to penetrate the MCP in these areas.[45] Prewar ties were turned into new insurgent groups, for better and for worse. The MCP's problems of leadership continuity and elite infiltration made it more difficult to build central control, but its vertical ties to labor and especially to squatter communities were helpful in creating local institutions it could control. The MCP at peace became the MCP at war.

The Briggs Plan and the Destruction of Local MCP Organization, 1951–1956

Despite this starting point, the MCP's vertical embeddedness was destroyed by British resettlement policies: local disembedding was pursued with remarkable force and persistence. In 1950, the British announced their Briggs Plan, which was based on the premise that the British needed to control the Chinese squatter population by resettling it in defensible, densely populated areas. The strategy was aggressively implemented in 1950–1952, often at a significant human cost to Chinese populations. This policy was very important; Coates observes that "the process changed substantially the human geography of Malaya."[46] As Harper notes, "Counter-insurgency slowly began to detach guerrillas from their main sources of intelligence, recruitment, and food," and "in many cases resettlement uprooted long-established communities."[47]

The social underpinnings of the MCP were forcibly changed by coercive state policies of resettlement, as Bayly and Harper note: "In the new settlements people often had little in common, not even a shared language. The trauma of removal did not encourage the formation of new community ties, whether through dialect associations, clubs or temples. Social trust was deeply damaged."[48] Eventually over 500,000 Chinese were resettled, generally from the jungle fringes and semi-rural areas into urban encampments that could be patrolled by the British. Access to food became an increasingly significant problem for the Min Yen and armed guerrillas.[49] While the MCP could still influence resettlement camps, it came to recognize just how severely British policy undermined their ability to maintain reliable manpower.[50] In 1951, the MCP readjusted its strategy to focus on a much longer struggle. From a high of 8,000–10,000, the number of MCP guerrillas had declined to 3,000 by 1956.[51]

Resettlement shattered the vertical social bonds that had kept local MCP institutions functioning. As Coates writes, "the new Malaya envisaged by the MCP was deprived, for the foreseeable future, of such social basis as it had."[52] Neither communism nor ethnicity were sufficient to keep the organization in the field. This was not a simple case of hearts and minds leading to insurgent marginalization, as Hack notes: "'Hearts and minds' tactics were an important, but auxiliary, part of the 'population control' paradigm."[53] The MCP had become disembedded from its core local communities. It withdrew further into the jungles and began to prepare to emulate a Maoist model of peripheral insurgency in expectation of a protracted conflict.[54] The physical geography of the jungle was perfect for insurgency.[55] Yet surrenders to the British accelerated during the mid-1950s as local control broke down. As Short notes, the surrender process often occurred within a unit when "the hard core and the leader himself ultimately surrendered not because their own morale was destroyed but because they realized that their organization was disintegrating."[56] The British operated in a particularly conducive context for disembedding the MCP from local areas: Malaya is a relatively small place surrounded by water on three sides, the MCP was restricted to the Chinese population, and the effective colonial bureaucracy and physical infrastructure could be expanded to penetrate and control social life.

Into the Periphery: An Isolated Vanguard, 1956–1989

As its attacks declined and the MCP found it harder to find recruits, the remaining leadership cohered around Chin Peng and withdrew further into the unpopulated jungles. A spate of surrenders in 1957–1958 ended the MCP threat.[57] The MCP came to resemble a vanguard organization as a tight core of leaders endured without local institutions or linkages in Malaya. Interestingly, the social isolation of the leadership improved central control, even if there were few people left to control on the ground. The organization set up shop in southern Thailand, with occasional forays into Malaysia that had no effect.[58] The organization became enmeshed in various local dynamics in Thailand, maintained links to China, suffered some splits in ensuing decades, and eventually formally ended its war in 1989. Explaining these dynamics seems beyond the scope of my theory since the MCP was no longer waging a guerrilla war, but my social-institutional theory helps explain the structure of the group during its period of active warfare.

Understanding the Trajectory of the MCP

The MCP was broken by an unusually intensive British local counterinsurgency campaign that physically separated communities from the MCP. It transitioned from an integrated/parochial hybrid over time into a vanguard group with a small group of leaders that lacked vertical ties in the war zone itself. Some argue that "the British did not win the Emergency so much as the Malayan Communist Party lost it,"[59] but the process was the result of the interaction of state policies and the MCP's insurgency. The MCP was built upon a historically determined set of networks that shaped its ability to deal with the British state. The state in turn tried to figure out the best ways of targeting the MCP's vulnerabilities. The MCP was greatly helped by its ability to mobilize and infiltrate local Chinese institutions and networks, which provided recruits and loyal members until the mid-1950s. It was badly harmed by its restriction to the Chinese community, the urban focus of its labor militancy campaign, and especially British counterinsurgency at the local level. Local disembedding was the central strategy that broke the MCP's back, even as its leadership core was becoming more consolidated.

The MCP case reveals several insights. First, even when state policy is centrally important in the demise of an insurgent organization, that importance lies in its effects on the social and organizational linkages that make insurgency possible. Second, communism did not seamlessly create an organizational structure. The MCP had to navigate an intricate mix of ethnic and urban-rural divisions in Malaysian society even before the 1948 war broke out, and these challenges grew more potent after 1948. Third, the requirements for successful counterinsurgency against a relatively integrated group are very demanding: the massive population-removal and resettlement policy the British instituted in Malaya would have been nearly impossible in most other wars. Even though the MCP was ultimately marginalized, it exacted a serious cost that a less potent armed group would not have. The massive counterinsurgency campaign fundamentally changed many aspects of Malaya's political and social life, a stark contrast to the similarly successful counterinsurgency campaign in the Philippines. Finally, like the Hizbul Mujahideen in Kashmir, the MCP's survival as a vanguard group was possible only because of external sanctuary that could protect the leadership. This case shows how insurgent structures and state policies can interact to create organizational change.

The Huks in the Philippines: Grassroots Mobilization and Organizational Collapse

Peasant rebellions in the Philippines were regular occurrences under Spanish and American rule.[60] A new form of leftist uprising occurred in central Luzon against the Japanese during 1942–1945 and then against the Philippine government from 1946 until the early 1960s. Both rebellions were waged by an insurgent organization broadly known as the Huks (which had a slightly different name during each of the two periods).[61] Here I study the organizational structure and evolution of the Huk rebellions, with a focus on 1946–1960. I argue that in both wars, the Huks were built around peasant associations with loose linkages to the Philippine Communist Party (Partido Komunista Pilipinas, PKP). Both the peasant groups and the PKP emerged in nonviolent forms during the 1930s and also had a period of nonviolent reformism in the mid-1940s, right after World War II.

The social bases created in these periods of nonviolent mobilization were made up of strong vertical but weak horizontal ties. Crucially, the Communist leadership had few links to the peasants, while the peasant organizations were bottom-up phenomena characterized by strong solidarity but not coherent overarching leadership. The communists sought to mobilize the urban working class while the peasants sought reform from landed elites; neither group was preparing for rural insurgency. When war unexpectedly arose in 1942 and 1946, the wartime organizations that emerged were parochial: they were strongly locally embedded but lacked consistent central control and a unified leadership.

The parochial organizational outcome became particularly problematic in the second rebellion. Though not dramatic, changes in Philippine counterinsurgency during the early 1950s proved sufficient to persuade local fighters and commanders to drop out of the fight. Central commanders were divided and unable to implement a coherent strategy, leading to the fragmentation of the Huks and eventually their organizational demise by the early 1960s. State policy was important but it succeeded primarily because it could exploit the vulnerabilities inherent in a parochial insurgent organization, as Goodwin notes: "The lack of discipline and the organizational weaknesses of the Huks and PKP contributed to the movement's decline."[62] Importantly, we can trace deep continuities across markedly different political contexts from the early 1930s through the 1950s.

Why could the Huks not change? A lack of external sanctuary made factional fusing difficult in the heat of the war, and improvements in Philippine counterinsurgency made the "cooperation under fire" mechanism of change irrelevant. The parochial structure militated against reform and made mistakes more difficult to overcome. It also caused serious challenges for communist leaders who were trying to graft Marxist ideology onto peasant grievances: urban leftists were generally not embedded in preexisting structures of collective action that could credibly carry Marxism to the local level. My argument makes sense of why particular Philippine government initiatives succeeded and failed, why we observe distinctive patterns of recruitment and defection, and why the Huk rebels often seemed to be ill prepared for the strategic demands of war despite the fact that they had substantial grassroots support.

Peasant Movements and Anti-Japanese Insurgency

The origins of the Huk insurgents "lie in the rural terrain of peasant movements that prevailed in the 1930s."[63] Peasant mobilization in the 1930s against landed elites, primarily in central Luzon, expressed itself in a variety of rural associations demanding reform. Challenging landlord dominance in a context of fraying ties between landlords and tenants, these associations engaged in protests and contentious politics aimed at wresting concessions related to rent and ownership. However, "not even in the late 1930s, after the KPMP and AMT [two peasant associations] had merged, could a central leadership orchestrate the peasantry."[64] Kerkvliet, author of the definitive study of the Huks, attributes this to social gaps within and between different strata of the leadership.[65] These were major new movements that imbued peasants with a new agency. Despite that importance, they "acquired right from the start an unfortunate tendency to fragmentize or change organizational names and goals. At the root of this chaos was the personalistic nature of Filipino grievance groups."[66] These organizations were not built for war: in 1935–1940 they were primarily nonviolent and "wanted to work through legitimate channels."[67]

Concurrent with the rural peasant mobilization in central and southern Luzon was urban mobilization by the PKP, which saw the urban working classes as the future of the party. As Kerkvliet notes, "The PKP lacked strong ties with the peasantry. Few of its members were peasants, and the party did little political work in the countryside. Most of the active members lived in towns and cities where they focused on labor unions, especially those in Manila."[68] In Chapman's words, "The PKP was a small, urban-based collection of intellectuals and union activists who, except for [Juan] Feleo, had little interest in or knowledge of the peasant struggle. Neither the Socialist nor the Communist parties exerted any significant ideological influence over the rank and file."[69] Even within the urban realm, the PKP was not wildly effective.[70] Overall, "urban and rural leftists had no significant history of cooperation before the war."[71] The PKP had a few linkages to the peasant movements through organizers such as Juan Feleo, but in general the party looked to Manila, and when it operated in rural areas it was primarily through loose alliances rather than direct linkages. From the 1930s on, an urban-rural distinction existed, as did divisions among the rural hotbeds of peasant collective action.[72] Kerkvliet notes that there was no intentional mobilization of cadres for the purposes of war: "Rural folks never anticipated, let alone planned, the rebellion that was to come."[73]

After the Japanese invasion of 1942, anti-Japanese insurgency was built around these peasant organizations. The Hukbalahap (Hukbo ng Bayan Laban sa Hapon; People's Anti-Japanese Army)[74] emerged in 1942 in response to Japanese repression. The KPMP peasant association played an important role in this insurgent mobilization.[75] World War II–era Huk leaders had been heavily involved in prewar peasant politics.[76] There was a deep "continuity between the peasant movement of the 1930s and the Hukbalahap,"[77] but the Huks also expanded beyond this base. There is abundant evidence of high levels of popular support for the Huks: Kerkvliet notes that "villagers worked hand in hand with the guerrillas" and that "the Hukbalahap was a popular-based guerrilla movement with political organizations in the villages."[78] According to Lachica, "The peasant organizations formed before the war—the AMT and the KPMP—provided the mass base for the guerrillas."[79]

During the war against the Japanese, "the Hukbalahap army became rather effective."[80] Lanzona's study of the involvement of women in the Huk rebellion "highlights the importance of social organizations and networks in the mobilization of social and revolutionary movements." The Huks represent what Jeremy Weinstein would call an "activist" organization, one engaged in grassroots mobilization that has mass popular support.[81] The Huks were embedded in communities in ways that clearly helped organization at the local level. As Huizer notes, "This system functioned particularly well in areas where the peasant organizations had gained strength before the war."[82] These networks were repurposed for new wartime purposes, as the KPMP and AMT had most certainly not been built during the 1930s in anticipation of anti-Japanese guerrilla warfare. Huizer notes that it was only after the Japanese invasion that "peasant organisations then accepted military aims. Many peasants carried arms for the first time."[83]

However, the horizontal ties of the Huks were weaker, which made it hard to centrally coordinate the movement during their anti-Japanese war. In addition, the various Huk local units did not regularly obey the PKP, which continued to be an unimpressive party with few links to the countryside: "the Communist Party lacked deep roots in Central Luzon and could add little to the resistance."[84] Although the PKP attempted to exert some influence over the insurgency, because of the "tenuous relations the party had with the peasant movement in Central Luzon ... major policies that PKP leaders made and asked the Hukbalahap to follow were, in large measure, ignored."[85] A variety of initiatives that the PKP leadership demanded were simply disregarded by the major local commanders and units, even though both groups were fighting a popular war against an oppressive foreign occupier. Also, the military influence of the Huks was limited to the group's native territory; the group did not have a central tier of clear command that was able to move forces around, coordinate activities, or make broader strategic decisions.[86] During the anti-Japanese years, the Huks were clearly a powerful but parochial organization that built upon prewar peasant mobilization.

The Onset of HMB Insurgency

The Huks fought alongside American forces after the U.S. invasion of the Philippines in 1944. However, at the end of the war the peasant organizations that underpinned the Hukbalahap organization were faced with the return of the landlord elites. Many of these elites had collaborated with the Japanese, often abandoning the restive rural areas for Manila. The Americans sided with the elites and began disarming Huk units in the countryside.[87] Edward Lansdale, an American military intelligence officer, viewed the Huks as "true disciples of Karl Marx,"[88] and this perception shaped the repressive U.S. response.

A postwar peasant movement, the Pambansang Kaisahan ng mga Magbukid (National Peasant Union, PKM), combined elements of the Hukbalahap, the PKP, and other peasant associations. There was some coalition building between the PKP and the PKM and other peasant groups in the form of the Democratic Alliance party,[89] but despite large-scale support, "the PKM was far from being a tightly integrated organization. Nor could its leaders dominate it from the top."[90] Moreover, the Democratic Alliance program was nonviolent and "moderate."[91] Key organizers and leaders of the alliance expected that the left would be incorporated into a reformed, independent Philippine government. They demobilized their military forces in 1945. Even in 1945–1946 we do not see network building in anticipation of war; in fact, we see quite the opposite. Though there was peasant consciousness and shared grievances, there was no robust organization because of the enduring localism of the peasant groups and the fact that the communist party was weak and based in urban areas. Prior to the recurrence of war in late 1946, the leftist social base retained strong vertical ties at the local level but lacked strong horizontal ties to link together these localities.

As the PKM advanced a peasant agenda in the countryside, the urban communists of the PKP focused on "parliamentary struggle"[92] in 1945–1948. As Lachica notes, "An urban insurrectionary force just did not exist in Manila. The CPP operatives, it must be recalled, were writers, printers, labor leaders, and academicians who would not know how to handle a gun if they had to. The likeliest course for the duration was a 'legal struggle' with the objective of winning footholds in the political establishment."[93] The PKP could not—and for its own reasons would not—take on the mantle of central leadership of the peasants in the immediate postwar period. Instead, it looked to urban labor struggle until 1948—at which point it had few ties to the peasantry (especially after Juan Feleo was killed by the government in August 1946).

Rural violence escalated in the summer and fall of 1946 as village-level clashes turned into a wider conflict. The state cracked down hard on the PKM and on elected politicians associated with the movement. Peasant support flowed to the Huk organization, now renamed the Hukbong Magpapalaya ng Bayan (Peoples' Liberation Army, HMB).[94] The group was revitalizing its war machine, particularly in central Luzon. Kerkvliet notes that "it was a people's army, composed of and supported by villagers."[95] However, the Huks also engaged in intra-community coercion and enforcement that reflected their power and interest in being a shadow government; this included killing and torture. Multiple armed bands emerged, each apparently built around prior Huk units and reflecting "the continuity between the rebellion and earlier years of the peasant movement."[96] This was a parochial structure without strong central command. It appears that by 1948, the HMB included between 5,000 and 10,000 insurgents, but it lacked external material support from any states or diasporas.[97] The Philippine state began to redirect security forces into areas of rebellion in Luzon with support from the United States.[98]

The PKP and Democratic Alliance partners continued to engage in some legal and electoral activity in 1946–1947, maintaining an opposition to the rebellion until 1948. After World War II, the party had believed that "the urban working class would provide the leadership for a future revolution"[99] and had focused its efforts accordingly, not expecting a rural uprising. Top leaders during 1944–1947 "were not closely involved with the peasant movement,"[100] instead devoting attention to urban labor and electoral politics. In 1947, the party was divided over whether or not to throw its political and organizational weight behind the peasant movement.[101] The HMB was launching a "spontaneous" rebellion on the back of previous military and social mobilization.[102] The localized nature of the social base limited the HMB leaders' ability to agree on or implement a coherent central command structure. Pomeroy, an American involved in the movement, later wrote that the communists were disorganized and that "at best, provincial organizations of the Communist Party, of the Democratic Alliance, of the PKM and the CLO, largely on their own, were giving direction to peasants arming themselves and fighting back against suppression."[103]

Even when the PKP committed to harnessing and mobilizing the Huk rebellion and was banned in 1948, however, the party's weaknesses made it impossible to provide leadership. Its involvement in trying to lead the rebellion was the result of a miscalculation about the future course of the Philippine economy and U.S. intervention; it was not a party that had been optimized for what was to come.[104] As had been true for decades, the PKP "membership was not homogeneous nor was it a tightly disciplined organization."[105] A shared commitment to resisting elite domination was not enough to create organizational solidarity; the revolt "lacked central coordination."[106] As during the anti-Japanese period, the HMB was a parochial organization that had robust local units but weak central control processes.

Kerkvliet clearly identifies how the PKP's weaknesses intersected with the problem of peasant localism to create a parochial armed movement:

> The [PKP's] national leaders knew ... that real leadership of the rebellion required more than an alliance between top PKP leaders and key HMB leaders. Nor was it enough that some important HMB leaders were also party members.... The PKP had never been a "mass-based" party, it had weak ties with the peasant movement in Luzon, and as a party memorandum stated in late 1949, even many supporters of the "armed struggle" had a "deep prejudice against communism and communists."[107]

The Rise and Fall of the Huks

What happened to the Huk rebellion? From its origins in 1946 through its peak in 1951 and disintegration in the mid-1950s, "it followed the course of most peasant revolts in history—it waned, then faded away. Many rebels simply left their HMB squads."[108] The parochial structure that characterized the HMB left it open to counterinsurgency that could not be easily defended against because of loose central control. After factional splits in 1953–1954 among the high command and a series of surrenders, the Huks essentially fell apart (though parts of their social organization were remobilized by the New People's Army in the 1960s). Some attribute this outcome to a clever counterinsurgency policy by the government. Land reform, changes in the security sector, and free 1951 elections are identified as causes of the insurgency's fragmentation and collapse.

Yet as Slater shows, Philippine government reforms were noticeable but minor. Land reform was limited and corrupt, while privileged elites continued to dominate politics.[109] There was improved treatment of civilians by the armed forces, which apparently convinced some Huks to slip away back into pure civilian life.[110] Ramon Magsaysay, who played a central role in counterinsurgency as defense secretary and then as president, was an inspirational and savvy leader, but there was not much objective change. Still, it was necessary to avoid massive indiscriminate violence to forestall the "cooperation under fire" mechanism that could change the HMB from a parochial group to an integrated organization, and in this the state succeeded.

State policy prevented the HMB from forming a tight coalition of insurgent leaders, but the underlying cause of Huk fragmentation was the social-institutional structure of the movement. Crucially, "the [PKP] had few roots in the villages and municipalities of Central Luzon,"[111] and its efforts to expand into new social terrain consistently failed because the peasantry there was not familiar with either the PKP or the HMB organizers. There was not much enthusiasm for these missions in the first place, since "Huk cadres had been reluctant to leave their home areas."[112] The "parochial character of the rebellion and the Huks' persistent internal tensions"[113] made the Philippine state's job much easier. The Huk leadership began to be locally disembedded; its own internal assessments showed shrinking local support and the defection of local units, starting especially in 1952.[114]

Even after it decided to take up the leadership of the rebellion in 1948, the PKP never solved its organizational problems, which stretched back to the 1930s, and its previous lack of focus on rural mobilization proved impossible to make up for in the context of an escalating war. The PKP was not stupid or myopic and its leaders were not cowards. The party explicitly tried to create discipline among insurgents, as its leadership felt that "left in this condition, the armed peasants would surely fail." With proper training and leadership from the PKP, the leadership believed, "the armed struggle would become an effective, tightly organized 'revolutionary movement.'"[115] PKP leaders took serious personal risks to put this model into practice.

Yet the weight of history made it hard to actually achieve this goal. Expansion was limited beyond central Luzon for social reasons, external sanctuary was not available to help the factions unite, and the reformed Philippine state made it possible for HMB fighters to believe they could escape punishment if they put down their guns. Embracing the Marxist-Leninist organizational strategy was not enough to actually create an integrated organization. The PKP's weak social structure made it an ineffective vessel of insurgent control and made the Philippine state's job much easier. As Kerkvliet notes, "Even at the movement's peak... one of the most troublesome problems from the national PKP leaders' viewpoint was that leaders of section committees, squadrons, and field commands frequently refused to comply with party directives. This happened even if these local leaders were party members.... [PKP/HMB] failed, despite their numerous efforts, to standardize procedures for recruiting people into the party."[116] This organizational outcome arose from the precarious nature of the alliance between the PKP and the HMB.[117] One of the most serious faults of peasant cadres, the PKP claimed, was that "people put their families, friendships, and local concerns ahead of the movement as a whole."[118] This is a classic parochial structure.

During the early 1950s, defections from the HMB accelerated. Some members surrendered to the government, but many just slipped away back home.[119] The deep social gaps in the movement that had been apparent since the 1930s came to the surface as the conflict endured, and "by 1953, the movement's remaining leaders were powerless to prevent even larger numbers of armed peasants from leaving."[120] As military and organizational pressures took their toll, the space available for conscious cohesion-building and grassroots politicization grew ever smaller, and "rebels had no more time for the movement's work; they were too busy trying to survive."[121]

In this context, open feuding erupted among factions.[122] In 1954, within the HMB "several important leaders split into two factions over this question of what to do."[123] By the mid-1950s, things had gotten worse, as Kerkvliet explains: "The movement had not one set of leaders but at least three, which developed as the unrest expanded.... Generally, leaders varied with respect to their connections to peasant organizations and with respect to their ideologies or outlooks."[124] The internal structure of conflict reflected the underlying social base of the movement. By the early 1960s, the HMB had become largely defunct, though local units and commanders continued to exist, often in collusive arrangements with politicians or power holders. Chapman summarizes the state of affairs: "By the 1960s, the Huk army had disintegrated into a collection of gangs."[125]

Explaining Huk Fragmentation

Kerkvliet sums up the social structure of the Huk rebellion:

> The alliances, when they did occur between peasant organizations or peasant rebels and the PKP, remained tenuous. This was another reason why the party had only limited influence on the course of the peasant movement. First, its ties to the peasant movement were mainly at the upper levels of the movement—primarily through national and middle-level leaders of the Hukbahalap, PKM, and HMB. The party had few roots in the villages and municipalities of Central Luzon.[126]

More broadly, Scott argues that the rebellion was a "classical case" of tension between peasants and urban revolutionary elites.[127] The peasants were organized into localized institutions and associations of their own;

this was not a case of rural anomie but instead of disjuncture between coalitions.

Arguments claiming that communists have particular organizational skills must deal with the ultimately fissiparous nature of the Huks.[128] In the Philippines, a site of peasant mobilization, rapacious rural elites, and the explicit embrace of a Marxist-Leninist model, the absence of social ties linking peasant associations and the PKP left the insurgency unable to hold itself together. Instead, "peasants and radicals glided past each other, each going the opposite way from the other and from the way each had been going before."[129] Understanding the roots of the Huk organization is essential to explaining the overall course of the war. Kessler suggests that the internal problems of the Huks organization were largely to blame. According to him, "in an important sense, they defeated themselves."[130]

My theory helps us understand the trajectory of the Huk rebellion because it illuminates why the PKP and HMB were unable to harness peasant unrest and forge an integrated and durable Marxist-Leninist insurgency. It does not deny that grievances, state policy, or ideology were relevant but it explains how these factors affected the insurgents. Most important of these other factors, Philippine counterinsurgency contributed to Huk defeat, but it did so at least in part because of the HMB's parochial organizational structure. We need to pay attention to political context and state policy, but we can fully understand rebellions only by examining how they are actually built and upon what kinds of social support they rely.

Forging the Insurgent State: ICP/Viet Minh Mobilization and Resilience, 1925–1954

The Indochinese Communist Party (ICP) was a powerful armed group that created North Vietnam after years of war with the French. The ICP and its Viet Minh military front were notable for their organizational cohesion; the party suffered no major internal splits that would undermine the armed struggle from 1946 to 1954. During that period it was clearly an integrated organization on a vast scale that eventually included hundreds of thousands of fighters in the Viet Minh. Yet before 1941, the ICP was a vanguard organization. In 1930–1931 and 1940 major ICP-linked revolts fell apart amid urban-rural and central-local disarray. There was important variation in organizational (and war) outcomes over time. In 1944–1946, the ICP was transformed from a vanguard group into an integrated organization. This raises a key question: What enabled an urban-based group of communists to overcome numerous past failures and successfully implant local institutions in previously alien soil?

This section argues that the ICP took advantage of a rural power vacuum in 1944–1946 that was opened by shifts in state policy that were exogenous to ICP activities. It then built local alliances by cutting deals with a wide variety of local power holders while remaining controlled by a core set of leaders. In doing so, it both seized and co-opted state power during 1945 and 1946. We see new institutions being built and consolidated, especially in Tonkin, prior to the onset of full-scale war with France in December 1946. This pivotal period laid the basis for massive warfare from late 1946 through 1954 and is the focus of this section.

The ICP/Viet Minh case provides support for my theory but also points to a much wider array of important variables. There are several limitations to my argument's explanation of the group's trajectory. First, the vacuum of rural power in 1944–1946 opened space for the ICP to escape the bonds of state repression. The political context was changing rather than being constant or fixed. Second, Ho Chi Minh's sharp understanding and implementation of the Marxist-Leninist organizational ideology (albeit with Maoist and nationalist edges) demonstrate the importance of human agency and strategy. Leadership was important, especially since during most of 1945–1946, the party could have pursued a variety of different strategies. Though we see local alliances as a key mechanism for transforming the ICP from a vanguard group to an integrated structure, nationalist-communist ideological appeals, Chinese external aid, and French policy—both in its absence (1944–1946) and in its brutal return to violence in 1946—also played important roles.

My argument therefore does not provide a full explanation for the ICP's course. It nevertheless offers key insights into the ICP's patterns of organization. First, the 1930–1931 and 1940 revolts looked very much like what we would expect from a vanguard group built around strong horizontal but weak vertical social linkages: local disarray in the face of a determined French counterinsurgent state. While it was eventually possible for the ICP to build new generations of local cadres, the process was difficult and time consuming. The fighters who took on France in 1946 were the result of two decades of effort. Second, my theory correctly identifies a crucial mechanism of expansion that the ICP used to become present in rural areas. Local alliances were a key route to changing vertical ties, though they were not the only one. The Viet Minh did not simply impose their will or rely on diffuse nationalism; instead, their cadres mobilized opposition to the French and to elite Vietnamese collaborators, exploited divisions in rural areas, and engaged in political co-optation to create new linkages that solidified their organization on the ground. This was a huge social-institutional project rather than a simple distilling of mass communist or nationalist sentiment into organization.

Third, the Viet Minh experienced significant problems of local control during their insurgent state building. There is extensive evidence of the bargaining and deals on the ground that made institutionalization possible. Local cadres, party factions, and different parts of state bureaucracy were all serious challenges to the ICP's "wobbly leviathan."[131] This process of gradual organization building confirms the importance of local alliances to ICP growth.

This section analyzes the ICP in peace and war from its founding through the formation of North Vietnam in 1954. It emphasizes the 1930–1946 period because it was then that the most truly "insurgent" processes operated. By the late 1940s, the ICP and Viet Minh were using armies and deploying strategies that more closely resembled massive conventional warfare than traditional guerrilla conflict. I seek to explain how this outcome was reached, but I do not delve into the operational details of the war against the French after 1948.

Building the ICP: Communist Mobilization through the Nghe Tinh Revolt, 1925–1931

French Indochina was ruled by a French administrative elite and a set of Vietnamese collaborators. A complex array of nationalist and communist organizations and networks stood in varying levels of opposition to the French presence in the mid-1920s.[132] These groups were largely dominated by urban, educated young men who had in many cases emerged from the French educational system in Indochina.[133] They constituted the dominant politicized social bases that could potentially be mobilized for war. Social structure and political economy mediated the effects of the growing nationalist sentiment, as Tai has noted: "Though the revolutionary tide swept through all three regions of Vietnam at the same time, its effect on the local political landscape was very different."[134] Nationalist and communist ideologies did not translate into any particular form of political organization.

In 1925, Ho Chi Minh returned from time in France to take control of an anticolonial Vietnamese organization based in southern China (the Revolutionary Youth League in Canton).[135] Ho Chi Minh was operating under Comintern guidance as he attempted to meld Marxism-Leninism with Vietnamese nationalism. Ho tried to appeal to nationalism while infusing it with Marxism-Leninism. He used the league as an infrastructure through which to build "a nucleus of radical intellectuals to serve as a source of future Party leaders."[136] This seemed promising, as "Leninism offered precisely what the Vietnamese liberation movement had heretofore lacked—organization, cohesion, external support, and a plan."[137] Ho also tried to mobilize affiliated and front organizations.[138]

Chapter 7

However, the league became locked in rivalries with other Vietnamese political organizations and was unable to ascend to a position of predominance, especially over the radical nationalist (but noncommunist) Viet Nam Quoc Dan Dang. In 1927, the escalation of violence between the Chinese Communist Party and the Kuomintang forced Ho to leave Canton for Moscow.[139] Ho's departure and schismatic ideological battles had taken a dramatic toll on the league by 1929.[140] Feuds and splits erupted in Ho's absence.[141] Khanh notes that the heterogeneity of the league undercut its organizational capacity,[142] while repression by Chinese authorities exacerbated these social and ideological divisions.[143]

Ho Chi Minh came back in 1930 and was able to sort out a compromise between the various groups under the banner of the Vietnamese Communist Party, supported by the clear directive of the Comintern, thus restoring a "delicate unity."[144] Individual leadership played an important role in this compromise.[145] The ICP's social base had some horizontal ties but few vertical linkages to local communities.[146] Like many other anticolonial movements, its members were the products of elite urban colonial education rather than members of a grassroots rural mobilization. In February 1930, an uprising by the Viet Nam Quoc Dan Dang was quashed; the noncommunist nationalists who had launched it were targeted by the hammer blows of the colonial regime.[147]

In 1930–1931, as the ICP/VCP was being cobbled back together under Ho's leadership, a peasant rebellion broke out in southern and north-central parts of French Indochina. This was the culmination of surging contentious politics during an economic downturn.[148] The rebellion was simultaneously widespread in scope and highly localized in character. As local elites and French officials were pushed out of villages, Communists and peasants formed the Nghe Tinh soviets; they also mounted a shorter rebellion in Cochinchina.[149] ICP mobilization had tapped into both urban and rural unrest, contributing to cascading violence.[150] This was not the intentional strategy of the Hong Kong–based leadership, but its policies had helped set the revolt in motion and the ICP scrambled to deal with the uprising.[151] This was the most serious uprising in decades, and it rocked Indochina for nearly two years.[152] By October 1930, the central leadership of the ICP was faced with the dilemma of whether or not to actively support the rebellion. The party tried to pull back its regional and local branches from the conflict, amid a broader debate about the purpose and theory of the communist movement in Indochina.[153] The war was unexpected, and it put pressure on the ICP.

Despite attempts to manage the rebellion, the ICP lacked the organization to control its regional and local forces. Scott notes that "within a few weeks at most the movement and many of its ill-trained cadre had

[204]

evaded the control of the party."[154] The disarray of the ICP's leadership left it unable to control the upsurge of violent mobilization or to counter the violent French repression that ensued.[155] The Nghe Tinh revolt shows that an intense sense of grievance, mass peasant mobilization, and Marxist-Leninist ideology were insufficient to build a resilient insurgent group in the face of a committed counterrevolutionary state. The "sporadic, localist" mobilization of "a series of distinct movements which correspond to local needs as much as to central direction"[156] overcame attempts by the ICP center to control and harness the rural revolt, revealing clear tensions between peasants and commissars. Given the urban core of the party and its prior weaknesses in the villages, this result is not surprising in the framework of my theory: the ICP's brief foray into rebellion created a vanguard group during this period that corresponded to the prior social structure of the movement.

Trying to Rebuild the Organizational Weapon, 1931–1940

The ICP was smashed. Lockhart writes that "the almost complete destruction of the ICP as soon as it was formed involved the execution or imprisonment of 90% of its leaders,"[157] and Duiker notes that "Ho Chi Minh's painstaking efforts to build up the nucleus of a loyal and disciplined organization were swept away."[158] The repression that the ICP experienced after the 1930–1931 uprising led to "years of persecution, isolation, and near-extinction of its organizational apparatus."[159] The ICP had to be almost entirely rebuilt, since "the inner party leaders [were] nearly all dead or in prison."[160] Ho Chi Minh was arrested by the British in Hong Kong, spent five years in the USSR, and did not return to leadership work with the ICP until 1940.[161]

Both Marxist-Leninist organizational ideology and nationalist sentiment played an important role in keeping the ICP's social base alive.[162] Many of the new ICP members were trained in Moscow in a process that enhanced their ideological commitment and social ties to one another.[163] Prisons also provided a space for the building of solidarity.[164] In 1935, the party convened a conference for the first time since the Nghe Tinh revolt.[165] Tensions continued to exist within the party, but the ICP was starting to coalesce again.[166]

A major breakthrough came with the creation of a Popular Front government in Paris, which loosened the restrictions on the ICP. This shift in political opportunity was completely exogenous to dynamics in Vietnam. The ICP launched an expansion campaign as a semi-legal organization.[167] This party worked on behalf of the party publicly while a secret apparatus continued to work in the background.[168] Because of this dual presence, "national and local ICP networks [were] restored and expanded to well beyond 1930 levels."[169] Much work remained to be done in rural areas, still a crucial site of weakness for the ICP at this stage.[170] Khanh argues that the Popular Front period opened a path for organization building but that the party did not sufficiently embrace or take advantage of this opportunity, in part because the shifting party line led to "confusion and dissension"[171] in the ICP.[172] However, the political opening rapidly disappeared with the coming of World War II. The USSR's alignment with Germany ended the French need to tolerate communist mobilization and they were now "determined to root out the communist movement."[173] In 1939, the French crackdown forced the party to the countryside; they effectively uprooted the urban networks where the ICP had strength.[174]

The French continued to administer the territory after the Japanese occupied French Indochina in 1940. At the end of 1939, the ICP had encouraged armed uprisings at its Sixth Plenum, and a series of revolts erupted against the Japanese and French during the fall of 1940. There a revolt in the Bac Son valley in the north, and in Cochinchina in the south another revolt emerged that was more clearly led by ICP regional leaders.[175] As the central party leadership watched the French wipe out the Bac Son revolt, they tried to restrain the southern cadres, but they were unable to get the word to Cochinchina, and the uprising there was quickly smashed.[176] Not only had the party leadership been surprised by these revolts but once again "they were unable to coordinate activities on a national scale."[177] French repression kept ICP organizers out of local communities. This left the party "somewhat confused and leaderless in the fall of 1940" and "in almost total disarray."[178] Constructing a social base that could harness and control local mobilization proved enormously difficult for the ICP as long as the French forces maintained vigilance. It was hard for the group to overcome its status as a vanguard organization during the 1930s because "French repression from 1930 to 1935, and again from 1939, prevented the establishment of durable party centres inside Indochina."[179]

World War II, Political Opportunities, and the Seizure
of Power, 1941–1945

The ICP was not annihilated by the revolts of 1940 (units in the north had been able to slip away), but it was badly damaged: "Organizationally it appeared to possess less potential than any of the other groups."[180] However, an increasingly organized ICP emerged from the ruins of World War II. Ho Chi Minh revitalized his work for the ICP in south China, where he helped broker alliances between nationalist and communist Vietnamese groups under the patronage of Chinese leaders.

Instead of building their organization under the watchful eyes of the colonial regime, the communists found and trained new recruits with the backing of an external set of powerbrokers, relying heavily on sanctuary. This process eventually created a vanguard group that could take advantage of new structural opportunities in 1944–1946 to transform itself into an integrated organization.

In 1941, the ICP established a new front organization, the Viet Minh.[181] It was an alliance of various anti-Japanese/anti-French forces that was controlled by an ICP core that melded nationalism with communism.[182] ICP leaders injected Maoist thinking into the Vietnamese context, with a focus on rural base areas and mobilization.[183] A new strategy was yoked to a new political context: an array of affiliate organizations was created to recruit and socialize new members under Viet Minh and ICP control.[184] Base areas that were established in the north along the Chinese border became the focus of the movement.[185] Nevertheless, the forging of a cohesive front organization was "more easily talked of than realized"[186] because of the distrust many had for the ICP. In addition, the party's roots in the countryside were shallow.[187] A massive investment in organizational infrastructure was needed. For most of the war, the Viet Minh were only a small obstacle to the Japanese, notwithstanding their new Maoist orientation.[188]

The ICP was ultimately able to outmaneuver its rivals and build deeper ties to the peasants because it took advantage of two significant changes in political context. The new strategy failed to build strong local links until 1944, but then it found itself perfectly primed to take advantage of a power vacuum. The first contextual change was the French colonial regime's increasing lack of interest in and then capacity for fighting the Viet Minh. The regime at first maintained a strong focus on order and control, and as late as May 1944 "the essential [ICP] network ... was a shambles"[189] because of French countermeasures. But by late 1944, "French operations were not systematically aimed at the ICP at all.... French military deployments were no longer dictated by the internal threat."[190] This was an exogenous change in political conditions that enabled the ICP to build networks in the rural areas.

As the French tried to anticipate their future in a post-Nazi France, their level of cooperation with the Japanese occupation forces decreased, and space opened for the ICP.[191] Toward the end of 1944, Vo Nguyen Giap was put in charge of creating a more formal armed structure that was the predecessor of the military of the First and Second Indochina Wars.[192] The ICP's vision could be put into action on the ground, creating new social and organizational ties rather than having to fall back on the weak links that had so badly failed it and its cadres in 1930 and 1940.[193] Thus, it was "able to break into the society at a point where

French power was weakened by World War II."[194] Local alliances were put into place with a wide variety of local power holders. The ICP did not impose a police state immediately but instead cut deals, incorporated new constituencies, and sent its cadres to the villages in order to form new relationships, establish new information flows, and lay the basis for organization. The local alliance mechanism operated here in a slow process of organization building.

1945–1946: Constructing the Insurgent State

The second shift in political opportunity that made local alliances easier came in 1945 when first the French and then the Japanese abandoned their attempts to control rural violence. The revolutionary moment for the ICP arrived when the Japanese launched a coup against the French colonial administration in March 1945. Until that point, the French had patrolled the countryside, while the Japanese had primarily focused on urban control.[195] After they dispensed with the French, the Japanese tried to prop up a puppet regime, but the power vacuum in the countryside created an opportunity for the Viet Minh.[196] From March 1945 through the Japanese seizure of power in August 1945 until the eventual outbreak of open war between France and the Viet Minh in late 1946, the Viet Minh and their ICP controllers faced low barriers to collective action.[197] Viet Minh mobilization prepared the party to seize power, in coalition with other political forces, after the Japanese surrendered in August 1945 and to set up a provisional government to rule Vietnam.[198] The organizational structure that coalesced in this period was the foundation of the Viet Minh that fought against the French from 1945 to 1954.[199]

This laid the basis for an unprecedented mass expansion, as Lockhart notes: "In the north the army ... enjoyed fifteen months of relative peace which enabled it to build on its already high level of political and military development."[200] Unlike in Malaya and the Philippines, Tonnesson notes that in the wake of the Japanese coup, "the risks of joining the revolution were suddenly dramatically reduced."[201] The power vacuum proved crucial because "the Party itself was small and still inexperienced."[202] However, even before their surrender, "the Japanese never really tried to control the countryside," and this enabled the ICP to use violence to target potential rivals and dissidents and punish collaborators without a countervailing armed force to blunt its onslaught.[203]

Yet the shift in political context, Marxist-Leninist organizational ideology, and Ho Chi Minh were not enough to immediately create Viet Minh integration, though all of these things mattered.[204] A process of local alliance building was necessary to push control out beyond the vanguard core. The Japanese coup led to a competitive scramble for mobilization among various contenders, and "a number of fortuitous circumstances contributed in no small measure to the Communist victory [in August 1945]."[205] Within the Viet Minh, there were tensions and clashes, as Vu notes: "In most cases, local Viet Minh militias did not fight the Japanese. Instead, it was 'old Viet Minh' fighting 'new Viet Minh,' Viet Minh militias exchanging fire with DP [Vietnamese Democratic Party] ones, and People's Committees challenging the authority of Viet Minh committees."[206] Various local divisions provided an excellent opportunity for the ICP to make alliances, but they were not seamless or without cost: the creation of alliances required compromise and time. The ICP now needed to overcome the organizational challenges created by the nature of its seizure of power; as Vu notes, "One source of the problem was clearly the way the Viet Minh government had been formed on the back of a popular but spontaneous movement."[207]

In 1945, the ICP faced the dual challenges of disunity within the core leadership and a "paucity of Party members."[208] The ICP had about 5,500 members in August 1945, a small revolutionary vanguard given the size of the revolution it was trying to control.[209] Even before the return of war, in 1945 and 1946 "the administration established by the Viet Minh in Hanoi became as much a prisoner of the thousands of revolutionary committees emerging around the country as the directing authority."[210] The strain of turning a vanguard into an integrated organization are clearly observable, providing support for my argument that local alliances are a crucial—though not the only—mechanism for creating such change. Duiker notes that "the mass base of the Vietminh front was broad—embracing peasants, workers, students, and some merchants and intellectuals in the major cities—but shallow, for the Communist coloration of the leadership was not as yet directly evident to the vast majority of supporters."[211] He points out that "the situation posed a serious challenge to the technique of the united front that the ICP had used."[212] As Vu notes, "The ICP was able to expand quickly but Party leaders at all levels seemed oblivious to the risks that rapid expansion might incur."[213] The ICP technically disbanded itself in favor of a broad front government, but its core continued to try to control the movement while integrating numerous local factions. The Viet Minh, though eventually highly disciplined, still had to actually build trust, connections, and institutions in local communities, and this "accommodation produced divided state leadership, fractured organizations, and a decentralized structure lacking both a cohesive social base and a crucial foreign alliance."[214]

To add to these problems of internal organization amid a fairly chaotic expansion, European power returned in the south, particularly around Saigon.[215] First British and then French forces were able to exert influence in the south. Cochinchina became the focus of French efforts to reconstruct their rule in Indochina, and this effort prefigured the north-south clashes that emerged in the following decades. The Viet Minh and the French engaged in a sporadic series of negotiations mixed with low-level clashes and disputes.[216] The Viet Minh cracked down on its nationalist (ostensible) allies and rivals in the summer of 1946.[217]

The Viet Minh and its Democratic Republic of Vietnam were forged between March 1945 and December 1946. The ICP was able to convert its organizational ideology into a tenuous but enduring reality due to the shift in political context occasioned by the geopolitics of 1944–1946.[218] The state structure that emerged became the base of a real state during the First Indochina War. The rise of the ICP as the social glue connecting previously disparate nodes of local mobilization was a long and difficult process, and the achievement of its ideological vision was contingent on state policies both within and outside of French Indochina. This shift toward integration was made possible by the power vacuum, by Ho Chi Minh's ability to craft a broad and appealing ideology, and by pervasive local conflicts that the Viet Minh could take advantage of. Yet the organizational change cannot be simply attributed to these factors, since the group needed to actually get on the ground and craft vertical linkages that made it possible for organizational processes to operate.

The vanguard—which was limited to urban revolutionaries in the 1930s—had transformed into an organization that far closer to an integrated form by 1946, but with growing pains that reflected its social underpinnings. The organizational project would not be fully complete until a series of brutal purges in the 1950s. Having laid the essential historical basis for the conflict, it is to the Viet Minh's war with France that we now briefly turn.

Mobilizing for War: Conflict with France, 1946–1954

The Viet Minh's organizational trajectory during the First Indochina War approaches that of an integrated group. The ICP at war was the social-organizational underpinning of Viet Minh military power. The Viet Minh's civilian administrative apparatus was not particularly cohesive, since it was reliant on non-ICP members who had been co-opted and brought in from the colonial apparatus.[219] The state that emerged was "bifurcated" and consisted of a mix of holdover colonial bureaucrats, Viet Minh leaders, co-opted nationalists, and local pockets of mobilization.[220] Vu describes the result: "A central feature of Vietnam's nationalist movement during the late 1940s was its organizational anarchy."[221]

However, the military side of the movement was significantly more cohesive and institutionalized. Village-level ICP members and representatives spearheaded recruitment and local monitoring, while ICP cadres dominated central command of the Viet Minh standing forces. The core horizontal linkages at the heart of the Viet Minh leadership, forged by decades of shared experiences, stabilized central institutionalization and made possible the increasing mobilization of local society. The skirmishes between the Viet Minh and the French flared into full-scale war in December 1946, and the most of the insurgents retreated from the cities in order to wage a rural war. This was not, however, a guerrilla war in a classical sense: there were up to 50,000 Viet Minh fighters, though they were certainly not particularly well trained or well armed. These forces took heavy losses as they attempted to withdraw.[222] As the ICP and the French tried to hold on to military strength, both attempted to build political alliances with other groups in Vietnamese society, especially in the countryside. The Viet Minh fighting forces maintained decent organization and capability.[223] The shifting tide of the Chinese Civil War made it possible for them to continue to rely on border areas for sanctuary. Limits on French manpower opened space for the Viet Minh to become further locally embedded.[224] The war tilted in favor of the Viet Minh as the intransigence and limited resources of the French and Mao's victories in China enabled the integrated Viet Minh to bolster its military and strategic power.

The victory of Mao in China led to an escalation in the ability of the ICP and its Viet Minh fighters to deploy military power.[225] The growing links between the Chinese Communist Party and the ICP had "momentous consequences"[226] for the evolution of the war in Indochina. A 1950 border offensive carved out further space in the north for the Viet Minh, forcing the French to tighten their perimeter.[227] Vu argues that Chinese aid enabled the ICP to consolidate its rule in 1949 by purging some of the other social forces that had been incorporated into the movement in hasty years of early expansion.[228] The ICP used its military prowess, political acumen, and external support to shatter potential rivals.[229] From roughly 1949, analyses treat the Viet Minh military apparatus as a unitary state actor.[230] A series of offensives and campaigns by both the Viet Minh and the French, culminating in the French defeat at Dien Bien Phu, led to a negotiated settlement and a partitioned Vietnam.

Explaining Viet Minh Cohesion

Important aspects of the ICP case accord with my argument. First, the ICP-linked 1930–1931 and 1940 revolts closely resembled what we would expect from an organization with its social base: it was chaotic and poorly disciplined at the local level and demonstrated endemic urban-rural gaps that reflect vanguard organization. Second, the group transformed from a vanguard to an integrated structure by using local alliances to create local institutions.[231] Though made possible by shifts in context, the specific processes through which the ICP changed were driven by social mechanisms and strategies and operated as my theory predicts. In this case, the social-institutional argument provides insights even when other variables are significant factors: the contextual changes made it possible for local alliances to occur. Third, even into the 1950s, the ICP experienced problems of local control in consolidating its rule over the new state because of the social heterogeneity of the coalition it had assembled.[232] Nationalism, communism, and leadership still needed to be grafted onto social life through organization, and none of these were seamless processes.

Despite the value of the social-institutional theory, ideology and state power continue to be necessary for any satisfying explanation of this case. Organizational ideology seems to have helped the ICP by providing a broad umbrella under which the Viet Minh could exploit and reframe local conflicts. Ideas did not straightforwardly build organization, but they did allow the party to survive in difficult times, to appeal to the mass public, and to expand central control on the ground. The ICP case is particularly interesting because of the way the leadership fused nationalism and Marxism, providing a framework for incorporating different social blocs into the movement and facilitating a rapid shift in organizational control. This shows a very different kind of ideational project than simply reading Lenin and Mao; the real challenge was grafting general ideas onto specific social and political circumstances.

The rural power vacuum in 1944–1946 is also essential for understanding the organization's course. The ICP's social structures in 1941 did not foretell the organization of 1945–1946. As Tønnesson notes, "When we consider the almost incredible cohesiveness of the little group of Vietnamese communist leaders who were to hold the reins from 1945 to 1986, it is striking to see how heterogeneous the movement was during its early history."[233] Large shifts in political opportunity intersected with a vanguard structure that could exploit the power vacuum. The rise of the Viet Minh was not a simple story of social bases and local alliances, but it cannot be understood without including the factors my theory emphasizes.

Goodwin's Alternative Argument: Political Context

Jeff Goodwin has offered an alternative explanation for these patterns of rebellion in post-1945 Southeast Asia.[234] Goodwin claims that political context—specifically state policy after the return of the colonial powers in 1945—is the crucial variable that explains the variation in the trajectories of the MCP, the ICP, and the Huks.[235] He argues that after the rise of anti-Japanese insurgent movements in all three colonies during World War II, inclusive and reformist colonial/neocolonial policies in the Philippines and Malaya defanged insurgent movements, while repression in French Indochina left dissidents with no other way out than to rally around the flag of the ICP. The degree of insurgent cohesion reflected the opportunities presented by the regime's policies. Regime accommodation led to insurgent fragmentation because key social blocs allied with a reforming state instead of joining a cohesive insurgent coalition held together by the grievances of colonialism and the exclusionary policy of the regime.

Goodwin's account is valuable for highlighting how state policies shape the options available to armed groups, echoing my conclusions from the Viet Minh case. My theoretical approach is weaker at incorporating the macrostructural environments in which insurgents operate; it focuses instead on the specific processes of mobilization and survival that characterize insurgent organization. Bringing insurgent groups into the picture is necessary but not always sufficient to explain change. With this caveat in mind, however, there are major problems with Goodwin's explanation of this pattern that illustrate how my theory improves our understanding of internal war.

First, there is remarkable continuity between pre-1939, 1942–1945, and post-1945 organizational mobilization in the Philippines and Malaya. The dislocations of World War II certainly provided a shock to state power but did not fundamentally alter the social terrain of the conflict: the MCP remained a Chinese organization linked to labor and squatters and the Huks remained a loose combination of urban leftists and rural peasants' groups. A changing political context does not appear to have shifted the social linkages through which armed groups could operate: radically different political contexts did not produce radically different social bases or organizational structures. This continuity makes it clear that state policy, while obviously important, is an unsatisfying sole theory of insurgent organization.

Second, the rise and consolidation of the Viet Minh actually happened *before* the return of the French to French Indochina. The sequencing of the Viet Minh organization building is the opposite of what Goodwin's theory predicts: the Viet Minh showed substantial organizational change and growing local cohesion even before the collapse of talks between the French and the Viet Minh in late 1946. The Viet Minh were able to build their organization in 1944–1946 precisely because of an absence of state repression, not because there was too much of it. A repressive, exclusionary French regime had kept the ICP an isolated vanguard in the 1930s. It was not "racially exclusionary and repressive colonialism"[236] that forged the Viet Minh as an integrated armed group; instead, it was the decay and collapse of that colonial apparatus during the later stages of World War II that enabled the ICP to build local alliances in the countryside that could then face down returning French forces in 1946 and beyond. Indeed, Goodwin acknowledges that the period of 1944–1946 involved "unprecedented, albeit short-lived, opportunities for political and military organization."[237]

The crucial change occurred when the French were not around and the Japanese were not willing to repress. Goodwin's account of why the Viet Minh later won gives little attention to the processes of organization building by the group. Political context mattered, but in the exact opposite way as he argues: it was important when it allowed entrepreneurial insurgent leaders to create new ties and alliances free of effective repression. Indeed, when the French actively tried to split the movement by mobilizing ethnic, regional, religious, and other divisions, it was Viet Minh cohesion that blunted these initiatives, showing the need to acknowledge the autonomous role of insurgent organization in shaping political contexts.

Third, as I have argued above, we must be careful not to exaggerate the inclusion and reform that were allegedly used as complements to counterinsurgency in Malaya and the Philippines. The British forcibly relocated hundreds of thousands of Chinese and fundamentally changed the social structure of the Malayan peninsula. The only path available to the Chinese was quiescence and collaboration. In the Philippines, the government's reform measures were enough to divide and degrade the parochial organization of the Huks but did not make deeper structural changes.

My claim is not that broader political factors are irrelevant. The salience and structure of prewar social bases are fundamentally affected by political beliefs and opportunities. Changes in organization can be made more likely by state policies. But the evidence clearly shows that insurgents were also constrained or helped by their own social and organizational structures rather than simply filling the space left behind by states. It is impossible to explain the outcomes of counterinsurgency campaigns without understanding insurgent groups.

CONCLUSIONS: INSURGENCY BEYOND SOUTH ASIA

This chapter shows that my argument can shed light on communist groups outside of South Asia. These organizations had a distinctive ideological profile, but like other armed groups, they faced challenges in turning goals into organized reality. The ability of the Southeast Asian organizations to do so varied both at their origins and over the course of their existences. These differences played an essential role in shaping the evolution of these countries: insurgency created North Vietnam, triggered a counterrevolutionary elite backlash in Malaya, and was unable to change exploitative rural relations in the Philippines. The ability of my social-institutional theory to help explain insurgent outcomes should increase confidence in its power across a broad range of cases.

The roots of these organizational trajectories are found in prewar politicized networks that mobilized for violence. State policy interacted with these starting points and the strategies of insurgent leaders to create varying patterns of insurgent organization. We saw change toward integration in Indochina that was in part caused by local alliances between the vanguard ICP core and local communities, a shift into fragmentation by the Huks that was driven by internal divisions, and change from an integrated/parochial structure to a vanguard party in the MCP caused by intense British counterinsurgency that sundered the group's vertical ties into local communities. The origins and evolution of these groups follow the predictions of my theory reasonably well.

Even when it is not a comprehensive explanation, my theory helps illuminate when and how other factors matter. First, the state was undoubtedly important in these cases, especially in Malaya. The roots of state policy there were extremely complex and they deserve careful attention in their own right. What my theory adds is a better understanding of why certain policies worked, why they worked in the ways that they did, and why others didn't. British counterinsurgency in Malaya had specific, observable effects on the MCP that can be best explained by my social-institutional framework. In the Philippines, state policy mattered less because of the Huks' organizational problems, while in Indochina even extensive French counterinsurgency was unable to break the Viet Minh. We should not try to eliminate the state from analysis, but we benefit from a better understanding of the insurgent side of wars.

Second, these cases reveal the limits and complexities of popular support. The Philippines is the clearest example of mass peasant grievances that could not be turned into an enduring insurgent organization. Prospective rebels need to be organized, and if the social and institutional resources needed for this task are absent, revolutionary enthusiasms will falter. Indochina is a far more intricate case; there Vietnamese nationalism provided a powerful basis for overcoming social divisions. Even in Indochina, however, organizational dynamics remained crucial: the ICP needed to elbow aside competitors, bargain with and co-opt powerful local actors, and figure out how to govern under fire. Mass support was key to the successes of the ICP and the Viet Minh, but a simple focus on that factor misses the important political action on the ground. Explaining when and how these communist insurgents could pose sustained, organized challenges to governments helps us understand the broader political evolution of Southeast Asia during the tumultuous Cold War.

[8]

Insurgency, War, and Politics

Insurgent groups are born from prewar politics. The social bases in which insurgent organizers are embedded shape initial organization. This explains why two communist insurgent groups might create radically different organizational structures even though they subscribe to the same doctrines and why groups with similar reliance on drug money may follow diverging trajectories. Key obstacles to collective action and organization building can be overcome only with the social resources of trust, information, and shared political meaning. Insurgents create strong institutions when they have social connections and fail to do so when these ties are weak or absent. The social bases of insurgency determine the structure of militant organizations in the early days of war.

These organizational starting points create different strengths and weaknesses. Pathways of change depend on whether groups begin with integrated, vanguard, parochial, or fragmented structures. Movement toward integration can be caused by innovative insurgent strategies, counterproductive government policies, and international involvement, while strategic miscalculation by insurgents and leadership decapitation and local disembedding by governments can trigger fragmentation. My social-institutional theory explains why some armed groups adapt to counterinsurgency while others collapse, when resources and ideas fuel fragmentation instead of cohesion, and why counterinsurgent strategies that succeed in some cases fail in others.

I have shown the value of this framework through systematic, structured comparisons within and across conflicts in southern Asia. The theory's typology of armed groups can be applied in many contexts and thus provides a new conceptual basis for studying rebellion. Careful study of history provides detail that is particularly useful for developing and testing theories. Most of the insurgent groups studied in this book emerged from prewar politics, and their initial structures reflected those roots. Over time, different kinds of groups changed in the ways

I specified: integrated groups were resilient but not impossible to break down, while parochial and vanguard groups faced distinctive challenges. Yet the research also uncovered cases that challenge my argument and provide new insights about how insurgency works. This chapter outlines key implications for future research and discusses lessons for policy.

Implications for Scholarship

This book, both in its successes and failures, identifies several important research frontiers for scholars of political violence. I want to make the case for a more dynamic, historical, and wide-ranging approach to political violence. Insurgency touches on phenomena as distinct as military strategy, state building, path dependence, ideological meaning making, institutional change, and social transformation. The key task for future work is to creatively pull these topics together into an integrated study of organization and violence that combines historical legacies with strategic interactions.

Taking History Seriously

The evidence in this book makes it clear that history creates powerful constraints on—as well as advantages for—insurgent leaders. Some outcomes are made impossible or at least extremely unlikely by historical conditions. This is why the pathways of organizational change are limited by starting points once war begins. Conflict does not play out on a blank slate that actors can make and remake as they wish. Instead, the past shapes leaders' options in the present. The Malayan Communist Party's decision to emphasize the mobilization of urban laborers in 1945–1947 determined how it could wage its war in 1948, while the loose connections between rural clerics in 1970s Afghanistan limited their ability to rapidly create a tight central command as the war escalated in 1978–1979. Without Afghanistan's war in the 1980s, the Taliban's social basis would not have been formed; without the rapid collapse of French control over rural areas after March 1945, the Viet Minh would have faced far greater challenges in building local presence. It is impossible to explain the trajectories of insurgent groups without understanding these preconditions.

This should make us rethink how research on civil wars is carried out. Cross-national quantitative research is often too aggregated to capture the details of the terrain upon which insurgency is actually waged, making it hard to understand the realistic choices that are available to political actors as they engage in violence. The main reaction against such research, "endogenous" microlevel studies of civil war, have created a different problem. By focusing so much on the intricate contingencies and interactions within conflicts, this work often misses the deeper, historically determined structure of possibilities that helps and hurts insurgents.[1] Politics do not start—or stop—when the first bullet is fired. We need to do a better job of merging history with comparative studies. By identifying different kinds of prewar social bases and using them to predict future outcomes, this book shows one way of taking history seriously while also deploying abstract conceptual categories that travel across contexts. This historicizes war without abandoning generalization.

Timing is similarly important once a conflict begins. The effectiveness of strategies depends in part on *when* they are applied. Leadership decapitation against a vanguard group will be far more effective in the early days of the group. When that group has built vertical ties and transformed itself into an integrated organization, decapitation will have less of an effect. Similarly, an international sponsor trying to shore up an insurgent group will have more success with a group that has a parochial structure than one that has already become fragmented due to leadership feuding. For a vanguard leader, adopting a strategy of local mobilization will pay off only if the state has not been able to resolve local disputes that provide fuel for local alliances. If the state has successfully shut down local feuds, insurgent organizers sent to these areas will be quickly eliminated. As Pierson has shown in other contexts, when particular variables enter the scene fundamentally influences what kind of impact they will have.[2]

Making War Dynamic

If history and structure matter, obviously so too do interactions between states and insurgents. States recover from early losses, insurgents gain strength and build institutions over time, organizational innovations occur that transform the central axis of the conflict, and external actors throw their power into the mix. By conceptualizing war as a sequence of processes operating within different structural possibilities, this book offers a framework for analyzing conflict over time.

Existing research on strategy tends to either use game theory to explore interrelated strategic choice or rely on static measurements of organizational behavior to empirically examine the outcomes of wars. Both are useful, but both have limits. The game theory work on civil war largely ignores actual processes of organization building and institutional evolution.[3] Choices are important, but so are the structures that leaders can call upon and try to change. By emphasizing the logics of decision making over explanations of organizational formation and innovation, much of this research does not speak to the central challenges that keep insurgents and counterinsurgents awake at night. In my experience in the field, states and their foes spend far more time and resources on organization building and institutional survival than on formulating intricate strategies of violence. This is because the former is necessary to make the latter even possible. Like logistics, organization consumes the attention of professional war-fighters. Empirical research that examines war outcomes also has overlooked organizational change. This is a problem in quantitative research that codes armed groups according to their characteristics in one way for the entirety of a war.[4] It also afflicts case study and subnational research, which does a better job of acknowledging change within insurgent groups but has not systematically explained it.[5]

These gaps create an opportunity to think of war as a clash of organizations attempting to protect themselves while influencing others, interacting with each other, and becoming intertwined over time. Insurgent groups face different constraints on how they can fight. Some insurgent organizations are capable of, for instance, mounting conventional warfare, launching suicide attacks, or providing public goods, while others are not. By studying the organizational preconditions for different strategies, we can add to our understanding of when these strategies are chosen and how they work. Insurgent behavior is not chosen or implemented in a vacuum. Capturing the organizational roots of strategic interaction is crucial to understanding how war is waged.

Counterinsurgency is similarly a force for change, but one that is constrained by how state forces and their rebel targets are organized. Understanding how government policies actually play out in interaction with insurgents is an important frontier for future research. Some counterinsurgency strategies are ineffective against integrated groups but effective against vanguards, and some strategies work against parochial groups but fail against vanguard groups. This is likely to be true of broader political strategies as well: buying off insurgents by turning them into local strongmen will be easier under some circumstances than others, campaigns of ethnic cleansing are more likely to succeed against some types of groups than others, and international mediation should have differing effects depending on the constellation of armed actors it needs to deal with.[6]

This leads to a broader point. The growth of work in economics and political science that relies on natural, field, and lab experiments has been useful in some contexts, but it will not bear fruit as the only way to study political violence. This is because the endogenous processes of interaction and historical change that are at the heart of war are precisely what we need to understand. Explaining the Anbar Awakening in Iraq in 2007 or the shifting forms of violence in the contemporary southern Philippines is possible only when we look at complex strategic interactions over time. This is messy, but the goal of scholarship should be to find ways to carefully analyze this complexity; endogenous processes should not be ignored simply because they are methodologically inconvenient. Pulling together history with dynamic organizational interaction is essential to creating theories that reflect what actually happens in war.[7]

Ideology and Organization

One of the key limits of this book is its underdeveloped understanding of how ideology relates to organization. Ideas motivate individuals and help constitute groups. The forces of nationalism, communism, and Islamism, among others, have been central to building networks in peace and war. They have kept fighters in the field even when all hope appears to have been lost, they can be tools of discipline and control, and they encourage individuals to take risks to join insurgencies. Ideological contestation has also encouraged vicious internecine feuding and deep legacies of distrust among insurgents. Ideological linkages were forces for network-building war in Sri Lanka and Indochina, and ideological gaps helped to explain the lack of social ties between urban Islamists and rural tribes in Afghanistan.

I did not theorize the origins or evolution of these ideological/social linkages and instead took them as a given, one of several causes of network formation and endurance: the social and the ideational were intertwined in the roots and evolution of social bases. The book brackets ideology by focusing on the social bases of politicized opposition and then using social networks to explain varying patterns of consequent organization. Beyond this assessment of prewar politics, I have been reluctant to deploy ideas as a full-fledged explanation because of the danger of essentializing ideologies and of making tautological arguments that do not reflect the diversity of organization across and within ideological categories. The comparison of communist groups in Southeast Asia in chapter 7 shows how complex the category "communist" was and how many types of organization are compatible with this overarching term. The same is true of Tamil nationalist groups in Sri Lanka and self-identified Islamist fighting forces in Kashmir and Afghanistan. My argument does not analyze the complexity of how ideas motivate, reshape, and structure organizational behavior: identities and shared beliefs are both absolutely necessary for the formation of insurgent groups and quite insufficient for explaining the structures those organizations take on.

Future work needs to do better. One promising path forward is to study how and when political leaders graft ideological programs onto social and organizational life. A variety of interesting strategies can be deployed to create political understandings within organizations and between insurgents and civilians and to use those meanings to gain adherence and loyalty. The methods armed groups use to present themselves to local communities—which range from elaborate performances of power to political consultation to brutal coercion—may be crucial in shaping how people on the ground understand the goals of leaders and their relationship to those goals. Socialization also plays a central role in creating a hegemonic "common sense" within organizations that makes decision making in conditions of uncertainty easier and enables members to better coordinate with each other. We know very little about when and how these strategies lead to particular outcomes in insurgency.[8]

The challenge for researchers is how to get inside these processes and how to compare them across groups. Each of these issues is a formidable obstacle. The problems of penetrating the inner workings of an armed group are numerous, especially since these organizations have powerful incentives to portray their operations in a biased and incomplete light. Exploring linkages between armed groups and communities is more doable but still presents major problems such as eliciting truthful responses from interviewees, dealing with heterogeneity across communities, and properly interpreting the data that is gathered. Doing this kind of work for even one group is difficult enough; doing it in several cases in order to engage in comparison is a very complex endeavor.[9]

Several possibilities present themselves. They include studies that mix cross-group comparisons with detailed knowledge of context, collaborative work that joins researchers who are experts on different groups, and innovative interpretations and/or coding of propaganda, confessions, trials, and training within armed groups and in their interactions between groups and communities. These strategies hold open the possibility of understanding how ideas are produced, reproduced, and transformed within armed organizations and the communities in which they operate. Serious commitments to fieldwork, contextual knowledge, and careful data collection need to be yoked to sophisticated theories about the intersection of ideational, material, and strategic processes in war. This is an area in which different methodological and theoretical approaches can be used to complement each other, from quantitative surveys to ethnography.

How States Manage Violence

The argument and evidence of this book show that insurgent groups can have autonomy and independence from states, though the extent of this autonomy varies. An endless focus on state-centric variables—from per capita GDP to regime type to counterinsurgent doctrine—in the study of civil war has overpromised and underdelivered. This is because this approach is inherently incomplete. Rebel movements rest on social and political pillars forged during prewar and wartime processes of identification and mobilization: ideological entrepreneurs, cynical operators, and committed activists all try to build and reshape political networks. The armed groups that emerge from these processes have to be taken seriously. Insurgents are fighting forces that should be analyzed on their own terms, not as pale reflections of state power and purpose. They possess agency that cannot be wished away.

This does not mean that states are irrelevant. I argued in chapter 3 and showed throughout the empirical chapters that counterinsurgency strategies can be very important, even if their effects depend on the nature of the insurgent group that is being targeted. The state should be integral to any study of war without being analytically hegemonic. One productive way of incorporating state policy is to consider the range of options states have for destroying, containing, and manipulating armed groups. Some insurgents and militias cannot be easily eliminated because of their social and organizational autonomy.

The question then becomes how governments grapple with insurgents—and other armed actors—that maintain organizational power and resist the imposition of central strategies. Many groups may be incorporated and managed only through using policies that do not look anything like what conventional wisdom demands, drawing on their autonomous strengths to push back against state policies. Regimes often realize this over time and adjust accordingly. In addition to brutal violence and escalation, we see the emergence of deals, bargains, and norms that make insurgents and other armed groups key players in political life.[10] The autonomy of insurgent groups may enable them to change the portfolio of plausible policies that is available to states. States constrain insurgents and insurgents constrain states. The building blocks of political order and governance are found in these interactions between armed actors.

We can study these fascinating politics by widening the comparative and theoretical scope of the study of violence. Civil wars are often not simple clashes of wills with a straightforward winner or a loser. Instead, armed groups can be incorporated into state structures, colluded with as armed political parties, tolerated below particular thresholds, or mobilized as allies for economic gain or against mutual enemies.[11] In Afghanistan and Burma/Myanmar, for instance, armed actors have become key political players who cut deals with states, carve out local economic

Chapter 8

power, and try to shape and control the lives of civilians in their areas of rule. In parts of Nigeria and the Philippines, electoral politics and local armed groups are intertwined. From insurgents transforming into mainstream politicians to states using ostensibly anti-state groups as partners in drug smuggling, the range of outcomes that emerge from the interactions of states and insurgents is remarkably broad.

A key implication of this book is that these political architectures of violence are likely to reflect the power of armed groups to defy, collude, and cooperate with state power. Integrated and vanguard groups may be more likely to directly bargain with states as equal political actors, while parochial groups are more likely to become involved in tacit, complex local arrangements with state forces. State strategies can be defied or manipulated by integrated groups, forcing strategic adjustment over time. A fine-grained analysis of insurgents speaks to questions well beyond the standard set of civil conflict topics, ranging from state building to wartime political orders to patronage politics. Building insurgent groups into a rich, wide-ranging research agenda is essential to grasping the politics of violence.

Collective Action and War

The evidence in this book finally suggests that we need to rethink how collective action occurs in war. The question scholars usually examine is why people can cooperate in the face of information and trust problems.[12] This is a valuable question, but the reality is that collective action is all around us: families, political parties, firms, unions, informal social networks, student associations, and NGOs are the lifeblood of societies. The question "Why collective action?" needs to be joined by the question "How and why does existing collective action take on new roles and identities?"[13] This transformation is central to the theoretical and empirical processes of this book: communist party organizers became militant leaders, Jamaat-e-Islami cadres became local commanders, Tamil caste networks became the underpinnings of new war-fighting organizations. My claim is not that actors began collective action out of nowhere, but instead that prior patterns of collective action structured the "social distribution of possibilities" for insurgent leaders both early in war and as wars progressed.[14]

The study of collective action therefore needs to shift its focus. First, we need to understand why existing social structures and organizations are turned to new purposes. I discussed the political salience of particular social bases, but I did not theorize their origins and endurance. Future work can move beyond simple categorization to explain the roots of oppositional political networks (violent or not) and especially how they are able to stay alive in the face of suppression or public indifference.[15] This endurance poses a potentially major challenge to some of our theories of internal conflict, which emphasize repression and opportunity more than preference and belief.

The origins of different political meanings, especially ideologies that can be yoked to warfare, is a fascinating area for mixing different forms of research to explain why some social blocs are more inclined to insurgency than others. Why did people become urban Islamists in the tumult of late-1960s Afghanistan? What did it mean to be part of a smuggling caste in northern Sri Lanka? How did peasants in the Philippines bear the costs of repression by landlords in the 1930s in order to maintain their involvement in agrarian mobilization? Beyond these cases, we can find fascinating examples of persistence and costly mobilization by non-insurgent social bases, from the Muslim Brotherhood in 1990s Egypt to the democratic opposition in contemporary China to Solidarity in Poland during the Cold War. These are obviously very different cases, but they all present the fascinating puzzle of what makes particular parties, organizations, networks, and the individuals within them willing to persevere against long odds.[16]

Equally important is explaining why some types of social networks may be locked in place even as political contexts shift. What kinds of social bases simply never go to war? There may be multiple pathways to political influence and varying strategies of survival that create important differences in how politicized networks manage their interactions with states and other actors. Some kinds of networks may be best suited to elite collective action, others to mass protest, and yet others to violent underground mobilization. There is a rich opportunity to explore which types of collective action are "portable" and along what boundaries. Everything from class interests to regime patronage networks to the career prospects of university graduates may shape how social bases become neutralized or co-opted.

Second, scholars should explore whether and how transformations occur when collective structures do become devoted to producing violence. The very process of change is likely to create new functions, connections, and political meanings. What happens when a group of clerics, for instance, goes to war? Does what it means to be a cleric change? Do people view these actors in new ways? Which responsibilities and actions retain their appropriateness and which new roles become accepted or condemned? What power do these clerics acquire from involvement in war-fighting and what is taken away? Combining comparisons over time with comparisons across societies and groups can begin to pinpoint what does and does not change when war occurs and members of preexisting structures pick up guns. Initial work suggests possibilities in areas as different as rural landholding patterns, gender roles, and political participation.[17]

IMPLICATIONS FOR POLICY

The promise of policy-relevant social science is that better analysis can lead to better policy. This book has a number of implications for how governments, insurgents, everyday citizens, and international organizations analyze political violence and make policies to deal with it. This work is most useful in identifying which dynamics to pay attention to, which assumptions to question, and which policy options to consider under what circumstances. I focus on three areas relevant to policy: the multiple challenges insurgent leaders face, the role of resources in shaping insurgent groups, and insurgent and counterinsurgent strategy.

The Complex Internal Life of Armed Groups

Organizations are the crucial actors in war, not the mass categories of ethnicity, religion, or class.[18] The Taliban is an actor that strategizes and carries out missions, whereas Afghan Pashtuns are not an actor in this sense. An organizational approach to civil war has the benefit of being able to specify the key actors, their capabilities, and their interests as the basis for policymaking. Several policy implications emerge from viewing conflict through this lens.

First, we should pay attention to the tenuous boundaries and balancing acts that insurgent groups face as they try to draw on but not become overwhelmed by social forces. Leaders attempt to pursue social solidarity, organizational expansion, and strategic goals, but their social networks, coalitions, and constituencies can create severe constraints. The leader of a parochial group may not be able to actually deliver on a peace deal because he cannot control his factions. A vanguard group may be unable to mount the type of ambitious, full-spectrum insurgent campaign it desires because of weak local control. An integrated group may be able to expand without fracturing, thus growing larger without becoming weaker, while a rival parochial group may spin into brutal fratricide while trying to keep up. The social sinews of insurgent power sometimes force trade-offs between violence and nonviolence as a strategic choice: networks and organizations that are well suited to insurgency may be ill equipped to manage transitions into normal politics, to shift into nonviolent protest, or to create

[226]

innovative governance. Opportunities are opened and closed by organizational structure.

Understanding how organization shapes strategies and capabilities makes possible discerning analysis of how insurgents are likely to operate. This does not mean that armed groups cannot escape structural limitations, but it does suggest more and less plausible strategic choices and policy successes. Integrated insurgents will have the broadest, most flexible portfolio of tactics and strategies; vanguards are likely to favor attacks that do not rely on widespread local mobilization and instead try to use high-visibility policies to surmount manpower constraints; and parochial groups will be characterized by weakly coordinated strategies that focus on localities. Patterns of violence, governance, and strategy are likely to be linked to insurgent organization.

Second, mass publics are less important than specific social networks and constituencies, from the perspective of counterinsurgents, insurgents, and international actors. Insurgent organizations do not float freely. Instead, they are reliant on particular sectors of society. Armed groups can establish some autonomy from "the people" writ large, but it is hard to become autonomous from their social base. This means that policy responses need to directly address the social core of armed groups. Urban vanguard groups, for instance, are unlikely to respond substantially to policies aimed at the average rural citizen, since that is not their social center of gravity. Elite political maneuverings in the metropole will have little effect on the localized fighting units of a parochial group.[19] Integrated groups that continue to draw on a robust social infrastructure can survive major shifts in political and military context without collapsing. Policymaking needs to move away from trying to influence a vague "population" and to instead recognize the heterogeneity and diversity within societies affected by war. The core constituencies of armed groups can keep fighting even if the state is pouring enormous resources into counterinsurgency. This linkage between the social and the institutional should make it clear that armed groups do not necessarily respond to the median citizen in a society; they respond to the specific networks that provide the organizational underpinnings for rebellion.

Resources and War

Since the end of the Cold War, a huge amount of attention has been devoted to the financing of wars.[20] This is because insurgents (and often states) have become linked to a wide range of sources of finance that include drug and commodity trading, state sponsors, and diaspora networks. Trying to understand how these resources affect how insurgents organize and behave has taken on particular importance in war zones rife with drugs, external involvement, and black markets. Some have argued that these resource endowments have clear effects in undermining and depoliticizing armed groups, while others suggest that resource wealth can enhance fighting power and control.

My argument suggests that both claims can be true, depending on the social and organizational characteristics of the group in question.[21] Which analysis describes a particular situation hinges on the social base underlying an organization. Groups built on strong horizontal and vertical networks are likely to use lucrative resource flows for military and state-like tasks, while those built on weak networks will face problems of indiscipline as resource flows exacerbate preexisting organizational divisions. Resources were certainly helpful to some groups, including the LTTE, the Taliban, and the Viet Minh, and deserve careful attention as possible "force multipliers" of organizational power. They did not play this role, however, in the TELO or the Al-Umar Mujahideen, which instead seem to have succumbed to the insurgent "resource curse"— wealth flowed through weak networks and ineffective institutions, encouraging thuggishness and predation.

This variation shows that we need to focus less on resources themselves than on the social and institutional contexts into which they flow. An interactive approach that considers multiple factors is necessary instead of relying on easy platitudes about criminalization and greed. There should be fewer sweeping claims about narco-insurgents and thuggish proxy armies and more attention to the actual and quite diverse ways that similar resource endowments can get used. In the political economy research on civil war, there is a real danger of turning insurgents into simple criminals out for loot and lucre.[22] The extraordinary costs many insurgents pay seem to belie this approach: it is implausible that the average insurgent in northwestern Pakistan is growing fabulously wealthy (though some of their leaders might be), but it is clear that they are facing the possibility of death, life-changing mutilation, or capture.[23] The "insurgents as criminals" approach also blends, perhaps inadvertently, with the discourse of counterinsurgents, who are eager to delegitimize and dismiss insurgent challenges as apolitical exercises in banditry. Sometimes armed groups are in fact solely driven by material urges, but building policy on this assumption risks misunderstanding the roots of rebellion and adding dubious intellectual legitimacy to the machinations of counterinsurgent regimes.

Insurgent and Counterinsurgent Strategies

This book shows that there are distinct organizational structures and possible strategies that insurgents and counterinsurgents can draw upon. We can see communist vanguard insurgents facing mass-killing states or separatist parochial armed groups facing off against states that rely heavily on careful leadership decapitation. The world of internal warfare is remarkably diverse. This means that neither insurgents nor counterinsurgents should expect any single set of doctrines or strategies to be optimal "best practices." Instead, military and political effectiveness is contingent on the particular constellation of forces that wage war. Policies, those of both insurgents and counterinsurgents, should be guided by careful consideration of how strategies might or might not work in different contexts.

The huge attention devoted to the creation and operation of counterinsurgency doctrine in the Afghanistan and Iraq wars made for good publicity, but the actual success of this doctrinal approach varied greatly across and within these wars. This variation occurred at least in part because of the factors that this book identifies: the Taliban has a different set of linkages to society than Al-Qaeda in Iraq, for instance. More broadly, counterinsurgency approaches should be adapted to the nature of an adversary. Providing public goods probably will not do much in the face of Hamas, which already has a powerful local infrastructure, but that strategy could be more effective against a vanguard organization struggling to attract popular support. Leadership targeting is much more useful against groups that look like the EROS than those that look like the LTTE. Thin troop deployments in an area will be insufficient to root out deep, overlapping networks that can evade the coercive infiltration of state power, but they may be highly effective against vanguards with weak local roots. Counterinsurgents can succeed only if they have the right mixture of capability and strategy to exploit the vulnerabilities of the insurgent group being targeted.

This helps explain why we have so few robust or rich findings on the determinants of counterinsurgency success. The problem of causal heterogeneity leads to platitudinous policy recommendations. The platitudes are a result of the impossibility of the task of finding simple, universal causal claims about why counterinsurgency succeeds. This problem is not one that can be accounted for with more case studies or statistical analyses; instead, the very nature of counterinsurgency campaigns fundamentally varies depending on the insurgent actor/s in questions. What works against one group may badly falter against another, which means that strategies need to be carefully tailored to insurgent organization. When facing a group with serious urban-rural divisions, state co-optation of rural localities may be the optimal strategy; when facing an organization full of feuding elites, the strategy of divide and conquer may be most appropriate; when taking on an integrated group, a mix of negotiations and directed force may be necessary. Strategy will work best if it is guided by the organizational structure of the insurgent group being targeted.

Most books on civil conflict devote their policy advice to counterinsurgents or the amorphous international community, but there is no reason why this bias should necessarily exist. If my argument is right, it should speak to the key policy dilemmas rebels themselves face. This book has clear lessons for both prospective and existing insurgents. The failures of so many would-be rebels who rely on the writing and examples of Mao and Che and Lenin (and, more recently, on Bin Laden) suggests that ideological precepts and organizational blueprints frequently run aground on the rocky shoals of social and political reality.[24] The technology of guerrilla warfare can be successfully set in motion only with trust, information, and cooperation embedded in social life. Too many insurgents launch doomed but bloody rebellions that reflect a triumph of hope over analysis. Without a careful understanding of their own social underpinnings and analysis of the strengths and weaknesses of their opponent state, insurgent leaders are liable to find themselves disorganized and on the run. They need to assess their likely opportunities for local alliances, factional fusing, and cooperation under fire and their likely vulnerabilities to decapitation, local disembedding, mismanaged expansion, and various forms of internal unrest. Will and vision are not substitutes for social (and consequently organizational) power.

Ignoring these social-institutional dynamics has been a severe problem for groups of activists and elites who try to mobilize rebellions. Their lack of actual connection to the mass publics they hope to mobilize has undermined rebel movements, even those that may have actually delivered benefits to those publics. A lesson from nineteenth-century Chinese revolts echoes in the present: "Utopian leadership must in the end face up to concrete problems of local administration."[25] Weak horizontal ties between local strongmen create a different kind of problem, as parochial groups emerge that undermine an insurgent struggle with violent divisions and internecine feuding. Fratricide and intense factional competition can create violent and chaotic political orders in which counterinsurgents end up backing flipped rebel splinters that commit horrific violence, and insurgents radicalize in the face of internal rivalries. Extensive research has shown that divided and fractious rebel movements find it more difficult to create a coherent strategy against the state, whether in terms of military operations or peace negotiations.[26] Foregoing rebellion may be better than a rebellion that devours its own and makes it easier for the state to penetrate and dominate society.

Insurgency is incredibly difficult to mobilize and sustain. Even the integrated armed groups in this book struggled to survive; only the Taliban and the Viet Minh had a real victory (and in the case of the Taliban, the victory was tenuous), while the LTTE was eventually wiped out and the MCP and the Hizbul Mujahideen were marginalized. Most of the other groups in this book met violent ends, despite bright ambitions and clever ideas. Organization either arises from prewar politics or has to be slowly and painstakingly built up over time; there are no shortcuts to enduring rebellion. The romanticism that is sometimes associated with guerrilla warfare neglects the extraordinary costs of insurgency and its low odds of success, just as the technocratic sheen granted to counterinsurgency doctrine ignores the coercion and domination that are intrinsic to it.

In the face of these challenges, prospective insurgents should keep in mind other possibilities for political action, such as nonviolent protest, when violence appears organizationally inauspicious.[27] Insurgents who are already in war should focus on building and maintaining organizational linkages to social forces that can keep them in the fight even against a powerful state. Expansion should be handled carefully, local conflicts need to be aggressively exploited to build up vertical ties and then local organization, and the balance of power within an organization should roughly mirror its social composition to avoid resentment and factional conflict. Resources can be helpful, but only when organizational mechanisms are in place to manage influxes of cash and weapons. Unity is no panacea, but it is undoubtedly better than the alternative, so trying to create mechanisms of consultation and cooperation among distinct factions is essential in order to prevent disastrous divide-and-conquer outcomes.

This book seeks to understand why some armed groups are better equipped to take up the tasks of rebellion and why others falter and collapse in the heat of conflict. States, insurgents, and the civilians caught in their paths constantly grapple with questions of organization and control. We can best explain the patterns that emerge during these rebellions by analyzing the social terrain of politics and identifying how armed groups reach into the past and try to reshape the present to create organizations able to handle the extraordinary pressures of war.

THE INTERNATIONAL INSTITUTE
FOR STRATEGIC STUDIES
ARUNDEL HOUSE
13-15 ARUNDEL STREET
LONDON WC2R 3DX

Notes

1. Organizing Insurgency

1. I use organizational cohesion, control, and discipline interchangeably. For conceptualizations of cohesion, see James Moody and Douglas White, "Structural Cohesion and Embeddedness," *American Sociological Review* 68 (2003): 103–127; Jasen Julio Castillo, "The Will to Fight: Explaining an Army's Staying Power" (PhD diss., University of Chicago, 2003); Edward Shils and Morris Janowitz, "Cohesion and Disintegration in the Wehrmacht in World War II," *Public Opinion Quarterly* 12, no. 2 (1948): 280–315.

2. Samuel P. Huntington, *Political Order in Changing Societies* (New Haven, CT: Yale University Press, 1968), 23. See also Patrick Johnston, "The Geography of Insurgent Organization and Its Consequences for Civil Wars: Evidence from Liberia and Sierra Leone," *Security Studies* 17, no. 1 (2008), 107–137; Abdulkader Sinno, *Organizations at War in Afghanistan and Beyond* (Ithaca, NY: Cornell University Press, 2008); and Barry Posen, "The Security Dilemma and Ethnic Conflict," *Survival* 35, no. 1 (1993): 31.

3. Cohesion affects the balance of power and control, which in turn explains key dynamics of violence. See Stathis Kalyvas, *The Logic of Violence in Civil War* (Cambridge: Cambridge University Press, 2006).

4. Dara Kay Cohen, "Explaining Sexual Violence during Civil War" (PhD diss., Stanford University, 2010); Macartan Humphreys and Jeremy M. Weinstein, "Handling and Manhandling Civilians in Civil War," *American Political Science Review* 100, no. 3 (August 2006): 429–447; Jeremy Weinstein, *Inside Rebellion: The Politics of Insurgent Violence* (Cambridge: Cambridge University Press, 2007).

5. Andrew Kydd and Barbara F. Walter, "Sabotaging the Peace: The Politics of Extremist Violence," *International Organization* 56, no. 2 (2002): 263–296; Stephen John Stedman, "Spoiler Problems in Peace Processes," *International Security* 22, no. 2 (1997): 5–53; Wendy Pearlman, *Violence, Nonviolence, and the Palestinian National Movement* (Cambridge: Cambridge University Press, 2011); David E. Cunningham, "Veto Players and Civil War Duration," *American Journal of Political Science* 50, no. 4 (2006): 875–892; Kathleen Gallagher Cunningham, Kristin M. Bakke, and Lee J. M. Seymour, "Shirts Today, Skins Tomorrow: Dual Contests and the Effects of Fragmentation in Self-Determination Disputes," *Journal of Conflict Resolution* 56, no. 1 (2012): 67–93.

6. Sarah Zukerman Daly, "Bankruptcy, Guns or Campaigns: Explaining Armed Organizations' Post-War Trajectories" (PhD diss., Massachusetts Institute of Technology, 2011).

7. Charles Tilly, *Coercion, Capital, and European States, AD 990–1992* (Cambridge, MA: Blackwell, 1992); William Reno, *Warlord Politics and African States* (Boulder, CO: Lynner Rienner Publishers); Paul Staniland, "States, Insurgents, and Wartime Political Orders," *Perspectives on Politics* 10, no. 2 (2012): 243–264.

8. Huntington, *Political Order in Changing Societies.*

9. Tuong Vu, *Paths to Development in Asia: South Korea, Vietnam, China, and Indonesia* (New York: Cambridge University Press, 2010).

10. For an overview, see Kristin M. Bakke, Kathleen Gallagher Cunningham, and Lee J. M. Seymour, "A Plague of Initials: Fragmentation, Cohesion, and Infighting in Civil Wars," *Perspectives on Politics* 10, no. 2 (2012): 265–283.

11. For a more extensive overview of the literature, see Paul Staniland, "Explaining Cohesion, Fragmentation, and Control in Insurgent Groups" (PhD diss., MIT, 2010).

12. Robert H. Bates, *When Things Fell Apart: State Failure in Late-Century Africa* (New York: Cambridge University Press, 2008); Theda Skocpol, *States and Social Revolutions: A Comparative Analysis of France, Russia, and China* (Cambridge: Cambridge University Press, 1979); Jeff Goodwin, *No Other Way Out: States and Revolutionary Movements, 1945–1991* (Cambridge: Cambridge University Press, 2001); James D. Fearon and David D. Laitin, "Ethnicity, Insurgency, and Civil War," *American Political Science Review* 97, no. 1 (2003): 75–90; William Reno, *Warfare in Independent Africa* (New York: Cambridge University Press, 2011).

13. On state sponsorship, see Daniel Byman, *Deadly Connections: States That Sponsor Terrorism* (Cambridge: Cambridge University Press, 2005), 3; Idean Salehyan, *Rebels without Borders: Transnational Insurgencies in World Politics* (Ithaca, NY: Cornell University Press, 2009), 36–40. On diasporas, see Fiona B. Adamson, "Globalisation, Transnational Political Mobilisation, and Networks of Violence," *Cambridge Review of International Affairs* 18, no. 1 (2005): 31–49. For arguments about the negative effects of resources, see Weinstein, *Inside Rebellion;* Paul Collier and Anke Hoeffler, "Greed and Grievance in Civil War," *Oxford Economic Papers* 56, no. 4 (2004): 563–595; Mary Kaldor, *New and Old Wars: Organized Violence in a Global Era* (Cambridge: Polity, 1999); and John Mueller, "The Banality of 'Ethnic War,'" *International Security* 25, no. 1 (2000): 42–70.

14. On the compatibility of illicit resources with discipline, see Vanda Felbab-Brown, *Shooting Up: Counterinsurgency and the War on Drugs* (Washington, DC: Brookings Institution, 2010); and Francisco Gutiérrez Sanin, "Criminal Rebels? A Discussion of Civil War and Criminality from the Colombian Experience," *Politics & Society* 32, no. 2 (2004): 257–285.

15. Doug McAdam, *Political Process and the Development of Black Insurgency, 1930–1970* (Chicago: University of Chicago Press, 1982), 21.

16. Paul Staniland, "Organizing Insurgency: Networks, Resources, and Rebellion in South Asia," *International Security* 37, no. 1 (2012): 142–177.

17. Classic works on revolution rely heavily on class and ethnic categories. See, for instance, Jeffery Paige, *Agrarian Revolution: Social Movements and Export Agriculture in the Underdeveloped World* (New York: Free Press, 1975); Skocpol, *States and Social Revolutions;* Carles Boix, *Democracy and Redistribution* (Princeton, NJ: Princeton University Press, 2003); Donald L. Horowitz, *Ethnic Groups in Conflict*

(Berkeley: University of California Press, 1985); and Roger Petersen, *Understanding Ethnic Violence: Fear, Hatred, and Resentment in Twentieth-Century Eastern Europe* (Cambridge: Cambridge University Press, 2002).

18. Mancur Olson, *The Logic of Collective Action: Public Goods and the Theory of Groups* (Cambridge, MA: Harvard University Press, 1965).

19. Nathan Leites and Charles Wolf, *Rebellion and Authority: An Analytic Essay on Insurgent Conflicts* (Chicago: Markham, 1970); Philip Selznick, *The Organizational Weapon: A Study of Bolshevik Strategy and Tactics* (New York: McGraw-Hill, 1952); Lucian W. Pye, *Guerrilla Communism in Malaya* (Princeton, NJ: Princeton University Press, 1956); Huntington, *Political Order in Changing Societies*, 335.

20. Zachariah Cherian Mampilly, *Rebel Rulers: Insurgent Governance and Civilian Life during War* (Cornell University Press, 2011); Weinstein, *Inside Rebellion*.

21. I define organizations as collective actors with formal membership boundaries; official, specialized goals; and routinized internal processes of decision-making, control, and allocation of resources that structure the interactions between members. For discussions of these concepts, see Jack Knight, *Institutions and Social Conflict* (Cambridge: Cambridge University Press, 1992), 3; and Jon Elster, *Explaining Social Behavior: More Nuts and Bolts for the Social Sciences* (Cambridge University Press, 2007), 428.

22. Though "vanguard" is sometimes portrayed as a strategy, here I show that it is also an organizational type that frequently persists even when leaders hope to transcend it.

23. Reno uses "parochial" to refer to a particular type of African armed groups that have a local agenda and often have ties to political networks of patronage. Reno, *Warfare in Independent Africa*. My book focuses on organizational structure rather than political goals, though in practice there is some overlap between the two concepts.

24. These insurgent types also do not make predictions about specific patterns of violence, and neither does my theory. Integrated groups may restrain violence or deploy huge amounts of it, depending on strategic context. For a different view, see Nils Metternich, Cassy Dorff, Max Gallop, Simon Weschle, and Michael Ward, "Anti-Government Networks in Civil Conflicts: How Network Structures Affect Conflictual Behavior," *American Journal of Political Science* (forthcoming).

25. "Fresh from Syria, Rebel Commanders Unite in Frustration," *New York Times*, July 13, 2012, http://www.nytimes.com/2012/07/14/world/middleeast/commanders-of-syrian-rebels-unite-in-frustration.html?_r = 1; accessed August 18, 2013.

26. This includes groups that began as guerrilla forces but later transitioned to conventional warfare.

27. For a careful discussion of political and criminal groups, see Ben Lessing, "The Logic of Violence in Criminal War: Cartel-State Conflict in Mexico, Colombia, and Brazil" (PhD diss., University of California, Berkeley, 2012).

28. Stathis N. Kalyvas and Laia Balcells, "International System and Technologies of Rebellion: How the End of the Cold War Shaped Internal Conflict," *American Political Science Review* 104, no. 3 (2010): 415–429.

29. See Steven Levitsky and Lucan A. Way, *Competitive Authoritarianism: Hybrid Regimes after the Cold War* (Cambridge: Cambridge University Press, 2010), 54, on disentangling organizational capacity from other variables using comparative research.

30. Leites and Wolf, *Rebellion and Authority*, 40.

31. Ashutosh Varshney, *Ethnic Conflict and Civic Life: Hindus and Muslims in India* (New Haven, CT: Yale University Press, 2002), 6; Elisabeth Wood, "Variation in Sexual Violence," *Politics and Society* 26, no. 3 (2006): 334.

32. I also did fieldwork in Northern Ireland during the summers of 2007 and 2008. The insights from this research were crucial to the development of my theory even though I did not end up including that conflict in this book. For a comparative study of insurgents in Northern Ireland, see Staniland, "Explaining Cohesion, Fragmentation, and Control in Insurgent Groups."

33. On process-tracing, see Henry Brady and David Collier, eds., *Rethinking Social Inquiry: Diverse Tools, Shared Standards* (Lanham, MD: Rowman & Littlefield, 2004); and Peter Hedstrom and Richard Swedberg, "Social Mechanisms: An Introductory Essay," in *Social Mechanisms: An Analytical Approach to Social Theory*, ed. Peter Hedstrom and Richard Swedberg (Cambridge: Cambridge University Press, 1998).

34. Sidney Tarrow, "Inside Insurgencies: Politics and Violence in an Age of Civil War," *Perspectives on Politics* 5, no. 3 (2007): 587–600; Nicholas Sambanis, "Using Case Studies to Expand Economic Models of Civil War," *Perspectives on Politics* 2, no. 2 (2004): 259–279.

35. Alexander George and Andrew Bennett, *Case Studies and Theory Development in the Social Sciences* (Cambridge, MA: MIT Press, 2005).

2. Insurgent Origins

1. Kathleen Thelen, "Historical Institutionalism in Comparative Politics," *Annual Review of Political Science* 2 (1999): 400.

2. Emirbayer and Goodwin define a social network as "the set of social relations or social ties among a set of actors (and the actors themselves thus linked)." Mustafa Emirbayer and Jeff Goodwin, "Network Analysis, Culture, and the Problem of Agency," *American Journal of Sociology* 99, no. 6 (1994): 1418.

3. Keith Darden, *Resisting Occupation: Mass Schooling and the Creation of Durable National Loyalties* (Cambridge: Cambridge University Press, forthcoming).

4. This focus on prewar dynamics allows us to avoid the problem that Thelen notes in a different context: "To argue that the groups institutionalized first were the ones that 'stuck' is to beg the question of why some were institutionalized and others not." Thelen, "Historical Institutionalism in Comparative Politics," 391.

5. Reno shows that in much of sub-Saharan Africa, states have deployed patronage and shadowy informal networks to co-opt, demobilize, and manipulate the political structures in society that could have become salient forces of opposition. William Reno, *Warfare in Independent Africa* (New York: Cambridge University Press, 2011).

6. Javier Auyero, *Routine Politics and Violence in Argentina: The Gray Zone of State Power* (Cambridge University Press, 2007); John Sidel, *Capital, Coercion, and Crime: Bossism in the Philippines* (Stanford, CA: Stanford University Press, 1999); David Art, "What Do We Know About Authoritarianism After Ten Years?" *Comparative Politics* 44, no. 3 (2012): 351–373.

7. Major exceptions to this claim are societies just before a regime change: pro-state forces (violent or not) may become anti-state in the wake of the shift in ruling power.

In this case, the most politicized pro-state forces are the most likely insurgents against a new regime. The mobilization of former Baathist and veterans' networks in Iraq in 2003–2004 is an example of this dynamic. On status reversal, see Roger Petersen, *Understanding Ethnic Violence: Fear, Hatred, and Resentment in Twentieth-Century Eastern Europe* (Cambridge: Cambridge University press, 2002).

8. I thank Elisabeth Wood for this phrase.

9. Donatella Della Porta, *Social Movements, Political Violence, and the State: A Comparative Analysis of Italy and Germany* (Cambridge: Cambridge University Press, 1995).

10. On types of politicized opposition, see Aspinall, *Opposing Suharto: Compromise, Resistance, and Regime Change in Indonesia* (Stanford, CA: Stanford University Press, 2005).

11. These movements may be led by intellectuals and politicians but can also be sustained by peasants and workers. James Scott, *Weapons of the Weak: Everyday Forms of Peasant Resistance* (New Haven, CT: Yale University Press, 1985); Ranajit Guha, *Elementary Aspects of Peasant Insurgency in Colonial India* (Durham, NC: Duke University Press, 1999).

12. Most studies of networks and social structures examine their effects on individuals, but "it is much rarer that the overall configuration of networks linking individual activists is assessed in order to evaluate the potential for collective action in a given collectivity." Mario Diani, "Networks and Social Movements: A Research Programme," in *Social Movements and Networks: Relational Approaches to Collective Action*, ed. Mario Diani and Doug McAdam (Oxford: Oxford University Press, 2003), 8. For research on networks and mobilization, see Karen Barkey and Ronan Van Rossem, "Networks of Contention: Villages and Regional Structure in the Seventeenth-Century Ottoman Empire," *American Journal of Sociology* 102, no. 5 (1997): 1345–1382; Mario Luis Small, *Unanticipated Gains: Origins of Network Inequality in Everyday Life* (Oxford: Oxford University Press, 2009); John F. Padgett and Christopher K. Ansell, "Robust Action and the Rise of the Medici, 1400–1434," *American Journal of Sociology* 98, no. 6 (1993): 1259–1319; Roger V. Gould, *Insurgent Identities: Class, Community, and Protest in Paris from 1848 to the Commune* (Chicago: University of Chicago Press, 1995); Roger Petersen, *Resistance and Rebellion: Lessons from Eastern Europe* (Cambridge: Cambridge University Press, 2001).

13. To count as social ties, these organizers must have actual connections to or through one another; agreement on political issues is not enough. Ideological preferences can be a component of but they are not the entirety of social relations.

14. On brokerage, Ronald S. Burt, *Brokerage and Closure: An Introduction to Social Capital* (Oxford: Oxford University Press, 2005).

15. Theda Skocpol identifies these types of horizontal linkages as the key to many political parties. Skocpol, "What Makes Peasants Revolutionary?," *Comparative Politics* 14, no. 3 (1982): 358.

16. Catherine Boone, *Political Topographies of the African State: Territorial Authority and Institutional Choice* (Cambridge: Cambridge University Press, 2003); and Anoop Sarbahi, "Insurgent-Population Ties and the Variation in the Trajectory of Peripheral Civil Wars" (PhD diss., UCLA, 2011); and author's interviews in Kashmir.

17. See Small, *Unanticipated Gains*; James Fearon and David Laitin, "Explaining Interethnic Cooperation," *American Political Science Review* 90, no. 4 (1996): 715–735; and James Habyarimana, Macartan Humphreys, Jeremy Weinstein, and Daniel Posner, "Why Does Ethnic Diversity Undermine Public Goods Provision?," *American Political Science Review* 101, no. 4 (2007): 709–725.

Notes to Pages 23–24

18. On politicized networks in a noninsurgent context, see Sheri Berman, "Civil Society and the Collapse of the Weimar Republic," *World Politics* 49, no. 3 (1997): 401–429; Ashutosh Varshney, *Ethnic Conflict and Civic Life: Hindus and Muslims in India* (New Haven, CT: Yale University Press, 2002).

19. Efforts to create simple theories to explain social structures such as parties, ethnic ties, and patronage networks have not succeeded. Numerous factors shape the rise and structure of social bases, and I use them as a theoretical starting point.

20. If a war does not break out, social bases are the movements, parties, organizations, and informal networks that fill out the politics of opposition to and support for a political status quo.

21. Geoffrey Blainey, *The Causes of War* (New York: Free Press, 1988); Barry R. Posen, "The Security Dilemma and Ethnic Conflict," *Survival* 35, no. 1 (1993): 27–47; and James D. Fearon, "Rationalist Explanations for War," *International Organization* 49, no. 3 (1995): 379–414, show that war onset is often the result of miscalculation and bad information.

22. Doug McAdam, Sidney Tarrow, and Charles Tilly, *Dynamics of Contention* (Cambridge: Cambridge University Press, 2001).

23. Skocpol, "What Makes Peasants Revolutionary?," 366.

24. I am not offering a theory of individual participation, which Viterna argues cannot be reduced to a single logic. See Jocelyn Viterna, "Pulled, Pushed, and Persuaded: Explaining Women's Mobilization into the Salvadoran Guerrilla Army," *American Journal of Sociology*, 112, no. 1 (2006): 1–45. On networks and participation, see Gould, *Insurgent Identities*; Petersen, *Resistance and Rebellion*; Marc Sageman, *Understanding Terror Networks* (Philadelphia: University of Pennsylvania Press, 2004); Dora Costa and Matthew E. Kahn, *Heroes & Cowards: The Social Face of War* (Princeton, NJ: Princeton University Press, 2008), and Elisabeth Jean Wood, "The Social Processes of Civil War: The Wartime Transformation of Social Networks." *Annual Review of Political Science* 11, no. 1 (2008): 539–561.

25. Sidney Tarrow, *Power in Movement: Social Movements and Contentious Politics*, 2nd ed. (Cambridge: Cambridge University Press, 1998), 124; and Scott Radnitz, *Weapons of the Wealthy: Elite-Led Protests in Central Asia* (Ithaca, NY: Cornell University Press, 2011).

26. Chester Irving Barnard, *The Functions of the Executive* (Cambridge, MA: Harvard University Press, 1938), 5, my italics.

27. On the difficulties of rapid network change, see Barry Wellman, "Network Analysis: Some Basic Principles," *Sociological Theory* 1 (1983): 173; John D. McCarthy, "Constraints and Opportunities in Adopting, Adapting, and Inventing," in *Comparative Perspectives on Social Movements: Political Opportunities, Mobilizing Structures, and Cultural Framings*, ed. Doug McAdam, John D. McCarthy, and Mayer N. Zald (Cambridge: Cambridge University Press, 1996), 147; Padgett and Ansell, "Robust Action and the Rise of the Medici," 1259.

28. Brian Downing, *The Military Revolution and Political Change: Origins of Democracy and Autocracy in Early Modern Europe* (Princeton: Princeton University Press, 1992), 252. This structural challenge faces even authoritarian government officials trying to build or reform ruling political parties. Steven Levitsky and Lucan Way, "Beyond Patronage: Violent Struggle, Ruling Party Cohesion, and Authoritarian Durability," *Perspectives on Politics* 10, no. 4 (2012): 880.

29. Overthrows of popular regimes, for example, happen when leaders get people on the street quickly. Charles Tilly, *From Mobilization to Revolution* (Reading, MA: Addison-Wesley, 1978); and Timur Kuran, "Now Out of Never: The Element of Surprise in the East European Revolution of 1989." *World Politics* 44, no. 1 (1991): 7–48.

30. Stathis N. Kalyvas, *The Logic of Violence in Civil War* (Cambridge: Cambridge University Press, 2006), 95–96.

31. Some survivors of this rebellion escaped and took to the jungles to painstakingly create vertical ties in India's interior. They succeeded to a great extent, but this took decades. It is certainly possible to change the structure of an organization but this does not happen quickly or easily.

32. Paul Pierson, *Politics in Time: History, Institutions, and Social Analysis* (Princeton, NJ: Princeton University Press, 2004).

33. Mancur Olson, *The Logic of Collective Action: Public Goods and the Theory of Groups* (Cambridge, MA: Harvard University Press, 1965). On "first actors" who trigger collective action, see Roger Petersen, *Resistance and Rebellion: Lessons from Eastern Europe* (Cambridge: Cambridge University Press, 2001).

34. In *Guerrillas and Revolution in Latin America: A Comparative Study of Insurgents and Regimes since 1956* (Princeton, NJ: Princeton University Press, 1992), Timothy P. Wickham-Crowley, argues that revolutionary organizers often come from shared social backgrounds, particularly universities and left-wing political parties.

35. Samuel P. Huntington, *Political Order in Changing Societies* (New Haven, CT: Yale University Press, 1968), 31.

36. Samuel L. Popkin, *The Rational Peasant: The Political Economy of Rural Society in Vietnam* (Berkeley: University of California Press, 1979).

37. This is especially an issue in parochial groups: once leaders are put in place, many prefer the status quo to becoming integrated into groups that they are not in charge of. This problem reflects the structures that forge parochial organizations, but the topic of how factional leaders compete with one another needs more careful study.

38. Eamonn McCann, "The Real IRA," *The Nation*, November 18, 2002, http://www.thenation.com/article/real-ira?page = full, accessed August 19, 2013.

39. Philip Selznick, *Leadership in Administration: A Sociological Interpretation* (Evanston, IL: Row, Peterson, 1957), 105–106.

40. Scott, "Peasants and Commissars."

41. McAdam, *Political Process*, 46.

42. Shaul Mishal and Avraham Sela, *The Palestinian Hamas: Vision, Violence, and Coexistence* (New York: Columbia University Press, 2006), 55.

43. On the dynamics of principals and agents in insurgent groups, see Weinstein, *Inside Rebellion*.

44. If my theory is wrong in a particular instance, the patterns of factionalism will instead reflect an alternative theoretical explanation, such as factions having different resource endowments or ideologies, or facing different state policies.

45. As I note in chapter 1, these subtypes are much closer to each another than to other broad categories, so I analyze them both as parochial groups.

46. Padgett and Ansell, "Robust Action and the Rise of the Medici."

47. International Crisis Group, "Iraq's Muqtada Al-Sadr: Spoiler or Stabiliser?" *Middle East Report* 55, 11 July 2006, 17.

48. This is the structure most similar to the dynamics addressed in Fotini Christia, *Alliance Formation in Civil Wars* (Cambridge: Cambridge University Press, 2012); and Kristin M. Bakke, Kathleen Gallagher Cunningham, and Lee J. M. Seymour, "A Plague of Initials: Fragmentation, Cohesion, and Infighting in Civil Wars," *Perspectives on Politics* 10, no. 2 (2012): 265–283.

49. Abigail Fielding-Smith, "Fractured Syrian Rebels Scour for Cash as Funders Dry Up," *Financial Times*, May 2, 2013, http://www.ft.com/cms/s/0/15844e92-ae48-11e2-8316-00144feabdc0.html#axzz2SFAdM5kF. As of this writing, the hunt for resources seems to have combined with the lack of an overarching prewar social base to create divisions within the overall movement and within specific organizations.

50. On veto points, see George Tsebelis, *Veto Players: How Political Institutions Work* (Princeton, NJ: Princeton University Press, 2002).

51. This claim disagrees with proponents of "netwar" who argue that highly decentralized and weakly organized networks can outwit and outcompete states and rivals. The need for scale, coordination, and discipline that fighting forces face do not vary markedly, and thus fragmented groups cannot achieve major policy goals under most circumstances. See John Arquilla and David F. Ronfeldt, *Networks and Netwars* (Santa Monica, CA: Rand, 2001).

52. Weinstein, *Inside Rebellion*.

53. Stephen Bloomer, "The History and Politics of the I.R.S.P. and I.N.L.A. from 1974 to the Present Day" (MA thesis, Queen's University Belfast, 1988).

54. INLA, "Future Strategy," February 1987, document in Northern Ireland Political Collection, Linen Hall Library, Belfast.

3. Insurgent Change

1. Exceptions include Elisabeth Jean Wood, "The Social Processes of Civil War: The Wartime Transformation of Social Networks," *Annual Review of Political Science* 11, no. 1 (2008): 539–561; and Paul D. Kenny, "Structural Integrity and Cohesion in Insurgent Organizations: Evidence from Protracted Conflicts in Ireland and Burma," *International Studies Review* 12, no. 4 (2010): 533–555; and Sarah Parkinson, "Organizing Rebellion: Rethinking High Risk Mobilization and Social Networks in War," *American Political Science Review* (forthcoming). For a valuable examination of shifts in alliances, see Fotini Christia, *Alliance Formation in Civil Wars* (Cambridge: Cambridge University Press, 2012); for a study of changes in how insurgent groups use violence against civilians, see Claire Metelits, *Inside Insurgency: Violence, Civilians, and Revolutionary Group Behavior* (New York: New York University Press, 2009). In *Inside Rebellion: The Politics of Insurgent Violence* (Cambridge: Cambridge University Press, 2007), 260–265, Jeremy Weinstein explores how shocks can induce change but reiterates that organizations are fairly resilient. He argues that "it is more likely that activist groups will turn into opportunistic organizations than vice versa" (264).

2. Paul Pierson, *Politics in Time: History, Institutions, and Social Analysis* (Princeton, NJ: Princeton University Press, 2004), 104.

3. A key benefit of this approach is that it can be used to examine specific organizational interactions over time instead of relying on level of an overall conflict or

time-invariant interactions. An example of an examination of the latter is David E. Cunningham, Kristian Skrede Gleditsch, and Idean Salehyan, "It Takes Two: A Dyadic Analysis of Civil War Duration and Outcome," *Journal of Conflict Resolution* 53, no. 4 (2009): 570–597; an analysis of the former is Ivan Arreguín-Toft, *How the Weak Win Wars: A Theory of Asymmetric Conflict* (Cambridge: Cambridge University Press, 2005).

4. Stathis Kalyvas, *The Logic of Violence in Civil War* (Cambridge: Cambridge University Press, 2006); Elisabeth Jean Wood, *Insurgent Collective Action and Civil War in El Salvador* (New York: Cambridge University Press, 2003).

5. Roger Petersen, *Resistance and Rebellion: Lessons from Eastern Europe* (Cambridge: Cambridge University Press, 2001).

6. On power and conflict in organizations, see Jack Knight, *Institutions and Social Conflict* (Cambridge: Cambridge University Press, 1992); and Terry M. Moe, "Power and Political Institutions," *Perspectives on Politics* 3, no. 2 (2005): 215–233.

7. Ronald Burt, *Structural Holes: The Social Structure of Competition* (Cambridge: Harvard University Press, 1992); Robert D. Putnam, *Making Democracy Work: Civic Traditions in Modern Italy* (Princeton, NJ: Princeton University Press, 1993); and David Kreps, "Corporate Culture and Economic Theory," in *Perspectives on Positive Political Economy*, ed. James Alt and Kenneth Shepsle (New York: Cambridge University Press, 1990), 90–143.

8. On the self-encapsulation of armed groups, see Donatella Della Porta, *Social Movements, Political Violence, and the State: A Comparative Analysis of Italy and Germany* (Cambridge: Cambridge University Press, 1995).

9. James Mahoney and Kathleen Thelen, "A Theory of Gradual Institutional Change," in *Explaining Institutional Change: Ambiguity, Agency, and Power*, ed. James Mahoney and Kathleen Thelen (Cambridge: Cambridge University Press, 2010), 8.

10. Nathan Constantin Leites and Charles Wolf, *Rebellion and Authority: An Analytic Essay on Insurgent Conflicts* (Chicago: Markham Pub. Co., 1970), 155.

11. On counterinsurgency, see Arreguín-Toft, *How the Weak Win Wars;* Jason Lyall and Isaiah Wilson III, "Rage against the Machines: Explaining Outcomes in Counterinsurgency Wars," *International Organization* 63, no. 1 (2009): 67–106; Andrew F. Krepinevich, *The Army and Vietnam* (Baltimore, MD: Johns Hopkins University Press, 1986); R. W. Komer, *Bureaucracy at War: U.S. Performance in the Vietnam Conflict* (Boulder, CO: Westview Press, 1986); John Nagl, *Learning to Eat Soup with a Knife: Counterinsurgency Lessons from Malaya and Vietnam* (Chicago: University of Chicago Press, 2005); Colin Jackson, "Defeat in Victory: Organizational Learning Dysfunction in Counterinsurgency" (PhD diss., Massachusetts Institute of Technology, 2008); Austin Long, "First War Syndrome: Military Culture, Professionalization, and Counterinsurgency Doctrine" (PhD diss., Massachusetts Institute of Technology, 2010).

12. Efforts to outline such best practices include Kalev I. Sepp, "Best Practices in Counterinsurgency," *Military Review* 85, no. 3 (2005): 8–12; Nagl, *Learning to Eat Soup with a Knife;* Peter W. Chiarelli and Patrick R. Michaelis, "Winning the Peace: The Requirement for Full-Spectrum Operations," *Military Review* 85, no. 4 (2005): 4–17.

13. Over time, wars may shift into deals between states and insurgents in which direct state repression is withdrawn. As long as the insurgent organization in question was born and had to survive for a substantial period of time (five years or more) in the face of substantial military pressure, however, my theory should tell us a lot about its organization. If the group was born and maintained in collusion with state

Notes to Pages 37–42

forces or in the absence of any repression, this argument will tell us much less. The mechanisms of change will be far more diverse, since the pressures on the group are less constraining. On wartime political orders, see Paul Staniland, "States, Insurgents, and Wartime Political Orders," *Perspectives on Politics* 10, no. 2 (2012): 243–264.

14. Kathleen Thelen, "Historical Institutionalism in Comparative Politics," *Annual Review of Political Science* 2 (1999): 397.

15. Theda Skocpol, "What Makes Peasants Revolutionary?," *Comparative Politics* 14, no. 3 (1982): 365, emphasis mine.

16. This theoretical move also allows for empirical research that includes the entire range of variation in organizational outcomes, including successful change and failed attempts. See Gary King, Robert O. Keohane, and Sidney Verba, *Designing Social Inquiry: Scientific Inference in Qualitative Research* (Princeton, NJ: Princeton University Press, 1994).

17. Even where military capacity exists, it needs to be linked to political will and resolve. Andrew Mack, "Why Big Nations Lose Small Wars: The Politics of Asymmetric Conflict," *World Politics* 27, no. 2 (1975): 175–200; Gil Merom, *How Democracies Lose Small Wars: State, Society, and the Failures of France in Algeria, Israel in Lebanon, and the United States in Vietnam* (Cambridge: Cambridge University Press, 2003); and Staniland, "States, Insurgents, and Wartime Political Orders."

18. Empirical studies of decapitation include Jenna Jordan, "When Heads Roll: Assessing the Effectiveness of Leadership Decapitation," *Security Studies* 18, no. 4 (2009): 719–755; Bryan C. Price, "Targeting Top Terrorists: How Leadership Decapitation Contributes to Counterterrorism," *International Security* 36, no. 4 (2012): 9–46; Patrick B. Johnston, "Does Decapitation Work? Assessing the Effectiveness of Leadership Targeting in Counterinsurgency Campaigns," *International Security* 36, no. 4 (2012): 47–79.

19. On local militias, see Paul Staniland, "Between a Rock and a Hard Place: Insurgent Fratricide, Ethnic Defection, and the Rise of Pro-State Paramilitaries," *Journal of Conflict Resolution* 56, no. 1 (2012): 16–40; and Stathis N. Kalyvas, "Ethnic Defection in Civil War," *Comparative Political Studies* 41, no. 8 (2008): 1043–1068.

20. See Parkinson, "Organizing Rebellion," for examples of these dynamics in the case of Palestinian armed groups in Lebanon.

21. See, for instance, Manoj Anand, "Bangla Safe Sanctuary for Northeast Rebels," *Asian Age,* April 18, 2013, http://archive.asianage.com/india/bangla-safe-sanctuary-northeast-rebels-944, accessed August 19, 2013.

22. On the distinctive characteristics of center-seeking and secessionist organizations, see Weinstein, *Inside Rebellion;* and Zachariah Mampilly, *Rebel Rulers: Insurgent Governance and Civilian Life during War* (Cornell University Press, 2011).

23. On dynamics in these fractious movements, see Wendy Pearlman, *Violence, Nonviolence, and the Palestinian National Movement* (Cambridge: Cambridge University Press, 2011).

24. Another option for pushing aside rivals and unifying movements is fratricide among insurgents. See Staniland, "Between a Rock and a Hard Place," on this policy and its consequences.

25. On problems of militant incorporation, see William Reno, *Warfare in Independent Africa* (New York: Cambridge University Press, 2011); and James C. Scott, "Revolution in the Revolution: Peasants and Commissars," *Theory and Society* 7, nos. 1–2 (1979): 97–134. On organizational socialization, see Philip Selznick, *Leadership in Administration: A Sociological Interpretation* (Evanston, IL: Row, Peterson, 1957).

Notes to Pages 42–47

26. Martin J. Smith, *Burma: Insurgency and the Politics of Ethnicity*, 2nd. ed. (London: Zed Books, 1999), 375.

27. Reno, *Warfare in Independent Africa*, discusses "reform rebels" able to shift from a vanguard to integrated structure. Weinstein, *Inside Rebellion*, provides detailed evidence on this process from Uganda. For local evidence of this process in South Vietnam, see Jeffrey Race, *War Comes to Long An: Revolutionary Conflict in a Vietnamese Province* (Berkeley: University of California Press, 1972); and David W. P. Elliott, *The Vietnamese War: Revolution and Social Change in the Mekong Delta* (Armonk, NY: M. E. Sharpe, 2000).

28. This strategy aims to yoke local cleavages to the "master cleavage" of a war. Stathis N. Kalyvas, "The Ontology of 'Political Violence': Action and Identity in Civil Wars," *Perspectives on Politics* 1, no. 3 (2003): 475–494.

29. Joel S. Migdal, *Peasants, Politics, and Revolution: Pressures toward Political and Social Change in the Third World* (Princeton, NJ: Princeton University Press, 1975); Scott, "Revolution in the Revolution."

30. Jeff Goodwin, *No Other Way Out: States and Revolutionary Movements, 1945–1991* (Cambridge: Cambridge University Press, 2001).

31. Skocpol, "What Makes Peasants Revolutionary?," 366.

32. For an example of how state interests can create space for insurgency, see Paul Staniland, "Cities on Fire: Social Mobilization, State Policy, and Urban Insurgency," *Comparative Political Studies* 43, no. 12 (2010): 1623–1649.

33. Reno, *Warfare in Independent Africa*; Weinstein, *Inside Rebellion*.

34. Timothy P. Wickham-Crowley, *Guerrillas and Revolution in Latin America: A Comparative Study of Insurgents and Regimes since 1956* (Princeton, NJ Princeton University Press, 1992).

35. Scott, "Peasants and Commissars."

36. In *Exploring Revolution: Essays on Latin American Insurgency and Revolutionary Theory* (Armonk, NY M. E. Sharpe, 1991), 33, Timothy Wickham-Crowley argues that many leftists in Latin America were "seized by an idea" that led to "inflexible awe" of politically ineffective strategies. On the challenges of applying Maoist strategies in war, see Mampilly, *Rebel Rulers;* on rebel governance, see Ana Arjona, "Social Order in Civil War" (PhD diss., Yale University, 2010).

37. This is a situation in which ideology can become crucial for an organization, though in terms of guiding attempts at institution building rather than in terms of creating organizations. See James C. Scott, *Seeing Like a State: How Certain Schemes to Improve the Human Condition Have Failed* (New Haven, CT: Yale University Press, 1998), chapter 5.

38. Philip Selznick, *The Organizational Weapon: A Study of Bolshevik Strategy and Tactics* (New York: McGraw-Hill, 1952), 84.

39. Wickham-Crowley, *Guerrillas and Revolution in Latin America*.

40. On selective violence, see Kalyvas, *The Logic of Violence in Civil War*; Stathis N. Kalyvas and Matthew Adam Kocher, "How 'Free' Is Free Riding in Civil Wars? Violence, Insurgency, and the Collective Action Problem," *World Politics* 59, no. 2 (2007): 177–216; Jason Lyall, "Does Indiscriminate Violence Incite Insurgent Attacks? Evidence from Chechnya," *Journal of Conflict Resolution* 53, no. 3 (2009): 331–362; and Jeff Goodwin, *No Other Way Out*.

41. Goodwin, *No Other Way Out*.

42. Pierson, *Politics in Time.*

43. Austin Long, "The Anbar Awakening," *Survival: Global Politics and Strategy* 50, no. 2 (2008): 67–94. Note that Al Qaeda in Iraq did not completely collapse but instead failed to expand into an integrated local armed group.

44. These disparate leaders can become "veto players" who block organizational change. On veto players, see George Tsebelis, *Veto Players: How Political Institutions Work* (Princeton, NJ: Princeton University Press, 2002).

45. Doug McAdam, *Political Process and the Development of Black Insurgency, 1930–1970* (Chicago, IL: University of Chicago Press, 1982).

46. Miguel Centeno makes the point that interstate war can be profoundly destructive of a group if no preexisting organization exists on which to build. Miguel Angel Centeno, *Blood and Debt: War and the Nation-State in Latin America* (University Park: Pennsylvania State University Press, 2002).

47. Interestingly, prison can have the same effect if states allow prisoners to congregate, collaborate, and interact. I focus on the international context here, but there may be some domestic spaces for factional fusing.

48. This is distinct from the more mundane military advantages that come with external sanctuary. These are different mechanisms, though they often point in the same direction. On the military benefits of external support, see Daniel Byman, Peter Chalk, Bruce Hoffman, William Rosenau, and David Brannan, *Trends in Outside Support for Insurgent Movements* (Washington, DC: RAND, 2001), xiv–xv; Jason Lyall and Isaiah Wilson III, "Rage against the Machines: Explaining Outcomes in Counterinsurgency Wars," *International Organization* 63, no. 1 (2009): 90; and Idean Salehyan, *Rebels without Borders: Transnational Insurgencies in World Politics* (Ithaca, NY: Cornell University Press, 2009), 36–40.

49. For a more detailed assessment of how international politics can affect insurgent movements, see Paul Staniland and Morgan Kaplan, "How Transnational Insurgents Emerge and Evolve: Theory and Evidence from the Middle East and South Asia," unpublished working paper, University of Chicago, 2013.

50. Will Reno, *Warfare in Independent Africa* (Cambridge: Cambridge University Press, 2011), 38.

51. Goodwin, *No Other Way Out;* Kalyvas, *The Logic of Violence in Civil War.*

52. Benjamin Valentino, *Final Solutions: Mass Killing and Genocide in the 20th Century* (Ithaca, NY: Cornell University Press, 2004).

53. Abdulkader Sinno, *Organizations at War in Afghanistan and Beyond* (Ithaca, NY: Cornell University Press, 2008).

54. This is essentially a form of militarized state building, which can be very costly and challenging for central regimes. Joel S. Migdal, *Strong Societies and Weak States: State-Society Relations and State Capabilities in the Third World* (Princeton, NJ: Princeton University Press, 1988); James Scott, *The Art of Not Being Governed: An Anarchist History of Upland Southeast Asia* (New Haven, CT: Yale University Press, 2009); Staniland, "States, Insurgents, and Wartime Political Orders."

55. C. Christine Fair, "Lessons from India's Experience in the Punjab, 1978–1993," in *India and Counterinsurgency: Lessons Learned,* ed. Sumit Ganguly and David P. Fidler (London: Routledge, 2009), Chapter 8.

56. For a related argument about alliance formation in civil wars, see Fotini Christia, *Alliance Formation in Civil Wars* (Cambridge: Cambridge University Press, 2012).

Notes to Pages 52–63

Christia's scope assumes existing groups and their interactions. This type of analysis seems most relevant to parochial groups, where distinct preexisting blocs operate in loose alliance with one another, though in the cases I examine they operate under a shared organizational banner.

57. Thanks to Jesse Dillon Savage for highlighting the strategic dilemmas this structure creates.

58. Staniland, "Between a Rock and a Hard Place."

59. This is likely when a state is trying to forge an exile army to wage war inside a rival neighbor. There is no guarantee it will work, but this strategy at least opens the possibility of coordinating a previously disparate rebel movement.

60. The rise of these kinds of warlords was integral to state building in Europe. See Charles Tilly, *Coercion, Capital, and European States, AD 990–1992* (Cambridge, MA: Blackwell, 1992).

61. Weinstein, *Inside Rebellion,* offers a defense of focusing on path-dependence and continuity. Other research codes insurgent movements as static over the course of a war. See David E. Cunningham, Kristian Skrede Gleditsch, and Idean Salehyan, "It Takes Two: A Dyadic Analysis of Civil War Duration and Outcome," *Journal of Conflict Resolution* 53, no. 4 (2009): 570–597.

4. Azad and Jihad

1. On these Pakistani groups, see Paul Staniland, "Explaining Cohesion, Fragmentation, and Control in Insurgent Groups" (PhD diss., Massachusetts Institute of Technology, 2010).

2. Rizwan Zeb, "Pakistan and Jihadi Groups in the Kashmir Conflict," in *Kashmir: New Voices, New Approaches,* ed. Waheguru Pal Singh Sidhu, Bushra Asif, and Cyrus Samii (Boulder, CO: Lynne Riener, 2006), 66.

3. For details of my narrative, I have relied on Manoj Joshi, *The Lost Rebellion: Kashmir in the Nineties* (New Delhi: Penguin Books, 1999); Sumantra Bose, *Kashmir: Roots of Conflict, Paths to Peace* (Cambridge, MA: Harvard University Press, 2003); Sumantra Bose, "The JKLF and JKHM: The Kashmir Insurgents," in *Terror, Insurgency and the State,* ed. Marianne Heiberg, Brendan O'Leary, and John Tirman, 229–255 (Philadelphia: University of Pennsylvania Press, 2007); Muhammed Amir Rana, *A to Z of Jehadi Organizations in Pakistan* (Lahore: Mashal Books, 2004); and David Devadas, *In Search of a Future: The Story of Kashmir* (New Delhi: Penguin, Viking, 2007). Much of the information I convey in this chapter has been corroborated in anonymous interviews.

4. Mridu Rai, *Hindu Rulers, Muslim Subjects: Islam, Rights, and the History of Kashmir* (London: Hurst, 2004).

5. For a revisionist assessment of this period, see Chitralekha Zutshi, *Languages of Belonging: Islam, Regional Identity, and the Making of Kashmir* (New York: Oxford University Press, 2003).

6. The NC was originally named the Muslim Conference. After the name change, the Muslim Conference reemerged as a distinct unit led by anti-Abdullah dissidents. See Victoria Schofield, *Kashmir in Conflict: India, Pakistan and the Unending War,* new ed. (London: I. B. Tauris, 2003), 23.

7. Andrew Whitehead, *A Mission in Kashmir* (New Delhi: Penguin, 2007).

Notes to Pages 64–67

8. There is a broad literature on conflict between India and Pakistan over Kashmir. Among many others, see Sumit Ganguly, *Conflict Unending: India-Pakistan Tensions since 1947* (New York: Columbia University Press, 2002); and Paul Kapur, *Dangerous Deterrent: Nuclear Weapons Proliferation and Conflict in South Asia* (Stanford, CA: Stanford University Press, 2007).

9. Alexander Evans, "The Kashmir Insurgency: As Bad as It Gets," *Small Wars and Insurgencies* 11, no. 1 (2000): 69–81.

10. There were of course innumerable networks in Jammu and Kashmir and ties that did not have clear political relevance to the question of whether India or Pakistan should control the state.

11. The Plebescite Front endured in the form of a loose alliance until it fractured into a variety of subgroups by the mid-1970s. It emerged as a forum in periods of tension, such as controversy over a religious relic in late 1963 and early 1964, but when Abdullah made his peace with the Indian state it withered away.

12. Husain Haqqani, "The Ideologies of South Asian Jihadi Groups," *Current Trends in Islamist Ideology* 1 (2005): 15.

13. Seyyed Vali Reza Nasr, *The Vanguard of the Islamic Revolution: The Jama'at-I Islami of Pakistan* (Berkeley: University of California Press, 1994). For the first amir, Sa'aduddin Tarabeli, and the first unofficial meeting in 1942, see Yoginder Sikand, "The Emergence and Development of the Jama'at-i-Islami of Jammu and Kashmir (1940s-1990)," *Modern Asian Studies* 36, no. 3 (2002): 717–718.

14. Devadas, *In Search of a Future*, 77.

15. Sikand, "The Emergence and Development of the Jama'at-i-Islami of Jammu and Kashmir," 720. See also G. N. Gauhar, "Jamat-I-Islami of Jammu and Kashmir," in *Conflict and Politics of Jammu and Kashmir: Internal Dynamics*, ed. Avineet Prashar and Paawan Vivek (Jammu: Saksham Books International, 2007), 77; and Devadas, *In Search of a Future*, 115.

16. Joshi, *The Lost Rebellion*, 11; Iffat Malik, *Kashmir: Ethnic Conflict, International Dispute* (Karachi: Oxford University Press, 2002), 270.

17. In Pakistan, organizational unity is built through meetings, ideological training, and recruitment of family members. Nasr, *The Vanguard of the Islamic Revolution*, 49.

18. Gilles Keppel, *Jihad: The Trail of Political Islam* (Cambridge, MA: The Belknap Press of Harvard University Press, 2002).

19. Gauhar, "Jamat-I-Islami of Jammu and Kashmir," 81. Even government bureaucrat Sati Sahni agrees; see Sahni, *Kashmir Underground*, 122.

20. Sikand, "The Emergence and Development of the Jama'at-i-Islami of Jammu and Kashmir," 710.

21. The Pakistani Jamaat provides insight into the Jammu and Kashmir Jamaat. In Pakistan, organizational units "envelope [sic] one another, producing an all-encompassing administrative and command structure, decentralized and yet closely knit to form the organizational edifice of the Jama'at"; Nasr, *Vanguard of the Islamic Revolution*, 51.

22. Bose, *Kashmir*, 130.

23. Basharat Peer, *Curfewed Night: One Kashmiri Journalist's Frontline Account of Life, Love, and War in His Homeland* (New York: Simon and Schuster, 2010), 186.

24. Devadas, *In Search of a Future*, 114 (first quote); Joshi, *The Lost Rebellion*, 11 (second quote); Sikand, "The Emergence and Development of the Jama'at-i-Islami of Jammu

and Kashmir," 730 (third quote). After the execution of Zulfiqar Bhutto in Pakistan in 1979, the mass appeal of Jamaat diminished. See Habibullah, *My Kashmir,* 45.

25. While Mawdudi was familiar with the communist model and drew upon it in emphasizing tight cells and a hierarchical structure, he did not focus on mobilizing the dispossessed or on violence. On the similarities of Jamaat to a communist style of organization, see Nasr, *Vanguard of the Islamic Revolution;* and Haqqani, *Between Mosque and Military,* 22.

26. Malik, *Kashmir,* 272. On how the Jamaat used schools and schoolteachers to spread its ideology, see Sikand, "The Emergence and Development of the Jama'at-i-Islami of Jammu and Kashmir," 735.

27. Devadas, *In Search of a Future,* 124; Bose, "JKLF and JKHM," 234, emphasis added. The same dynamic exists in Pakistan; Nasr, *Vanguard of the Islamic Revolution,* 81.

28. Amelie Blom, "A Patron-Client Perspective on Militia-State Relations: The Case of the Hizbul-Mujahidin of Kashmir," in *Armed Militias of South Asia: Fundamentalists, Maoists and Separatists,* ed. Laurent Gayer and Christophe Jaffrelot (New York: Columbia University Press, 2009), 139.

29. Sahni, *Kashmir Underground,* 122.

30. Navnita Chadha Behera, *State, Identity & Violence: Jammu, Kashmir, and Ladakh* (New Delhi: Manohar Publishers & Distributors, 2000), 142.

31. Peer, *Curfewed Night,* 183.

32. Phone interview, May 2009.

33. Interview, Srinagar, July 2009. Of course, some do leave, and they are not barred from doing so.

34. There is ambiguity in the secondary sources about where the JKLF name was first used—some argue it was not used until 1977. See Praveen Swami, *India, Pakistan and the Secret Jihad: The Covert War in Kashmir, 1947–2004* (London: Routledge, 2007), 129; and Devadas, *In Search of a Future,* 135.

35. Schofield, *Kashmir in Conflict,* 114.

36. Devadas, *In Search of a Future,* 113. It is worth noting that JKLF mobilization would nevertheless have included Islamic symbols and rhetoric.

37. Joshi, *The Lost Rebellion,* 13.

38. See, among others, Patricia Ellis and Zafar Khan, "The Kashmiri Diaspora: Influences in Kashmir," in *New Approaches to Migration?,* ed. Nadje Sadig Al-Ali and Khalid Koser (London: Routledge, 2002), 169–185; Patricia Ellis and Zafar Khan, "Kashmiri Displacement and the Impact on Kashmiriyat," *Contemporary South Asia* 12, no. 4 (2003): 523–538; and Nasreen Ali, "Diaspora and Nation: Displacement and the Politics of Kashmiri Identity in Britain," *Contemporary South Asia* 12, no. 4 (2003): 471–480.

39. Bose, "JKLF and JKHM," 233.

40. Bose, *Contested Lands,* 179.

41. Joshi, *The Lost Rebellion,* 14.

42. Interview, Srinagar, July 2009.

43. Devadas, *In Search of a Future,* 139. For a detailed discussion of Al Fatah from the perspective of Indian sources, see Swami, *India, Pakistan and the Secret Jihad.*

44. Amin Tahir, *Mass Resistance in Kashmir: Origins, Evolution, Options* (Islamabad: Institute of Policy Studies, 1995), 85.

45. Noorani, "Contours of Militancy."

46. Interview, Srinagar, July 2009.

47. Interviews, Srinigar, May 2008 and July 2009. Also interviews, Delhi, 2008 and 2009. Some interviewees in Delhi argue that this kind of factionalization is endemic in Kashmir politics.

48. Devadas, *In Search of a Future,* 169.

49. See Bose, *Kashmir;* and Tavleen Singh, *Kashmir: A Tragedy of Errors* (New Delhi: Viking, 1995).

50. Bose, "JKLF and JKHM," 231.

51. Bose, *Kashmir,* 125.

52. Malik, *Kashmir,* 293.

53. Joshi, *The Lost Rebellion,* 52.

54. Ibid., 86.

55. Malik, *Kashmir,* 293. See also Bose, "JKLF and JKHM," 240.

56. Devadas, *In Search of a Future,* 159.

57. Bose, "JKLF and JKHM," 233.

58. Pradeep Thakur, *Militant Monologues: Echoes from the Kashmir Valley* (New Delhi: Parity Paperbacks, 2003), 35.

59. On socioeconomic background, see Behera, *Demystifying Kashmir,* 145. See also Sumit Ganguly, "Explaining the Kashmir Insurgency: Political Mobilization and Institutional Decay," *International Security* 21, no. 2 (1996): 76–107.

60. For how Javed Mir joined with a group of friends, see Thakur, *Militant Monologues,* 121–122.

61. Bose, *Kashmir,* 109; Bose, "JKLF and JKHM," 233 (quote).

62. Malik, *Kashmir,* 300. Jonah Blank writes that "most observers agree that if a plebiscite were held today, residents of the Valley (if not Jammu and Ladakh) would still opt for independence from both India and Pakistan." See "Kashmir: Fundamentalism Takes Root," *Foreign Affairs* 78, no. 6 (1999), 40.

63. Balraj Puri, *Kashmir towards Insurgency* (New Delhi: Orient Longman, 1993), 4.

64. Ashutosh Varshney, "Three Compromised Nationalisms: Why Kashmir Has Been a Problem," in *Perspectives on Kashmir: The Roots of Conflict in South Asia,* ed. Raju G. C Thomas (Boulder, CO: Westview Press, 1992), 221.

65. Sahni, *Kashmir Underground,* 37. In 1994, Baweja estimated that "90 per cent of the Kashmiris back [Yasin Malik's] organisation's demand for independence." Harinder Baweja, "The War Within," *India Today,* July 15, 1994.

66. "Till Freedom Come," *Outlook India,* October 18, 1995, http://www.outlookindia.com/article.aspx?200005.

67. It had "by far the widest indigenous support in the Kashmir valley." Julian Schofield and Reeta Tremblay, "Why Pakistan Failed: Tribal Focoism in Kashmir," *Small Wars & Insurgencies* 19, no. 1 (2008): 33.

68. Interviews, Srinagar, May 2008 and July 2009.

69. Alexander Evans, "Kashmir: The Past Ten Years," *Asian Affairs* 30, no. 1 (1999): 23–24.

70. Behera, *Demystifying Kashmir,* 149. A similar point is made in Bose, *Kashmir,* 111.

Notes to Pages 74–77

71. Beg is sometimes spelled Baig.

72. Interviews, Srinagar, May 2008. See also Peer, *Curfewed Night;* and Singh, *A Tragedy of Errors.*

73. Amanullah Khan was actually from Baltistan, part of the Pakistani Northern Areas, not from the Valley; the HAJY group had no prior connections to the PJK.

74. S. Verma, *Jammu and Kashmir at the Political Crossroads* (Delhi: Vikas, 1994), 277.

75. Bose, "JKLF and JKHM," 240–241.

76. Devadas, *In Search of a Future,* 162.

77. Ibid., 164.

78. Sinha, *Death of Dreams,* 25.

79. Joshi, *The Lost Rebellion;* Devadas, *In Search of a Future,* 164.

80. Sinha, *Death of Dreams,* 45.

81. Interview, Srinagar, May 2008.

82. Devadas, *In Search of a Future,* 159.

83. Joshi, *The Lost Rebellion,* 17. See also Bose, *Kashmir,* 126.

84. A. G. Noorani, "The Betrayal of Kashmir: Pakistan's Duplicity and India's Complicity," in *Perspectives on Kashmir: The Roots of Conflict in South Asia,* ed. Raju G. C Thomas (Boulder: Westview Press, 1992), 263. See also "A Profile in Passion," *Newsline,* February 2001, 34.

85. Joshi, *The Lost Rebellion,* 26.

86. Evans, "Kashmir: The Past Ten Years," 24.

87. Devadas, *In Search of a Future,* 214; Joshi, *The Lost Rebellion,* 49.

88. Joshi, *The Lost Rebellion;* Devadas, *In Search of a Future.*

89. Schofield, *Kashmir in Conflict,* 145. See also Harinder Baweja, "Spiralling Downwards," *India Today,* May 15, 1993, 751; and Bose, "JKLF and JKHM," 243.

90. Varshney, "Three Compromised Nationalisms," 221.

91. Noorani, "Contours of Militancy."

92. Rana, *A to Z of Jehadi Organizations,* 440.

93. Behera, *Demystifying Kashmir,* 154.

94. Deepa Ollapally, *The Politics of Extremism in South Asia* (Cambridge: Cambridge University Press, 2008), 125.

95. Behera, *Demystifying Kashmir,* 167.

96. Interview, Srinagar, May 2008.

97. There is some lack of clarity about its original name. Joshi argues that Hizbul Mujahideen was originally named Al Badr (*The Lost Rebellion,* 48,); Devadas says that it was originally the Ansar-ul Islam (this is also mentioned in Joshi, *The Lost Rebellion,* 15) and that Al Badr was merely one name considered (Devadas, *In Search of a Future,* 180).

98. Joshi, *The Lost Rebellion,* 47. Much of the early pro-Pakistan mobilization occurred (in Amin's pro-Jamaat language) "independent of the Jamaat discipline." Amin, *Mass resistance in Kashmir,* 90.

99. Jaleel, "Spawning Militancy: The Rise of Hizbul," *Indian Express,* May 22, 2003.

Notes to Pages 77–79

100. Geelani fits the socioeconomic profile of many influential Jamaat members: "another Pirzada and school teacher"; Gauhar "Jamat-I-Islami of Jammu and Kashmir," 77.

101. Devadas, *In Search of a Future,* 213.

102. Ibid., 214.

103. Harinder Baweja, *Most Wanted: Profiles of Terror* (New Delhi: Lotus Collection, Roli Books, 2002), 116–117. Yusuf Shah became a schoolteacher and a politician; he also became a full-fledged Jamaat *rukn,* or member, sometime soon after 1972.

104. This splinter group was also known as the "Green Army." Praveen Swami says that the Jamiat was "soon marginalized"; see "The Tanzeems and Their Leaders," *Frontline,* September 19, 2000. See also Thakur, *Militant Monologues,* 132. Ghulam Rasool Shah, a senior commander of Jamiat, is profiled in "A Profile in Passion," *Newsline,* February 2001, 33–34.

105. Bose, "JKLF and JKHM," 235.

106. Schofield, *Kashmir in Conflict,* 202–203.

107. Jaleel, "Spawning Militancy."

108. Swami, *India, Pakistan and the Secret Jihad,* 178.

109. Devadas, *In Search of a Future,* 240.

110. See Verma, *Jammu and Kashmir,* 278; Devadas, *In Search of a Future,* 256.

111. Thakur, *Militant Monologues,* 127.

112. Behera, *State, Identity & Violence,* 178–179.

113. Jaleel, "Spawning Militancy."

114. Sikand, "The Emergence and Development of the Jama'at-i-Islami of Jammu and Kashmir," 749; Interview, Delhi, November 2007.

115. Interviews, Srinagar, May 2008 and July 2009; interviews, Delhi, September 2007–May 2008 and July 2009.

116. Peer, *Curfewed Night,* 184.

117. Example from ibid., 184–185.

118. Joshi, *The Lost Rebellion,* 201, 186; Aamer Ahmed Khan, "Kashmir Chalo," *The Herald* (Karachi) (Karachi), November 1994, 33. *The Herald* is a major Pakistani monthly newsmagazine.

119. Bose, *Kashmir,* 129.

120. Joshi, *The Lost Rebellion,* 51.

121. K. V Krishna Rao, *The Genesis of the Insurgency in Jammu and Kashmir, and in the North East, and Future Prospects* (New Delhi: United Service Institution of India, 1997), 42; Arjun Ray, *Kashmir Diary: Psychology of Militancy* (New Delhi: Manas Publications, 1997), 160.

122. According to Zaffar Abbas this group had fought under Gulbuddin Hekymatyar's Hizbul Mujahideen-e-Islami in Afghanistan, which was linked to the Jamaat. See "A Who's Who of Kashmir Militancy," *The Herald* (Karachi), August 2000, 30,

123. Rana, *A to Z of Jehadi Organizations,* 460.

124. Zaigham Khan, "'The People Who Have Announced the Cease-Fire Have Fallen Prey to Indian Conspiracy,'" *The Herald* (Karachi), August 2000, 36–37.

125. Singh, *A Tragedy of Errors,* 235.

126. Joshi, *The Lost Rebellion,* 48.

127. Zahid Hussain, *Frontline Pakistan: The Struggle with Militant Islam* (New York: Columbia University Press, 2007), 132. See also Mubashir Zaidi, "The Himalayan Implosion," *The Herald* (Karachi), June 2003, 59.

128. One Hizbul Mujahideen fighter is quoted as saying, "The JKLF is not even a true Islamic group. Their manifesto is in English, meant for Europeans, and talks of a secular Kashmir." "Exporting Terror," *India Today,* May 15, 1994, 50–51.

129. Joshi, *The Lost Rebellion,* 86.

130. Geelani's prison diaries from the early 1990s reflect the Hizbul Mujahideen's obsession with controlling the insurgent movement. See Yoginder Sikand, "The Jama'at-i-Islami of Jammu and Kashmir," in *Competing Nationalisms in South Asia,* ed. Paul R. Brass and Achin Vanaik (Hyderabad: Orient Blackswan, 2002), 279. See also Yoginder Sikand, "For Islam and Kashmir: The Prison Diaries of Sayyed Ali Gilani of the Jama'At-I-Islami of Jammu and Kashmir," *Journal of Muslim Minority Affairs* 18, no. 2 (1998): 241–249.

131. Bose, "JKLF and JKHM," 237.

132. Arif Jamal, *Shadow War: The Untold Story of Jihad in Kashmir* (New York: Melville Publishing House, 2009).

133. Bose, "JKLF and JKHM," 238.

134. Ibid. 241. This was in part because of the relative poverty of the diaspora in the United Kingdom, where many were linked to the PJK, and the fact that members of the diaspora in the United States tended to be more nonpolitical, more wealthy, and Hindu.

135. Bose, "JKLF and JKHM," 238 (quote); Joshi, *The Lost Rebellion,* 77. See also Bose, *Contested Lands,* 180.

136. According to Indian security sources, the ratio of security forces to militants eventually reached a staggering 1,000:1 in the Valley. Muzamil Jaleel, "Hold Fire," *Indian Express,* April 14, 2007.

137. To give a sense of how decisions were being made, see Devadas, *In Search of a Future,* 247–248.

138. Ibid., 248.

139. Ibid., 262.

140. Bose, "JKLF and JKHM," 240–241.

141. Ibid., 238.

142. Bose, *Kashmir,* 126.

143. Devadas, *In Search of a Future,* 181. According to Sahni, Amanullah Khan then proceeded to denounce Beg's JKSLF/Ikhwan; *Kashmir Underground,* 44.

144. Joshi dates the formal split to April 1991; see *The Lost Rebellion.*

145. Ibid., 51.

146. The Ikhwan actually attempted to get the JKLF and Al Umar to sort out their feud in March 1992, but this effort failed. Ibid., 105.

147. Behera, *State, Identity & Violence,* 204.

148. Arun Joshi, *Eyewitness Kashmir: Teetering on Nuclear War* (Singapore: Marshall Cavendish Academic, 2004), 167.

Notes to Pages 83–86

149. Amanullah Khan and Javed Mir began arguing that India and Pakistan were both the JKLF's enemies. For Khan's view, see "Both Nawaz and Rao Are Our Enemies," *India Today,* December 31, 1992, 100.

150. Evans, "The Kashmir Insurgency," 69; Thakur, *Militant Monologues,* 127.

151. Some believe that Malik was released by the Indians in hopes that he could "resolve the disunity in the ranks of the JKLF" and thus balance the now-dominant Hizbul Mujahideen. Harinder Baweja, "A Calculated Gamble," *India Today,* June 15, 1994, 67. For the JKLF prior to the release of Malik, see Harinder Baweja, "A High Risk Gamble," *India Today,* March 31, 1993.

152. See interview with him in Harinder Baweja, "Give Me Forty Days," *India Today,* June 15, 1994, 69: "If there are differences of opinion in the JKLF, it doesn't make it a divided house."

153. Opinions vary about the overall balance of personality and ideology in this split. See Joshi, *The Lost Rebellion,* 431; Behera, *Demystifying Kashmir,* 158; Malik, *Kashmir,* 300.

154. Joshi, *The Lost Rebellion,* 431.

155. Noorani also suggests that there was tension within the JKLF in Pakistan. See "Contours of Militancy."

156. Sikand, "The Emergence and Development of the Jama'at-i-Islami of Jammu and Kashmir," 748.

157. See, for instance, "JKLF Splits for Second Time," *Indian Express,* October 31, 2002. See a dissident splitter's explanation for his break at Shabir Choudry, "Why I Said Goodbye to the JKLF," Counter Currents Web site, July 25, 2008, www.countercurrents.org/choudhry250708.htm.

158. "The Rediff Interview: Abdul Majid Dar," *Rediff.com,* April 2001, http://www.rediff.com/news/2001/apr/06inter.htm.

159. See Singh, *A Tragedy of Errors,* 220; Muzamil Jaleel, "Hizb Rebel Dar Shot at Sopore House," *Indian Express,* March 24, 2003; and "The Rediff Interview: Abdul Majid Dar."

160. Majid's Tehrik-e Jehad Islami was linked to a People's League faction (Qureshi). See Devadas, *In Search of a Future,* 237; and Joshi, *The Lost Rebellion,* 46.

161. Jaleel, "Spawning Militancy."

162. Interview, Srinagar, July 2009.

163. Devadas, *In Search of a Future,* 237.

164. Jaleel "Spawning Militancy."

165. Similarly, a senior loyalist of Nasir-ul Islam, Abdullah Bangroo, had been trained in JKLF camps.

166. Baweja, *Most Wanted,* 123.

167. Joshi, *The Lost Rebellion,* 87.

168. Joshi argues that the Hizbul Mujahideen's "leadership problems [were] settled" by 1992. See ibid., 103.

169. Ibid., 203. For more on Doda, see Harjeet Singh, *Doda: An Insurgency in the wilderness* (New Delhi: Lancer Publishers, 1999), 77–79.

170. Bose, "JKLF and JKHM," 240–241.

Notes to Pages 86–89

171. Joshi, *The Lost Rebellion*, 422. For more on "fratricidal flipping," see Paul Staniland, "Between a Rock and a Hard Place: Insurgent Fratricide, Ethnic Defection, and the Rise of Pro-State Paramilitaries," *Journal of Conflict Resolution* 56, no. 1 (2012): 16–40.

172. Evans, "The Kashmir Insurgency," 75. See also Bose, "JKLF and JKHM," 244; and Devadas, *In Search of a Future*, 279.

173. Gauhar, "Jamat-I-Islami of Jammu and Kashmir," 81.

174. Jaleel mentions 2,000 Jamaat deaths; see Jaleel, "Spawning Militancy." This number was repeated in interviews in Delhi and Srinagar but its original source is unclear.

175. Schofield, *Kashmir in Conflict*, 199. Confirmed in interviews in Delhi and Srinagar.

176. Sikand, "The Emergence and Development of the Jama'at-i-Islami of Jammu and Kashmir," 751.

177. Jamaat's distancing of itself from the Hizbul Mujahideen is discussed in Bose, "JKLF and JKHM," 245.

178. Gauhar, "Jamat-I-Islami of Jammu and Kashmir," 81–83. See also Bose, "JKLF and JKHM," 244. The party's active role left it particularly vulnerable. On backing away, see Jamal, *Shadow War*.

179. Interviews, Srinagar, May 2008 and July 2009.

180. Bose, "JKLF and JKHM," 247.

181. Devadas, *In Search of a Future*, 322.

182. Zaigham Khan, "'The People Who Have Announced the Cease-Fire Have Fallen Prey to Indian Conspiracy,'" *The Herald* (Karachi), August 2000, 36.

183. Zaigham Khan, "Losing Control," *The Herald* (Karachi), May 2000, 56.

184. Rana, *A to Z of Jehadi Organizations*, 460. More broadly, Rana claims that "Al Badar resented the strong influence of Jama'at-e-Islami on Hizb," Rana, *A to Z of Jehadi Organizations*, 451.

185. Zaigham Khan, "Fumbling Towards irrelevance?" *The Herald* (Karachi), August 2000, 35.

186. Bose, "JKLF and JKHM," 248. See also Singh, *A Tragedy of Errors*, 219–224.

187. Zaffar Abbas, "Peace in Kashmir?" *The Herald* (Karachi), August 2000, 25.

188. Ibid., 24–34.

189. Sarfraz set up Hizbul Mujahideen-E-Islami as commander of the Pir Panjal Regiment; Rana, *A to Z of Jehadi Organizations*, 452–453. On hard-liners' disagreements with Dar over the ceasefire in 2000 see ibid., 453. See also Azmat Abbas, "Factional Fighting between Kashmiri Militants Leaves 10 dead," *The Herald* (Karachi), November 2000, 25.

190. Devadas, *In Search of a Future*, 331.

191. This despite Majid Dar's April 2001 claim that "there is no problem [with Salahuddin]. Up till now, all steps that we have taken were taken after discussions"; "The Rediff Interview: Abdul Majid Dar."

192. Bose, "JKLF and JKHM," 249. He was killed and then replaced by a Jamaati. Mir quoted in Rana, *A to Z of Jehadi Organizations*, 64.

193. There is disagreement about the extent of the split. Behera suggests it was large (*Demystifying Kashmir,* 158), while Rana suggests it was fairly contained (*A to Z of Jehadi Organizations,* 453). Interviewees in Delhi and Srinagar leaned toward Rana's assessment.

194. Zaffar Abbas, "The Militant Brigade," *The Herald* (Karachi), February 2004, 55.

195. Amir Mir, "The Swelling Force of Extremism," *The News,* March 22, 2009.

196. Joshi, *The Lost Rebellion,* 88. *Islampasand* here refers to groups favoring Pakistan that had an Islamist tinge.

197. Joshi argues that "the ISI encouraged all of them, its only condition being that they maintain a relentless pace of attack on Indian security forces." Joshi, *The Lost Rebellion,* 78.

198. A first-hand account by the MJF's primary commander, Firdous Syed Baba (nom de guerre Babar Badr), provides more information on this group than would otherwise be available in the secondary literature, though it must be read with some skepticism. Aditya Sinha, *Death of Dreams: A Terrorist's Tale* (New Delhi: HarperCollins Publishers, India, 2000) is his biography.

199. Interviewees in Kashmir said that the MJF had a major following in Baramulla in the north, for instance.

200. Devadas, *In Search of a Future,* 164.

201. Joshi, *The Lost Rebellion,* 51. See also Sinha, *Death of Dreams,* 59.

202. Sahni, *Kashmir Underground,* 153. That said, a former militant interviewee in Kashmir claimed that there were 10,000 men in MJF. This seems even more implausible.

203. Baramulla, chief of PL(S), was used for recruiting. See Joshi, *The Lost Rebellion,* 151.

204. Sinha, *Death of Dreams,* 48, 58–59. Sinha also claims that "when the trained militants returned [from Pakistan], Babar had no choice but to assimilate them into what was slowly growing into an unwieldy outfit. All he could do was try and slowly consolidate the organization, which was a tough job." Sinha, *Death of Dreams,* 60.

205. Sinha, *Death of Dreams,* 77.

206 Ibid.

207. Ibid., 104.

208. "The Jamaat's sympathizers took over, merged the tanzeem with the Jehad Force, and called the new group Al Jehad"; Sinha, *Death of Dreams,* 154.

209. Bose, *Kashmir,* 125.

210. Sahni, *Kashmir Underground,* 153.

211. Interview, Srinagar, May 2008. This is the same word a different interviewee used to describe the JKLF's social base in July 2009.

212. Joshi, *The Lost Rebellion,* 237.

213. Ibid., 249.

214. Sinha, *Death of Dreams,* 155.

215. Ibid., 157.

216. Thakur, *Militant Monologues,* 70 and 57. Abbas describes the Al Fatah Force as "a relatively small group." Al Jihad is said to be headed by M. Aslam Wani, and

Abbas said that "in recent months no one has heard anything about its activities"; Abbas, "A Who's Who of Kashmir Militancy," 31. One faction of the group defected to the Indian security forces.

217. Sinha, *Death of Dreams*, 195.

218. Devadas, *In Search of a Future*, 310.

219. Rana, *A to Z of Jehadi Organizations*, 488–489.

220. Joshi, *The Lost Rebellion*, 245. Note that Joshi was close to the Indian security forces and would have powerful incentives to exaggerate Pakistani influence.

221. Devadas, *In Search of a Future*, 179.

222. The *mirwaiz* of the Jama Masjid in Srinagar is a Kashmiri religious figure with substantial political influence.

223. Syed Ali Dayan Hasan, "Costly Freedom," *The Herald* (Karachi), January 2000, 48.

224. The South Asia Terrorism Portal argues there was "tacit endorsement." "Al Umar Mujahideen (AuM)," http://www.satp.org/satporgtp/countries/india/states/jandk/terrorist_outfits/Al_Umar.htm. Interviews made it clear that this relationship was extremely murky and unclear.

225. Muzamil Jaleel, "Days After He Called for End to Violence, Mirwaiz Meets Lashkar, Jaish, Al-Umar Top Guns," *Indian Express*, January 26, 2007.

226. Joshi notes that "being in the main in Srinagar, the Al Umar's activity was providing security to the Jasma Masjid area, the headquarters of the Awami Action Committee to which it was linked." Joshi, *The Lost Rebellion*, 78.

227. Devadas, *In Search of a Future*, 236.

228. Al-Umar Commandos split over weapons; Joshi, *The Lost Rebellion*, 78.

229. Interview, Srinagar, May 2008; Bose, *Kashmir*, 126.

230. Joshi, *The Lost Rebellion*, 79.

231. Devadas, *In Search of a Future*, 238.

232. It would pop back into notice briefly between 1999 and 2002, when Mushtaq Zargar was released from prison as part of a deal to free a hijacked Indian airliner. See Abbas "A Who's Who of Kashmir Militancy," 31.

233. Joshi, *The Lost Rebellion*, 63.

234. Devadas, *In Search of a Future*, 160.

235. This is McAdam, Tarrow, and Tilly's "brokerage" in action. See Doug McAdam, Sidney Tarrow, and Charles Tilly, *Dynamics of Contention* (Cambridge: Cambridge University Press, 2001).

236. Thakur, *Militant Monologues*.

237. Ibid., 45.

238. There was also a "central body coordinating with the ISI and organizing the training of personnel in Azad Kashmir"; Joshi, *The Lost Rebellion*, 80, see also 106.

239. Ibid., 423.

240. Ibid., 245.

241. Thakur, *Militant Monologues*. Sources in Delhi suggest that Parrey was actually much closer to the Jamaat than he claimed.

242. Devadas, *In Search of a Future*, 286.

243. Sahni, *Kashmir Underground*, 201.

244. Thakur, *Militant Monologues*, 50–51.

245. Joshi, *The Lost Rebellion*, 425.

246. Thakur, *Militant Monologues*, 50. See also Joshi, *The Lost Rebellion*, 426.

247. Joshi, *The Lost Rebellion*, 426.

248. Thakur, *Militant Monologues*, 89.

249. Usman Majid similarly flipped from Ikhwan after clashes with Hizbul Mujahideen. Thakur, *Militant Monologues*, 115.

250. On Ikhwan factionalism, see Joshi, *The Lost Rebellion*, 415 and 425–426.

251. Ibid., 415.

252. Ibid., 175–176.

253. Ibid. On the formation of the JKIF, see ibid., 429–430.

254. On the JKIF's fate by 1998, see Swami, "Terrorism in Jammu and Kashmir," 82. In 2000, Zaffar Abbas wrote that "it is not very active these days"; Abbas, "A Who's Who of Kashmir Militancy," 31.

255. Jamal, *Shadow War*, 150–151.

5. Organizing Rebellion in Afghanistan

1. Gilles Dorronsoro, *Revolution Unending: Afghanistan, 1979 to the Present* (New York: Columbia University Press in association with the Centre d'Etudes et de Recherches Internationales, Paris, 2005), 15.

2. Kristian Berg Harpviken, "Transcending Traditionalism: The Emergence of Non-State Military Formations in Afghanistan," *Journal of Peace Research* 34, no. 3 (1997): 283.

3. Barnett R. Rubin, *The Fragmentation of Afghanistan: State Formation and Collapse in the International System* (New Haven, CT: Yale University Press, 1995).

4. There were also a few royalists who sought to recapture power after the 1973 coup, but they were a small and declining social base. For a brief discussion of this social base and the minor armed groups it produced, see Olivier Roy, *Islam and Resistance in Afghanistan* (Cambridge: Cambridge University Press, 1986), 117–118.

5. On the decline of clerical power between 1929 and 1960s, see Dorronsoro, *Revolution Unending*, 35–36.

6. Roy, *Islam and Resistance in Afghanistan*, 47.

7. Roy, *Islam and Resistance in Afghanistan*, 48.

8. David B. Edwards, *Before Taliban: Genealogies of the Afghan Jihad* (Berkeley: University of California Press, 2002), 210.

9. Dorronsoro, *Revolution Unending*, 69.

10. Edwards, *Before Taliban*, 200–203.

11. Rubin, *The Fragmentation of Afghanistan*, 76. This is truer of 1978–1988 than afterward.

12. Roy, *Islam and Resistance in Afghanistan*, 69.

Notes to Pages 107–112

13. Edwards, *Before Taliban*, 209.

14. Roy, *Islam and Resistance in Afghanistan*, 73.

15. Ibid.

16. Edwards, *Before Taliban*, 203; Dorronsoro, *Revolution Unending*, 69–70.

17. Edwards, *Before Taliban*, 215–216.

18. This included Burhanuddin Rabbani, Gulbuddin Hekmatyar, and Ghulam Rasul Sayyaf. Rabbani would lead Jamiat, Hikmatyar the Hezb-Gulbuddin, and Sayyaf the Ittehad. Sayyaf later changed his name to Abd al-Rab al-Rasul Sayyaf. Ahmed Rashid, *Taliban: Militant Islam, Oil and Fundamentalism in Central Asia*, 2nd ed. (New Haven, CT: Yale University Press, 2010), 86; Jason Burke, *Al-Qaeda* (London: Penguin, 2004), 68–70.

19. Roy, *Islam and Resistance in Afghanistan*, 70.

20. Ibid., 72.

21. Harpviken, "Transcending Traditionalism," 277.

22. Rashid, *Taliban*, 19.

23. Rubin, *The Fragmentation of Afghanistan*, 76.

24. Olivier Roy, *Afghanistan: From Holy War to Civil War* (Princeton, NJ: Darwin Press, 1995), 46–49, 54–57, 85–87. On the urban-rural divide, see Dorronsoro, *Revolution Unending*, 69; and Antonio Giustozzi, *War, Politics and Society in Afghanistan, 1978–1992* (Washington, DC: Georgetown University Press, 2000), 241.

25. Rubin, *The Fragmentation of Afghanistan*, 202.

26. Dorronsoro, *Revolution Unending*, 68.

27. Thomas J. Barfield, *Afghanistan: A Cultural and Political History* (Princeton, NJ: Princeton University Press, 2010), 215–216; Rubin, *The Fragmentation of Afghanistan*, 103; Dorronsoro, *Revolution Unending*, 79.

28. Roy, *Islam and Resistance in Afghanistan*, 112.

29. Rubin, *The Fragmentation of Afghanistan*, 202.

30. Harpviken, "Transcending Traditionalism," 277.

31. Ibid., 275.

32. Edwards, *Before Taliban*, 243.

33. Dorronsoro, *Revolution Unending*, 83.

34. Ibid., 74.

35. Roy, *Islam and Resistance in Afghanistan*, 77.

36. Ibid., 112–113.

37. Dorronsoro, *Revolution Unending*, 82; Edwards, *Before Taliban*, 235–239.

38. Rubin, *The Fragmentation of Afghanistan*, 184.

39. Ibid., 185.

40. Abdulkader H. Sinno, *Organizations at War in Afghanistan and Beyond* (Ithaca, NY: Cornell University Press, 2008), 155.

41. Dorronsoro, *Revolution Unending*, 162.

42. Ibid., 97, 105.

43. Ibid., 122–123.

44. As I discuss below, an early tribal split also created Hezb-Khalis in the southeast.

45. Edwards, *Before Taliban*, 276.

46. Dorronsoro, *Revolution Unending*, 163–165.

47. Rashid, *Taliban*, 86.

48. Dorronsoro, *Revolution Unending*, 169; Roy, *Islam and Resistance in Afghanistan*, 128; Rashid, *Taliban*, 19.

49. Dorronsoro, *Revolution Unending*, 165.

50. Roy, *Islam and Resistance in Afghanistan*, 111–112.

51. Ibid., 111; Rubin, *The Fragmentation of Afghanistan*, 215.

52. Roy, *Islam and Resistance in Afghanistan*, 133.

53. Antonio Giustozzi, *Empires of Mud: War and Warlords of Afghanistan* (New York: Columbia University Press, 2009), 46.

54. Rubin, *The Fragmentation of Afghanistan*, 214.

55. Dorronsoro, *Revolution Unending*, 154. See also Giustozzi, *War, Politics, and Society in Afghanistan*, 247.

56. Rubin, *The Fragmentation of Afghanistan*, 214.

57. Edwards, *Before Taliban*, 277.

58. Ibid., 178.

59. Steve Coll, *Ghost Wars: The Secret History of the CIA, Afghanistan, and Bin Laden, from the Soviet Invasion to September 10, 2001* (New York: Penguin, 2004), 119.

60. Roy, *Islam and Resistance in Afghanistan*, 134; Sinno, *Organizations at War in Afghanistan and Beyond*, 165.

61. Roy notes that "the determination and discipline of Gulbuddin's men is well known." Roy, *Islam and Resistance in Afghanistan*, 109.

62. Ibid., 133.

63. Dorronsoro, *Revolution Unending*, 163.

64. Harpviken, "Transcending Traditionalism," 283. This was true even after Pakistan began supporting Hekmatyar as a response to Daoud's pro-Pashtunistan policies. Roy, *Islam and Resistance in Afghanistan*, 75.

65. Rubin, *The Fragmentation of Afghanistan*, 232.

66. Dorronsoro, *Revolution Unending*, 109.

67. "Hizb's performance was impressive only when compared to most of the other, extremely disorganized opposition parties. Although (alone among the opposition) it did have something resembling a general strategy, its capacity to carry it out on the ground was limited." Giustozzi, *War, Politics, and Society in Afghanistan*, 248.

68. Harpviken, "Transcending Traditionalism," 277.

69. Ibid., 278.

70. Roy, *Islam and Resistance in Afghanistan*, 133; Dorronsoro, *Revolution Unending*, 217.

71. Edwards, *Before Taliban*, 277–8.

72. Rashid, *Taliban*, 87.

73. Rubin, *The Fragmentation of Afghanistan*, 214.

Notes to Pages 116–122

74. Giustozzi, *Empires of Mud*, 46.
75. Sinno, *Organizations at War in Afghanistan and Beyond*, 156.
76. Roy, *Islam and Resistance in Afghanistan*, 133.
77. Rubin, *The Fragmentation of Afghanistan*, 213.
78. Ibid., 78.
79 Ibid.
80. Harpviken, "Transcending Traditionalism," 277.
81. Roy, *Islam and Resistance in Afghanistan*, 141.
82. Rubin, *The Fragmentation of Afghanistan*, 218.
83. Barfield, *Afghanistan*, 250.
84. Rubin, *The Fragmentation of Afghanistan*, 218.
85. Ibid.; Giustozzi, *Empires of Mud*, 46; Dorronsoro, *Revolution Unending*, 165.
86. Dorronsoro, *Revolution Unending*, 216.
87. Barfield, *Afghanistan*, 240.
88. Peter Tomsen, *The Wars of Afghanistan: Messianic Terrorism, Tribal Conflicts, and the Failures of Great Powers* (New York: Public Affairs, 2011), 323.
89. Giustozzi, *Empires of Mud*, 47.
90. Giustozzi, *War, Politics, and Society in Afghanistan*, 241.
91. Roy, *Afghanistan*, 72.
92. Ibid., 73.
93. Rubin, *The Fragmentation of Afghanistan*, 234.
94. Ibid., 235.
95. Roy, *Afghanistan*, 73; Rubin, *The Fragmentation of Afghanistan*, 235.
96. Rubin, *The Fragmentation of Afghanistan*, 233.
97. Roy, *Afghanistan*, 74,
98. Ibid., 75.
99. Giustozzi, *Empires of Mud*, 288.
100. Rubin, *The Fragmentation of Afghanistan*, 235.
101. Ibid.
102. Ibid., 237.
103. Rubin notes that there were recurring local challenges to the organization. Ibid., 237.
104. Tomsen, *The Wars of Afghanistan*, 217.
105. Dorronsoro, *Revolution Unending*, 137.
106. Edwards, *Before Taliban*, 247.
107. William Maley, *The Afghanistan Wars* (Houndmills: Palgrave Macmillan, 2002), 63.
108. Roy, *Islam and Resistance in Afghanistan*, 129.
109. Edwards, *Before Taliban*, 246–7.
110. Rubin, *The Fragmentation of Afghanistan*, 212.

111. Edwards, *Before Taliban*, 275; Rashid, *Taliban*, 84.

112. Roy, *Islam and Resistance in Afghanistan*, 114; Rubin, *The Fragmentation of Afghanistan*, 212.

113. Roy, *Islam and Resistance in Afghanistan*, 113.

114. Dorronsoro, *Revolution Unending*, 113.

115. See ibid., 113–115.

116. Roy, *Islam and Resistance in Afghanistan*, 111–112; Dorronsoro, *Revolution Unending*, 154–155.

117. Roy, *Islam and Resistance in Afghanistan*, 112.

118. Rashid, *Taliban*, 19.

119. Roy, *Islam and Resistance in Afghanistan*, 114.

120. Giustozzi, *Empires of Mud*, 45.

121. Larry Goodson, *Afghanistan's Endless War: State Failure, Regional Politics, and the Rise of the Taliban* (Seattle: University of Washington Press, 2001), 62. See also Dorronsoro, *Revolution Unending*, 215.

122. Rubin, *The Fragmentation of Afghanistan*, 213.

123. Ibid., 212.

124. Ibid.

125. Harpviken, "Transcending Traditionalism," 276.

126. Roy, *Islam and Resistance in Afghanistan*, 129.

127. Rashid, *Taliban*, 19.

128. Harpviken, "Transcending Traditionalism," 276.

129. Dorronsoro, *Revolution Unending*, 162; Roy, *Islam and Resistance in Afghanistan*, 130.

130. Rubin, *The Fragmentation of Afghanistan*, 212.

131. Roy, *Islam and Resistance in Afghanistan*, 130.

132. Dorronsoro, *Revolution Unending*, 138; Barfield, *Afghanistan*, 237. My theory does not explain this animosity; it only explains the underlying divisions along which it emerged.

133. Roy, *Islam and Resistance in Afghanistan*, 78, 128; Edwards, *Before Taliban*, 248.

134. Edwards, *Before Taliban*, 251.

135. Roy, *Islam and Resistance in Afghanistan*, 128.

136. Rubin, *The Fragmentation of Afghanistan*, 216. See also Dorronsoro, *Revolution Unending*, 166–167; Goodson, *Afghanistan's Endless War*, 62.

137. Dorronsoro, *Revolution Unending*, 155.

138. Roy, *Islam and Resistance in Afghanistan*, 129. Rubin confirms this: "Haqqani's front was a traditionally organized, religiously led tribal coalition with many elements of modern infrastructure"; Rubin, *The Fragmentation of Afghanistan*, 218. Haqqani was a cleric deeply embedded in the Jadran tribe, and his group was one of the key social building blocks of the Hezb-Khalis. For a recent study of Haqqani, see Vahid Brown and Don Rassler, *Fountainhead of Jihad: The Haqqani Nexus, 1973–2012* (Oxford: Oxford University Press, 2013).

139. Dorronsoro, *Revolution Unending*, 138.

140. Edwards, *Before Taliban*, 248; Roy, *Islam and Resistance in Afghanistan*, 128.

141. Edwards, *Before Taliban*, 275.

142. Rubin, *The Fragmentation of Afghanistan*, 192.

143. Ibid., 220.

144. Giustozzi, *Empires of Mud*, 45.

145. Rubin, *The Fragmentation of Afghanistan*, 221. See also Roy, *Islam and Resistance in Afghanistan*, 136.

146. Edwards *Before Taliban*, 275.

147. Ibid., 275–276. See also Rubin, *The Fragmentation of Afghanistan*, 221.

148. Roy, *Islam and Resistance in Afghanistan*, 136 (first quote); Giustozzi, *Empires of Mud*, 45 (second quote).

149. On the consequences of this opposition structure, see Sinno, *Organizations at War in Afghanistan and Beyond*.

150. Giustozzi, *Empires of Mud*, 44.

151. Dorronsoro, *Revolution Unending*, 109.

152. For instance, Ismail Khan in Herat "inherited much of the state structure in Herat." Giustozzi, *Empires of Mud*, 212. My theory offers insights into even this array of groups, but they are not its focus. In *Empires of Mud*, Giustozzi argues that Dostum's group was "fragmented among the vassals" (121) because of its roots in former regime militias. As a result, "trust was not sufficient to infuse in the system a sufficient degree of discipline and responsiveness to the 'orders' of the warlord" (128). Dorronsoro in *Revolution Unending* notes that "the militia chiefs retained close links with their villages of origins, where they had built up a clientele. There was a sense of distance from the towns as a result of the militia commanders' local roots" (261–262). This description clearly points to the features of a parochial group.

153. Dorronsoro, *Revolution Unending*, 240. See also Rubin, *The Fragmentation of Afghanistan*, 247.

154. Sinno, *Organizations at War in Afghanistan and Beyond*, 174.

155. Dorronsoro, *Revolution Unending*, 258.

156. Sinno, *Organizations at War in Afghanistan and Beyond*, 189.

157. Maley, *The Afghanistan Wars*, 213.

158. Dorronsoro, *Revolution Unending*, 240.

159. Barfield, *Afghanistan*, 254.

160. Rubin, *The Fragmentation of Afghanistan*, 252.

161. Ibid., 253.

162. Sinno, *Organizations at War in Afghanistan and Beyond*, 201–202.

163. Giustozzi, *Empires of Mud*, 81.

164. Abdulkader Sinno, "Explaining the Taliban's Ability to Mobilize the Pashtuns," in *The Taliban and the Crisis of Afghanistan*, ed. Robert Crews and Amin Tarzi (Cambridge, MA: Harvard University Press, 2008), 63.

165. Dorronsoro, *Revolution Unending*, 239.

166. Giustozzi, *Empires of Mud*, 288.

167. Ibid., 287.

168. Ibid., 282; Dorronsoro, *Revolution Unending,* 266.

169. Rubin, *The Fragmentation of Afghanistan,* 276.

170. Giustozzi, *Empires of Mud,* 284.

171. Ibid., 283.

172. Dorronsoro, *Revolution Unending,* 255.

173. Giustozzi, *Empires of Mud,* 286–287.

174. Rashid, *Taliban,* 33.

175. Harpviken, "Transcending Traditionalism," 282.

176. Thomas Ruttig, "How Tribal Are the Taliban?," in *Under the Drones: Modern Lives in the Afghanistan-Pakistan Borderlands,* ed. Shahzad Bashir and Robert Crews (Cambridge, MA: Harvard University Press, 2012), 109.

177. Edwards, *Before Taliban,* 292.

178. For some dramatic statistics on the increase of Afghans studying in these schools, see Dorronsoro, *Revolution Unending,* 277.

179. Barnett R. Rubin, *The Fragmentation of Afghanistan: State Formation and Collapse in the International System,*. 2nd ed. (New Haven, CT: Yale University Press, 2002), xiii. Rashid concurs; see Rashid, *Taliban,* 89.

180. Dorronsoro, *Revolution Unending,* 278.

181. Maley, *The Afghanistan Wars,* 225; Barnett Rubin, "The Political Economy of War and Peace in Afghanistan," *World Development* 28, no. 10 (2000): 1794; Harpviken, "Transcending Traditionalism," 280.

182. Ruttig, "How Tribal Are the Taliban?,"114.

183. Dorronsoro, *Revolution Unending,* 275; Goodson, *Afghanistan's Endless War,* 107.

184. Barfield, *Afghanistan,* 255; Sinno, "Explaining the Taliban's Ability to Mobilize the Pashtuns," 63; Rashid, *Taliban,* 26.

185. Harpviken, "Transcending Traditionalism," 281.

186. Rashid, *Taliban,* 90.

187. Ibid., 22. See also Thomas Ruttig, "The Haqqani Network as an Autonomous Entity," in *Decoding the New Taliban,* ed. Antonio Giustozzi (New York: Columbia University Press, 2009), 73.

188. Mariam Abou Zahab and Olivier Roy, Islamist Networks: The Afghan-Pakistan Connection (New York: Columbia University Press, 2004), 13.

189. Edwards, *Before Taliban,* 291. See also Sinno, "Explaining the Taliban's Ability to Mobilize the Pashtuns," 70–1.

190. Maley, *The Afghanistan Wars,* 224.

191. Dorronsoro, *Revolution Unending,* 245–250.

192. Sebastien Trives, "Roots of the Insurgency in the Southeast," in *Decoding the New Taliban,* ed. Antonio Giustozzi, 57–88. (New York: Columbia University Press, 2009), 91. See also Ruttig, "The Haqqani Network as an Autonomous Entity," 80–81; and Goodson, *Afghanistan's Endless War,* 189. These networks were linked to clerics in Pakistan who advocate a particular form of Islam with its roots in South Asia's Deobandi movement.

193. Rubin, "The Political Economy of War and Peace in Afghanistan," 1794.

194. Barfield, *Afghanistan,* 263.

Notes to Pages 132–134

195. Rubin, "The Political Economy of War and Peace in Afghanistan," 1797; Rashid, *Taliban*, 87.

196. Rubin, *The Fragmentation of Afghanistan*, 2nd ed., xiii (quote); Giustozzi, *War, Politics, and Society in Afghanistan*, 242; Maley, *The Afghanistan Wars*, 221.

197. Ruttig, "How Tribal Are the Taliban?," 113–114.

198. Gilles Dorronsoro, "The Transformation of the Afghanistan-Pakistan Border," In *Under the Drones: Modern Lives in the Afghanistan-Pakistan Borderlands*, ed. Shahzad Bashir and Robert Crews (Cambridge MA: Harvard University Press, 2012), 39. See also Rubin, *Fragmentation of Afghanistan*, 2nd ed., xiv.

199. Dorronsoro, *Revolution Unending*, 274.

200. Goodson, *Afghanistan's Endless War*, 107; Dorronsoro, *Revolution Unending*, 267; Rashid, *Taliban*, 98; Ruttig, "The Haqqani Network as an Autonomous Entity," 58; Rubin, "The Political Economy of War and Peace in Afghanistan," 1795.

201. Maley, *The Afghanistan Wars*, 223. Rashid concurs, noting that he had "little charismatic appeal"; Rashid, *Taliban*, 24.

202. Rashid, *Taliban*, 95.

203. Dorronsoro, *Revolution Unending*, 275.

204. Ibid., 273.

205. Ibid., 267.

206. Ibid., 270.

207. On rural reach, see Sinno, "Explaining the Taliban's Ability to Mobilize the Pashtuns," 84.

208. Harpviken, "Transcending Traditionalism," 282.

209. Barfield, *Afghanistan*, 257.

210. Rubin, "The Political Economy of War and Peace in Afghanistan," 1794.

211. Barfield, *Afghanistan*, 252–253.

212. Haqqani, for instance, was not incorporated into the command core; Ruttig, "The Haqqani Network as an Autonomous Entity," 65.

213. Rashid, *Taliban*, 97.

214. Sinno, "Explaining the Taliban's Ability to Mobilize the Pashtuns," 80. For a detailed study of the Taliban's rise in a local area, as well as its return, see Carter Malkasian, *War Comes to Garmser: Thirty Years of Conflict on the Afghan Frontier* (Oxford: Oxford University Press, 2013).

215. Ruttig, "How Tribal Are the Taliban?," 115.

216. Barfield, *Afghanistan*, 258.

217. Maley, *The Afghanistan Wars*, 219; see also Rashid, *Taliban*, 34.

218. Sinno, "Explaining the Taliban's Ability to Mobilize the Pashtuns," 74.

219. Barfield, *Afghanistan*, 259.

220. Sinno, "Explaining the Taliban's Ability to Mobilize the Pashtuns," 81.

221. Maley, *The Afghanistan Wars*, 203–204; Sinno, "Explaining the Taliban's Ability to Mobilize the Pashtuns," 65–66.

222. Sinno, "Explaining the Taliban's Ability to Mobilize the Pashtuns," 86.

223. Sinno, "Explaining the Taliban's Ability to Mobilize the Pashtuns," 66.

224. Sinno, *Organizations at War in Afghanistan and Beyond*, 249.

225. Rashid, *Taliban*, 39.

226. Giustozzi, *Empires of Mud*, 253.

227. Dorronsoro, *Revolution Unending*, 251.

228. Dorronsoro, *Revolution Unending*, 252 (quote); Giustozzi, *Empires of Mud*, 253.

229. Ibid., 114; Rashid, *Taliban*, 57; Maley, *The Afghanistan Wars*, 170–171.

230. Barfield, *Afghanistan*, 258.

231. Sinno, *Organizations at War in Afghanistan and Beyond*, 223.

232. Rashid, *Taliban*, 98.

233. Goodson, *Afghanistan's Endless War*, 115–116; Rashid, *Taliban*, 60.

234. Goodson, *Afghanistan's Endless War*, 180; Rashid, *Taliban*, 79–80, 103–104; Maley, *The Afghanistan Wars*, 255,

235. Rashid, *Taliban*, 104.

236. Goodson, *Afghanistan's Endless War*, 112.

237. Rashid, *Taliban*, 185.

238. Sinno, "Explaining the Taliban's Ability to Mobilize the Pashtuns," 87; Rubin, *Fragmentation of Afghanistan*, 2nd ed., xv; and Dorronsoro, *Revolution Unending*, 278–281.

239. Sinno, *Organizations at War in Afghanistan and Beyond*, 245.

240. A detailed account of this relationship can be found in Coll, *Ghost Wars*.

241. Robert Pape, "The True Worth of Air Power," *Foreign Affairs* 83, no. 2 (2004): 116–130.

242. Giustozzi, *Empires of Mud*, 290–293.

243. Rashid, *Taliban*, 223–225.

244. Martine van Bijlert, "Unruly Commanders and Violent Power Struggles: Taliban Networks in Uruzgan," in *Decoding the New Taliban*, ed. Antonio Giustozzi (New York: Columbia University Press, 2009), 159.

245. Ruttig, "How Tribal Are the Taliban?,"128.

246. Mohammad Osman Tariq Elias, "The Resurgence of the Taliban in Kabul: Logar and Wardak," in *Decoding the New Taliban*, ed. Antonio Giustozzi (New York: Columbia University Press, 2009), 48.

247. On the attempted split, see Dorronsoro, *Revolution Unending*, 323; and van Bijlert, "Unruly Commanders and Violent Power Struggles," 159.

248. Ruttig, "How Tribal Are the Taliban?,"132–133.

249. Barfield argues that this is "a divided movement whose leaders had different interests and bases of support"; Barfield, *Afghanistan*, 328. Yet there are few public indications of major splits or feuds, which makes it clear that in comparative perspective this was a reasonably integrated group. See also Sinno, "Explaining the Taliban's Ability to Mobilize the Pashtuns," 89.

250. Dorronsoro, *Revolution Unending*, 338. See also International Crisis Group, "The Insurgency in Afghanistan's Heartland," *Asia Report No. 207*, June 27, 2011, 13.

251. Dorronsoro, "The Transformation of the Afghanistan-Pakistan Border," 41.

252. Ruttig, "How Tribal Are the Taliban?," 119.

253. Ruttig, "The Haqqani Network as an Autonomous Entity."

254. Barfield, *Afghanistan*, 326.

255. William Reno, *Warlord Politics and African States* (Boulder, CO: Lynner Rienner Publishers, 1998); Stathis N. Kalyvas and Laia Balcells, "International System and Technologies of Rebellion: How the End of the Cold War Shaped Internal Conflict," *American Political Science Review* 104, no. 3 (2010): 415–429; Kimberly Marten, *Warlords: Strong-Arm Brokers in Weak States* (Ithaca, NY: Cornell University Press, 2012).

256. An impressive study of these dynamics is Fotini Christia, *Alliance Formation in Civil War* (Cambridge: Cambridge University Press, 2012).

6. Explaining Tamil Militancy in Sri Lanka

1. Sri Lanka has also had two major leftist-nationalist rebellions by the JVP, in 1971 and 1987–1990.

2. Dagmar Hellmann-Rajanayagam, *The Tamil Tigers: Armed Struggle for Identity* (Stuttgart: F. Steiner, 1994), 1.

3. William Clarance, *Ethnic Warfare in Sri Lanka and the UN Crisis* (London: Pluto Press, 2007), 41.

4. For a discussion of the limited sources, see Stephen Hopgood, "Tamil Tigers, 1987–2002," in Diego Gambetta, ed., *Making Sense of Suicide Missions* (Oxford: Oxford University Press, 2005), 44.

5. See Colonel (ret.) R. Hariharan, "Who Will Lead LTTE after Prabhakaran?" http://www.colhariharan.org/2009/06/who-will-lead-ltte-after-prabhakaran.html.

6. Mark P. Whitaker, *Learning Politics from Sivaram: The Life and Death of a Revolutionary Tamil Journalist in Sri Lanka* (London: Pluto Press, 2007), 123.

7. Muslims often speak Tamil or both Tamil and Sinhala.

8. This background section relies on K. M. De Silva, *A History of Sri Lanka*, rev. and updated ed. (New Delhi: Penguin Books, 2005); A. Jeyaratnam Wilson, *Sri Lankan Tamil Nationalism: Its Origins and Development in the Nineteenth and Twentieth Centuries* (New Delhi: Penguin, 2001); and Jonathan Spencer, ed., *Sri Lanka: History and the Roots of Conflict* (London: Routledge, 1990).

9. Jane Russell, *Communal Politics under the Donoughmore Constitution, 1931–1947* (Dehiwala, Sri Lanka: Tisara Prakasakayo, 1982), 7.

10. Dagmar Hellmann-Rajanayagam, "From Difference to Ethnic Solidarity among the Tamils," in *Sri Lankan Society in an Era of Globalization*, ed. S. H. Hasbullah and Barrie M. Morrison (New Delhi: SAGE, 2004), 106. See also Dennis McGilvray, *Crucible of Conflict: Tamil and Muslim Society on the East Coast of Sri Lanka* (Durham, NC: Duke University Press, 2008), 9.

11. Chris McDowell, *A Tamil Asylum Diaspora: Sri Lankan Migration, Settlement and Politics in Switzerland* (Providence, RI: Berghahn Books, 1996), 208.

12. McGilvray, *Crucible of Conflict*; Dennis McGilvray, *Caste Ideology and Interaction* (Cambridge: Cambridge University Press, 1982); and Mark P. Whitaker, *Amiable Incoherence: Manipulating Histories and Modernities in a Batticaloa Tamil Hindu Temple* (Amsterdam: V.U. University Press, 1999).

13. Bryan Pfaffenberger, "The Political Construction of Defensive Nationalism: The 1968 Temple-Entry Crisis in Northern Sri Lanka," *The Journal of Asian Studies* 49, no. 1 (1990), 81, 94; Øivind Fuglerud, *Life on the Outside: The Tamil Diaspora and Long Distance Nationalism* (London: Pluto Press, 1999), 24.

14. "Since about the mid-1980s, they have come to rank very high, socially, as patriots and warriors in the forefront of the war of Tamil independence. That the Karaiyars constitute an independent and powerful entity in Tamil society is further reinforced by records of their historical progress." Wilson, *Sri Lankan Tamil Nationalism*, 19. For background, see Sinnappah Arasaratnam, "Sri Lanka's Tamils," in *The Sri Lankan Tamils: Ethnicity and Identity*, ed. Chelvadurai Manogaran and Bryan Pfaffenberger (Boulder, CO: Westview Press, 1994).

15. Arasaratnam, "Sri Lanka's Tamils," 39–40.

16. Ibid. See also Fuglerud, *Life on the Outside*, 27.

17. Wilson, *Sri Lankan Tamil Nationalism*, 19. More recently, McGilvray notes that in areas of the east and despite their "stigmatic profession as fishermen," Karaiyars are viewed as having "generally acknowledged prosperity and political influence." McGilvray, *Crucible of Conflict*, 156.

18. Wilson, *Sri Lankan Tamil Nationalism*, 20.

19. Arasaratnam, "Sri Lanka's Tamils," 40; Russell, *Communal Politics*, 82, 13–14.

20. Wilson, *Sri Lankan Tamil Nationalism*, 21.

21. "As Pfaffenberger shows, the insecurity about their pre-eminence, primarily among the Vellalar themselves, resulted from the system's own premises and mechanisms which assisted in undermining it. We can illustrate this with the well-known proverb 'Slowly, slowly, they all become Vellalar'. Anybody can become a Vellalar by acquiring Vellalar attributes." Hellmann-Rajanayagam, "From Difference to Ethnic Solidarity," 103.

22. Fuglerud, *Life on the Outside*, 149 and passim.

23. Bruce Matthews, "Religious and Ideological Intransigence among the Sinhalese," in *Sri Lankan Society in an era of Globalization*, ed. S. H. Hasbullah and Barrie M. Morrison (New Delhi: SAGE, 2004), 85.

24. Stanley Tambiah, *Buddhism Betrayed? Religion, Politics, and Violence in Sri Lanka* (Chicago: University of Chicago Press, 1992).

25. Russell, *Communal Politics*.

26. Neil DeVotta, *Blowback: Linguistic Nationalism, Institutional Decay, and Ethnic Conflict in Sri Lanka* (Stanford, CA: Stanford University Press, 2004).

27. Wilson, *Sri Lankan Tamil Nationalism*, 12.

28. The historical validity of these claims is contested. Compare Chelvadurai Manogaran, *Ethnic Conflict and Reconciliation in Sri Lanka* (Honolulu: University of Hawaii Press, 1987) with K. M. De Silva, *Regional Powers and Small State Security: India and Sri Lanka, 1977–1990* (Washington, DC: Woodrow Wilson Center Press, 1995); and De Silva, *A History of Sri Lanka*.

29. De Silva, *A History of Sri Lanka*, 76.

30. Stanley Tambiah, *Sri Lanka: Ethnic Fratricide and the Dismantling of Democracy* (Chicago: University of Chicago Press, 1986); and DeVotta, *Blowback*.

31. M. R. Narayan Swamy points to the Tamil Liberation Organization as the first protomilitant group; others offer different acronyms. There was also a Tamil Youth

Notes to Pages 148–151

League. See Swamy, *Tigers of Lanka, from Boys to Guerrillas,* 7th ed. (Colombo: Vijitha Yapa Publications, 2006), 25.

32. The PLOT's history is touched on only briefly here since it had begun its existence by 1983. I do not focus on the EPRLF in this section because its activities do not appear to have begun in earnest until 1982.

33. John M. Richardson, *Paradise Poisoned: Learning about Conflict, Terrorism, and Development from Sri Lanka's Civil Wars* (Kandy, Sri Lanka: International Center for Ethnic Studies, 2005), 479.

34. Swamy, *Tigers of Lanka,* 174.

35. Clarance, *Ethnic Warfare in Sri Lanka,* 42.

36. McDowell, *A Tamil Asylum Diaspora,* 89.

37. Wilson, *Sri Lankan Tamil Nationalism,* 126.

38. Clarance, *Ethnic Warfare in Sri Lanka,* 43; and Bryan Pfaffenberger, "Introduction," in *The Sri Lankan Tamils: Ethnicity and Identity,* ed. Chelvadurai Manogaran and Bryan Pfaffenberger (Boulder, CA: Westview Press, 1994), 11.

39. Richardson, *Paradise Poisoned,* 479.

40. Zachariah Mampilly, *Rebel Rulers: Insurgent Governance and Civilian Life during War* (Ithaca, NY: Cornell University Press, 2011).

41. Richardson, *Paradise Poisoned,* 480.

42. Michael Roberts, *Blunders in Tigerland,* Heidelberg Papers in South Asian and Comparative Politics (Heidelberg: South Asia Institute and Department of Political Science, University of Heidelberg, 2007), 21. See also Michael Roberts, "Ideological and Caste Threads in the Early LTTE," 9. I thank Michael Roberts for his permission to cite this unpublished work.

43. Fuglerud, *Life on the Outside,* 35.

44. Fuglerud supports this argument: "There is a certain degree of correlation between caste origin and militant groups seems clear, e.g. PLOTE in the early 1980s had a relatively large following of Vellala members, LTTE's leadership came from the Karaiyar caste.... It is also clear, however, that this correlation is not complete, either on a caste, region or village level." Fuglerud, *Life on the Outside,* 35.

45. Brendan O'Duffy, "LTTE: Liberation Tigers of Tamil Eelam," in *Terror, Insurgency, and the State,* ed. John Tirman, Marianne Heiberg, and Brendan O'Leary (Philadelphia: University of Pennsylvania Press, 2007), 268.

46. Wilson, *Sri Lankan Tamil Nationalism,* 20.

47. Hellmann-Rajanayagam, *The Tamil Tigers,* 39.

48. Roberts, "Ideological and Caste Threads in the Early LTTE." See also Michael Roberts, "Caste in modern Sri Lankan politics," *transCurrents,* February 22, 2010, http://transcurrents.com/tc/2010/02/caste_in_modern_sri_lankan_pol.html.

49. Hellman-Rajanayagam identifies Kittu as a Vellalar, but from Velvethithurai, a Karaiyar bastion; she also identifies Yogi as a Karaiyar, not a Vellalar. Hellman-Rajanayagam, *The Tamil Tigers,* 36–41. Soosai became the leader of the Sea Tigers; Mahattaya the deputy commander of the LTTE; and Kumaran Pathmanathan (KP) and Castro were leaders at different times of the crucial international operations department.

50. Kittu was also a childhood friend of Prabhkaran. Swamy, *Tigers of Lanka,* 52.

Notes to Pages 151–153

51. Clarance, *Ethnic Warfare in Sri Lanka,* 44.

52. Hellmann-Rajanayagam, "From Difference to Ethnic Solidarity," 109. See also Hellmann-Rajanayagam, *The Tamil Tigers,* 36. Peiris also notes that Velvethithurai is "regarded as the cradle of the LTTE.... Among its special attractions was its cohesive community, held together by ties of kinship and caste. There were links between its smugglers, fisher folk, and ordinary tradesman." G. H. Peiris quoted in Vijay Sakhuja, *The Dynamics of LTTE's Commercial Maritime Infrastructure* (Delhi: Observer Research Foundation, 2006), 7.

53. Donald Horowitz, *The Deadly Ethnic Riot* (Berkeley: University of California Press, 2001), 427.

54. Other sources that indicate that I am coding this properly include Richardson, *Paradise Poisoned,* 28; Hellmann-Rajanayagam, "From Difference to Ethnic Solidarity," 110; and J. N. Dixit, *Assignment Colombo* (Delhi: Konark Publishers, 1998), 67.

55. Chris Smith, "The LTTE: A National Liberation and Oppression Movement," in *Armed militias of South Asia: Fundamentalists, Maoists and Separatists,* ed. Laurent Gayer and Christophe Jaffrelot (New York: Columbia University Press, 2009), 93.

56. S. D. Muni, *Pangs of Proximity: India and Sri Lanka's Ethnic Crisis* (Oslo, Norway: PRIO, 1993), 140.

57. Swamy, *Tigers of Lanka,* 50.

58. For the Tamil Students' Federation evolution into the LTTE, see Wilson, *Sri Lankan Tamil Nationalism,* 124–125,.

59. Catholic networks played some role as well. See Dagmar Hellmann-Rajanayagam, "Religious Ideology among the Tamils," in *Sri Lankan Society in an Era of Globalization,* ed. S. H. Hasbullah and Barrie M. Morrison (New Delhi: SAGE, 2004), 81.

60. Swamy, *Tigers of Lanka,* has a blow-by-blow account of the militant actions of the Tigers during this period.

61. On rhetoric, see Liberation Tigers of Tamil Eelam, *Towards Liberation: Selected Political Documents of the Liberation Tigers of Tamil Eelam* ([Sri Lanka?]: Liberation Tigers of Tamil Eelam, 1984). Underground publication.

62. M. R. Narayan Swamy, *Inside an Elusive Mind: Prabhakaran, the First Profile of the World's Most Ruthless Guerrilla Leader* (Delhi: Konark Publishers, 2003), 44.

63. Ambalavanar Sivarajah, *Politics of Tamil Nationalism in Sri Lanka* (New Delhi: South Asian Publishers, 1996), 139.

64. Hellmann-Rajanayagam, *The Tamil Tigers,* 38.

65. Uma was accused of sleeping with Urmila, which would have been a breach of discipline; Swamy, *Inside an Elusive Mind,* 51. Prabhakaran expelled Uma in 1979, but Uma continued to claim to be chairman of the LTTE; ibid., 54.

66. On Prabhakaran working with the TELO, see Swamy, *Tigers of Lanka,* 41.

67. Wilson, *Sri Lankan Tamil Nationalism,* 127. Matthews writes that "Uma Maheswaran's PLOT is largely Vellalar, whereas V. Prabhakaran's LTTE is Karaiyar"; Bruce Matthews, "Radical Conflict and the Rationalization of Violence in Sri Lanka," *Pacific Affairs* 59, no. 1 (1986): 34. In addition, "its members mainly come from the highest caste, the Vellalar"; Hellmann-Rajanayagam, *The Tamil Tigers,* 43.

68. Whitaker, *Learning Politics from Sivaram,* 87.

69. McDowell, *A Tamil Asylum Diaspora,* 88.

70. Hellmann-Rajanayagam, *The Tamil Tigers,* 38.

[268]

71. Matthews, "Radical Conflict," 35.
72. Whitaker, *Learning Politics from Sivaram*, 87.
73. Hellmann-Rajanayagam, *The Tamil Tigers*, 44.
74. Wilson, *Sri Lankan Tamil Nationalism*, 127.
75. On the EROS, see Swamy, *Tigers of Lanka*, 30.
76. Ibid., 102.
77. Swamy, *Tigers of Lanka*, 104.
78. Rohan Gunaratna, *Indian Intervention in Sri Lanka: The Role of India's Intelligence Agencies* (Colombo: South Asian Network on Conflict Research, 1993), 137.
79. Wilson, *Sri Lankan Tamil Nationalism*, 129.
80. Smith, "The LTTE," 92.
81. Swamy, *Tigers of Lanka*, 96.
82. Ibid., 175.
83. Dixit offers a rationalization for this policy from a former Indian ambassador to Sri Lanka; see J. N. Dixit, *Assignment Colombo*.
84. De Silva, *Regional Powers and Small State Security*, 113.
85. Swamy, *Tigers of Lanka*, 102.
86. Richardson, *Paradise Poisoned*, 527.
87. Swamy, *Tigers of Lanka*, 109.
88. Muni, *Pangs of Proximity*, 66.
89. Swamy, *Tigers of Lanka*, 142.
90. Swamy, *Tigers of Lanka*, 183.
91. O'Duffy, "LTTE," 257.
92. On the one hand, Little argues that "The Liberation Tigers of Tamil Eelam (LTTE) were the major beneficiaries of Indian intervention"; David Little, *Sri Lanka: The Invention of Enmity* (Washington, D.C: United States Institute of Peace Press, 1994), 7. However, Swamy asserts that the TELO was the most favored militant group; Swamy, *Tigers of Lanka*, 109.
93. O'Duffy, "LTTE," 272; Hellmann-Rajanayagam, *The Tamil Tigers*, 106.
94. Gunaratna offers a detailed discussion of these operations; see Gunaratna, *Indian Intervention in Sri Lanka*.
95. Pratap, *Island of Blood*, 68.
96. Hellmann-Rajanayagam, *The Tamil Tigers*, 52.
97. Hopgood, "Tamil Tigers, 1987–2002," 73.
98. Swamy, *Inside an Elusive Mind*, 143.
99. Ibid., 94.
100. Richardson, *Paradise Poisoned*, 482.
101. Smith, "The LTTE," 93.
102. Hellmann-Rajanayagam, *The Tamil Tigers*, 139.
103. Swamy, *Tigers of Lanka*, 174.
104. Hellmann-Rajanayagam, *The Tamil Tigers*, 66.

105. Ibid.

106. Dixit, *Assignment Colombo* 61.

107. Pratap, *Island of Blood*, 70.

108. Sivarajah, *Politics of Tamil Nationalism*, 130.

109. Swamy, *Inside an Elusive Mind*, 132.

110. Swamy, *Tigers of Lanka*, 129; see also Hellmann-Rajanayagam, *The Tamil Tigers*, 129.

111. Swamy, *Tigers of Lanka*, 109.

112. Ibid., 104.

113. Wilson, *Sri Lankan Tamil Nationalism*, 127.

114. "The members of TELO have been called 'India's little soldiers'"; Dagmar Hellmann-Rajanayagam, "The Tamil Militants—Before the Accord and After," *Pacific Affairs* 61, no. 4 (1989–1988): 607.

115. Ketheshwaran Loganathan, *Sri Lanka: Lost Opportunities, Past Attempts at Resolving Ethnic Conflict* (Colombo: Centre for Policy Research and Analysis, University of Colombo, 1996), 119.

116. Richardson, *Paradise Poisoned*, 531.

117. Richardson contents that "its members lacked discipline, exploited civilians and were given to ostentatious displays." Richardson, *Paradise Poisoned*, 531.

118. Swamy, *Tigers of Lanka*, 186.

119. Swamy, *Tigers of Lanka*, 190 (quote); see also University Teachers for Human Rights (Jaffna), *Broken Palmyra*, Chapter 5, http://www.uthr.org/BP/volume1/Chapter5.htm. University Teachers for Human Rights (Jaffna) is a Tamil NGO group that has documented many aspects of the war.

120. This was confirmed by interviews with EPRLF members in Colombo, spring 2008. See also Gunaratna, *Indian Intervention in Sri Lanka*, 143.

121. Gunaratna says that the split happened 1981; Wilson simply says "the EPRLF was founded during 1981–84"; Wilson, *Sri Lankan Tamil Nationalism*, 128. Gunaratna refers to another EROS split at some point in the mid-1980s (before the Balakumar vs. Shankar split in the late 1980s) but I have not found other confirmation of this. Gunaratna, *Indian Intervention in Sri Lanka*, 138.

122. Gunaratna, *Indian intervention in Sri Lanka*, 138.

123. Hellmann-Rajanayagam, *The Tamil Tigers*, 81.

124. Ibid., 83.

125. Swamy, *Tigers of Lanka*, 186.

126. Hellmann-Rajanayagam, *The Tamil Tigers*, 75.

127 Ibid.

128. Hellmann-Rajanayagam, *The Tamil Tigers*, 78. See also Hellmann-Rajanayagam, *The Tamil Tigers*, 39, 47.

129. According to McDowell, "the EPRLF, who later became an east-coast based group, became known (not entirely in jest) as 'Eelatti Pallar' or the 'Eelam *Pallar* Revolutionary Liberation Front' reflecting a genuine support base in the urban Pallar caste communities"; McDowell, *A Tamil Asylum Diaspora*, 90.

Notes to Pages 161–164

130. Swamy, *Tigers of Lanka*, 104.

131. Gunaratna, *Indian Intervention in Sri Lanka*, 146.

132. Hellmann-Rajanayagam, *The Tamil Tigers*, 108.

133. Ibid., 77.

134. Swamy, *Tigers of Lanka*, 178.

135. Whitaker, *Learning Politics from Sivaram*, 95.

136. According to UTHR(J), "the P.L.O.T.E. in Jaffna had a strong base amongst the high caste, middle-class Tamils in Valigamam North and Central. They also had a political programme which emphasised work amongst the masses"; UTHR(J), *Broken Palmyra*, chapter 5, University Teachers for Human Rights Web site, http://www.uthr.org/BP/volume1/Chapter5.htm.

137. Hellmann-Rajanayagam, *The Tamil Tigers*, 42–43.

138. Swamy, *Inside an Elusive Mind*, 91.

139. Swamy, *Tigers of Lanka*, 180.

140. Hellmann-Rajanayagam, *The Tamil Tigers*, 42–43.

141. Sivarajah, *Politics of Tamil Nationalism*, 135.

142. UTHR(J), *Broken Palmyra*, chapter 5.

143. Whitaker, *Learning Politics from Sivaram*, 92.

144. Swamy, *Tigers of Lanka*, 181.

145. Ibid., 179.

146. Swamy, *Tigers of Lanka*, 182; Whitaker, *Learning Politics from Sivaram*, 94.

147. Hellmann-Rajanayagam, *The Tamil Tigers*, 42–43.

148. Ibid., 42; Whitaker, *Learning Politics from Sivaram*, 95.

149. UTHR(J), *Broken Palmyra*, chapter 5.

150. Since most of the EPRLF leadership was killed in 1990, much of this history has unfortunately been lost. Two Tamil experts on (and former participants in) the armed groups, Sivaram and Ketheeswaran Loganathan, were killed before I began my fieldwork, though I do rely on their written work and Whitaker's biography of Sivaram.

151. Swamy, *Inside an Elusive Mind*, 91.

152. Richardson, *Paradise Poisoned*, 528.

153. Swamy, *Inside an Elusive Mind*, 131.

154. Swamy, *Tigers of Lanka*, 185.

155. Swamy, *Tigers of Lanka*, 158.

156. Hellmann-Rajanayagam, *The Tamil Tigers*, 42.

157. Dayan Jayatilleka, *The Indian Intervention in Sri Lanka, 1987–1990: The North-East Provincial Council and Devolution of Power* (Kandy, Sri Lanka: International Centre for Ethnic Studies, 1999), 21.

158. Swamy, *Tigers of Lanka*, 192. Wilson suggests that this attack may have had something to do with the fact that the TELO received more of the diaspora funding than the Tigers believed appropriate; see *Sri Lankan Tamil Nationalism*, 127.

159. Hellmann-Rajanayagam, *The Tamil Tigers*, 44.

160. Ibid.

161. UTHR(J), *Broken Palmyra*, chapter 5.

162. Richardson, *Paradise Poisoned*, 531.

163. Ibid.

164. "Kittu called them clowns"; Hellmann-Rajanayagam, *The Tamil Tigers*, 123.

165. Muni, *Pangs of Proximity*, 72.

166. The induction of Indian combat forces on Sri Lankan soil triggered a violent backlash against the Sri Lankan government among Sinhalese nationalists; a second JVP rebellion raged from 1987 until 1990.

167. Hellmann-Rajanayagam, *The Tamil Tigers*, 101.

168. Muni, *Pangs of Proximity*, 142.

169. Depinder Singh, *The IPKF in Sri Lanka* (Noida: Trishul Publications, 1991); and Harkirat Singh, *Intervention in Sri Lanka: The IPKF Experience Retold* (New Delhi: Manohar, 2007) are accounts from former commanding officers of the IPKF that emphasize the poor preparation of the force and the mediocre quality of the intelligence it received.

170. Richardson, *Paradise Poisoned*, 547.

171. Clarance, *Ethnic Warfare in Sri Lanka*, 57.

172. Ibid. 54.

173. Wilson, *Sri Lankan Tamil Nationalism*, 128.

174. Hellmann-Rajanayagam, *The Tamil Tigers*, 121.

175. Dagmar Hellmann-Rajanayagam, "The Tamil Militants-Before the Accord and After," *Pacific Affairs* 61, no. 4 (1988–1989): 611.

176. A new 13th Amendment and provincial councils were part of political package in the Indo-Sri Lanka Agreement.

177. Former senior EPRLF spokesman Kethesh Loganathan (later assassinated by the LTTE while working for the Sri Lankan government) discusses this partnership; Loganathan, *Sri Lanka*, 139–140. He notes that "the EPRLF knew its strength in the Eastern Province. The expulsion of the LTTE from Jaffna also gave EPRLF an opportunity to reactivate its traditional support base in parts of Jaffna Peninsula, and amongst the depressed castes and underprivileged sections of Jaffna society" (140).

178. Hellmann-Rajanayagam, *The Tamil Tigers*, 120.

179. Ibid., 140.

180. Muni, *Pangs of Proximity*, 144–145.

181. Chelvadurai Manogaran, *Ethnic Conflict and Reconciliation in Sri Lanka* (Honolulu: University of Hawaii Press, 1987), 172.

182. Muni, *Pangs of Proximity*, 140.

183. On the rise of new fighters from the Wanni and processes of internal socialization, see D. B. S. Jeyaraj, "Theepan of the LTTE: Heroic Saga of a Northern Warrior," http://dbsjeyaraj.com/dbsj/archives/318.

184. Hellmann-Rajanayagam, "From Difference to Ethnic Solidarity," 106.

185. Muni, *Pangs of Proximity*, 169.

186. Hellmann-Rajanayagam, *The Tamil Tigers*, 79–80.

187. Ibid., 122.

188. Loganathan, *Sri Lanka,* 154–155.

189. Hellmann-Rajanayagam, *The Tamil Tigers,* 122.

190. Hellmann-Rajanayagam, "Tamil Militants"; and Hellmann-Rajanayagam, *The Tamil Tigers,* 77.

191. The EPRLF later split into two: one led by Suresh Premachandran, the other led by Srithiran. The Premachandran faction became linked to the LTTE-controlled Tamil National Alliance parliamentary group; the EPRLF (Srithiran) maintained an anti-LTTE position.

192. On the EROS breaking apart, see Gunaratna, *Indian Intervention in Sri Lanka,* 361; and Whitaker, *Learning Politics from Sivaram,* 142.

193. Wilson, *Sri Lankan Tamil Nationalism,* 24.

194. Hopgood, "Tamil Tigers, 1987–2002," 66.

195. De Silva, *Regional Powers and Small State Security,* 322.

196. Diaspora aid came heavily from Europe and North America.

197. Mampilly *Rebel Rulers,* Chapter 4, provides an excellent account of LTTE governance that moves well beyond this study.

198. Hellmann-Rajanayagam, *The Tamil Tigers,* 136.

199. See Pushpa Iyer, "Coming to the Table: Decisions and Decision-Making in a Non-State Armed Group, the Liberation Tigers of Tamil Eelam (LTTE)" (PhD diss., George Mason University, 2007); and Mampilly, *Rebel Rulers.*

200. An excellent discussion of LTTE suicide mission targeting can be found in Hopgood, "Tamil Tigers, 1987–2002."

201. Ibid., 75.

202. McDowell, *A Tamil Asylum Diaspora,* 179.

203. Richardson, *Paradise Poisoned,* 28; Hellmann-Rajanayagam, "From Difference to Ethnic Solidarity," 109.

204. Hellmann-Rajanayagam, "From Difference to Ethnic Solidarity," 110. Fuglerud writes that "several informants argue that the LTTE's national project is nothing but a clever strategy of caste-climbing"; Fuglerud, *Life on the Outside,* 88. It is important not to overstate the extent of these changes, since interviews with individuals who have spent significant time in LTTE territory report that while change was perceptible, it was not revolutionary or overwhelming.

205. McDowell, *A Tamil Asylum Diaspora,* 89.

206. D. B. S. Jeyaraj, "Brigadier Thamilselvan: 'Smiling' Face of the LTTE," *The Nation,* http://www.nation.lk/2007/11/04/newsfe6.htm.

207. Fuglerud, *Life on the Outside,* 160.

208. McDowell, *A Tamil Asylum Diaspora,* 88–89.

209. Hellmann-Rajanayagam, *The Tamil Tigers,* 141.

210. McGilvray, *Crucible of Conflict,* 17.

211. Similarly, the northern-dominated LTTE tried to shape social coalitions during expansion into the east. McDowell, *A Tamil Asylum Diaspora,* 110.

212. Swamy, *Inside an Elusive Mind,* 242.

213. A dubious discussion of this episode is found in Adele Balasingham's purely pro-LTTE account. Adele Balasingham, *The Will to Freedom: An Inside View of Tamil Resistance* (Mitcham, UK: Fairmax Publishing, 2003). See also Pratap, *Island of Blood,* 95–96.

214. O'Duffy, "LTTE," 266.

215. Ibid.

216. C. Christine Fair, "Diaspora Involvement in Insurgencies: Insights from the Khalistan and Tamil Eelam Movements," *Nationalism and Ethnic Politics* 11, no. 1 (2005): 145.

217. For background on the peace process, see Jonathan Goodhand, Jonathan Spencer, and Benedict J. Korf, eds. *Conflict and Peacebuilding in Sri Lanka: Caught in the Peace Trap?* (London: Routledge, 2010).

218. D. B. S. Jeyaraj, "Tiger vs Tiger in Eastern Sri Lanka," *The Hindu,* March 15, 2004, http://www.hindu.com/2004/03/15/stories/2004031504231400.htm.

219. Ibid.

220. There had been some leadership shuffles in the east in the past, but Karuna was unaffected by these maneuvers. Jeyaraj notes that in the east Prabhakaran had previously "allowed functional autonomy to a great degree." D. B. S. Jeyaraj, "A Face-Saving Manoeuvre," *Frontline* 19, no. 17 (August 17–30, 2002), http://www.frontline.in/static/html/fl1917/19170600.htm.

221. Clarance, *Ethnic Warfare in Sri Lanka,* 221.

222. O'Duffy, "LTTE," 271.

223. Jeyaraj, "Tiger vs. Tiger."

224. O'Duffy, "LTTE," 271.

225. Interviews in Colombo in 2008 suggested that Karuna's exposure to the peace process had mellowed him and introduced him to the comforts of peace. An apocryphal story is that Sri Lankan intelligence became convinced that Karuna did not want a return to war when they found that he had built a swimming pool outside his home.

226. McGilvray, *Crucible of Conflict,* 328.

227. Whitaker, *Learning Politics from Sivaram,* 198.

228. The government was also paralyzed by a struggle between the president and prime minister at this time.

229. I discuss the Karuna split in comparative perspective in Paul Staniland, "Between a Rock and a Hard Place: Insurgent Fratricide, Ethnic Defection, and the Rise of Pro-State Paramilitaries," *Journal of Conflict Resolution* 56, no. 1 (2012): 16–40.

230. McGilvray, *Crucible of Conflict,* 329.

231. Paul Staniland, "Organizing Insurgency: Networks, Resources, and Rebellion in South Asia," *International Security* 37, no. 2 (2012): 42–70.

232. De Silva, *Regional Powers and Small State Security,* 247.

233. Michael Mann, *The Sources of Social Power,* vol. 1, *A History of Power from the Beginning to AD 1760* (Cambridge: Cambridge University Press, 1986), 22.

7. "Peasants and Commissars"

1. James Scott, "Revolution in the Revolution: Peasants and Commissars," *Theory and Society* 7, nos. 1–2 (1979): 97–134.

2. Jeff Goodwin, *No Other Way Out: States and Revolutionary Movements, 1945–1991* (Cambridge: Cambridge University Press, 2001).

3. Though local units continued to operate that were later mobilized by the leftist New People's Army, I view the organization as having collapsed by the early 1960s.

4. The territory of the Malay Peninsula in which the MCP operated was known as British Malaya until 1946, the Malayan Union from 1946 to 1948, the Federation of Malaya from 1948 to 1963, and Malaysia after 1963. Singapore became independent in 1965.

5. C. F. Yong, "Origins and Development of the Malayan Communist Movement, 1919–1930," *Modern Asian Studies* 25, no. 4 (1991): 625–648.

6. T. N. Harper, *The End of Empire and the Making of Malaya* (Cambridge: Cambridge University Press, 2001), 33.

7. For studies of the roots of the MCP and its links to the Kuomintang, see Png Poh Seng, "The Kuomintang in Malaya, 1912–1941," *Journal of Southeast Asian History* 2, no. 1 (1961): 21 and 27; on the Kuomintang left's evolution into the MCP, see C. F. Yong and R. B. McKenna, "The Kuomintang Movement in Malaya and Singapore, 1925–30," *Journal of Southeast Asian Studies* 15, no. 1 (1984): 95–96.

8. Yong, "Origins and Development of the Malayan Communist Movement," 647; C. F. Yong, *The Origins of Malayan Communism* (Singapore: South Seas Society, 1997), 152.

9. Harper, *The End of Empire and the Making of Malaya*, 34.

10. There were some leftist Malays and Indians, but not very many. There were also anti-British Malays, but many subscribed to a nationalist/Islamist ideology and did not cooperate with the MCP in a serious way.

11. Harper, *The End of Empire and the Making of Malaya*, 34; Michael Stenson, *Industrial Conflict in Malaya: Prelude to the Communist Revolt of 1948* (London: Oxford University Press, 1970), 19–20.

12. Stephen Leong, "The Kuomintang-Communist United Front in Malaya during the National Salvation Period, 1937–1941," *Journal of Southeast Asian Studies* 8, no. 1 (1977): 34.

13. Stenson, *Industrial Conflict in Malaya*, 21–24; Richard Stubbs, *Hearts and Minds in Guerilla Warfare: The Malayan Emergency, 1948–1960* (Singapore: Eastern Universities Press, 2004), 47–49; Yong, *The Origins of Malayan Communism*, 201.

14. Yong Ching Fatt, "Leadership and Power in the Chinese Community of Singapore during the 1930s," *Journal of Southeast Asian Studies* 8, no. 2 (1977): 202. See also Stubbs, *Hearts and Minds in Guerilla Warfare*, 49.

15. Anthony Short, *The Communist Insurrection in Malaya, 1948–1960* (London: Muller, 1975), 22.

16. Stenson, *Industrial Conflict in Malaya*, 55. During the Japanese occupation, the MCP was "not only militarily but also organizationally weak"; Cheah Boon Kheng, *The Masked Comrades: A Study of the Communist United Front in Malaya, 1945–48* (Singapore: Times Books International, 1979), 21. See also Stubbs, *Hearts and Minds in Guerilla Warfare*, 56.

17. Cheah Boon Kheng, *Red Star over Malaya: Resistance and Social Conflict During and After the Japanese Occupation of Malaya, 1941–1946* (Singapore: Singapore University Press, 1983), 100.

18. Kheng, *The Masked Comrades*, 46–47.

19. Stenson, *Industrial Conflict in Malaya*, 62.

20. Coates, *Suppressing Insurgency*, 15.

Notes to Pages 186–190

21. Harper, *The End of Empire and the Making of Malaya*, 142.

22. Ibid., 110–111, 159.

23. Stubbs, *Hearts and Minds in Guerilla Warfare*, 49.

24. Harper, *The End of Empire and the Making of Malaya*, 122.

25. Ibid., 143.

26. Bayly and Harper, *Forgotten Wars*, 416.

27. Stubbs, *Hearts and Minds in Guerilla Warfare*, 58; Kheng, *The Masked Comrades*, 151.

28. Michael Stenson, *Industrial Conflict in Malaya: Prelude to the Communist Revolt of 1948* (London: Oxford University Press, 1970); Michael Stenson, *Repression and Revolt: The Origins of the 1948 Communist Insurrection in Malaya and Singapore* (Athens: Ohio University, Center for International Studies, 1969).

29. Stenson, *Repression and Revolt*, 12.

30. Harper, *The End of Empire and the Making of Malaya*, 149; Stubbs, *Hearts and Minds in Guerilla Warfare*, 61, 86–87.

31. Harper, *The End of Empire and the Making of Malaya*, 143.

32. Short, *The Communist Insurrection in Malaya*, 96.

33. Stubbs, *Hearts and Minds in Guerilla Warfare*, 61; Bayly and Harper, *Forgotten Wars*, 430.

34. Stubbs, *Hearts and Minds in Guerilla Warfare*, 61.

35. Ibid., 252.

36. Ibid., 248.

37. Coates, *Suppressing Insurgency*, 64. See also Harper, *The End of Empire and the Making of Malaya*, 161; and Short, *The Communist Insurrection in Malaya*, 311.

38. Stubbs, *Hearts and Minds in Guerilla Warfare*, 62.

39. Bayly and Harper, *Forgotten Wars*, 477.

40. Stubbs, *Hearts and Minds in Guerilla Warfare*, 90.

41. Karl Hack, "'Iron Claws on Malaya': The Historiography of the Malayan Emergency," *Journal of Southeast Asian Studies* 30, no. 1 (1999): 104; Harper, *The End of Empire and the Making of Malaya*, 174; Stubbs, *Hearts and Minds in Guerilla Warfare*, 100.

42. Hack, "'Iron Claws on Malaya,'" 102. See also Bayly and Harper, *Forgotten Wars*, 474–475.

43. Coates, *Suppressing Insurgency*, 58.

44. Ibid., 55–56.

45. Short, *The Communist Insurrection in Malaya*, 362–363.

46. Coates, *Suppressing Insurgency*, 93. Harper concurs; see *The End of Empire and the Making of Malaya*, 177.

47. Harper, *The End of Empire and the Making of Malaya*, 162, 177.

48. Bayly and Harper, *Forgotten Wars*, 491.

49. Stubbs, *Hearts and Minds in Guerilla Warfare*, 123.

50. Short, *The Communist Insurrection in Malaya*, 394; Stubbs, *Hearts and Minds in Guerilla Warfare*, 148. On MCP perceptions of resettlement, see Karl Hack and C. C. Chin, eds., *Dialogues with Chin Peng: New Light on the Malayan Communist Party* (Singapore: Singapore University Press, 2004), 160.

51. Stubbs, *Hearts and Minds in Guerilla Warfare*, 225.

52. Coates, *Suppressing Insurgency*, 94.

53. Hack, "'Iron Claws on Malaya,'" 124.

54. Short, *Communist Insurrection in Malaya*, 439.

55. Coates, *Suppressing Insurgency*, 143.

56. Short, *Communist Insurrection in Malaya*, 490.

57. Stubbs, *Hearts and Minds in Guerilla Warfare*, 240.

58. Karl Hack, "The Long March to Peace of the Malayan Communist Party in Southern Thailand," in *Thai South and Malay North: Ethnic Interactions on a Plural Peninsula*, ed. Michael John Montesano and Patrick Jory (Singapore: NUS Press, 2008).

59. Humphrey quoted in Stubbs, *Hearts and Minds in Guerilla Warfare*, 252.

60. David Sturtevant, *Popular Uprisings in the Philippines, 1840–1940* (Ithaca, NY: Cornell University Press, 1976).

61. During the anti-Japanese war, they were known as the Hukbalahap, or Hukbo ng Bayan Laban sa Hapon (Anti-Japanese Army). During the 1946–1960 war, they were called the Hukbong Mapalaya ng Bayan (HMB).

62. Jeff Goodwin, "The Libidinal Constitution of a High-Risk Social Movement: Affectual Ties and Solidarity in the Huk Rebellion, 1946 to 1954," *American Sociological Review* 62, no. 1 (1997): 59.

63. Richard J. Kessler, *Rebellion and Repression in the Philippines* (New Haven, CT: Yale University Press, 1989), 16.

64. Benedict J. Kerkvliet, *The Huk Rebellion: A Study of Peasant Revolt in the Philippines* (Berkeley: University of California Press, 1977), 47.

65. Ibid., 49.

66. Eduardo Lachica, *Huk: Philippine Agrarian Society in Revolt* (Manila: Solidaridad Publishing House, 1971), 93.

67. Kerkvliet, *The Huk Rebellion*, 44.

68. Ibid., 50.

69. William Chapman, *Inside the Philippine Revolution* (New York: W. W. Norton, 1987), 56.

70. Lachica, *Huk*, 94.

71. Dan Slater, *Ordering Power: Contentious Politics and Authoritarian Leviathans in Southeast Asia* (Cambridge: Cambridge University Press, 2010), 95.

72. Lachica, *Huk*, 100.

73. Kerkvliet, *The Huk Rebellion*, 60.

74. Gerrit Huizer, *Agrarian Unrest and Peasant Organisations in the Philippines* (The Hague: Institute of Social Studies, 1972), 4.

75. Kerkvliet, *The Huk Rebellion*, 67. The KPMP was the Kalipunang Pambansa ng mga Magsasaka sa Pilipinas (National Society of Peasants in the Philippines).

76. Ibid., 78; see also the tables on 84–85.

77. Ibid., 80.

78. Ibid., 72, 115.

79. Lachica, *Huk*, 109. For data on the prewar social roots of wartime leaders, see Kerkvliet, *The Huk Rebellion*, 84–87.

80. Kerkvliet, *The Huk Rebellion*, 93.

81. Jeremy Weinstein, *Inside Rebellion: The Politics of Insurgent Violence* (Cambridge: Cambridge University Press, 2007). Vina Lanzona, *Amazons of the Huk Rebellion: Gender, Sex, and Revolution in the Philippines* (Madison: University of Wisconsin Press), 69, 44.

82. Huizer, *Agrarian Unrest and Peasant Organisations in the Philippines*, 5.

83. Ibid.

84. Kerkvliet, *The Huk Rebellion*, 99.

85. Ibid., 100.

86. Lachica, *Huk*, 108.

87. Kerkvliet, *The Huk Rebellion*, 110–118.

88. Ibid., 147.

89. Ibid., 142.

90. Ibid., 132.

91. Ibid., 140.

92. Chapman, *Inside the Philippine Revolution*, 60.

93. Lachica, *Huk*, 119.

94. Ibid., 122.

95. Kerkvliet, *The Huk Rebellion*, 157.

96. Ibid., 169.

97. Ibid., 174, 176.

98. Ibid., 191.

99. Ibid., 180.

100. Ibid., 184.

101. Ibid., 188.

102. Pomeroy, quoted in ibid., 179.

103. William Pomeroy, *Guerrilla and Counter-Guerrilla Warfare* (New York: International Publishers, 1964), 62–63.

104. The PKP leadership expected a massive economic crisis that their revolt would take advantage of. Lachica, *Huk*, 126–127.

105. Kerkvliet, *The Huk Rebellion*, 181, 184.

106. Slater, *Ordering Power*, 97.

107. Kerkvliet, *The Huk Rebellion*, 218.

108. Ibid., 203.

109. Slater, *Ordering Power*, 99–102. Thomas McKenna notes that the government's policy of resettling Huks and their sympathizers in Mindanao was "the only element of its agrarian reform program that was effectively implemented." See *Muslim Rulers and Rebels: Everyday Politics and Armed Separatism in the Southern Philippines* (Berkeley: University of California Press, 1998), 115.

110. Kerkvliet, *The Huk Rebellion*, 208.

111. Ibid., 265.

112. Kessler, *Rebellion and Repression in the Philippines*, 61.

113. Slater, *Ordering Power*, 103.

Notes to Pages 199–204

114. Kerkvliet, *The Huk Rebellion*, 232.

115. Ibid., 219.

116. Ibid., 223.

117. Ibid., 223–224.

118. Ibid., 228.

119. Ibid., 237, 241. Though Goodwin attributes this to the "libidinal constitution" of Philippine society, it is a common dynamic among fragmenting insurgent groups, regardless of their libidinal status.

120. Kerkvliet, *The Huk Rebellion*, 234.

121. Ibid., 245.

122. Lachica, *Huk*, 135.

123. Kerkvliet, *The Huk Rebellion*, 246.

124. Ibid., 262. Some of course were linked to both party and peasants, including Taruc, who quit in 1954. Ibid., 263.

125. Chapman, *Inside the Philippine Revolution*, 65.

126. Kerkvliet, *The Huk Rebellion*, 265.

127. Scott, "Revolution in the Revolution," 113.

128. An example of this claim is Phillip Selznick, *The Organizational Weapon: A Study of Bolshevik Strategy and Tactics* (New York: McGraw-Hill, 1952).

129. Kerkvliet, *The Huk Rebellion*, 266.

130. Kessler *Rebellion and Repression in the Philippines*, 35.

131. Tuong Huu Vu, "Late Leviathans: State Formation, Nationalism and Postcolonial Transformation in Pacific Asia" (PhD diss., University of California, Berkeley, 2004); Tuong Vu, *Paths to Development in Asia: South Korea, Vietnam, China, and Indonesia* (New York: Cambridge University Press, 2010).

132. Huynh Kim Khanh,. *Vietnamese Communism, 1925–1945* (Ithaca, NY: Cornell University Press, 1983), 45–47; David Marr, *Vietnamese Tradition on Trial, 1920–1945* (Berkeley: University of California Press, 1981); Hue-Tam Ho Tai, *Radicalism and the Origins of the Vietnamese Revolution* (Cambridge, MA: Harvard University Press, 1992).

133. Stein Tønnesson, *The Vietnamese Revolution of 1945: Roosevelt, Ho Chi Minh, and De Gaulle in a World at War* (Oslo: International Peace Research Institute, 1991), 100, 418; see also 99–103.

134. Tai, *Radicalism and the Origins of the Vietnamese Revolution*, 173.

135. Khanh, *Vietnamese Communism*, 63.

136. William Duiker, *The Communist Road to Power in Vietnam*, 2nd ed. (Boulder, CO: Westview Press, 1996), 23.

137. Duiker, *The Communist Road to Power*, 20.

138. William Duiker, *Ho Chi Minh* (New York: Hyperion, 2000), 121.

139. Duiker, *The Communist Road to Power in Vietnam*, 29.

140. There was particular weakness in the Cochinchina south. Tai, *Radicalism and the Origins of the Vietnamese Revolution*, 214, 241; Duiker, *Ho Chi Minh*, 154.

141. Duiker, *The Communist Road to Power*, 31.

142. Khanh, *Vietnamese Communism*, 113–117.

143. Tai, *Radicalism and the Origins of the Vietnamese Revolution*, 182.

144. William Duiker, *The Rise of Nationalism in Vietnam, 1900–1941* (Ithaca, NY: Cornell University Press, 1976), 215.

145. Duiker, *The Communist Road to Power*, 27. Ho at this point "emphasized the Leninist organizational blueprint rather than the Marxist theory of history." Tai, *Radicalism and the Origins of the Vietnamese Revolution*, 225.

146. Duiker, *Ho Chi Minh*, 156. See also Duiker, *The Rise of Nationalism in Vietnam*, 205.

147. Khanh, *Vietnamese Communism*, 94–95.

148. For a discussion of the revolt in comparative perspective, see James Scott, *The Moral Economy of the Peasant: Rebellion and Subsistence in Southeast Asia* (New Haven, CT: Yale University Press, 1976).

149. Duiker, *The Communist Road to Power*, 36–37.

150. Khanh, *Vietnamese Communism*, 152; Duiker, *Ho Chi Minh*, 177.

151. Scott, "Revolution in the Revolution," 107. On the origins of this rebellion, see Duiker, *The Rise of Nationalism in Vietnam*, 218–222. On its local roots, see Scott, *The Moral Economy of the Peasant*, 148.

152. Duiker, *The Rise of Nationalism in Vietnam*, 230.

153. Khanh, *Vietnamese Communism*, 126–128.

154. Scott, "Revolution in the Revolution," 108. See also Duiker, *The Rise of Nationalism in Vietnam*, 221–222 and Duiker, *The Communist Road to Power*, 42.

155. Khanh, *Vietnamese Communism*, 159.

156. Scott, *The Moral Economy of the Peasant*, 126 (first quote); Scott, "Revolution in the Revolution," 112.

157. Greg Lockhart, *Nation in Arms: The Origins of the People's Army of Vietnam* (Sydney: Asian Studies Association of Australia in Association with Allen and Unwin, 1989), 61. For the evolution of the People's Army of Vietnam over time, see Douglas Pike, *PAVN: People's Army of Vietnam* (Novato, CA: Presidio Press, 1986).

158. Duiker, *The Communist Road to Power*, 42.

159. Duiker, *The Rise of Nationalism in Vietnam*, 233.

160. Ibid., 235.

161. Ibid., 272.

162. Khanh outlines the ICP's organizational structure, at least as it was supposed to be on paper. Khanh, *Vietnamese Communism*, 134–137.

163. Duiker, *The Communist Road to Power*, 48–49.

164. Tønnesson, *The Vietnamese Revolution*, 418.

165. Duiker, *The Rise of Nationalism in Vietnam*, 238.

166. Khanh, *Vietnamese Communism*, 178. There was also an external rivalry with Vietnamese Trotskyists.

167. Duiker, *The Rise of Nationalism in Vietnam*, 242.

168. Marr, *Vietnamese Tradition on Trial*, 389n50, 390.

169. Ibid., 389.

170. Duiker, *The Communist Road to Power*, 55.

171. Khanh, *Vietnamese Communism*, 223.

Notes to Pages 206–208

172. Ibid., 190.

173. Duiker, *The Rise of Nationalism in Vietnam*, 258.

174. Duiker, *The Communist Road to Power*, 60–61; Khanh, *Vietnamese Communism*, 250.

175. Duiker, *The Rise of Nationalism in Vietnam*, 267. David G. Marr links the premature timing of the revolt to the lack of communication with the Central Committee and pressure from Vietnamese units in the French colonial military. See *Vietnam 1945: The Quest for Power* (Berkeley: University of California Press, 1995), 161.

176. Vu, *Paths to Development in Asia*, 110; Duiker, *The Rise of Nationalism in Vietnam*, 268–269; Khanh, *Vietnamese Communism*, 253.

177. Duiker, *The Rise of Nationalism in Vietnam*, 270.

178. Duiker, *The Rise of Nationalism in Vietnam*, 271 (first quote); Duiker, *Ho Chi Minh*, 246 (second quote).

179. Tønnesson, *The Vietnamese Revolution*, 99.

180. Marr, *Vietnamese Tradition on Trial*, 415. Marr says of the remnant army in the north that "for the next forty months, it proved impossible for this 'army' to operate at more than squad level." See Marr, *Vietnam 1945*, 164.

181. Duiker, *The Rise of Nationalism in Vietnam*, 275. Its formal name was the Viet Nam Doc Lap Dong Minh (Vietnam Independence League).

182. Marr, *Vietnam 1945*, 240.

183. Lockhart, *Nation in Arms*, 64.

184. Marr, *Vietnam 1945*, 170.

185. Ibid., 179; Tønnesson, *The Vietnamese Revolution*, 418–419, 410.

186. Duiker, *The Rise of Nationalism in Vietnam*, 278.

187. Ibid., 284; Tønnesson, *The Vietnamese Revolution*, 344. The north-south divisions were important in this regard.

188. As Marr notes, during this period "very few Viet Minh groups attempted armed resistance." Marr, *Vietnam 1945*, 184.

189. Ibid., 184.

190. Lockhart, *Nation in Arms*, 92.

191. See Marr, *Vietnam 1945*, 314–319; Lockhart, *Nation in Arms*, 88.

192. Marr, *Vietnam 1945*, 198.

193. Lockhart, *Nation in Arms*, 124.

194. Ibid., 75.

195. "Japanese forces as a rule occupied only the major urban centers and made little effort to establish their authority in the countryside." Duiker, *The Communist Road to Power*, 86.

196. Ibid., 105.

197. Lockhart, *Nation in Arms*, 104.

198. Tai, *Radicalism and the Origins of the Vietnamese Revolution*, 255.

199. "This provided the Viet Minh with the unique opportunity to set up the local framework for a new state." Tønnesson, *The Vietnamese Revolution*, 419. See also Vu, "Late Leviathans," 170.

200. Lockhart, *Nation in Arms*, 145.

201. Tønnesson, *The Vietnamese Revolution*, 419.
202. Duiker, *The Communist Road to Power*, 111.
203. Tønnesson, *The Vietnamese Revolution*, 351 (quote); Marr, *Vietnam 1945*, 234.
204. Vu, "Late Leviathans," 178.
205. Duiker, *The Communist Road to Power*, 104.
206. Vu, "Late Leviathans," 186.
207. Ibid., 140.
208. Marr, *Vietnam 1945*, 238.
209. Ibid.
210. Ibid., 402.
211. Duiker, *The Communist Road to Power*, 111.
212. Ibid., 112.
213. Vu, "Late Leviathans," 187.
214. Vu, *Paths to Development in Asia*, 105.
215. Duiker, *The Communist Road to Power*, 118–121.
216. An overview is Duiker, *The Communist Road to Power*, 124–125.
217. Duiker, *The Communist Road to Power*, 126.
218. Marr, *Vietnam 1945*, 552.
219. Vu argues that "the spontaneous and decentralized nationalist movement created in its image a bifurcated and fragmented state." Vu, "Late Leviathans," 174.
220. Ibid., 183.
221. Ibid., 174.
222. Duiker, *The Communist Road to Power*, 138.
223. Ibid., 140.
224. Ibid., 142.
225. Ibid., 146–147.
226. Ibid., 147.
227. Ibid., 152.
228. Vu, "Late Leviathans," 172. Vu adds that "communist leaders [in 1945] in fact had a precarious control over the movement and over their own party" (173).
229. Massive purges occurred in the early 1950s. Ibid., 205.
230. See Bernard Fall, *Street without Joy: Indochina at War, 1946–54* (Harrisburg, PA: Stackpole, 1961); Ted Morgan, *Valley of Death: The Tragedy at Dien Bien Phu that Led America into the Vietnam War*, 1st ed. (New York: Random House, 2010); Colin Jackson, "Defeat in Victory: Organizational Learning Dysfunction in Counterinsurgency" (PhD diss., Massachusetts Institute of Technology, 2008).
231. Tønnesson, *The Vietnamese Revolution*, 416.
232. Ibid., 424.
233. Ibid., 99.
234. Goodwin, *No Other Way Out*.
235. I do not deal with Indonesia here because it did not have a communist revolutionary movement. The Indonesian revolutionary movement seems to have been a

parochial organization built around localized political groups. On its origins, see Benedict R. O'G. Anderson, *Java in a Time of Revolution; Occupation and Resistance, 1944–1946* (Ithaca, NY: Cornell University Press, 1972).

236. Goodwin, *No Other Way Out*, 132.

237. Ibid., 92.

8. Insurgency, War, and Politics

1. Stathis Kalyvas, *The Logic of Violence in Civil War* (Cambridge: Cambridge University Press, 2006); Elisabeth Jean Wood, *Insurgent Collective Action and Civil War in El Salvador* (New York: Cambridge University Press, 2003).

2. Paul Pierson, *Politics in Time: History, Institutions, and Social Analysis* (Princeton, NJ Princeton University Press, 2004).

3. An excellent and insightful example of this approach is Ethan Bueno de Mesquita, "Conciliation, Counterterrorism, and Patterns of Terrorist Violence," *International Organization* 59, no. 1 (2005): 145–176.

4. Ivan Arreguin-Toft, "How the Weak Win Wars: A Theory of Asymmetric Conflict," *International Security* 26, no. 1 (2001): 93–128; Jason Lyall and Isaiah Wilson III, "Rage Against the Machines: Explaining Outcomes in Counterinsurgency Wars," *International Organization* 63, no. 1 (2009): 67–106; David E. Cunningham, Kristian Skrede Gleditsch, and Idean Salehyan, "It Takes Two: A Dyadic Analysis of Civil War Duration and Outcome," *Journal of Conflict Resolution* 53, no. 4 (2009): 570–597; Barbara Walter, *Reputation and Civil War: Why Separatist Conflicts Are so Violent* (Cambridge: Cambridge University Press, 2009).

5. Macartan Humphreys and Jeremy M. Weinstein, "Handling and Manhandling Civilians in Civil War," *American Political Science Review* 100, no. 3 (August 2006): 429–447; Elisabeth Jean Wood, "The Social Processes of Civil War: The Wartime Transformation of Social Networks," *Annual Review of Political Science* 11, no. 1 (2008): 539–561. A partial exception is Fotini Christia, *Alliance Formation in Civil Wars* (Cambridge: Cambridge University Press, 2012).

6. On these dynamics in conventional warfare, see Caitlin Talmadge, "Explaining Military Effectiveness: Political Intervention and Battlefield Performance" (PhD diss., Massachusetts Institute of Technology, 2011).

7. Anna Grzymala-Busse, "Time Will Tell? Temporality and the Analysis of Causal Mechanisms and Processes," *Comparative Political Studies* 44, no. 9 (2011): 1267–1297; James Mahoney, and Kathleen Ann Thelen, eds. *Explaining Institutional Change: Ambiguity, Agency, and Power* (Cambridge: Cambridge University Press, 2010).

8. On the spread of ideas, see Robert Wuthnow, *Communities of Discourse: Ideology and Social Structure in the Reformation, the Enlightenment, and European Socialism* (Cambridge, MA: Harvard University Press, 1989).

9. Ana Arjona, "Social Order in Civil War" (PhD diss., Yale University, 2010); Zachariah Mampilly, *Rebel Rulers: Insurgent Governance and Civilian Life during War* (Ithaca, NY: Cornell University Press, 2011).

10. Paul Staniland, "States, Insurgents, and Wartime Political Orders," *Perspectives on Politics* 10, no. 2 (2012): 243–264.

11. For a discussion of these state strategies toward armed groups, see Paul Staniland, "The State and the Monopoly of Violence," unpublished working paper, University of Chicago, 2013.

12. Mancur Olson, *The Logic of Collective Action: Public Goods and the Theory of Groups* (Cambridge, MA: Harvard University Press, 1965).

13. Thanks to Dan Nexon for clearly articulating this insight. See also Doug McAdam, Sidney Tarrow, and Charles Tilly, *Dynamics of Contention* (Cambridge: Cambridge University Press, 2001).

14. Barry Wellman, "Network Analysis: Some Basic Principles," *Sociological Theory* 1 (1983): 163.

15. Jason Wittenberg, *Crucibles of Political Loyalty: Church Institutions and Electoral Continuity in Hungary* (New York: Cambridge University Press, 2006).

16. On opposition movements of different sorts, see Timothy P. Wickham-Crowley, *Guerrillas and Revolution in Latin America: A Comparative Study of Insurgents and Regimes since 1956* (Princeton, NJ: Princeton University Press, 1992); Edward Aspinall, *Opposing Suharto: Compromise, Resistance, and Regime Change in Indonesia* (Stanford, CA: Stanford University Press, 2005).

17. Wood, "The Social Processes of Civil War"; and Roger V. Gould, *Insurgent Identities: Class, Community, and Protest in Paris from 1848 to the Commune* (Chicago: University of Chicago Press, 1995).

18. Abdulkader Sinno, *Organizations at War in Afghanistan and Beyond* (Ithaca, NY: Cornell University Press, 2008).

19. On this dynamic in the peacekeeping context, see Séverine Autesserre, *The Trouble with the Congo: Local Violence and the Failure of International Peacebuilding* (Cambridge: Cambridge University Press, 2010).

20. Stathis N. Kalyvas, "'New' and 'Old' Civil Wars: A Valid Distinction?" *World Politics* 54, no. 1 (October 2001): 99–118.

21. Paul Staniland, "Organizing Insurgency: Networks, Resources, and Rebellion in South Asia," *International Security* 37, no. 1 (2012): 142–177.

22. On dangers of this approach, see Mike McGovern, "Popular Development Economics—An Anthropologist among the Mandarins," *Perspectives on Politics* 9, no. 2 (2011): 345–355.

23. For evidence on just how little Iraqi insurgents were paid, see Benjamin W. Bahney, Radha K. Iyengar, Patrick B. Johnston, Danielle F. Jung, Jacob N. Shapiro, and Howard J. Shatz, "Insurgent Compensation: Evidence from Iraq," *American Economic Review: Papers and Proceedings* 103, no. 3 (2013): 518–522.

24. Mampilly, *Rebel Rulers*; Jeremy Weinstein, *Inside Rebellion: The Politics of Insurgent Violence* (Cambridge: Cambridge University Press, 2007).

25. Philip Kuhn, *Rebellion and Its Enemies in Late Imperial China: Militarization and Social Structure, 1796–1864* (Cambridge, MA Harvard University Press, 1980), 84.

26. Adria Lawrence, "Triggering Nationalist Violence: Competition and Conflict in Uprisings against Colonial Rule," *International Security* 35, no. 2 (2010): 88–122; Wendy Pearlman, *Violence, Nonviolence, and the Palestinian National Movement* (Cambridge: Cambridge University Press, 2011).

27. Erica Chenoweth and Maria J. Stephan, *Why Civil Resistance Works: The Strategic Logic of Nonviolent Conflict* (New York: Columbia University Press, 2011).

Index

9/11 terrorist attacks in United States, 105, 136–38

AAC (Awami Action Committee), 65, 93, 98
Abbas, Zaffar, 250n122, 254–55n216
Abdullah, Farooq, 70–71
Abdullah, Sheikh Mohammed, 63–64, 69–70; death of, 71
Abou Zahab, Mariam, 131
activist organizations, 195, 223, 230
Afghanistan, 12, 223; pre-1975 political mobilization and social change, 105–9; 1973–1978, first uprising and aftermath, 110–11; 1973–1988, origins and evolution of insurgency, 109–26; 1978 PDPA coup, Soviet intervention, and escalation, 111–13; 1989–1994, state failure in, 126–29; 1994–2001, Taliban, rise of, 129–36; 1995–2001, Taliban's pursuit of national power, 133–36; 9/11, Taliban after, 133–36; clerics, 105–6, 113, 117, 121–24, 130, 132–34, 136, 218; communists, 108, 110–11, 121; counterinsurgency, 112, 120–21, 138–39, 229; coups, 110–11, 121; education in, 107, 114, 119, 122, 129–30, 133; ethnic divisions, 103, 117, 123; external state sponsorship, 139; fragmented groups, 101, 110, 112, 126; funding from Saudi Arabia, 101, 124–26; history, 103–4; horizontal linkages, 101; ideology, 111, 139, 221; integrated groups, 101, 109, 112, 126, 135; Islamists, 100, 104, 106–8, 113–17, 121, 139, 221, 225; leaders, 112; leaders of insurgent groups, 139; material resources, 139; militias, 139; modernizers, middle-class, 108, 110; mujahideen groups, 126–27, 130; Najibullah regime, 104, 126; nationalism, 126; overview of conflicts, 100–102; Pakistani aid, 111–12; parochial groups, 101, 109–10, 112, 126, 135; patterns of organization, 103, 125–29; politicized opposition, 107–9, 138; refugees, 129; religion, 106–8, 126; research methodology, 102; revolutionary planning, 107; rural communities, 107–9; social bases, pre-1975, 105–9; social resources, 112, 138; Soviet war, 104, 109, 111–13, 118, 120–21, 124–25, 130, 138; tribal leaders, 124, 131–33; ulama networks (clerics), 106, 113, 117, 121–24, 130; United States war, 37, 136–37; urban communities, 107–8; vanguard groups, 101, 109–10, 112, 126, 135; vertical linkages, 101; warlords, 133, 139
Africa, 236n5; anticolonial rebels, 50
agency of insurgent organizations, 23–25, 41, 99, 223
Ahmad, Ahsan, 86
aid to insurgents, 219; China, 202; India, 141, 155–61, 165–67, 176–77; Pakistan, 72, 80, 89–92, 98, 111–12, 116, 123–24, 126, 128, 131, 133, 139; Pakistan to Afghanistan, 111–12, 123–24,

[285]

Index

aid to insurgents *(continued)*
  126; United States, 126; United States to Afghanistan, 126
Al Badr, 79, 88, 249n97
Al Barq, 82
Al Fatah, 70
Ali, Liaquat (Hilal Haider), 96
Al Jehad, as parochial group, 59, 61, 92
Alliance of Democratic Forces for the Liberation of Congo, 8
alliances, 25
Al Madad, 93
Al Qaeda, 7, 48, 135, 229; Taliban and, 135–36
Al-Umar Mujahideen, 76, 90; fragmentation of, 59–61, 93–94, 96, 98–99; resources, 228; split from JKLF, 82, 93
Amman, Pottu, 171, 173
AMT (peasant association in Philippines), 194–95
Anbar Awakening, 48, 220
Ansar-ul Islam, 249n97
anticolonial movements, 19, 50, 181, 203–4
Asaratnam, Sinnappah, 146
Assam state, India, 40
Athulathmudalai, Lalith, 153
autonomy of insurgent organizations, 222–23
Awami Action Committee (AAC), 65, 93, 98
Aziz, Sheikh Abdul, 70

Baba Badr (Firdous Syed Baba), 91–92
Bac Son valley, 206
Baig, Bilal Ahmed, 96
Balakumar, Velupillai, 160
Balasingham, Adele, 273n213
Balasingham, Anton, 152
Balochistan, Pakistan, 130
Bandaranaike, S.W.R.D., 147–48
Barfield, Thomas J., 118, 127, 131, 135, 264n249
Barnard, Chester Irving, 24
Batticaloa, Sri Lanka, 146, 160, 173
Bayly, Christopher, 187, 189–90
Beg, Hilal, 74, 76, 82, 94–95
Behera, Navnita Chadha, 78, 254n193
Bhutto, Benazir, 75
Bin Laden, Osama, 136, 230
Black July pogroms, 155–56

Bobby (TELO leader), 159
Bolsheviks, 7, 29
bombings, 160, 169, 220
Bose, Sumantra, 67, 72–74, 81, 92
Briggs Plan, 190–91
British colonial rule in Sri Lanka, 146
British counterinsurgency: in French Indochina, 209; Malaya, 215; MCP, 184, 188, 191–92
British Malaya, 275n4
British resettlement of Chinese in Malaya, 190–92, 214
brokerage leadership, 30, 255n235
Buddhists, Sinhalese, 147
Burma, Communist Party of, 42
Burma/Myanmar, 223
Butt, Maqbool, 68–69

Canton, China, 203–4
case selection, research methodology of, 11–14
caste in Sri Lanka, 142, 145–47, 149, 154–55, 171, 175–76, 224–25
Castro, 267n49
Catholic Church: Brazilian branch of, 18; in Sri Lanka, 146
cease-fire: Hizbul Mujahideen, 88–90; between India and Pakistan, 64, 99
Centeno, Miguel, 244n46
central control, 5–8; Hizbul Mujahideen, 77–78, 88; HMB, 198; LTTE, 150; MCP, 189–91; Shura-yi Nazar, 120
Ceylon, 145, 147. *See also* Sri Lanka
change in organizations, 225; fragmented, 35, 38, 53–54; integrated, 35–42, 217; parochial, 35–37, 49–53, 217; vanguard, 35–37, 43–49, 217
Chapman, William, 194, 200
Chiang Kai-Shek, 184
China: aid to ICP, 202; Ho Chi Minh in, 203–4; Japanese invasion of, 185
Chinese Civil War, 183, 211
Chinese Communist Party, 184–85, 204, 211
Chinese in Malaya, 184–92, 214
Chin Peng, 187–89, 191
Christia, Fotini, 244–45n56
Christianity, 146
Civilian Volunteer Force (CVF), 167
civil wars, 6, 11–12, 19–20, 55, 144,

[286]

Index

167; Kashmir, 12, 60; organizational approach to, 226–27; Sri Lanka, 12–13; study of, 218–21, 223, 226, 228
Clarance, William, 148, 151
clerics: Afghanistan, 105–6, 113, 117, 121–24, 130, 132–34, 136, 218; in Taliban leadership, 136
coalitions, 25
Coates, John, 186, 189–90
Cochinchina, 204, 206, 279n140
cohesion, 2–3, 8, 33; Viet Minh, 211–12, 214, 216
Cold War, 4, 216, 225, 227
Coll, Steve, 114
collective action, 217; during war, 224–26
collective leadership, 28
Colombo, Sri Lanka, 172; Tamil insurgents in, 1
colonialism: in Kashmir, 62–63; Malaya, 213–14; Philippines, 213–14; Southeast Asia, 181 *See also* anticolonial movements
Comintern, 185–86, 203–4
communism, 221, 224, 247n25; Afghanistan, 108, 110–11, 121; Ho Chi Minh and, 203–4; Indochina, 13; Malaya, 13; organizational structures and, 192; Philippines, 13
Communist Party of Burma, 42
Communist Party of Thailand, 29–30
comparative method (research methodology), 11–14
Congress party. *See* Indian National Congress
contingency, 23
control. *See* central control; institutional control; local control
cooperation under fire: Huks, 193, 199; parochial, 49–51
counterinsurgency, 26, 55, 138, 217; Afghanistan, 112, 120–21, 138–39, 229; Huks, 183, 198; indiscriminate violence, 50–51; insurgent organization structure and, 227; against integrated groups, 220; Iraq, doctrine on, 229; against parochial groups, 49–53, 220; Philippines, 193, 198; policy advice, 226–31; research on, 220; strategies of, 228–31; against vanguard groups, 44–49, 220; vulnerability to, 36–37

coups: Afghanistan, 110–11, 121; Japanese in Indochina, 208
criminals, 32–33, 93–94; insurgents as, 228
CVF (Civilian Volunteer Force), 167

Dar, Abdul Majid, 85, 88–89
Dar, Ahsan, 77–78, 85, 88
Dar, Ashraf, 85, 87
Das (TELO leader), 159, 164
Daud Khan, 104, 107–8, 110, 121
decision making, logics of, 219–20
Democratic Alliance party, 196–97
Democratic Republic of Vietnam, 210
Deobandi networks, 131, 134
Devadas, David, 67–68, 75, 85, 94, 249n97
Devananda, Douglas, 160, 164
diaspora networks, 227–28; JKLF, 69; parochial leaders, 50; Tamils, 176–77
Dien Bien Phu, 211
discipline, 2–3, 90; Hizbul Mujahideen, 79–80; PKP, 199; PLOT, 161–62
divide-and-conquer strategy, 42, 52, 229, 231
Dixit, J. N., 158
Doda, 78, 86
Dorronsoro, Gilles, 100, 109–11, 113–14, 124, 127, 130, 132–33, 261n152
Dostum, Abdul Rashid, 104, 127, 133, 135, 139, 261n152
DP (Vietnamese Democratic Party), 209
drug and commodity trading, 227–28
Duiker, William, 205, 209, 281n195
Durrani Pashtuns, 123, 136
dynamic organizational interaction and history, 219–21

education: in Afghanistan, 107, 114, 119, 122, 129–30, 133; in French Indochina, 203–4; in Pakistan, 67–69, 129; political, 27; in Sri Lanka, 147–48
Edwards, David B., 115, 122, 124–25, 131
Eelamist left, 159
Eelam People's Revolutionary Liberation Front. *See* EPRLF
Eelam Revolutionary Organisation of Students. *See* EROS
Eelam War II, 170

[287]

Eelam War III, 170, 173
Egypt, 18, 106
Ejército de Liberación Nacional de Bolivia, 7
endogenous processes, 35, 219–21
EPRLF (Eelam People's Revolutionary Liberation Front), 1, 141; attacks by LTTE, 163–65, 167–68; CVF fighters, 167; formation of, 148; horizontal ties, strong, 160; Indian aid, 158–61, 165–67, 176–77; leadership decapitation, 163, 168; organization type, 143, 162; split from EROS, 155; vanguard organization, 167–68; vertical links, weak, 160
EROS (Eelam Revolutionary Organisation of Students), 141; absorption into LTTE, 169; counterinsurgency strategies, 229; formation of, 148; horizontal ties, 149; Indian aid, 158–60; leftist ideology, 176; in London, 148–49, 154, 160; organization type, 143, 162; vanguard organization, 155, 160; vertical ties, 149
Ethiopia, 45
ethnic cleansing, 3
ethnic groups: Afghanistan, 103, 117, 123; Sri Lanka, 144, 171–73, 176
Evans, Alexander, 64, 86
evolution of organizations, 9–10, 14
expansion, 231; Hezb-e Islami, 116; Hizbul Mujahideen, 78–79; Huks, 199; ICP, 202; JKLF, 74–75; LTTE, 157; mismanaged, 39, 41–43, 230; PLOT, 161–62; Shura-yi Nazar, 119–20, 128–29

factions, 30–32, 42; feuding among, 200; parochial, 49–53
Fatt, Yong Ching, 185
Federal Party, 147–48
Federation of Malaya, 275n4
Feleo, Juan, 194, 197
First Indochina War, 207, 210
fragmented groups, 8, 10, 219; Afghanistan, 101, 110, 112, 126; Al Umar Commandos, 93–94, 96, 98–99; Al-Umar Mujahideen, 59–61, 93–94; change in, 35, 38, 53–54; control in, 53–54; external actors, 54; Harakat-e Inqelab, 112, 121, 126; Hezb-Khalis, 125; horizontal ties, 53–54; Huks, 199–201, 215; Ikhwan-ul Muslimeen, 94–96, 98; from integrated groups, 10, 38–42; JKLF, 81–84; Kashmir, 90, 96–97; leaders of insurgent groups, 32–33; origins of, 17, 32–33; from parochial groups, 49, 51–53, 90; pathways of change and, 217; PLOT, 143, 155, 161–63; TELO, 159; from vanguard groups, 43–44, 46–49; warlords, emergence of, 54
France: defeat at Dien Bien Phu, 211; Popular Front government, 205–6
fratricide, 230; Hezb-e Islami, 128; Hizbul Mujahideen, 84, 86; LTTE, 155; in parochial groups, 49, 52–53; in vanguard groups, 48, 52
French Communist Party, 18
French counterinsurgency and repression in Indochina, 202, 205–7, 209, 213–15
French Indochina. *See* Indochina
Fuglerud, Øivind, 150, 273n204

game theory, 219
Gandhi, Indira, 64, 69
Gandhi, Rajiv, 165, 170
Gauhar, G. N., 87
Geelani, 85, 250n100, 251n130
Ghilzai Pashtuns, 136
Giustozzi, Antonio, 114, 120, 122, 128, 135, 261n152
Goodson, Larry, 130
Goodwin, Jeff, 51, 181, 183, 193, 212–14, 279n119
Green Army, 250n104
guerrilla warfare, 36, 230–31
Guevara, Che, 29, 230
Gunaratna, Rohan, 270n121

Hack, Karl, 191
HAJY group, 73–74, 82
Hamas, 27–28, 229
Hamid, S., 70, 92
Haq, Sami ul-, 130
Haqqani, Jalaluddin, 124, 134
Haqqani network, 105, 138
Harakat-e Inqelab, 101–2, 109–13, 119, 121–24, 127, 131, 133; fragmentation, 112, 121, 126; horizontal linkages,

[288]

Index

weak, 121–22; leadership, 122; material resources, 139; parochial organization, 121; Pashtuns and, 133; in southern Afghanistan, 130; splinter groups, 123; vertical ties, 122

Harper, T. N., 187, 189–90

Harpviken, Kristian Berg, 101, 107, 110, 115, 123, 129–30

Hassan, Mullah, 131

Hazaras, Shiite, 103–4

Hekmatyar, Gulbuddin, 100, 104–5, 107, 109, 111–16, 119–21, 126–29, 133, 138–39, 250n122; Pashtuns and, 134; in southern Afghanistan, 130

Hellman-Rajanayagam, Dagmar, 141, 151, 157–58, 160, 164, 166, 171

Herat, Afghanistan, 127, 133

Hezb-e Islami, 100–102, 104–5, 109, 111, 113–16, 127–29, 133, 138; control in, 113–16; expansion, 116; fratricide, 128; horizontal ties, strong, 113–14, 116; ideology, 116; leadership, 114–15; local networks, 115–16, 134; Pakistani aid, 116, 128, 139; Pashtuns and, 133–34; vanguard organization, 112–13, 116; vertical ties, weak, 113, 115

Hezb-i Wahdat, 104, 133, 135

Hezb-Khalis, 110, 131, 133–34, 138, 258n44; fragmentation, 125; organizational function, 125; parochial organization, 124–25

Hezbollah, 6

hijackings, 255n232

Hindus and Muslims in Kashmir, 62–63

history, dynamic organizational interaction and, 219–21

Hizbul Mujahideen, 230; Al Badr faction, 79, 88; cease-fire, 88–90; central control, 77–78, 88; consolidation and dominance, 85–86; discipline in, 79–80; fratricide, 84, 86; Ikhwan and, 95; Indian counterinsurgency, 80–81, 86–87, 89; as integrated group, 59, 61, 72, 76–77, 79–80, 86; integration, 177; intelligence on, 84, 86–87; JKLF and, 82–83; leadership decapitation, 84, 86–87; local disembedding, 81, 84; local expansion, 78–79; mobilization for war, 76–80; Pakistan: aid from, 80, 89, 98; sanctuary in, 86; popular support, 97; recruitment, 79; as vanguard group, 60, 81, 84–90, 192; vertical ties, 87

Hizbul Mujahideen-e-Islami, 89, 250n122

HMB (Hukbong Mapalaya ng Bayan), 197–201, 277n61; central control, 198; feuding among factions, 200; parochial organization, 197–98, 201

Ho Chi Minh, 183, 205–6, 208, 210; in China, 203–4; communist mobilization by, 203–4; Marxist-Leninist organizational ideology, 202

horizontal ties and linkages, 9, 13, 21–22, 25, 33–34; Afghanistan, 101; changes in, 35; EPRLF, 160; EROS, 149; in fragmented groups, 53–54; Harakat-e Inqelab, 121–22; Hezb-e Islami, 113–14, 116; Huks, 195; ICP, 202, 204; in integrated groups, 26–27; Jamaat-e-Islami (JI), 66–68; JKLF, 69; LTTE, 151, 169, 172, 175–76; MCP, 184–85, 187; in parochial groups, 30–32; Philippines, 193; PLOT, 153; Shura-yi Nazar, 119; Taliban, 129, 137; in vanguard groups, 43, 48; Viet Minh, 211

Horowitz, Donald, 151

Huizer, Gerrit, 195

Hukbalahap (Hukbo ng Bayan Laban sa Hapon; People's Anti-Japanese Army), 195–96, 277n61

Hukbong Mapalaya ng Bayan. *See* HMB

Huks, 13, 181–83, 192–201; cooperation under fire, 193, 199; counterinsurgency, 183, 198; expansion, 199; external sanctuary, 199; fragmentation, 199–201, 215; horizontal ties, weak, 195; killings by, 197; local disembedding, 199; Marxist-Leninist organizational ideology, 193, 199, 201; parochial organization, 182–83, 196–98, 200–201; peasant mobilization, 194–96, 199–201; popular support, 215; social bases, 193, 196; state policy and, 213–14; torture by, 197; women's involvement in, 195

Huntington, Samuel P., 2, 25

Hurriyat Conference, 99

ICP (Indochinese Communist Party), 181–83; 1925–1931, communist mobilization through Nghe Tihn Revolt, 203–5; 1925–1954, mobilization and resilience, 201–3; 1930–31 revolt, 202, 204–5, 211; 1931–1940, rebuilding organization, 205–8; 1940 revolt, 202, 211; 1945–1946, constructing insurgent state, 208–10; 1946–1954, conflict with France, 210–11; Chinese aid, 202; expansion, 202; horizontal linkages, strong, 202, 204; ideology, 212; local alliances, 202, 208–9, 212, 214; Marxist-Leninist organizational ideology, 203, 205, 208, 212; popular support, 215–16; rebuilding of, 205–6; recruitment, 207; shift from vanguard to integrated organization, 201–2, 209–10, 212, 215; social base, 204; socialization of soldiers, 207; state policy and, 213; vanguard organization, 182, 201, 205–7, 212; vertical linkages, weak, 202, 204

ideology, 3–4, 25–26, 28–29, 33, 225, 243n37; Afghanistan, 111, 139, 221; Hezb-e Islami, 116; ICP, 212; Indochina, 221; Jamaat-e-Islami (JI), 67; Kashmir, 97–98; LTTE, 152, 177; organization and, 221–22; Sri Lanka, 221

Ikhwan-ul Muslimeen, 80, 86, 90; creation of, 82; feuds between leaders, 95; fragmentation of, 94–96, 98; local disembedding, 59; as parochial group, 59, 61; war with Hizbul Mujahideen, 95–96

Ikhwan-ul Muslimoon, 95–96

Ilahi, Maqbool, 85

India: aid to Tamil insurgents, 141, 155–61, 165–67, 176–77; Assam state, 40; counterinsurgency in Kashmir, 59–60, 63–64, 80–81, 84, 86–87, 89–90, 92–96, 98; Indian-administered Jammu and Kashmir, 59; Maoist uprising in West Bengal, 24; Ministry of External Affairs, 160; Punjab, 52; RAW (Research and Analysis Wing), external intelligence agency, 156, 165, 177

Indian National Congress, 63–65, 71, 167

Indochina, 14, 203–11; communist rebellion, 13; education in, 203–4; French counterinsurgency and repression, 202, 205–7, 209, 213–15; ideology, 221; Japanese coup, 208; Japanese occupation, 206–8; peasant rebellions, 204–5; rural power vacuum, 202, 207–8, 210, 212, 218; war with France, 202

Indochinese Communist Party. *See* ICP

Indonesian revolutionary movement, 282–83n235

Indo-Sri Lanka Accord, 165, 272n176

information, 9, 17, 20–23, 27–29, 36, 39, 81, 217, 224, 230

Inquilabi, Azam, 70

institutional control: in fragmented groups, 53–54; Jamiat-e Islami, 117–18; social linkages and, 54–55, 89; Taliban, 137

insurgent organizations: agency of, 23–25, 41, 99, 223; autonomy from states, 222–23; as criminals, 228; definition of, 5; origins of, 17, 33–34; pathways of change, 37–38, 54–55, 217–18; policy implications, 226–27; resources and, 227–28; sources of change, 35–36; strategies of, 217, 228–31

integrated groups, 6, 34, 59, 218; Afghanistan, 101, 109, 112, 126, 135; change in, 35–42, 217; counterinsurgency against, 39–41, 220; fragmentation of, 10, 38–42; Hizbul Mujahideen, 59, 61, 72, 76–77, 79–80, 86, 177; horizontal ties, 26–27; incorporation of new leaders, 41–42; interaction with states, 224; leadership decapitation, 39–40, 219; leaders of, 27, 226–27; local disembedding, 39–41; local networks, 27; LTTE, 142–44, 158, 162, 170, 175–77; MCP, 183; mismanaged expansion, 39, 41–43; origins of, 17, 26–28; from parochial groups, 10, 49–51; socialization processes, 41; Sri Lanka, 143; Taliban, 139–40, 177; from vanguard groups, 10, 43–46; vertical ties, 26–27; Viet Minh, 208, 210

integrated/parochial hybrid groups (MCP, Malayan Communist Party), 182–84, 189, 191, 215

[290]

Index

intelligence gathering, 39–40, 84, 86–87
internal cooperation, 36
internal unrest, 230
international aid. *See* aid to insurgents
International Crisis Group, 31
Inter-Services Intelligence (ISI), Pakistan, 82, 89, 92, 95, 98, 112
IPKF (Indian Peace Keeping Force), 143, 145, 156, 163–68; withdrawal from Sri Lanka, 167–68
IPKF, attacks on, LTTE, 165–66
Iraq, 2, 8, 37, 220, 229
Irish National Liberation Army (INLA), 8, 33, 54
Islam, Nasir-ul, 78, 85
Islamic Students' League, 73
Islamists: Afghanistan, 100, 104, 113–17, 121, 139, 221, 225; Kashmir, 90, 96
Ittehad of Sayyaf, 101, 110, 115, 125, 257n18

Jaffna, Sri Lanka, 142, 146, 151, 164–65, 169–72
Jamaat (Pakistani), 246n21
Jamaat-e-Islami (JI), 59–60, 65–66, 71, 73, 106, 224; attacks on, 86–87; horizontal ties, 66–68; ideology, 67; JKLF and, 75, 95; local notables in, 66–68; middle class in, 66–68; militancy, 77–78; model of, 113–14; in Muslim United Front, 72; overview of, 66–68; Pakistani, 88; religious organization, 63, 66; as social base for Hizbul Mujahideen, 72, 76–79, 84, 88–89; social influence, 67–68; vertical ties, 66–68
Jamiat-e Islami, 101–2, 109, 111, 116–18, 127; institutional control, 117–18; local power centers, 117–18; Pakistani aid, 117; parochial organization, 112, 117–18
Jamiat Ulema-e-Islam, 130
Jamiat-ul-Mujahideen, 78
Jammu, 62
Jammu and Kashmir Liberation Front. *See* JKLF
Jammu and Kashmir Students' Liberation Front (JKSLF), 76, 82, 94–95
Japan: anti-Japanese insurgency in Malaya, 184–86; anti-Japanese insurgency in Philippines, 192, 195–96; anti-Japanese insurgent movements, 181, 213; coup in Indochina, 208; invasion of China, 185; occupation of French Indochina, 206–8
Jayatilleka, Dayan, 163
Jayewardene, J. R., 148, 155, 165
Jaysh al-Mahdi, 8
Jehad Force, 90, 92
Jeyaraj, D.B.S., 274n220
JI. *See* Jamaat-e-Islami
JKLF (Jammu and Kashmir Liberation Front): agency, human, 99; Al Umar and, 94; diaspora networks, 69; expansion, challenges of, 74–75; fighting units, 73; fragmentation of, 81–84; growth of, 77; "HAJY" group, 73–74, 82; Hizbul Mujahideen and, 82–83; horizontal ties, 69; independence, goal of, 73; Indian counterinsurgency, 80–81; Jamaat-e-Islami (JI) and, 75, 95; leadership decapitation, 60, 75, 81–84; mobilization for war, 71–76; overview of, 68–69, 71; Pakistani aid, 75–76, 81–83; People's League and, 75; politicized opposition of, 65–66, 68–69; popular support for, 74, 97; social linkages, 69; splinter groups from, 76, 81, 94–96; training of fighters, 74–75; as vanguard group, 59, 61, 72–76, 80, 84; vertical ties, weak, 69, 72, 74
JKSLF (Jammu and Kashmir Students' Liberation Front), 76, 82, 94–95
Jombesh, 133
Joshi, Manoj, 75, 79, 83, 85–86, 90–92, 94–95, 249n97

Kabul, Afghanistan, 103–8, 110–13, 119, 125–28, 130, 133, 135–38
Kabul University, 111
Kadalodiekal, 150–51
Kahn, Amanullah, 252n149
Kalipunang Pambansa ng mga Magsasaka sa Pilipinas (National Society of Peasants in the Philippines). *See* KPMP
Kandahar, Afghanistan, 131
Kandy, Kingdom of (Sinhalese), 145, 147
Karaiyar fishing caste, 146, 148–50, 155, 157, 166, 169, 171, 176

Index

Karuna Group, 143, 169, 172–74, 176
Karzai, Hamid, 137
Kashmir, 59–99, 221; cease-fire between India and Pakistan, 64, 99; civil war, 12, 60; colonialism, history of, 62–63; diaspora, 251n134; fragmentation of insurgent groups, 96–97; ideology in, 97–98; independence, public support for, 73–74; Indian counterinsurgency, 59–60, 63–64, 80–81, 84, 86, 90, 92–96; effectiveness of, 98; instability and protests, 64; insurgency, overview of, 59–60, 62–64; Islamist ideology, 90, 96; Line of Control (LOC), 62–63, 69, 72–73, 75–76, 83, 85, 89, 91, 93; material resources, 96; Muslims and Hindus, 62–63; nationalists, 62–63; networks of politics in, 71; Pakistan and, 60, 62–64, 90; Pakistani aid, 72, 90–92, 98; political divisions, 62–64; politicized opposition, 65–66; popular support, 97; pro-independence activists, 68–69; pro-state social bases, 64–65; research methodology, 61; social bases, prewar, 59–60, 64–71, 97; state sponsorship, 96; street militancy and violence, 72; urban-rural social divide, 74 *See also* Hizbul Mujahideen; JKLF
Kashmir Valley, 62, 64, 68–69, 73, 78
Kerkvliet, Benedict J., 194–95, 197–99
KHAD (Afghan intelligence agency), 120, 123
Khalis, Yunis, 101, 105, 110, 114–15, 124, 133–34, 138
Khan, Amanullah, 68–69, 72–73, 83–84
Khan, Ismail, 104, 117–18, 127, 133, 139, 261n152; Taliban, opposition to, 135
Khan, Naeem, 70
Khanh, Huynh Kim, 204, 206, 280n162
killing: by Huks, 197; of Prabhakaran, Velupillai, 145
Kittu, 151, 171
Kosovo Liberation Army, 45
KPMP (Kalipunang Pambansa ng mga Magsasaka sa Pilipinas) (National Society of Peasants in the Philippines), 194–95, 277n75
Kumaran Pathmanathan (KP), 267n49
Kumaratunga, Chandrika, 170
Kuomintang, 184, 204
Kuttimani, 152–53, 159

labor organizations, 28, 181. *See also* urban labor mobilization
Lachica, Eduardo, 195–96
Ladakh, 62
Lai Teck, 185–87, 189
landed elites in Philippines, 194, 196, 200–201
language policies of Sri Lanka, 147–48
Lansdale, Edward, 196
Lanzona, Vina, 195
Lashkar-e-Taiba, 89
Lashkar-i Isar (Army of Sacrifice), 128
Latin America, leadership decapitation in, 47
leadership decapitation, 217, 219, 229–30; EPRLF, 163, 168; Hizbul Mujahideen, 84, 86–87; in integrated groups, 39–40, 219; JKLF, 60, 75, 81–84; in Latin America, 47; state policy, 47; Taliban, 137; in vanguard groups, 46–47, 219
leaders of insurgent groups: Afghanistan, 112, 139; complexities faced by, 226–27; creation of organizations, 26; feuds between, 95; fragmented groups, 32–33; Harakat-e Inqelab, 122; Hezb-e Islami, 114–15; integrated groups, 27, 226–27; links to communities, 36–37; MCP, 189–91; parochial groups, 30–32, 226–27; vanguard groups, 28–30, 226–27
leftist ideology. *See* communism; Marxist-Leninist organizational ideology
Leites, Nathan, 12
Leninist "combat party," 4, 28
Leninist ideology. *See* Marxist-Leninist organizational ideology
Liberation Tigers of Tamil Eelam. *See* LTTE
Libya, anti-Qaddafi military opposition, 7–8
Line of Control (LOC) in Kashmir, 62–63, 69, 72–73, 75–76, 83, 85, 89, 91, 93
Little, David, 269n92
local alliances, 219, 230; ICP, 202, 208–9, 212, 214; LTTE, 157, 177; parochial

[292]

groups and, 45; state policy and, 44–45; vanguard groups, 43–47
local communities and networks, 9, 21–22, 25–31, 36, 43, 47–48, 222
local control, 5–8, 10, 27, 29–30, 32, 36, 38, 40, 42, 45–46
local disembedding, 217, 230; Hizbul Mujahideen, 81, 84; Huks, 199; Ikhwan-ul Muslimeen, 59; integrated groups, 39–41; MCP, 183, 191–92; Muslim Janbaz Force (MJF), 60; parochial groups, 49, 51–52
Lockhart, Greg, 205, 208
Loganathan, Ketheshwaran, 159, 168, 271n150, 272n177
Loya Paktia, Afghanistan, 131
LTTE (Liberation Tigers of Tamil Eelam), 1, 8, 13, 230; annihilation of, 175; attacks on rival insurgent groups, 163–65; caste base, 154–55; central control, 150; conflict with Sri Lankan government, 145; counterinsurgency strategies, 229; ethnic cleansing campaigns, 3; expansion, 157; formation of, 149–52; fratricide, 155; horizontal linkages, 151, 169, 172, 175–76; ideology, 152, 177; Indian aid, 155–58; integrated organization, 142–44, 158, 162, 170, 175–77; IPKF, attacks on, 165–66; Karuna split, 172–74; local alliances, 157, 177; military effectiveness, 161, 169; organization type, 143; overview of, 141–42; popular support, 166, 177; proto-state, 1990–2002, 169–72; recruits, 157; resources, 228; shift from vanguard to integrated organization, 158; social base, 149, 177; socialization of soldiers, 157, 177; suicide bombings, 169; vanguard organization, 150, 155, 158; vertical linkages, 152, 169–70; war with Sri Lanka Army, 174–75
Luzon, Philippines, 192, 194–95, 197, 199

madrasas, 106, 111, 116, 122–23, 130–31, 133
Magsaysay, Ramon, 198
Mahattaya, 143, 151, 169, 171–72, 267n49
Mahendrajaah, Gopalaswamy. *See* Mahattaya

Mahoney, James, 36
Majid, Usman, 96
Malaya, 183–92; British counterinsurgency, 215; British resettlement of Chinese, 190–92, 214; Chinese in, 184–87; colonial/neocolonial policies, inclusive and reformist, 213–14; communist rebellion, 13; rural insurgency, 184, 188; state policy, 192, 215; war against Japanese, 184
Malayan Communist Party, 13
Malayan National Liberation Army (MNLA), 183
Malayan People's Anti-Japanese Army, 185–86
Malaysia, 275n4
Maley, William, 127, 131–32
Malik, Yasin, 73, 82–84
Manila, Philippines, 196
Mann, Michael, 177
Maoist ideology, 4, 107, 139, 207; MCP, 191
Maoist uprising in West Bengal, India, 24
Mao Zedong, 211, 230
Marr, David G., 281n175, 281n180, 281n188
Marxist-Leninist organizational ideology, 33, 107, 110, 139, 143, 152, 160–61, 183, 189, 230; Ho Chi Minh, 202; Huks, 193, 199, 201; ICP, 203, 205, 208, 212; Sri Lanka, 176
Masood, Sarfraz, 88
Massoud, Shah Ahmed, 109, 112, 117–18, 121, 126–28, 133; assassination of, 135; Taliban, opposition to, 135
material resources, 3–4, 26, 33, 96, 166; Afghanistan, 139; Harakat-e Inqelab, 139; Kashmir, 96
Matthews, Bruce, 153
Mawdudi, Syed Abul Ala, 66–67
McAdam, Doug, 255n232
McCann, Eamonn, 26
McDowell, Chris, 148, 171, 270n129
McKenna, Thomas, 278n109
MCP (Malayan Communist Party), 181–92, 230; 1948–1951, war onset and militant origins, 188–90; 1951–1956, Briggs Plan and destruction of local organization, 190–91;

[293]

Index

MCP *(continued)*
  1956–1989, isolated vanguard period, 191; British counterinsurgency, 184, 188, 191–92; central control, 189–91; Chinese roots of, 185; Chinese squatter communities: mobilization of, 186–90; resettlement of, 190–91; exile in Thailand, 184, 191; external sanctuary, 192; horizontal linkages, moderate, 184–85, 187; integrated/parochial hybrid group, 182–84, 189, 191, 215; integration, 183; leadership, 189–91; local disembedding, 183, 191–92; Maoist ideology, 191; mobilization, 1945–1948, 186–87; nonviolence, policy of, 186–87; state policy and, 213; urban labor mobilization, 184–90, 218; vanguard organization, 183, 189, 191; vertical ties: strong, 184–85, 187, 189–90; weak, 192
Mendis, 164
methodology. *See* research methodology
middle class, 66–68, 73–74, 105, 107–8, 121
Mindanao, Philippines, 278n109
Min Yuen (People's Movement), 189–90
Mir, Javed, 73, 82, 252n149
mirwaiz of Srinagar, 93
Mishal, Shaul, 28
mismanaged expansion, 39, 41–43, 230
MNLA (Malayan National Liberation Army), 183
mobile warfare, 135–36
modernizers in Afghanistan, 105, 108, 110
Muhammadi, Mawlawi, 131
Mujaddidi family, 106
mujahideen groups in Afghanistan, 126–27, 130
Mullaitivu area (Sri Lanka), 166
Muni, S. D., 155, 165–66
Muralitharan, Vinayagamoorthy (Colonel Karuna), 172
Muslim Brotherhood, 18, 27, 106, 113, 225
Muslim Janbaz Force (MJF), 80, 90; local disembedding, 60; as parochial group, 59, 61, 92; popular support, 97; recruitment, 91
Muslims: and Hindus in Kashmir, 62–63; in Sri Lanka, 144, 172–73 *See also* Islamists

Muslim United Front, 72, 77
Muslim Youth Organization, 107, 124

Nabi Muhammadi, Maulavi Muhammad, 121–22
Najibullah Ahmadzai regime (Afghanistan), 100, 104, 112, 126
Nanhaji, Saleem, 82
National Conference (NC), 63–65, 71
nationalism, 221; Afghanistan, 126; Kashmir, 62–63; Sinhalese, 272n166; Southeast Asia, 183; Tamils, 143; TELO, 176; Vietnamese, 212, 215
National Peasant Union (Pambansang Kaisahan ng mga Magbukid). *See* PKM
National Resistance Army (Uganda), 43
National Society of Peasants in the Philippines (Kalipunang Pambansa ng mga Magsasaka sa Pilipinas). *See* KPMP
Naxalites, 7
Nehru, Jawaharlal, 63
NEPC (Northeastern Provincial Council), 166–67
New People's Army, 198, 274n3
Nghe Tinh revolt, 204–5
Nigeria, 224
nonviolence, 19–20, 65, 231; MCP, 186–87; Philippines, 193
Noorani, A. G., 61, 70, 76
Northern Alliance, 105, 135–36
Northern Ireland, 236n32
North Vietnam, 201, 203, 215
Northwest Frontier Province, Pakistan, 130
Nuristanis, 103

O'Duffy, Brendan, 150, 173
Omar, Mullah, 130, 132, 136–38
opium economy, 128, 134, 136
organization, patterns of: Afghanistan, 103, 125–29; Kashmir, 61–62; Southeast Asia, 181–83; Sri Lanka, 143
organizations: pathways of change, 37–38, 54–55, 217–18; prewar social bases and wartime organization, 9–10; types of, 1–2, 5–8, 25, 217, 226–27

Padmanabha, K., 160
Pahlawan, Abdul Malik, 135

[294]

Index

Pakistan: Afghan Islamists' exile in, 110; education in, 67–69, 129; Inter-Services Intelligence (ISI), 82, 89, 92, 95, 98, 112; Jamaat-e-Islami, 88; Kashmir insurgency and, 60, 62–64, 90; refugees, 129; sanctuary in, 86, 101; Taliban and, 7, 136–37

Pakistani aid: Afghanistan, 111–12; Hezb-e Islami, 116, 128, 139; Hizbul Mujahideen, 80, 89, 98; to insurgents in Afghanistan, 123–24, 126; Jamiat-e Islami, 117; JKLF, 75–76, 81–83; Kashmir, 72, 90–92, 98; Taliban, 131, 133

Pallar caste, 270n129

Pambansang Kaisahan ng mga Magbukid (National Peasant Union). *See* PKM

Panjshiris, 118–20, 128

parochial groups, 7–8, 34, 218, 261n152; Afghanistan, 101, 109–10, 112, 126, 135; Al Jehad, 59, 61, 92; change in, 35–37, 49–53, 217; cooperation under fire, 49–51; counterinsurgency against, 49–53, 220; diaspora leaders, 50; external sanctuaries, 50; factional fusing, 49–51; factions, 52–53; fragmentation of, 49, 51–53, 90; Harakat-e Inqelab, 121; Hezb-Khalis, 124–25; HMB, 197–98, 201; Huks, 182–83, 196–98, 200–201; Ikhwan-ul Muslimeen, 59, 61; indiscriminate violence against, 51–52; integration of, 10, 42, 49–51; interleadership fratricide, 49, 52–53; international aid to, 219; Jamiat-e Islami, 112, 117–18; leaders of, 30–32, 226–27; local alliances and, 45; in local communities, 31; local disembedding, 49, 51–52; Muslim Janbaz Force (MJF), 59, 61, 92; origins of, 17, 30–32; Philippines, 193; PKP, 200; Sri Lanka, 141, 143; states, interaction with, 224; TELO, 153, 155

Parrey, Mohammed Yusuf "Kukka," 95–96

Pashtuns, 101, 103, 107, 113, 115, 121, 131, 226; Durrani, 123; education in Pakistan, 129; Harakat-e Inqelab and, 133; Hekmatyar, Gulbuddin and, 134; Hezb-e Islami and, 133–34; support for Taliban, 136

path dependence, 35, 37, 55, 218

Pathmanabha, 164

pathways of change for insurgent organizations, 37–38, 54–55, 217–18

PDPA (People's Democratic Party of Afghanistan), 104, 108–9, 111–13, 120

peace processes, 3, 172–74

peasant mobilization and rebellions, 181; Indochina, 204–5; Philippines, 192–96, 199–201, 225

Peer, Basharat, 67

Peiris, 268n52

People's Committees, 209

People's Conference, 65, 82; in Muslim United Front, 72

People's Democratic Party of Afghanistan. *See* PDPA

People's League, 59, 65–66, 68, 71, 85, 90; JKLF, training by, 75; Muslim Janbaz Force of, 97; in Muslim United Front, 72; overview of, 70; popular support for, 93; recruitment, 91; Rehmani faction of, 92

People's Liberation Organisation of Tamil Eelam. *See* PLOT

People's Movement (Min Yuen), 189–90

Perumal, Varatharajah, 160

Peshawar, 111, 118, 121–22, 125, 139; sanctuary in, 104

Philippine Communist Party (Partido Komunista Pilipinaas). *See* PKP

Philippines, 192–201, 215, 221, 224; anti-Japanese insurgency, 192, 195; colonial/neocolonial policies, inclusive and reformist, 213–14; communist rebellion, 13; counterinsurgency, 193, 198; horizontal ties, weak, 193; insurgency, 181–83; landed elites, 194, 196, 200–201; "libidinal" status, 279n119; nonviolent mobilization, 193; parochial organizations, 193; peasant rebellions, 192, 225; peasants and land reform, 193, 215; social bases, 193; state policy, 193; United States intervention, 196–98; urban-rural distinction, 194–95; vertical ties, strong, 193; violence, 197

Pierson, Paul, 219

Pir Panjal Regiment, 88

PKM (Pambansang Kaisahan ng mga Magbukid, National Peasant Union), 196–97

[295]

PKP (Philippine Communist Party, Partido Komunista Pilipinaas), 193, 196–201; discipline, 199; parochial organization, 200; urban working class, mobilization of, 193–95
Plebiscite Front, 65, 68–70
PLOT (People's Liberation Organisation of Tamil Eelam), 1, 141; attacks by LTTE, 163–64; discipline, 161–62; expansion, 161–62; formation of, 148; fragmented organization, 155, 161–63; horizontal linkages, weak, 153; Indian aid, 159–60; leftist ideology, 176; murders, 162; organization type, 143; social base, 149; split from LTTE, 150, 152–53; vertical linkages, weak, 153
policy implications of research, 226–31
political violence, scholarship on, 218–26
politicized opposition: Afghanistan, 107–9, 138; JKLF, 65–66, 68–69; Kashmir, 65–66; social bases, 19–20, 221, 225
politics, prewar. *See* prewar politics
Pomeroy, William, 197
Popular Front government (France), 205–6
popular support, 3–4; Hizbul Mujahideen, 97; Huks, 215; ICP, 215–16; JKLF, 74, 97; Kashmir, 97; limits and complexities of, 215–16; LTTE, 166, 177; Muslim Janbaz Force (MJF), 97; People's League, 93
Prabhakaran, Velupillai, 142, 148–52, 156–57, 163, 169, 171, 173, 175, 177; killing of, 145
Premachandran, Suresh, 160, 273n191
Premadasa, Ranasinghe, 167, 170
prewar politics, 2, 9–10, 12–13, 23, 25, 33, 39, 54, 217, 221, 231
prewar social bases. *See* social bases
prisons, 244n47
pro-state social bases, 18–19; Kashmir, 64–65
Provisional Irish Republican Army, 4, 6, 26
Punjab, India, 52
putsch, Sri Lanka, 171

Qaddafi, military opposition to, 7–8
Qureshi, Hashim, 72

Rabbani, Burhanuddin, 101, 107, 109, 111–12, 116–18, 121, 127, 132–33
Rajee, Shankar, 160
Rana, Muhammed Amir, 79, 88, 254n193
Rashid, Ahmed, 107, 115, 122, 131
RAW (Research and Analysis Wing), India, 156, 165, 177
recruitment, 29; Hizbul Mujahideen, 79; ICP, 207; LTTE, 157; Muslim Janbaz Force (MJF), 91; People's League, 91
Red Brigades, 8
refugees, Afghanistan and Pakistan, 129
Rehmani, Farooq, 70, 85, 92
religion: Afghanistan, 106–8, 126; Jamaat-e-Islami (JI), 63, 66
Reno, Will, 45, 50, 236n5
research methodology: Afghanistan, 102; case selection and comparative method, 11–14; Kashmir, 61; scope conditions, 10–11, 61; Sri Lanka, 143–44
resources: insurgent organization and, 227–28 *See also* material resources; social resources
revolutionary plotters, 19–20, 65, 68, 107, 188
Revolutionary Youth League, 203
Richardson, John M., 148–49, 159
Roberts, Michael, 150–51
Roy, Olivier, 107, 109, 111, 113–14, 116, 119, 122, 131
Rubin, Barnett R., 117, 119–20, 123–25, 128, 130, 133
rural communities: Afghanistan, 107–9; Indochina, 202, 207–8, 210, 212, 218; Kashmir, 74; Malaya, 184, 188; Philippines, 194–95
Ruttig, Thomas, 129, 132, 134, 137
Rwandan Patriotic Front, 6

Sabaratnam, Sri, 159
al-Sadr, Moktada, 2, 8, 30–31
Saigon, 209
Salahuddin, Syed, 77–78, 85, 88
sanctuary: Huks, 199; MCP, 192; in Pakistan, 86, 101; parochial groups, 50; in Peshawar, 104

Index

Saudi Arabia: Afghan Islamists' exile in, 110; Afghanistan, funding to, 101, 124–26
Sayyaf, Ghulam Rasul, 101, 110, 115, 125, 257n18
Schofield, Victoria, 77–78
Scott, James, 200, 204
Sea Tigers, 267n49
Second Indochina War, 207
Sela, Avraham, 28
Selznick, Philip, 47
Shah, Ghulam Rasool, 250n104
Shah, Shabir, 70, 91–92
Shah, Yusuf, 77
Sheikh, Hamid, 73, 82
Sheikh, Wahid, 85
Short, Anthony, 191
Shura-yi Nazar, 100–102, 104, 109–10, 113, 118–21, 124, 128–29; central control, 120; expansion, 119–20, 128–29; horizontal ties, 119; shift from vanguard to integrated organization, 118–20, 126; Taliban, opposition to, 135; vertical linkages, 118–20
Siddiqui, Shabir, 83–84
Sikand, Yoginder, 66, 87
Sikh militants, 52
Singapore, 186, 188–89, 275n4
Singh, Maharajah Hari, 63
Singh, V. P., 167
Sinha, Aditya, 91–92
Sinhalese, 144, 172–73; Buddhists, 147; kingdom in Sri Lanka, 145; nationalists, 272n166
Sinno, Abdulkader H., 116, 127–28
Sivaram, 174, 271n150
Skocpol, Theda, 38
Slater, Dan, 198
Smith, Chris, 151
social bases, 9, 13, 49, 54, 224; Afghanistan, 105–9; appropriation for organization building, 96–97; conversion into wartime organizations, 23–25; definition of, 17–18; Huks, 193, 196; ICP, 204; Kashmir, 59–60, 64–71, 97; LTTE, 149, 177; organizational structures and, 217; Philippines, 193; PLOT, 149; politics and, 17–20, 23–24; prediction of outcomes from, 219; pro-state, 18–19; Southeast Asia insurgency, 182, 215–16; Sri Lanka, 142, 148–49; state policy and, 213–14; structures of horizontal and vertical ties, 20–26; Taliban, 129–33, 218, 229; TELO, 149; unpoliticized, 18–19
social embeddedness, 2, 36–37
social-institutional theory of insurgent organization, 1–2, 9–10, 25–26, 54–55, 212, 217; empirical data, 11–14; limits of existing research, 3–5
socialization processes, 222; ICP, 207; in integrated organizations, 41; LTTE, 157, 177
social linkages: importance of, 36–37; JKLF, 69; organizational control and, 54–55, 89 *See also* horizontal ties and linkages; vertical ties and linkages
social networks, 225, 227, 230–31; description of, 9; organizations and, 23, 36; patterns of organization and, 221
social resources, 2, 17, 21–27, 31, 39, 42, 217; Afghanistan, 112, 138; Kashmir, 74, 78–79, 99
soldiers: promotion of, 41–42; socialization of, 157, 177, 207; training of, 74–75
Soosai, 267n49
Sopore, 86, 88
Southeast Asia: nationalism, 183; patterns of organization, 181–83; social bases, 182, 215–16
Soviet-Afghan war, 104, 109, 111–13, 118, 120–21, 124–25, 130, 138
splinter groups: Al-Umar Mujahideen, 82, 93; EPRLF, 155; Harakat-e Inqelab, 123; JKLF, 76, 81, 94–96; PLOT, 150, 152–53
Sri Lanka: British colonial rule, 146; caste divisions, 171; caste networks, 142, 149, 154–55, 175–76; caste structure, 145–47, 225; civil war, 12–14; education in, 147–48; ethnic groups, 144, 172–73, 176; fragmented organizations, 143; history, 145–47; ideology, 221; Indian aid, 141; integrated organizations, 143; language policies, 147–48; Marxist-Leninist organizational ideology, 176; parochial groups, 141, 143; patterns of organization, 143; peace process, 172–74; president, 167; putsch, 171; research methodology, 143–44; social bases,

[297]

Index

Sri Lanka *(continued)*
142, 148–49; sources, 144; urban bombings, 160; vanguard organizations, 141, 143, 148; war with LTTE, 174–75 *See also* Tamil insurgency
Sri Lanka Army, 174–75
Sri Lanka Freedom Party, 147–48
Srinagar, 63, 73, 93
Srithiran, 273n191
state building, 3, 41, 108, 170, 203, 213–14, 218, 224
state-centric theories, 3–4, 223
state policy, 26, 213–15, 217, 222–24; Indochina, 213; leadership decapitation, 47; local alliances among insurgents, 44–45; Malaya, 192, 213, 215; Philippines, 193, 213–14; repression, absence of, 213–14, 241n13
state sponsorship, 4, 50, 53, 60, 81, 84, 90, 96–98, 139, 165, 177, 227–28. *See also* aid to insurgents
strategies, insurgent and counterinsurgent, 228–31
Stubbs, Richard, 186–87, 189
Students' and Youth League, 70
Sufi networks, 116–17
suicide bombings, 169, 220
Sunni nationalists, 48
Swami, Praveen, 250n104
Swamy, M. R. Narayan, 155, 157, 161, 269n92
Syria, 9, 31

Tai, Hue-Tam Ho, 203
Tajiks, 103, 107, 117–18
Taliban, 4, 100–102, 105, 123, 226, 230; 1994–2001, rise of, 129–36; 1995–2001, national power, 133–36; after 9/11 terrorist attacks in U.S., 136–38; Al Qaeda and, 135–36; clerics in leadership, 136; command and control, 134, 137; horizontal ties, strong, 129, 137; integrated organization, 139–40, 177; leadership decapitation, 137; mobile warfare, 135–36; opposition to, 135; origins of, 129–33; Pakistan and, 7, 131, 133, 136–37; resources, 228; social base of, 129–33, 218, 229; vertical embeddedness, 139

Tamil Eelam Liberation Organization. *See* TELO
Tamil insurgency, 1, 148–49, 221; 1972–1983, origins of, 154–55; 1983–1986, escalating militancy, 162–63; 1986–1990, rivalry and Indian counterinsurgency, 163–68; 1990–2002, LTTE proto-state, 169–72; 2002–2009, peace, war, and annihilation, 172–75; findings, 175–77; Indian support, 155–61, 176–77; pogroms against, 155–58
Tamil Makkal Viduthalai Pulikal, 143, 174
Tamil Nadu, 156
Tamil National Alliance, 273n191
Tamil National Army, 167–68
Tamil New Tigers, 148
Tamils, 144, 172; caste networks, 224; diaspora, 176–77; ethnic and caste identity, 171; kingdom in Sri Lanka, 145; nationalism, 143
Tamilselvan, 151
Tamil Students' Federation, 151
Tamil Tigers. *See* LTTE
Tamil United Front, 148
Tamil United Liberation Front, 148–49
tanzeems (armed groups), 78, 91–92, 94
Tarrow, Sidney, 255n232
Tehrike-Jihad-e-Islami (TJI), 85, 88
TELO (Tamil Eelam Liberation Organization), 141, 152–53; attacks by LTTE, 163–64; formation of, 148; fragmentation, 159; Indian aid, 158–59; nationalism, 176; organization type, 143, 162; parochial organization, 153, 155; resources, 228; social base, 149
Thailand: Communist Party of, 29–30; MCP exile in, 184, 191
Thangadurai, 152–53, 159
Thelen, Kathleen, 17, 36–37
Thilakar, Lawrence, 151
thuggishness, 80, 167, 228
Tigers. *See* LTTE
Tigrayan People's Liberation Front (Ethiopia), 43
Tilly, Charles, 255n232
Tito's communist partisans in World War II Yugoslavia, 6
Tomsen, Peter, 118
Tonkin, 202

[298]

Index

Tønnesson, Stein, 208, 212, 281n199
torture, 164, 197
tribal leaders in Afghanistan, 124, 131–33
trust, 9–10, 17, 22–23, 25, 29–31, 36, 39, 44–47, 49–52, 217, 224, 230
Turkmens, 103
typology of insurgent groups, 1–2, 5–8, 25, 217, 226–27

Uganda, 45
ulama networks (clerics) in Afghanistan, 106, 113, 117, 121–24, 130
Uma Maheswaran, 150, 152–53, 161–62, 164
uncontested territory, 45–46
United Kingdom, 69; colonial rule in Sri Lanka, 146; EROS, 148–49, 154, 160; French Indochina, counterinsurgency in, 209; Kashmir diaspora in, 251n134; Malaya, counterinsurgency in, 184, 188, 191–92, 215; resettlement of Chinese in Malaya, 190–92, 214
United Liberation Front of Asom, 40
United National Party, 148
United States: Afghanistan war, 37, 136–37; aid to insurgent organizations in Afghanistan, 126; counterinsurgency in Afghanistan, 138; intervention in Philippines, 196–98; Iraq war, 37; Kashmir diaspora in, 251n134
unpoliticized social bases, 18–19
urban and rural communities: Afghanistan, 107–8; Kashmir, 74; Philippines, 194–95
urban bombings in Sri Lanka, 160
urban labor mobilization: MCP, 184–90, 218; PKP, 193–95
Uzbeks, 103

Vaddamarachchi, 151, 164
Vaddukkoddai Resolution of 1976, 148
vanguard groups, 7, 33–34, 218; Afghanistan, 101, 109–10, 112, 126, 135; change in, 35–37, 43–49, 217; control over uncontested territory, 45; counterinsurgency against, 44–49, 220; emergence from integrated groups, 42; EPRLF, 167–68; EROS, 155, 160; fragmentation of, 43–44, 46–49; fratricide, 48, 52; Hezb-e Islami, 112–13, 116; Hizbul Mujahideen, 60, 81, 84–90, 192; horizontal linkages, 43, 48; ICP, 182, 201, 205–7, 212; interaction with states, 224; JKLF, 59, 61, 72–76, 80, 84; leadership decapitation, 46–47, 219; leaders of, 28–30, 226–27; local alliances, 43–47; local imposition, 43, 46; LTTE, 150, 155, 158; MCP, 183, 189, 191; origins of, 17, 28–30; shift to integration, 10, 43–46; ICP, 201–2, 209–10, 212, 215; LTTE, 158; Shura-yi Nazar, 118–20, 126; Viet Minh, 182; Sri Lanka, 141, 143, 148; vertical linkages, 43–45, 48; vulnerabilities of, 134
Vellalar land-owning caste, 145–46, 149–53, 161, 166
Velvethithurai, 148, 151, 153
vertical embeddedness, 67, 139, 189–90
vertical ties and linkages, 9, 13, 22–23, 33–34; Afghanistan, 101; changes in, 35; EPRLF, 160; EROS, 149; Harakat-e Inqelab, 122; Hezb-e Islami, 113, 115; Hizbul Mujahideen, 87; ICP, 202, 204; integrated organizations, 26–27; Jamaat-e-Islami (JI), 66–68; JKLF, 69, 72, 74; LTTE, 152, 169–70; MCP, 184–85, 187, 189–90, 192; Philippines, 193; PLOT, 153; Shura-yi Nazar, 118–20; vanguard organizations, 43–45, 48; Viet Minh, 210
veto players, 31
Viet Cong, 6
Viet Minh, 13, 43, 181–83, 218, 230; 1925–1954, mobilization and resilience, 201–3; cohesion, 211–12, 214, 216; establishment of, 207; horizontal linkages, 211; integration, 208, 210; local control, 203; mobilization by, 202, 208–10; resources, 228; shift from vanguard to integrated organization, 182; state repression, absence of, 213–14; vertical linkages, 210; war with France, 210–11
Vietnamese Democratic Party (DP), 209
Vietnamese nationalism, 203–4, 212, 215

Vietnamese Trotskyists, 280n166
Viet Nam Quoc Dan Dang, 204
violence: change in collective structures, 225; indiscriminate, 10, 40, 50–53, 199; Kashmir, 72; Philippines, 197; prediction of patterns, 235n24; preparation for, 18; scholarship on, 218–26
Vo Nguyen Giap, 207
Vu, Tuong, 3, 209–11, 282n219
vulnerability to counterinsurgency, 36–37, 134

Wahhabi group, 124
Wani, Ashfaq Majid, 73, 82
Wani, M. Aslam, 254n216
Wanni jungles, 165–66, 173
Wardak, Amin, 124

warlords: Afghanistan, 133, 139; emergence of, 54
Waza, Abdul Ahad, 74–75
Weinstein, Jeremy, 32, 195
Whitaker, Mark P., 144, 174
Wickremasinghe, Ranil, 172
Wilson, Isaiah, 146, 151, 159, 270n121, 271n158
Wolf, Charles, 12
women, involvement in Huks insurgency, 195
World War II, 195, 206–8, 213

Yogi, Yogaratnam, 151

Zahir Shah, 104, 110
Zargar, Mushtaq, 76, 93–94, 96
Zia, Zia ul-Haq, 75

THE INTERNATIONAL INSTITUTE
FOR STRATEGIC STUDIES
ARUNDEL HOUSE
13-15 ARUNDEL STREET
LONDON WC2R 3DX